Contents

THE
TIPPERARY
WAR DEAD

HISTORY OF THE CASUALTIES OF THE FIRST WORLD WAR

TOM & RUTH BURNELL

NONSUCH

First published 2008

Nonsuch Publishing
73 Lower Leeson Street
Dublin 2
Ireland
www.nonsuchireland.com

British Library Cataloguing in Publication Data.
A catalogue record for this book is available from the British Library.

ISBN 978 1 84588 938 8

Typesetting and origination by Nonsuch Publishing
Printed and bound in Great Britain by Athenaeum Press, Ltd, Gateshead, Tyne & Wear.

Items should be returned on or before the last date shown below. Items not already requested by other borrowers may be renewed in person, in writing or by telephone. To renew, please quote the number on the barcode label. To renew online a PIN is required. This can be requested at your local library.
Renew online @ www.dublincitypubliclibraries.ie
Fines charged for overdue items will include postage incurred in recovery. Damage to or loss of items will be charged to the borrower.

Foreword

What follows are records of Tipperary soldiers or soldiers who listed their next of kin as being from Tipperary. These men died during the First World War or following it, while in the service of the British Army, the Australian Army, the New Zealand Army, the American Army, the Indian Army, the Canadian Army, the South African Army, the Royal Navy or the British Mercantile Marine.

Introduction

I consider myself blessed to live in the beautiful little village of Holycross, in Co. Tipperary, a village with an interesting ancient history and a strong religious backdrop. It is also quite a peaceful village, a far cry from the famous wartime locations to be found in other parts of Europe. Yet even in this peaceful place, there are graves of the fallen from the Great War of 1914-1918. There are few places in this county that do not contain the resting-place of at least one such serviceman. Some came home wounded and died here, while others may have died in England from wounds received in France, the Dardanelles or Flanders. Over 400 of the 1,400 Tipperary men who fell in this conflict have no graves at all and their commemorations remain as small inscriptions on foreign Memorials to the Missing. They fell in the service of the British Army, the Canadian Army, the Australian Imperial Force (the A.I.F.), the South African Army, the Indian Army, the New Zealand Army or the American Army. Some were sailors serving in one of several navies including the British Mercantile marine.

I was born in Finglas in the 1950s, long after the Great War (and many others wars) had ended. Like most Dubs, I was the offspring of a Dublin mother and a father from outside the Pale, known in Dublin as a Culchie. My father was from a little place called Camas, in Co. Galway, near Meelick, Eyrecourt.

In the late 1940s, after the Second World War, he gave up the drudgery of the farming life. At that time our family was farming and also selling turf cut from the Meelick bogs and sent by canal to Dublin where they got the best price. In the summer of 1949 he left his plough stuck in a furrow, said 'Feck this' or something similar and with a fiver in his pocket left for the Dublin, where there was more work and more music. He was a talented musician and formed the Galway Rovers Céilí Band with the world famous Joe Cooley. He got a job with the Lucan Dairies and afterwards with Kennedy's Bread in Parnell Street opposite the 'Hill' Saturday morning market.

In the 1950s Finglas was still rural, surrounded by farms and fields and lots and lots of places for a kid to explore. The village was a small place with one shop, a post office, a bank, a church, a few pubs, a dentist's and a few other shops that I cannot remember. However I do remember playing music in The Duck Inn opposite The Drake Inn with the music I inherited from my Dad.

In those days it was customary for Catholic families like ourselves to kneel down each evening and say the Rosary and as my father had a special devotion to the Blessed Virgin this was included in our nightly devotions.

It's well I remember us all kneeling down in front of high-backed chairs with my parents, four brothers and two sisters 'doing' the decades of the Rosary just before bedtime. As children we did not understand it and sniggers and giggles were commonly heard which made it difficult for our parents. The coal fire burned bright in the corporation tiled fireplace grate and burned our backs as we studied our shadows on the wall counting the decades on our fingers.

At the end of it all there was a part where each of us could add our own special dedication of three Hail Marys to anything we liked. I don't remember anyone's particular dedication but what has stuck in my mind is the special dedication of three prayers that I specifically wanted to be said. I was most insistent and did it many times. I wanted them said for all the soldiers who died in battle (no matter where that battle was or which side they were on) who had no one to say a prayer for them when they took their last breath. As a child I could not understand why a soldier about to die without a priest to say the final absolution or the last rites, could not die 'proper'. Did that mean that men who died on the battlefield without the last rites would not go to heaven?

I remember my father initially staying silent for a short while he absorbed my request. I am sure he remembered his Granny sticking the spade into the roasting cinders lest the 'Tans' call and she could sort them out. Anyway, my father said, 'Three Hail Marys for all the soldiers who died with no one to pray for them.'

I must have been about eight years old or so at that time. It may be a tiny particle of inherited memory or *déjà-vu* – I don't have an explanation – but the predisposition was still there. I insisted and there was no objection from anyone present. What did my siblings know anyway? It was as much a mystery to me as it was to them. My special dedication was done many times. My father was a special man and very tolerant. After a few years, the feeling of the lost and forgotten souls began to dig deeper and I decided to amass the largest collection of 'War Dead' databases available in Ireland so I could help anyone searching for their kin.

The idea of some poor soldier dying in a foreign field, his people not knowing where he had died, where he had been buried or why he had been buried in that particular place, was not right. During the summer of 2005 and 2006 my wife Ruth and I decided to visit all the Tipperary cemeteries and record the Great War graves contained in them. This is no mean feat in itself as it took us most of those summers and a heck of a lot of petrol. We photographed any we found and believe me there is no one faster at recognising a war grave than the elegant

Ruth. Now, whenever we pass a cemetery, she is eagle-eyed for a war grave. All First World War soldiers buried in Tipperary are included in this book including a photograph of their headstone if it exists.

At one time St Mary's Famine and War Museum was given on loan of a set of medals of a Navan soldier who had died in the Great War. Among his ephemera was a copy of a letter from his parents published in a Meath newspaper asking soldiers of his regiment returning from the battlefields to please tell them how he had died. I wish I had lived in those days with the access to information now available, to tell them what they needed to know. This is the beginning and these are the Tipperary men who were the casualties of the Great War – also known as 'The War to end all Wars'. It must have seemed a great saying at the time.

If no one else remembers them they will be remembered here in this little book, *Tipperary War Dead*.

Tom Burnell and Ruth Burnell

Terminology

Killed in action: The soldier was killed during engagement with the enemy.

Died of wounds: The soldier was not killed outright and may have made it back to the Regiments Aid post or Casualty Clearing Station before he eventually died of his wounds.

Died at home: death by drowning, suicide, accident or illness in the UK. Home in these cases means back in England and not necessarily where he lived. Many times I have been misled by this as it turned out to be a soldier that died in a UK hospital.

Died of wounds at home: The soldier was not killed outright and may have made it back to the Regiments Aid Post or Casualty Clearing Station before he eventually died of his wounds back in the UK or Ireland.

A

ABBOTT, Charles: Rank: C. S. (C. Q. M. S). Regiment or Service: Royal Irish Regiment. Unit: 2nd Bn. Date of death: 24 May 1915. Service No.5805. Born in Secunderabad, East India. Enlisted in Birr while living in Carrick-on-Suir, Co. Tipperary. Killed in action. Age at death: 34.

Supplementary information: Son of the late H.G. Abbott: husband of Margaret Helen Abbott of 9 The Terrace, Tramore, Co. Waterford. He has no known grave but is listed on Panel 33 on the Ypres (Menin Gate) Memorial in Belgium.

ABRAHAM, John: Rank: Private. Regiment or Service: Royal Inniskilling Fusiliers. Unit: 1st Bn. Date of death: 19 May 1915. Service No.15058. Born in Cashel. Enlisted in the Curragh while living in Cashel. Died of wounds at sea. Gallipoli.

Supplementary information: Brother of Mrs Mary Quinn, of Brownstown, Curragh Camp, Co. Kildare. He has no known grave but is listed on Panel 97 to 101 on the Helles Memorial in Turkey.

ABRAHAM, Sydney Herbert: Rank: Corporal. Regiment or Service: Royal Irish Rifles. Unit: 1st Bn. Age at death: 20. Date of death: 7 February 1916. Killed in action. Service No.16803. Born in Nenagh. Enlisted: Birr, Co. Offaly while he was living in Limerick.

Supplementary information: Son of Charlotte Browne (formerly Abraham) of 4 Zetland Street, Belfast. Native of Nenagh, Co. Tipperary. Grave or Memorial Reference: I. D. 33. Cemetery: Rue-Du-Bois Military Cemetery, Fleurbaix in France.

ADAIR, Thomas: Rank: Private. Regiment or Service: Machine Gun Corps (Infantry). Unit: 123rd Coy. Age at death: 39. Date of death: 20 February 1917. Killed in action. Service No.43291. Born: Roscrea. Enlisted in Roscrea. He was formerly with the Royal Irish regiment where his number was 8,000.

Supplementary information: Son of William and Isabella Adair, of Carroll's Row, Roscrea, Co. Tipperary. Grave or Memorial Reference: L. 28. Cemetery: Dickebusch New Military Cemetery in Belgium.

AHEARNE, Michael: Rank: Gunner. Regiment or Service: Machine Gun Corps (Motors). Unit: 18th Bty. Date of death: 11 March 1916. Killed in action. Service No.897. Born: St Mary's, Tipperary. Enlisted: Galway, while he was living in Marlfield.

Supplementary information: Son of Mrs Mary Ahearne, of Markfield, Clonmel, Co. Tipperary. Grave or Memorial

Arthur H. Allen.
Photogragh courtesy of Karen Black, USA.

Reference: XVII. H. 42. Cemetery: Cabaret-Rouge British Cemetery, Souchez in France.

AHERN, Patrick Joseph: Rank: Lieutenant (Quartermaster). Regiment or Service: Leinster Regiment. Unit: 7th Bn. Age at death: 41. Date of death: 9 September 1916.

Supplementary information: Son of Mrs M. Ahern, of Thurles, Co. Tipperary: husband of Mary Ellen Ahern, of 2 Townsend Street House, Birr, King's Co. Grave or Memorial Reference: Has no known grave but is commemorated on Pier and Face 16 C. Memorial: Thiepval Memorial in France.

ALLEN, Arthur Haviland: Brother of **ALLEN, John de Renzi** below. Rank: 2nd Lt. Regiment or Service: Royal Dublin Fusiliers. Unit: 11th Bn, attached 1st Bn. Date of death: 4 October 1917. Age at death: 27.

Supplementary information: Son of Mr B. W. and Harriette Allen, of Tipperary. Grave or Memorial Reference: He has no known grave but is listed on the Tyne Cot Memorial on Panel 144 to 145. Below is a letter to his parents:

Dear Mr Allen,

I am unfortunately the bearer of very sad news. Your son was killed on the morning of the 4th inst. While very gallantly leading his men in an attack. He has been reported as 'Missing believed killed,' but I am afraid there is absolutely no hope of his being a prisoner. During the attack, they had to advance a long distance, your son went to the right to try to maintain touch with our next Company. He was seen to fall and the men say, that is those who were with him who are left, that he was killed instantly. At the time of course everyone was moving and although a thorough search was made your son's body was not discovered. It would be very hard for for you to realize what the ground is like up there, it is churned up and pitted with shell

John De Renzi Allen.
Photograph courtesy of Karen Black, USA.

holes. Your son behaved in a most gallant manner, he has always done so. He was very popular with all, and respected. He and I were great friends, and used to have a stroll together most days. Of late I have never seen him in better form, and he went up the line in great spirits. Up there the men tell me he was laughing and joking. Zero hour was at 6 a. m. and as the barrage came down your son turned around and said to his men 'Come on now I am off.' He jumped over the parapet and led them like a true man with fine courage.

I cannot tell you how sorry I am for you all in your great sorrow, and what a great loss it is to me personally. I am, I am afraid, very bad at expressing myself in a letter, so please forgive if I have broken this awful news to you very clumsily. I offer you and all your family my true and deep
sympathy.
Yours sincerely,
Talbot Considine.

ALLEN, Christopher: Rank: Private. Regiment or Service: Leinster Regiment. Unit: 1ˢᵗ Bn. Date of death: 28 February 1915. Service No.10113. Born in Tipperary. Enlisted in Tipperary. Killed in action. He has no known grave but is listed on Panel 44 on the Ypres (Menin Gate) Memorial in Belgium.

ALLEN, John de Renzi: Rank: Private. Regiment or Service: Canadian Machine Gun Corps Unit: 2ⁿᵈ Bn. Age at death: 32. Born 12 December 1885. Date of death: 29 August 1918. Service No.2600830. Died of wounds at the battle of Arras. Data from the reverse of the enlistment document: Age on Enlistment: 31 Years 9 Months. Height: 5'8". Eye colour: Grey. Complexion: Fair. Hair colour: Brown. Religion: C. of E.. Chest expansion: 2". Girth: 35". Vision: Normal. Hearing: Normal. Date of Enlistment: 20 September, 1917. Place of Enlistment: Calgary.

Supplementary information: Son of B. W. and Mrs H. Allen, of Bank of

Ireland House, Tipperary, Ireland. Grave or Memorial Reference: III. A. 19. Cemetery: Ligny-St Flochel British Cemetery, Averdoingt in France.

ANDERSON, William: Rank: Private. Regiment or Service: Royal Fusiliers (City of London Regiment). Unit: 23rd Bn. Date of death: 27 July 1916. Service No.SPTS-1692. Born in Peebles. Enlisted in Edinburgh while living in Clogheen, Co. Tipperary. Killed in action.

Supplementary information: He has no known grave but is listed on Pier and Face 8 C, 9 A and 16 A on the Thiepval Memorial in France. He is also commemorated on the Cahir War Memorial.

ANGLIN, John: Rank: Private. Regiment or Service: Somerset Light Infantry. Unit: 1st Bn. Date of death: 1 July 1916. The first day of the battle of the Somme. Service No.9828. Born in Cahir. Enlisted in Taunton while living in Bridgewater. Killed in action.

Supplementary infromation: He has no known grave but is listed on Pier and face A on the Thiepval Memorial in France.

APPLEYARD, Herbert: Rank: Private. Regiment or Service: Royal Army Medical Corps. Age at death: 37. Born in Morley in Yorkshire. Enlisted in Morley in Yorkshire. Died at home. Date of death: 30 October 1917. Service No.121479.

Supplementary information: Son of Francis and Elizabeth Appleyard and husband of Annie Appleyard of 8

Cross Street, Morley Leeds. Cemetery, Mary's Churchyard, Tipperary. Grave location: The old military plot to the west of the church.

ARDILL, John: Rank: Private. Regiment or Service: Royal Irish Regiment. Unit: 7th Bn. Age at death: 25. Date of death: 23 August 1918. Service No.25007 Awards: Mentioned in Despatches. Born: Aghanacon, Co. Tipperary. Enlisted: Coolderry in Queens County while he was living in Roscrea.

Supplementary information: Son of John and Alice Ardill, of Ballysallagh, Newtownards, Co. Down. Born at Aghancon, Roscrea, Co. Tipperary. Grave or Memorial Reference: Sp. Mem. 3. Cemetery: Roisel Communal Cemetery Extension in France.

ARDILL, Albert William: Rank: Private. Regiment or Service: Duke of Wellington's (West Riding Regiment). Unit: 2nd Bn. Age at death: 19. Date of death: 3 February 1917. Killed in action. Service No.20219. Born: Aghanacon, Co. Tipperary. Enlisted: Roscrea while he was living in Aghancon.

Supplementary information: Son of John and Alice Ardill, Garryhill, Aghancon, Roscrea, Co. Tipperary. Grave or Memorial Reference: VII. G. 22. Cemetery: Fins New British Cemetery, Somme in France.

ARMSTRONG, William Maurice (Pat): Rank: Captain. Regiment or Service: 10th (Prince of Wales's Own Royal) Hussars Secondary. Unit: (Bde. Major. 29th Div.) Age at death: 27. Date

Albert Edward Baker and daughter.
Photograph courtesy of Christy Archer
(Albert's only grandson), Galway.

of death: 23 May 1917. Awards: M C, Mentioned in Despatches.

Supplementary information: Son of Marcus Beresford Armstrong and Rosalie Cornelia Armstrong, of Moyaliffe, Thurles, Co. Tipperary. Grave or Memorial Reference: V. F. 18. Cemetery: Faubourg D'Amiens Cemetery, Arras in France. Extract from De Ruvigny's Roll of Honour:

William Maurice Armstrong, M. C, Capt, 10th (Prince of Wales's Own Royal) Hussars, only son of Marcus Beresford Armstrong, Capt, D. L, J. P, of Moyaliffe, Co. Tipperary: Chaffpool, Co. Sligo, and Clodagh, Folkestone, Co. Kent, by his wife, Rosalie Cornelia, daughter of the late Maurice Ceely Maude, of Lenaghan, Co. Fermanagh, and cousin to the late Lieut. General Sir F. Stanley Maude, K. C. B, C. M. G, D. S. O. : b. Chaffpool afore-said, 20 Aug. 1889: educ. at Stoke House, Slough: Eton and the Royal Military College, Sandhurst:

was gazetted 2nd Lieut. 23 Feb. 1910: promoted Lieut 1 Feb 1914, and Capt. 7 May, 1917. : served with his regiment in India and South Africa : was in England on leave on the outbreak of war, and left for France in Aug. 1914, with the original Expeditionary Force, being attached to the staff of the 2nd Cavalry Brigade : after serving in France and Flanders, was sent to Gallipoli in June 1915, where he served as Staff Captain with the famous 29th Division, taking part in the evacuation of both Suvia and Helles; was sent to Egpyt and returned to France in March 1916, to serve as Brigade Major, and had just been recommended for the D. S. O. when he was killed in action on 23 May, 1917, while on duty in a front-line trench near Arras. Buried in Fambourg d'Amiens Cemetery, Arras. Capt. Armstrong was awarded the Military Cross (*London Gazette*, 2 Feb. 1916), and was four times mentioned in

William Maurice Armstrong

Despatches (*London Gazette*, 9 Dec 1914: 28 Jan 1916: 13 July 1916, and 15 May 1917), for gallant and distinguished service in the field. He was a keen sportsman and very successful in his big-game shooting expeditions; had won many races and horse-jumping competitions; was a promising polo player, and had hunted with most of the English and Irish packs. The General Commanding the Cavalry Corps wrote: "As an old Tenth Hussar, too, I can tell you how very distressed the whole regiment will be, and what a loss he will be to them. He had done so awfully well during this war, and showed such great promise for the future, that he is a great loss, not only to his regiment and the cavalry, but to the whole Army. I do not know of anyone of his age who had a more promising future before him, as not only did he love his profession, and show most of the qualities needed for him to shine in it, but he had such a charming personality that all he came in contact with loved him, and were able to show their best work when working with him or under him." General

_____ wrote: "He was so absolutely fearless, he was bound to be hit sooner or later, but I had always hoped it would be to be wounded only… I cannot help sending you enclosed, it is so very typical, and no better tribute could be paid to a man. You see the boy is referred to as 'Dear old Pat', he always will be to all the 29th Division, who knew and appreciated him so well, he will never be forgotten." The enclosed letter stated: "Dear General, You will have been terribly grieved by the news of dear old Pat's death. I know how proud you were of him. He was so far above the crowd of us, it seems so hard to lose him. Hope things go well with you and your division." Another General also wrote: "I had met him hunting in the Meynell country, but I had never realised his sterling worth until I found him here as my Brigade Major: he has been my right-hand man… believe me, he is a real loss, not only to you, but to the Army. He was the best and bravest lad that ever lived. " A Colonel on the Staff wrote: "I was convinced that he had a great future ahead of him, for the moment he took on a job he always saw it through. Of his gallantry others have doubtless told you, but what I admired most in him was his unselfishness and kindness: he never said an unkind word of anybody, and that, in the stress and worry of a campaign, is not an easy thing. I saw 'Pat' last on the afternoon of the 22nd, the day before he was killed, and I was awfully struck then at the manner in which his presence brightened the sordid dug-out of Brigade Headquarters." The Chaplain wrote: "I have just returned from your son's funeral, where a unique gathering of senior officers testified to what we all feel." General _____ wrote: "He is indeed a loss to us all, as he was one of the most lovable characters I have ever met, unselfish, always cheery under the most trying circumstances, and the bravest of the brave. All the time he was with me in Gallipoli he helped me enormously to get through that trying time with his unvariable cheerfulness and good humour: besides that, his energy was astonishing: no day or work was ever too long or too hard for him: the Service has lost one of its very best" General _____ wrote: "As my A. D. C. said this afternoon, 'Pat is the best man we have in the Division': I think that expresses the feeling throughout: there is a gloom over the whole division to-night over this bereavement. I have seen him grow from boy to man, and a man who gained the respect of the other men who came in contact with him." General _____ wrote: "He was one of those gallant, unselfish people who had little chance of living through this war. Anyone who has had anything to do with them classifies them at once, and wonders they have lasted so long: there are not many of them left now, so they are valued all the more. This is not idle talk, it might have helped you a little if you had seen the people round our dinner-table when we got the news: he has never been in this brigade, but no one would have guessed it…. His action in risking his life the previous night to try and find the body of a friend was typical of him." Major _____ wrote: "I don't suppose there ever was a more popular, keener soldier and sportsman than Pat… but there it is, you have lost one of the very best, and his loss to the Brigade and Division is enormous." An N. C. O. wrote: "We are all just deep down in the dumps, how much we all miss him I dare not say, other good fellows are gone and we mourn their loss, but with Pat it was so different. At present we all just think but dare not speak… We must try and keep his memory green by endeavouring to follow his noble, unselfish life.

ARTHUR, John Alexander: Rank: Sergeant. Regiment or Service: 66th Dragoons (Inniskilling) Secondary Regiment: 1st Life Guards Secondary.

Unit: attd. Age at death: 32. Date of death: 30 October 1914. Killed in action. Service No.4520. Born: St John's in Cashel. Enlisted in Templemore while living in Cricklewood. N.W.

Supplementary information: Son of Richard James and Honora Arthur, of Cashel, Co. Tipperary. Husband of Margaret Hetherington (formerly Arthur), of 22 Mitchell Way, Willesden, London. Served in the South African Campaign. Grave or Memorial Reference: Has no known grave but is commemorated on Panel 5. Memorial: Ypres (Menin Gate) Memorial in Belgium.

B

BABBAGE, Christopher Thomas: Regiment or Service: Norfolk Regiment. Rank: Company Sergant Major. Unit: 8th Bn. Date of death: 22 October 1917. Service No.4662.

Supplementary information: Born in Templemore and enlisted in Norwich in Norfolk. Killed in action. He has no known grave but is listed on Panels 34, 35 and 162A on the Tyne Cot Memorial in Belgium.

BACON, Thomas: Rank: Private. Regiment or Service: Royal Munster Fusiliers. Unit: 2nd Bn. Date of death: 22 September 1916. Service No.6167. Born in Carrigmore, Co. Tipperary. Enlisted in Cork while living in Tallow, Co. Waterford. Killed in action. Age at death: 37.

Supplementary information: Son of John and Euen Bacon, of West Street, Tallow, Co. Waterford. He has no known grave but is listed on Pier and Face 16 C on the Thiepval Memorial in France.

BAIRD, David Eugene: Rank: Company Sergeant Major. Regiment or Service: Border Regiment. Unit: 1st Bn. Age at death: 34. Date of death: 6 July 1916. Service No.7516. Born: Aldershot. Hants. Enlisted: Woolwich in Kent while he was living in Berris Co. Carlow. Died of wounds.

Supplementary information: Son of Capt. David Baird, of Ullard House, Borris, Co. Carlow. Husband of Elizabeth M. F. Baird, of Ash Brook, Roscrea, Co. Tipperary. Grave or Memorial Reference: F.7. Cemetery: Beauval Communal Cemetery in France.

BAKER, Albert Edward: Rank: Gunner. Regiment or Service: Royal Garrison Artillery. Unit: 5th Siege Battery. Date of death: 26 December 1915. Service No.21869. Age at death: 29. Born in Tipperary. Enlisted in Ennis Co. Clare. Died. Grave or Memorial Reference: VIII. C. 74. Cemetery: Boulogne Eastern Cemetery in France.

BAKER, Frederick: Rank: Driver. Regiment or Service: Royal Field Artillery and Royal Horse Artillery.

William Baker's death report.

Unit: D Battery, 14th Brigade. Age at death: 30. Date of death: 31 August 1918. Enlisted in Camelford in Cornwall. Killed in action.

Supplementary information: Husband of Ellen Baker of 6 William Street, Clonmel. He is listed as being born in Calmelford in Cornwall and also in Clonmel. Grave or Memorial Reference: VI. A. 8. Cemetery: Quarrt Cemetery, Montaban in France.

BAKER, William: Rank: Private. Regiment or Service: Australian Imperial Force. Unit: 49th Bn. Date of death:. 5 April 1917. Service No.3763. Served in Plymouth, Folkstone, England, Heliopolis, Serapeum, Tel-El-Kebir, Alexandria. Previously rejected for service due to bad teeth. Born in Tipperary, Ireland. Enlisted 13 April 15 aged 31 Years 7 Months in Brisbane, Queensland. Height, 5' 6", Weight, 9st 5lbs, Complexion: fair. Hair: dark brown. Eyes: blue.

Supplementary information: Occupation on enlistment, horse driver. Mother Mrs E Baker, Bally Poreen P. O. Via Cahir, County Tipperary, Ireland. Sister Mrs M Stallwood, 'Ellesmere' 458 Upper Roma Street, Brisbane. Died of wounds. Religious Denomination: R.C. Killed in action. He has no known grave but is listed on the Villers Bretonneux Memorial in France.

BANKS, Francis: Rank: Private (Lance Corporal). Regiment or Service: Royal Irish Regiment. Unit: B Coy, 2nd Bn. Date of death: 16 August 1917. Service No.2566. Born

in Carrick-on-Suir, Co. Tipperary. Enlisted in Tipperary while living in Carrick-on-Suir, Co. Tipperary. Killed in action. Age at death: 31.

Supplementary information: Son of Martin and Mary Banks, of Carrick-on-Suir. He has no known grave but is listed on Panels 51 to 52 on the Tyne Cot Memorial in Belgium. He won the Military Medal and is listed in the *London Gazette*.

BANNON, Denis: Rank: Private. Regiment or Service: Connaught Rangers. Unit: 6th Bn. Date of death: 10 September 1916. Service No.6946. Born in Tipperary. Enlisted in Liverpool while living in Birkinhead. Killed in action. He has no known grave but is listed on Pier and Face 15A on the Thiepval Memorial in France.

BANNON, John: Rank: Private. Regiment or Service: Irish Guards. Unit: 1st Bn. Age at death: 27. Date of death: 9 October 1917. Service No.8333.

Supplementary information: Son of John and Elizabeth Bannon, of Glentara Cottage, Roscrea, Co. Tipperary. Grave or Memorial Reference: Has no known grave but is commemorated on Panel 10 to 11. Memorial: Tyne Cot Memorial in Belgium.

BANNON, Michael: Rank: Private. Regiment or Service: Irish Guards. Unit: 2nd Bn. Age at death: 21. Date of death: 27 September 1915. Killed in action. Service No.6880. Born in Roscrea and enlisted there also.

Supplementary information: Son of Mr and Mrs John Bannon, of Glentara Cottage, Roscrea, Co. Tipperary. Grave or Memorial Reference: Has no known grave but is commemorated on Panel 9 and 10. Memorial: Loos Memorial in France.

BANNON, Michael: Rank: Sergeant. Regiment or Service: Cheshire Regiment. Unit: 23rd Bn. Date of death: 6 November 1918. Service No. 304 and W-304. Born in Roscrea. Enlisted in Port Sunlight in Cheshire.

Supplementary information: He won the Military Medal and is listed in the *London Gazette*. Grave or Memorial Reference: II. E. 21, Roisel Communal Cemetery Extension in France.

BARAGO, Henry: Rank: Private. No 5357, Royal Irish Regiment, 6th Bn. Date of death: 18 December 1916. Son of Mrs L. Barago, of William Street, Cashel. Co. Tipperary. Born in Cashel and enlisted in Cashel also. Killed in action, France. Grave Reference G. 8. Cemetery: Pond Farm Cemetery in Belgium.

BARDWELL, Walter: Rank: Gunner. Regiment or Service: Royal Garrison Artillery. Unit: 9th Heavy Battery. Date of death: 3 September 1918. Service No. 43341. Born in Templemore. Enlisted in Dublin while living in the Curragh, Co. Kildare. Died of wounds. Age at death: 25.

Supplementary information: Son of Walter Wm. and Annie Bardwell, of 3, Maddenstown Terrace, Curragh Camp, Ireland. Grave or Memorial

Reference: III. F. 29. Cemetery: Ligny-St Flochel British Cemetery, Averdoingt in France.

BARNES, Henry: Rank: Fireman. Regiment or Service: Mercantile Marine. Unit: S.S. *Ivernia* (Liverpool). Age at death: 36. Date of death: 1 January 1917.

Supplementary information: Son of the late Henry Barnes, and Margaret Barnes, of Cloghssegg, Thomastown, Co. Kilkenny. Husband of the late Kate Barnes. Born in Co. Tipperary. Memorial: Has no known grave but is commemorated on the Tower Hill Memorial, London.

BARNETT, John William: Rank: Private. Regiment or Service: Royal Irish Fusiliers. Unit: 2nd Bn. Date of death: 6 April 1915. Service No. 16350. Born in Cahir. Enlisted in Winchester while living in Aldershot. Killed in action. He has no known grave but is listed on Panel 42 on the Ypres (Menin Gate) Memorial in Belgium.

BARRETT, Daniel: Rank: Private. Regiment or Service: Royal Irish Regiment. Unit: 2nd Bn. Date of death: 19 October 1914. Service No. 6047 and 6017. Born in St Mary's, Clonmel, Co. Tipperary. Enlisted in Clonmel. Died of Wounds. Age at death: 21.

Supplementary information: Son of the late Michael and Nora Barrett. He has no known grave but is listed on Panels 11 and 12 on the Le Touret Memorial in France.

BARRY, Christopher: Rank: Private. Regiment or Service: Royal Fusiliers (City of London Regiment). Unit: 45th Bn. Formerly he was with the Leinster Regiment where his number was 3830. Date of death: 10 August 1919. Service No. 130804. Born in Roscrea. Enlisted in Dublin while living in Roscrea. Killed in action in Russia. He has no known grave but is listed on the Archangel Memorial in the Russian Federation.

BARRY, Thomas: Rank: Private. Regiment or Service: Royal Irish Regiment. Unit: 'A' Coy. 1st Bn. Age at death: 24. Date of death: 20 June 1915. Killed in action. Service No. 9536. Born in Clonmel and enlisted there also.

Supplementary information: Son of Philip and Margaret Barry, of 1, King Street, Clonmel, Co. Tipperary. Grave or Memorial Reference: III. C. 5. Cemetery: Houplines Communal Cemetery Extension in France.

BARRY, Michael: Rank: Fireman and Trimmer. Regiment or Service: Mercantile Marine. Unit: S.S. *Haulwen* (Cardiff). Age at death: 52. Date of death: 9 June 1917.

Supplementary information: Son of the late Patrick and Mary Barry: husband of Mary Barry (*née* Kelly), of Parish Height, Carrickbeg, Co. Tipperary. Born at Tramore, Co. Waterford. Memorial: Has no known grave but is commemorated on the Tower Hill Memorial, London.

BARRY, Michael: Rank: Private.

Regiment or Service: Royal Irish Fusiliers. Unit: 5th Bn. Date of death: 16 September 1915. Service No. 17035. Formerly he was with the Royal Irish Regiment where his number was 1681. Born in Clonmel. Enlisted in Clonmel while living in Kilmanahan, Co. Waterford. Died of wounds in Gallipoli. Grave or Memorial Reference: III. C. 7. Cemetery: Lala Baba Cemetery in Turkey.

BARRY, Patrick: Rank: Private. Regiment or Service: Connaught Rangers. Unit: 'D' Coy. 5th Bn. Age at death: 29. Date of death: 11 November 1915. Service No. 5693. Born in Carrigbeg in Co. Waterford and enlisted in Carrick-on-Suir while living there. Died in Salonika.

Supplementary information: Son of Michael and Ellen Barry and husband of Annie Barry, of Mass Rd, Carrick Beg, Carrick-on-Suir, Co. Tipperary. Born at Carrick-on-Suir. Grave or Memorial Reference: C. 39. Cemetery: Alexandria (Chatby) Military and War Memorial Cemetery in Egypt.

BARRY, William Francis: Rank: Private. Regiment or Service: Royal Inniskilling Fusiliers. Unit: 8th Bn. Age at death: 22. Date of death: 1 May 1916. Service No. 25223. Born in Cappawhite, enlisted in Tipperary Town while living in Cappawhite. Died of wounds.

Supplementary information: Son of Patrick and Ellen Barry, of Cappawhite, Co. Tipperary. Grave or Memorial Reference: V. B. 48. Cemetery: Lilliers Communal Cemetery in France.

BEACH, Arthur: Rank: Gunner. Regiment or Service: Royal Horse Artillery and Royal Field Artillery. Unit: D Battery, 25th Brigade. Date of death: 18 July 1916. Service No.69812. Born in Tipperary. Enlisted in Hounslow, Middlesex. Killed in action. Grave or Memorial Reference: X. C. 6. Cemetery: Flatiron Cemetery: Flatiron Copse Cemetery. Mametz in France.

BEARY, David: served as **COONEY**, Rank: Private. Regiment or Service: Royal Munster Fusiliers. Unit: 2nd Bn. Date of death: 1 January 1915. Born in St John's, Limerick, enlisted in Tralee, Co. Kerry, while living in Thurles, Co. Tipperary.

Supplementary information: Son of M. Beary of the Post Office, Thurles. Died of wounds at home. This man was one of two casualties buried in the Hospital Cemetery at the rear of the County Home in Thurles. They were removed to Grangegorman Military Cemetery some time after the war. The graveyard at the County Home was levelled and shows no sign of any internments there now. Grave or Memorial Reference: Church of Ireland Section. Grave No.1003. Cemetery: Grangegorman Military Cemetery.

BEIRNE, John: Rank: Private. Regiment or Service: Leinster Regiment. Unit: 1st Bn. Date of death: 1 March 1915. Service No.9559. Born in Tipperary. Enlisted in Ipswich, Suffolk. Died of wounds. Grave or Memorial Reference: 2. 29. Cemetery: Le Gonards Cemetery, Versailles in France.

BEIRNE, John: Rank: Private. Regiment or Service: Royal Irish Regiment. Unit: 1st Bn. Age at death: 22. Date of death: 10 February 1915. Service No.10049. Born in Ballyhaunis in Co. Mayo, enlisted in Clonmel while living in Thurles. Died of wounds.

Supplementary information: Brother of Miss Bridget Beirne, of 6 Cottage, Ballycurrane, Thurles, Co. Tipperary. Grave or Memorial Reference: Has no known grave but is commemorated on Panel 33. Memorial: Ypres (Menin Gate) Memorial in Belgium.

Grave of Frederick Bennett.

BEIRNE, Patrick: Served as **BYRNE**. Rank: Sergeant. Regiment or Service: Connaught Rangers. Unit: 2nd Bn. Date of death: 19 September 1914. Service No.6574. Born in Castlerea, Co. Roscommon. Enlisted in Galway while living in Roscrea. Killed in action. Age at death: 34.

Supplementary information: Son of Thomas and Mary Beirne (*née* Murray), Furfield, Castlerea, Co. Roscommon. Served in South African War. He has no known grave but is listed on the La Ferte-Sous-Jouarre-Memorial in France.

BELL, Robert: Rank: Private. Regiment or Service: Royal Dublin Fusiliers. Unit: 2nd Bn. Date of death: 24 May 1915. Service No.8501 and 85001. Born in Templemore. Enlisted in Dublin while living in Magherymore, Co. Wicklow. Killed in action. Age at death: 18.

Supplementary information: Son of Mr and Mrs William Bell, of Magherymore, Wicklow. He has no known grave but is listed on Panel 44 and 46 on the Ypres (Menin Gate) memorial in Belgium.

BELL, Robert William Popham: Rank: Captain. Regiment or Service: Royal Irish Regiment. Unit: 3rd Bn. attd. 2nd Bn. Age at death: 32. Date of death: 5 July 1916. He was the son of the Revd Robert Popham Bell of St Mary's church, Tipperary Town.

Supplementary information: Son of the late Robert Popham Bell, of Pegsborough, Tipperary. Grave or Memorial Reference: Has no known grave but is commemorated on Pier and Face 3 A. Memorial: Thiepval Memorial in France. He is also commemorated on the Memorial window in St Mary's church in Tipperary.

BENN, John: Rank: Private. Regiment or Service: Middlesex Regiment. Unit: 13th Bn. Age at death: 19. Date of death: 20 June 1917. Service No.G-41865. Born in Roserea, enlisted in Waterford while living in Roscrea. Killed in action.

Supplementary information: Son of

Michael Bergin.

John and Sarah Benn, of Clonan, Roscrea, Co. Tipperary. Grave or Memorial Reference: Has no known grave but is commemorated on Panel 49 and 51. Memorial: Ypres (Menin Gate) Memorial in Belgium.

BENNETT, Frederick: Rank: Private. Regiment or Service: Irish Guards. Age at death: 24. Date of death: 10 December 1920. Service No. 7636. Cemetery: St Cronan, COI Graveyard, Roscrea. Grave location: North-west of the middle path.

BENNETT, Robert: Rank: Private. Regiment or Service: Lancashire Fusiliers. Unit: 12th Bn. Date of death: 12 September 1916. Service No. 7838. Born in Roscrea. Enlisted in Burnley in Lancashire while living in Salford in Lancashire. Died in Salonika.

Supplementary information: Father of William Bannett of 101 Kew Road, Birkdale, Southport. Grave or Memorial Reference: 398. Cemetery: Salonika (Lembet Road) Military Cemetery in Greece.

BENTON, Thomas: Rank: Private. Regiment or Service: Royal Dublin Fusiliers. Unit: 1st Bn. Date of death: 7 August 1915. Service No. 18172. Born in Kilcommon Co. Tipperary. Enlisted in Manchester while living in Kilcommon. Killed in action in Gallipoli. Age at death: 45.

Supplementary information: Son of John and Margaret Benton. He has no known grave but is listed on Panel 190 to 196 on the Helles Memorial in Turkey.

BERGIN, Michael: Rank: Appointed Chaplain 4th Class (Major). Initially taken on strength on 12 May 1915 in Fagala in Egypt and was taken sick. Placed in a hospital in Mudros and released 22 June 1915. Attested in the 5th Light Horse Regiment and taken on strength in ANZAC, Turkey on 12 July 1915. Educated in the Convent School, Mungret, Limerick and University of Ireland. Linguist, French Arabic and English. He became a Jesuit Novice in Tullabeg in September 1897. Age on enlistment: 35 years and 11 months. Complexion: fresh. Hair: fair. Eyes: blue. Occupation on enlistment: professor and school teacher in Holy Family College, Cairo. Date of birth: 18 August 1879. Next of kin listed as his brother, John Bergin, Fancroft, Roscrea, Co. Tipperary. Religious denomination: R.C. Date of death: 12 October 1917. Born in the Parish of St Kieran, Roscrea, Co. Tipperary.

Fr Bergin joined the Catholic Military Chaplains in January 1915 and was dressed by the soldiers in the uniform of a private and left with the 5th Light Horse for Gallipoli where he was sworn in and taken on as Chaplain. Upgraded to Chaplain 3rd Class. Under A. I. F. Order No 677 on 5 June 1917. Awarded the Military Cross posthumously on 1 January 1918 and was listed in the *London Gazette* Supplement No 30450 and in the Commonwealth of Australia Gazette, No. 57, dated 18 March 1918. Fr Bergin was a Jesuit Priest working in Syria he was interned by the Turks. He contracted Smallpox and was ejected by the Turks. He then volunteered to serve as a stretcher bearer. A book written about him was entitled, *Sister S, a Son of St Patrick* by Patrick Bergin, SJ, Dublin 1932. Working near a first aid post he died of wounds (shrapnel wound to the shoulder) when a heavy shell burst near where he was working at No. 3 Australian Field Ambulance located in an ANZAC back area of Passchendaele. He is the only member of the Australian Imperial Force I know that never set a foot on Australian soil.

Letter from Lt Col Christie:
Father Bergin, of the Jesuit Fathers, accompanied us as Padre. He remained with us until October, when he was evacuated. Many well-known members of the A. I. F. were killed on tracks about this battlefield, among them. Father M. Bergin (Rosscrea, Ireland), a missionary, who joined the force in Egypt and of whom a soldier said at Pozieres, 'If ever an angel walked among men, it was he.' , a man made great through the complete subordination of self...He was killed near Zonnebeke, N. E. of Ypres on 11th Oct. Our battalion was in the front line, and as was his usual custom, he went up to the find out if there was anything he could do for the men. On the way to the front a piece of shell caught him in the chest, killing him instantly. He was buried the day he died in Reninghelst Churchyard Extension in Row 1 in Belgium.
From the Australian Dictionary of Biography.

BERGIN, Michael: (1879-1917), Jesuit priest and military chaplain, was born in August 1879 at Fancroft, Tipperary, Ireland, son of Michael Bergin, mill-owner, and his wife Mary, *née* Hill. Educated at the local convent school and the Jesuit College at Mungret, Limerick, he entered the Jesuit noviceship at Tullabeg in September 1897. Two years later he was sent to the Syrian mission where English-speakers were needed. He felt the break from home and country very keenly but became absorbed in his missionary work and the exotic customs of the local peoples. After learning Arabic and French he studied philosophy at Ghazir, and in October 1904 began teaching at the Jesuit College in Beirut.

In 1907 Bergin was sent to Hastings, England, to complete his theology studies and was ordained a priest on 24 August 1910. After a short time at home he returned to Hastings for further study and then gave missions and retreats in the south of England. He returned to the Middle East in January 1914 and was in charge of Catholic schools near Damascus until the outbreak of the First World War along with other foreigners in Syria, he was then imprisoned and later expelled by the Turkish government. By the time he reached the French Jesuit College in Cairo in January 1915 the first Australian troops had arrived in Egypt, and Bergin offered to assist the Catholic military chaplains. Though still a civilian, he was dressed by the men in the uniform of a private in the Australian Imperial Force and when

Grave of P. Bingley.

the 5th Light Horse Brigade left for Gallipoli he went with it. Sharing the hardships of the troops, he acted as priest and stretcher-bearer until his official appointment as chaplain came through on 13 May 1915. He remained at Anzac until September when he was evacuated to the United Kingdom with enteric fever.

Bergin's arrival home in khaki, complete with emu feather in his slouch-hat, caused a sensation among his family and friends. Though tired and weak after his illness, he was anxious to get back to his troops for Christmas. He returned to Lemnos but was pronounced unfit and confined to serving in hospitals and hospital-ships. Evacuated to Alexandria in January 1916, he worked in camps and hospitals in Egypt and in April joined the 51st Battalion, A.I.F., at Tel-el-Kebir. He accompanied it to France and served as a chaplain in all its actions in 1916-17: these included the battles of Pozières and Mouquet Farm, the advance on the Hindenburg Line and

the battle of Messines. He was killed at Passchendaele on 11 October 1917 when a heavy shell burst near the aid-post where he was working. He was buried in the village churchyard at Renninghelst, Belgium.

Bergin was awarded the Military Cross posthumously. The citation praised his unostentatious but magnificent zeal and courage. Though he had never seen Australia he was deeply admired by thousands of Australian soldiers, one of whom referred to him as 'a man made great through the complete subordination of self'.

BEST, Thomas Andrew Dunlop: Rank: Lieutenant Colonel. Regiment or Service: Royal Inniskilling Fusiliers. Unit: 1st-2nd Bn. Age at death: 38. Date of death: 20 November 1917. Awards: D. S.O. and Bar. Killed at the Battle of Cambrai.

Supplementary information: Son of William J. and Annie Best, husband of Amy M. Best, of Annerville, Clonmel, Co. Tipperary. Native of Scotland.

Grave of Thomas Bishop.

Grave or Memorial Reference: F. 8. Cemetery: Ruyaulcourt Military Cemetery in France.

BILLETT, George Herbert: Rank: Private. Regiment or Service: Northumberland Fusiliers. Unit: 1st-6th Bn (Territorials). Date of death: 15 September 1916. Service No. 8022. Born in Tipperary. Enlisted in Hull. Killed in action.

Supplementary information: He has no known grave but is listed on Pier and Face 10 B, 11 B and 12 B on the Thiepval Memorial in France.

BINGLEY, P: Rank: Gunner. Regiment or Service: Royal Field Artillery. Date of death: 12 May 1921. Service No. 1026116. Cemetery, Cahir Old Graveyard. Grave location: South-west of the ruins near the west boundary.

BIRD, Harry Eli: Rank: Private. Regiment or Service: Worcestershire Regiment. Unit: 1st Bn. Age at death: 38. Date of death: 21 August 1915. Service No. 5242. Born in Birmingham and enlisted there also. Died of wounds.

Supplementary information: Son-in-law of Mrs Mary Maguire, of College Hill, Templemore, Co. Tipperary. Native of Birmingham. Served in the South African Campaign. Grave or Memorial Reference: III. A. 8. Cemetery: Sailly-Sur-La-Lys-Canadian Cemetery in France.

BIRMINGHAM, Patrick: Rank: Private. Regiment or Service: Irish Guards. Unit: 1st Bn. Age at death: 24. Date of death: 6 November 1914. Service No. 3802. Born in Thurles and enlisted in Waterford City. Killed in action.

Supplementary information: Son of John and Margaret Birmingham, of Drish Bridge, Thurles, Co. Tipperary.

Grave or Memorial Reference: IV. C. 38. Cemetery: Santuary Wood Cemetery in Belgium.

BISHOP, Thomas: Rank: Private. No 4754, Royal Irish Regiment, 1ˢᵗ Bn. Died 25 March 1915,.Born: Cashel, Co. Tipperary and enlisted in Cashel. Died at home aged 61. Buried in St John the Baptist Cemetery in Cashel in the middle of the cemetery. He does not have a Commonwealth War Grave headstone.

BLACKSTOCK, Robert T.: Rank: Lance Corporal. Regiment or Service: Royal Scots Fusiliers. Unit: 7ᵗʰ Bn. Date of death: 6 September 1915. Service No. 16153. Born in Roscrea. Enlisted in Dunbarton while living in Helensburgh in Dumbartonshire. Grave or Memorial Reference: He has no known grave but is listed on the Loos Memorial in France on Panel 46 to 49.

BOLAND, Daniel: Rank: Private. Regiment or Service: Royal Irish Regiment. Unit: 2ⁿᵈ Bn. Date of death: 3 September 1916. Service No. 6550 and 2-6650. Born in Carrickbeg, Co. Waterford. Enlisted in Clonmel while living in Carrick-on-Suir, Co. Tipperary. Killed in action. Grave or Memorial Reference: XIV. J. 7. Cemetery: Delville Wood Cemetery, Longueval in France.

BOLAND, William: Rank: Private. Regiment or Service: Irish Guards. Unit: 1ˢᵗ Bn. Date of death: 10 October 1915. Service No. 5779. Born in Clonmel. Enlisted in Clonmel. Killed in action. He has no known grave but is listed on Panels 9 and 10 on the Loos Memorial in France.

BOLES, Robert Stephen: Rank: Lieutenant. Regiment or Service: Royal Dublin Fusiliers. Unit: 1ˢᵗ Bn. Age at death: 22. Born in Killenaule. Date of death: 6 May 1918.

Supplementary information: Son of Mrs Mary J. Boles, of Main Street, Killenaule, Co. Tipperary. Grave or Memorial Reference: I. E. 25. Cemetery: Ebblinghem Military Cemetery in France. He is also commemorated on the Cahir War Memorial.

BOLGER, George: Rank: Private. Regiment or Service: Royal Irish Regiment. Unit: 5ᵗʰ Bn. Age at death: 33. Date of death: 20 September 1916. Service No. 1117. Born in Nenagh and enlisted there also. Died of fever contracted in Mesopotamia.

Supplementary information: Son of William and Winifred Bolger, of Nenagh and husband of Ellen Bolger, of Birr Rd, Nenagh, Co. Tipperary. Grave or Memorial Reference: III. H. 15. Cemetery: Struma Military Cemetery in Greece.

BOLGER, James: Rank: Sergeant. Regiment or Service: Royal Munster Fusiliers. Unit: 1ˢᵗ Bn. Age at death: 37. Date of death: 28 November 1915. Service No. 5851 Awards: D C M. Born in Tipperary Town, enlisted in London while living in Nenagh. He won the Distinguished Conduct Medal before

Grave of A. Bowes.

he died in Gallipoli.

Supplementary information: Son of Mrs Winifred Bolger, of Birr Rd, Nenagh, Co. Tipperary. Grave or Memorial Reference: Has no known grave but is commemorated on Panel 185 to 190. Memorial: Helles Memorial in Turkey.

BOND, Samuel Thomas: Rank: Gunner. Regiment or Service: Royal Field Artillery. Unit: 'A' Bty. 320th Bde. Age at death: 19. Date of death: 23 January 1918. Service No. 119903. Born in Rahan in King's County and enlisted in Birr. Died at home.

Supplementary information: Son of Samuel T. Bond (late of Royal Irish Constabulary), and Margaret Frances Bond, of Parochial Hall, Mary Street, Clonmel, Co. Tipperary. Grave or Memorial Reference: G. 72. Cemetery: Aylesham Cemetery in Norfolk, UK.

BOURKE/BURKE, James: Rank: Lance Corporal. Regiment or Service: Leinster Regiment. Unit: 2nd Bn. Age at death: 27. Date of death: 31

July 1917. Service No. 10743. Born in Thurles and enlisted in Templemore. Killed in action. He was formerly with the Royal Irish Regiment where his number was 10379.

Supplementary information: Son of Pierce and Alice Burke, of Stradavoher Street, Thurles, Co. Tipperary. Grave or Memorial Reference: Has no known grave but is commemorated on Panel 44. Memorial: Ypres (Menin Gate) Memorial in Belgium.

BOURKE, John: Rank: Gunner. Regiment or Service: Royal Horse Artillery and Royal Field Artillery. Unit: 52nd Battery. Date of death: 21 October 1917. Service No. 5426. Born in Carrick, Co. Tipperary. Enlisted in Camp Camden. Died of wounds. Grave or Memorial Reference: III. L. 27. Cemetery: Menin Road South Military Cemetery in Belgium.

BOURKE, Patrick: Rank: Private. Regiment or Service: Royal Munster Fusiliers. Unit: 1st Bn. Age at death:

24. Date of death: 30 June 1915. Service No.6319. Born in Tipperary and enlisted in Limerick while living in Tipperary. Died of wounds in Gallipoli.

Supplementary information: Son of William Bourke, of Slone-Parke, Aherlow, Co. Tipperary. Grave or Memorial Reference: Has no known grave but is commemorated on Panel 185 to 190. Memorial: Helles Memorial in Turkey.

BOURKE/BURKE: Stephen: Rank: Private. Regiment or Service: Leinster Regiment. Unit: 2nd Bn. Age at death: 27. Date of death: 9 November 1914. Service No.7192. Born in Templemore and enlisted there also. He died of wounds at home.

Supplementary information: Son of Thomas and Johanna Burke, of Templemore: husband of Johanna Burke (*née* Leahy), of New Rd, Templemore, Co. Tipperary. Grave or Memorial Reference: Soldiers' Plot. 171 (Screen Wall). Cemetery: Moston (St Joseph's) Roman Catholic Cemetery, UK.

BOWE, Bernard: Rank: Private. Regiment or Service: Royal Irish Regiment. Unit: 2nd Bn. Date of death: 14 July 1916. Service No.7450. Born in Templemore. Enlisted in Templemore. Killed in action. Grave or Memorial Reference: III. C. 12. Cemetery: Flatiron Copse Cemetery. Mametz in France.

BOWES, A: Rank: Private. Regiment or Service: Yorkshire Regiment.

Unit: Date of death: 20 May 1920. Service No.66896. Cemetery, Mary's Churchyard, Tipperary. Grave location: the old military plot to the west of the church.

BOWMAN, Walter: Rank: Private. Regiment or Service: Hampshire Regiment. Unit: 1st Bn. Date of death: 22 May 1915. Service No.9480. Born in Piltown, Carrick-on-Suir, Co. Tipperary. Enlisted in Clonmel while living in Waterford. Killed in action. Age at death: 35. He has no known grave but is listed on Panel 35 on the Ypres (Menin Gate) Memorial in Belgium.

BOYLAN, Laurence: Rank: Sergeant. Regiment or Service: Leinster Regiment. Unit: 2nd Bn. Age at death: 24. Date of death: 12 April 1917. Service No.5403. Born in Moyne in Tipperary, enlisted in Dublin while living in Roscrea. Killed in action.

Supplementary information: Son of Elizabeth Boylan, of Limerick Street, Roscrea, Co. Tipperary John Boylan. Grave or Memorial Reference: IV. A. 15. Cemetery: Lievin Communal Cemetery Extension in France.

BRABSTON, James: Rank: Private. Regiment or Service: Royal Irish Regiment Unit: 1st Bn. Age at death: 26. Date of death: 14 February 1915. Service No.10352. Born in Ardfinnan in Tipperary, enlisted in Clonmel while living in Cahir. Killed in action.

Supplementary information: Son of Denis Brabston and Bridget Fennessey, his wife, of Ballindoney,

Cahir, Co. Tipperary. Grave or Memorial Reference: Has no known grave but is commemorated on Panel 33. Memorial: Ypres (Menin Gate) Memorial in Belgium. He is also commemorated on the Cahir War Memorial.

BRACKEN, Edward: Rank: Private. Regiment or Service: Connaught Rangers. Unit: 1st Bn. Age at death: 23. Date of death: 24 June 1915. Service No.9965. Born in Nenagh, enlisted in Nenagh while living there also. Killed in action.

Supplementary information: Son of George and Maggie Bracken, of Silver Street, Nenagh, Co. Tipperary. Grave or Memorial Reference: Has no known grave but is commemorated on Panel 43. Memorial: Le Touret Memorial in France.

BRADSHAW, Patrick: Rank: Gunner. Regiment or Service: Royal Garrison Artillery. Unit: 187th Siege Battery. Date of death: 7 July 1918. Service No.170034. Born in Tipperary. Enlisted in Birmingham. Grave or Memorial Reference: I. D. 43 Cemetery: Terlincthun British Cemetery, Wimille in France.

BRADSHAW, Thomas: Rank: Private. Regiment or Service: Royal Munster Fusiliers. Unit: 1st Bn. Date of death: 21 August 1915. Service No.5350. Born in Newport Co. Tipperary. Enlisted in Limerick while living in Newport. Killed in action in Gallipoli. Age at death: 23.

Supplementary information: Son of William Bradshaw, of Shower, Newport, Limerick, and the late Margaret O'Shea Bradshaw. He has no known grave but is listed on Panel 185 to 190 on the Helles Memorial in Turkey.

BRADY, Peter: Rank: Private. Regiment or Service: Connaught Rangers. Unit: 5th Bn. Date of death: 23 September 1915. Service No.5063. Born in Nenagh Co. Tipperary.

Private Braham/Brahan. Photograph courtesy of Martin Dwyer, Cashel.

Enlisted in Boyle while living in Boyle Co. Roscommon. Died in Gallipoli. Grave or Memorial Reference: E. EA. A. 655. Cemetery: Addolorata Cemetery in Malta.

BRAHAM/BRAHAN, Thomas: Rank: Private. Regiment or Service: Leinster Regiment. Unit: 1st Bn. Age at death: 24. Date of death: 27 December 1917. Service No.9574. Born in Cashel and enlisted in Clonmel. Killed in action, Egypt. Killed while attempting to drive the Turks from Nabus.

Supplementary information: Son of Bridget Carthy (formerly Braham), of Boherclough Street, Cashel, Co. Tipperary, and the late Thomas Braham. Grave or Memorial Reference: Y. 81. Cemetery: Jerusalem War Cemetery, Israel.

BREEN, Denis: Rank: Sergeant. Regiment or Service: Royal Garrison Artillery. Unit: 88th Siege Bty. Date of death: 14 August 1917. Service No.479. Born in Tipperary Town, enlisted in Clonmel while living in Golden. Died of wounds.

Supplementary information: Son of Mrs J. Ryan, of Sergeant Hut, Golden, Co. Tipperary. Grave or Memorial Reference: H. 25. Cemetery: Bruay Communal Cemetery Extension in France.

BREEN, Matthew: Rank: Lance Corporal. Regiment or Service: Guards Machine Gun Regiment. Unit: 4th Bn. Date of death: 11 October 1918. Service No.1844. Formerly he was with the South Irish Horse where his number was 9529. Born in Templetown, Co. Wexford. Enlisted in Ayrshire while living in Fethard, Co. Tipperary. Died of wounds. Age at death: 23.

Supplementary information: Son of Mrs Margaret Breen, of Herrylock, Fethard, Waterford. Grave or Memorial Reference: I. D. 5. Cemetery: Masnieres British Cemetery, Marcoing in France.

BRENNAN, James: Rank: Private. Regiment or Service: Royal Irish Regiment. Unit: 1st Garr. Bn. Age at death: 43. Date of death: 22 February 1916. Service No.2124. Born in St Mary's in Clonmel. Enlisted in

Joseph Brennan.

Philip Brennan.

Tipperary while livng in Clonmel. Died in Egypt.

Supplementary information: Son of the late James and Marguerite Brennan. Born at Clonmel, Co. Tipperary. Grave or Memorial Reference: C. 129. Cemetery: Alexandria (Chatby) Military and War Memorial Cemetery in Egypt.

BRENNAN, James Francis: Rank: Corporal. Regiment or Service: Lancashire Fusiliers. Unit: 1st-5th Bn, (T. F.). Date of death: 6 September 1917. Service No.235518. He had previously been with the Liverpool Regiment where his number was 4761. Born in Templemore. Enlisted in Liverpool. Killed in action. He has no known grave but is listed on Panels 54 to 60 and 163A. on the Tyne Cot Memorial in Belgium.

BRENNAN, Joseph: Rank: Sapper. Regiment or Service: Australian Engineers Unit: 7th Field Coy. Age at death: 25. Date of death: 10 January 1917. Service No.6662. He was born in Kilcommon, worked as a fettler, was 5' 7 ½" tall had blue eyes black hair and a fair complexion.

Supplementary information: His wife Ester lived at various addresses, 62 Margaret Street, Petersham in New South Wales, 'Benicia', Cambridge Street, Watson's Bay, New South Wales and later moved to 70c Darlinghurst Road, Darlinghurst. Enlisted on 15 of November 1915. It was said that he enlisted to avenge his brother Philip Brennan's death. The date of his brothers death and Joseph's enlistment would seem to bear this out. He went to Tel-el-Kabir, Marseilles and also trained in the famous Etaples bull ring. He died of wounds in the 36th Casualty Clearing Station and buried in Albert. Josephs other brother John Brennan was a Police Constable in Australia. His mothers address (Mary Brennan) after his death was High Street Killarney. The death plaque and medals were sent to his widow Ester. Son of John Brennan and his wife Mary Carey, husband of Esther Brennan, of 'Benicia', Cambridge Street, Watson's Bay, New South Wales. Native of Tipperary, Ireland. Grave or Memorial Reference: V. F. 38. Cemetery: Heilly Station Cemetery, Mericourt-l'Abbe in France.

BRENNAN, Philip Joseph: Rank: Lance Corporal (Promoted on the 15 January 1915). Regiment or Service: Australian Infantry, A. I. F. Unit: 3rd Bn. Age at death: 26. Date of death: between 7 August 1915 and 12 August 1915. Service No.104. Rose Cottage, Dean Street Sydney was the address Phillip left on the 17 August 1914 and enlisted.

Supplementary information: He was a twenty-five year old labourer and listed his father, John Brennan, Foilnadrough, Kilcommon, Thurles as his next of kin. He listed in his will his Mother to receive all his property. Weight 162lbs, 5ft 9 inches tall, grey eyes and brown hair, fair complexion and a Roman Catholic. On his enlistment documents it states that he served with the Connaught Rangers for three months. In Gallipoli he was wounded in the upper left thigh on 2 May 1915. He was reported wounded and missing on the famous attack on the lone Pine on the 6 of November 1915. On 12 January 1916 this report was upgraded to a killed in action. This usually happens after a soldier is seen to have been wounded (not killed) but is not accessible and the body is recovered after the incident. The location of this is ANZAC COVE in the Gallipoli Peninsula. His parents were awarded a pension of ten shillings a week from the Australian Government. Son of John and Mary Brennan, of Kilcommon, Thurles, Co. Tipperary, Ireland. Grave or Memorial Reference: III. B. 44. Cemetery: Lone Pine Cemetery, Anzac in Turkey.

BRENNAN, Robert: Rank: Driver. Regiment or Service: Royal Field Artillery. Unit: 5th 'C' Reserve Bde. Age at death: 38. Date of death: 10 November 1916. Service No.L-31723. Born in Tipperary and enlisted in Deptford S. E. Died at home.

Supplementary information: Son of Mrs Robert Brennan, of Lisvarrinane, Co. Tipperary, husband of Emily C. Brennan, of 3, Blackheath Vale, London. Grave or Memorial Reference: Screen Wall. D. 3184. Cemetery: Lewisham (Ladywell) Cemetery, UK.

BRENNAN, Thomas: Rank: Private. Regiment or Service: Leinster Regiment. Unit: 2nd Bn. Date of death: 20 October 1914. Service No.6395. Born in Templemore. Enlisted in Birr. Killed in action. He has no known grave but is listed on Panel 10 on the Ploegsteert Memorial in Belgium.

BRERETON, William Kingsley: Rank: Lance Corporal. Regiment or Service: Royal Inniskilling Fusiliers. Unit: 9th Bn. Age at death: 21. Date of death: 14 April 1917. Service No.28390. Born in Roscrea and enlisted in Tullamore. Killed in action.

Supplementary information: Son of Charlotte Brereton, of Spruce Hill, Roscrea, Co. Tipperary, and the late George Brereton. Grave or Memorial Reference: I. H. 24. Cemetery: Dranoutre Military Cemetery in Belgium.

BRETT/BRITT James: Rank: Private. Regiment or Service: Scottish Rifles. Unit: 2nd Bn. Date of death: 12

March 1915. Service No.10483. Born in Tipperary. Enlisted in Hamilton while living in Shettleston. Died of wounds. Age at death: 21.

Supplementary information: Son of Richard and Helen Brett, of 50 McNair Street, Shettleston, Glasgow. Grave or Memorial Reference: I. A. 53. Cemetery: Longuenesse (St Omer) Souvenir Cemetery in France.

BRETT, John: Rank: Driver. Regiment or Service: Royal Horse Artillery and Royal Field Artillery. Unit: D Battery. Date of death: 19 October 1916. Service No.76997. Born in Thurles. Enlisted in Clonmel. Died of wounds. Grave or Memorial Reference: I. N. 24, Grove Town Cemetery, Meaulte in France.

BRETT, Michael: Rank: Private. Regiment or Service: Royal Irish Regiment. Unit: B Company, 2nd Bn. Date of death: 21 March 1918. Service No.3376. Born in Mullinahone. Enlisted in Clonmel while living in Mullinahone. Age at death: 23.

Supplementary information: Son of Bridget Brett, of Chapel Street, Mullinahone, Co. Tipperary, and the late Daniel Brett. Enlisted March, 1915. He has no known grave but is listed on Panel 30 and 31 on the Pozieres Memorial in France.

BRETT, Patrick: Rank: Lance Bombardier. Regiment or Service: Royal Garrison Artillery. Unit: 261st Siege Bty. Date of death: 27 August 1918. Service No.30985. Born in Templederry and enlisted in Nenagh.

Killed in action.

Supplementary information: Son of James and Mary Brett, of Nenagh, Co. Tipperary. Grave or Memorial Reference: XXV. A. A. 27A. Cemetery: Lijssenthoek Military Cemetery in Belgium.

BRETT, Timothy: Rank: Private. Regiment or Service: Royal Irish Regiment. Unit: 6th Bn. Date of death: 18 December 1916. Service No.7692. Born in Thurles and enlisted there also. Killed in action.

Supplementary information: Husband of Mrs N. Brett, of Stradvoker Street, Thurles, Co. Tipperary. Grave or Memorial Reference: G. 7. Cemetery: Pond Farm Cemetery in Belgium.

BRIDGE, William Purefoy: Rank: Private. Regiment or Service: Royal Dublin Fusiliers. Unit: 7th Bn. Age at death: 34. Date of death: 10 August 1915. Service No.14220. Born in Roscrea and enlisted in Dublin. Died of wounds in Gallipoli.

Supplementary information: Son of the late Joshua Smith Bridge and Jane Angel Bridge, formerly of Barnagree, Roscrea, Co. Tipperary. Educated at St Stephen's Green School, Dublin. Graduate of Trinity College. Solicitor by profession. He was the nephew of Dr Purefoy, Merrion Square, Dublin. Before enlisting William was a solicitor with the firm of Messrs, Maunsell, Darby and Orpen. Grave or Memorial Reference: Has no known grave but is commemorated on Panel 190 to 196. Memorial: Helles Memorial in Turkey. He is also listed on the Solicitors Memorial in the Four Courts in Dublin. The Memorial heading is, 'THIS TABLET IS ERECTED TO THE MEMORY OF THE IRISH SOLICITORS AND APPRENTICES TO IRISH SOLICITORS WHO GAVE THEIR LIVES FOR THEIR KING AND COUNTRY IN THE GREAT WAR'.

BRIEN, Henry: Rank: Private. Regiment or Service: Royal Irish Regiment. Unit: 2nd Bn. Age at death: 20. Date of death: 24 May1915. Service No.10715. Born in Templemore. Enlisted in Templemore while living in Roscrea. Killed in action.

Supplementary information: Son of James and Mary Brien, of Gurtnagoona, Roscrea, Co. Tipperary. Grave or Memorial Reference: Has no known grave but is commemorated on Panel 33. Memorial: Ypres (Menin Gate) Memorial in Belgium.

BRIEN, Thomas: Rank: Private. Regiment or Service: Royal Munster Fusiliers. Unit: 1st Bn. Date of death: 11 September 1917. Service No.2769. Born in Clonmel. Enlisted in Cork while living in Clonmel. Died of wounds. Grave or Memorial Reference: II. B. 5. Cemetery: Bacquoy Road Cemetery, Ficheux, in France.

BRIEN/O'BRIEN Thomas: Rank: Private. Regiment or Service: Royal Irish Regiment. Unit: 5th Bn. Date of death: 27 October 1915. Service No.4967. Born in Cahir. Enlisted in Killcatin, Co. Tipperary while living in Clogheen, Co. Tipperary. Age at death: 29. Died in Gallipoli.

Supplementary information: Son of Mrs Mary O'Brien, of St Joseph's Hospital, Clogheen, Co. Tipperary. Grave or Memorial Reference: 1593. Cemetery: Salonika (Lambet Road) Military Cemetery in Greece.

BRIGGS, Lionel John: Rank: Wireless Operator. Regiment or Service: Mercantile Marine. Ship: SS

Grave of Martin Brindley.

Grave of William Browne.

Poylmnia. Age at death: 21. Date of death: 15 May 1917.

Supplementary information: Son of Andrew and Mary Briggs of Crannagh, Queens County, Ireland. Born at Roscrea, Ireland. He has no known grave but is listed on the Tower Hill Memorial, UK.

BRINDLEY, Martin: Rank: Private. Regiment or Service: Royal Irish Regiment. Unit: 3rd Bn. Date of death: 14 February 1916. Service No.9022. Born in Nenagh. Enlisted in Nenagh. Died at home.

Supplementary information: Husband of M Brindley, 165 St James Street Dublin. He died in a Dublin Hospital after a brief illness. Grave or Memorial Reference: In the South East part of the ruins. Cemetery: Lisbunny Cemetery located two miles from Nenagh on the Dublin Road.

BRITT/BRETT James: Rank: Private. Regiment or Service: Scottish Rifles. Unit: 2nd Bn. Date of death: 12 March 1915. Service No.10483. Born in Tipperary. Enlisted in Hamilton while living in Shettleston. Died of wounds. Age at death: 21.

Supplementary information: Son of Richard and Helen Brett, of 50 McNair Street, Shettleston, Glasgow. Grave or Memorial Reference: I. A. 53. Cemetery: Longuenesse (St Omer) Souvenir Cemetery in France.

BRITT, Patrick: Rank: Private. Regiment or Service: Royal Irish Regiment. Unit: 1st Bn. Secondary. Unit: attd. 31st General Hospital Age at death: 28. Date of death: 27 October 1916. Service No.10623. Born in Killenaule. Enlisted in Clonmel while livng in Clonoulty. Died in Egypt.

Supplementary information: Son of Ellen F. Costello (formerly Britt), of Clonoulty, Co. Tipperary. Native of Killenaule, Co. Tipperary. Grave or Memorial Reference: N. 23. Cemetery: Port Said War Memorial Cemetery, Egypt.

Robert Brownlow.

BRITT, Rody: Rank: Lance Corporal. Regiment or Service: Irish Guards. Unit: 1st Bn. Date of death: 1 November 1914. Service No.2663. Born in Templemore. Enlisted in Templemore. Killed in action. He has no known grave but is listed on Panel 11 on the Ypres (Menin Gate) Memorial in Belgium.

BROPHY, Denis: Rank: Driver. Regiment or Service: Royal Horse Artillery and Royal Field Artillery. Unit: 24th Brigade. Date of death: 5 July 1915. Service No.47660. Born in Tipperary. Enlisted in Tipperary. Died of wounds at home. Grave or Memorial Reference: B. 1893. Cemetery: Southend-On-Sea (Sutton Road) Cemetery, UK.

BROWN, Edward: Rank: Private. Regiment or Service: Royal Dublin Fusiliers. Unit: 7th Bn. Age at death: 44. Date of death: 10 November 1914. Service No.12320. Born in Templemore and enlisted there also. Died at home.

Supplementary information: Husband of Margaret Brown, of Church Street, Templemore, Co. Tipperary. Grave or Memorial Reference: 573. Cemetery: Curragh Military Cemetery in Co. Kildare.

BROWNE/BROWN Joseph: Rank: Private. Regiment or Service: Leinster Regiment. Unit: 2nd Bn. Date of death: 27 October 1916. Service No.8212. Born in Templemore. Enlisted in Templemore. Killed in action. Age at death: 24.

Supplementary information: Son of William and Mary Brown, of 81 Nab Lane, Blackburn. Grave or Memorial Reference: I. K. 8. Cemetery: Maroc British Cemetery, Grenay in France.

BROWNE, William: Rank: Gunner. Regiment or Service: Royal Garrison Artillery. Unit: 164th Siege Battery. Date of death: 29 May 1917. Service No.34280. Born in Tipperary. Enlisted in Tipperary. Killed in action.

Supplementary information: Grave or Memorial Reference: I. B. 5. Cemetery:

43

Nine Elms Military Cemetery, Thelus in France.

BROWNE, William: Rank: Pte. Regiment or Service: Connaught Rangers. Unit: Depot. Date of death: 18 November 1918, one week after the war ended. Service No. 10967. Age at death: 28. Grave or Memorial Reference: E. H. 106. Cemetery: Tipperary (St Michael's) New Cemetery, Tipperary.

BROWNLOW, Robert: Rank: Private. Regiment or Service: South Irish Horse. Age at death: 24. Date of death: 4 December 1914. Service No. 634. Born in Nenagh, enlisted in Nenagh and resided there also. Entitled to the 1914 Star, the War Medal and the Victory Medal.

Supplementary information: Son of George F. and Alicia Brownlow, of Nenagh, Co. Tipperary. Grave or Memorial Reference: III. A. 9. Cemetery: Hazebrouck Communal Cemetery, Nord, in France.

Extract from the *Tipperary Star*, December 1914:

Nenagh journalist killed in Belgium by an Aeroplane Bomb

On Saturday morning the sad news reached Nenegh that Trooper Robert Brownlow of the South Irish Horse, was killed, amongst others on Sunday last by a bomb thrown from an aeroplane at the front. The deceased, who was on the reporting staff of the *Nenagh Guardian* was a young man who gained for himself the respect and esteem of all whith whom he came in contact with and much regret has been occasioned in his native town by his untimely death. In his family circle he was idolised, and the poignant grief of his relations is of the keenest. The sympathy of the entire town is tendered to them in their sad bereavement. The deceased had a few narrow escapes previous to his death. His horse was shot under him, and on another occasion while sitting at breakfast in an outhouse with some other troops a shell burst and blew away portion of the 'hotel' as he described it, and killed two men close to him. He escaped by being covered with mortar and falling 'debris'. In a letter some days previous to his death he wrote home telling his sisters how a little French child made love to him, and how forcibly she reminded of 'his own dear little Nancy at home' and how much he would have given to see her dear little face again. But, alas, fate decreed it otherwise, and he gave up his young life and a promising career for his country. The deceased was Secretery to the Nenagh Dance Class, and in this capacity he was responsible for many a social gathering, and at which he was the soul of mirth and fun. He was possessed of a very kindly and genial disposition, which made for him hosts of friends by whom his sad death is deeply mourned.

BRYAN, Arthur Patrick: Rank: Private. Regiment or Service: Royal Irish Regiment. Unit: 7th (South Irish Horse) Bn. Age at death: 26. Date of death: 21 March 1918. Service No.25057. Born in Kilvemnon and enlisted in Clonmel while living in Drangan. Killed in action. Entitled to the War Medal and the Vicotry Medal He was formerly with the South Irish Horse where his number was 2087.

Supplementary information: Son of Anna Kathleen Bryan, of Priestown House, Drangan, Co. Tipperary, and the late Arthur Bryan. Grave or Memorial Reference: Has no known grave but is commemorated on Panel 30 and 31. Memorial: Pozieres Memorial in France.

BUCKLEY, John: Rank: Private. Regiment or Service: Gloucestershire Regiment. Unit: 1st Bn. Age at death: 24. Date of death: 9 May 1915. Service No.10011. Born in Cahil Tipperary and enlisted in Bristol. Killed in action.

Supplementary information: Son of John and Catherine Buckley, of Garranlea, New Inn, Cahir, Co. Tipperary. Grave or Memorial Reference: Has no known grave but is commemorated on Panel 17. Memorial: Le Touret Memorial in France.

BUCKLEY, Patrick: Rank: Private. Regiment or Service: Royal Irish Fusiliers. Unit: 2nd Garrison Bn. Date of death: 19 September 1917. Service No.1279 and G-1279. Formerly he was with the Royal Irish Regiment where his number was 9069. Enlisted in Clonmel while living in Ballyporeen. Died In Salonika. Grave or Memorial Reference: 1892. Cemetery: Mikra British Cemetery, Kalamaria in Greece. He is also commemorated on the Cahir War Memorial.

BURKE, Alexander: Rank: Private. Regiment or Service: Royal Irish Regiment. Unit: 4th Bn. Age at death: 42. Date of death: 12 February 1916. Service No.5436. Born in Ballylooby

Grave of Alexander Burke.

and enlisted in Clonmel while living in Ardfinnan. Died at home.

Supplementary information: Husband of Mrs Bridget Burke, of Lady Abbey, Ardfinnan, Co. Tipperary. Grave or Memorial Reference: South-West of ruins. Cemetery: Ballydrinan Old Graveyard, Tipperary. He is also commemorated on the Cahir War Memorial.

BURKE, Andrew: Rank: Private. Regiment or Service: Royal Munster Fusiliers. Unit: 2nd Bn. Date of death: 13 December 1916. Service No.6301. Born in Ballyboy Co. Tipperary. Enlisted in Birkenhead while living in Birkenhead. Killed in action. He has no known grave but is listed on Pier and Face 16C on the Thiepval Memorial in France.

BURKE/BOURKE, James: Rank: Lance Corporal. Regiment or Service: Leinster Regiment. Unit: 2nd Bn. Age at death: 27. Date of death: 31 July 1917. Service No.10743. Born in Thurles and enlisted in Templemore. Killed in action. He was formerly with the Royal Irish Regiment where his number was 10379.

Supplementary information: Son of Pierce and Alice Burke, of Stradavoher Street, Thurles, Co. Tipperary. Grave or Memorial Reference: Has no known grave but is commemorated on Panel 44. Memorial: Ypres (Menin Gate) Memorial in Belgium.

BURKE, James Leo: Rank: Private. Regiment or Service: Oxford and Bucks Light Infantry. Unit: 2nd-4th Bn. Age at death: 20. Date of death: 22 August 1917. Service No.203442. Born in Clogheen, Co. Tipperary and enlisted in New Court Middlesex while living in Clogheen. Killed in action. He was formerly with the Royal Buckinghamshire Hussars where his number was 2730.

Supplementary information: Son of Joanna Mary Burke, of Mountanglesby, Clogheen, Co. Tipperary, and the late Michael E. Burke. Grave or Memorial Reference: Has no known grave but is commemorated on Panel 96 to 98. Memorial: Tyne Cot Memorial in Belgium. He is also commemorated on the Cahir War Memorial.

BURKE, John: Rank: Private. No 8937, Royal Irish Regiment, 2nd Bn. Date of death: 5 July 1916, Born: Cashel, Co. Tipperary and enlisted in Cashel. Killed in action during the battle of the Somme, France. Has no known grave but is commemorated on Pier and Face 3 A. on the Thiepval Memorial in France.

BURKE, John: Rank: Private. Regiment or Service: Royal Irish Regiment. Unit: 2nd Bn. Date of death: 19 October 1914. Service No.6266. Born in St Peter's and St Paul's, Clonmel, Co. Tipperary. Enlisted in Clonmel. Killed in action. He has no known grave but is listed on Panels 11 and 12 on the Le Touret Memorial in France.

BURKE, J. C.: Rank: Private. Regiment or Service: Machine Gun Corps. Unit:: Infantry. Age at death: 26. Date of death: 21 June 1920. Service

No. 18035.

Supplementary information: Son of Mrs Catherine Burke of 33 River Street, Clonmel. Cemetery, Clonmel, St Patricks Cemetery. Grave location: 5. N. 152.

BURKE, Michael: Rank: Private. Regiment or Service: Irish Guards. Unit: 1st Bn. Date of death: 5 October 1916. Service No. 9437. Born in Ballylooby, Co. Tipperary. Enlisted in Dublin while living in Ardfinnan, Co. Tipperary. Died of wounds. Grave or Memorial Reference: XI. F. 5A. Cemetery: Etaples Military Cemetery in France. He is also commemorated on the Cahir War Memorial.

BURKE, Patrick: Rank: Private. Regiment or Service: Royal Irish Regiment. Unit: 1st Bn. Age at death: 28. Date of death: 25 May 1915. Service No. 6956. Born in Templemore and enlisted in Dublin while living in Templemore. Died of wounds.

Supplementary information: Son of Thomas and Mary Burke, of Templemore; husband of Elizabeth Burke, of Church Street, Templemore, Co. Tipperary. Grave or Memorial Reference: I. F. 140. Cemetery: Bailleul Communal Cemetery Extension (Nord) in France.

BURKE/BOURKE, Stephen: Rank: Private. Regiment or Service: Leinster Regiment. Unit: 2nd Bn. Age at death: 27. Date of death: 9 November 1914. Service No. 7192. Born in Templemore and enlisted there also. He died of wounds at home.

Supplementary information: Son of Thomas and Johanna Burke, of Templemore: husband of Johanna Burke (*née* Leahy), of New Rd, Templemore, Co. Tipperary. Grave or Memorial Reference: Soldiers' Plot. 171 (Screen Wall). Cemetery: Moston (St Joseph's) Roman Catholic Cemetery, UK.

BURKE, Thomas: Rank: Private. Regiment or Service: Leinster Regiment. Unit: 2nd Bn. Date of death: 11 February 1916. Service No. 3748. Born in Templemore. Enlisted in Templemore. Killed in action. Grave or Memorial Reference: I. G. 18. Cemetery: Menin Road South Military Cemetery in Belgium.

BURKE, William: Rank: Lance Corporal. Regiment or Service: Royal Munster Fusiliers. Unit: 2nd Bn. Date of death: 27 April 1916. Service No. 10206. Born in St John's in Limerick and enlisted in Limerick while living in Ennis Co. Clare. Killed in action.

Supplementary information: Husband of Louisa Tierney (formerly Burke), of John Street, Nenagh, Co. Tipperary. Grave or Memorial Reference: A. 82. Cemetery: Bully-Grenay Communal Cemetery, French Extension in France.

BURNS, Garret: Rank: Private. Regiment or Service: Royal Irish Regiment. Unit: 5th Bn. Date of death: 4 November 1918. Service No. 21. Born in St Michael's, Co. Tipperary. Enlisted in Clonmel while living in

Tipperary. Killed in action. Age at death: 22.

Supplementary information: Son of Michael and Ellen Burns, of Bansha Rd, Tipperary. Grave or Memorial Reference: I. B. 15. Cemetery: Cross Roads Cemetery, Fontaine-Au-Bois in France.

BURNS, James: Rank: Donkeyman. Regiment or Service: Mercantile Marine. Unit: S.S. *Alfalfa* (London) Age at death: 44. Date of death: 6 May 1917.

Supplementary information: Born at Tipperary. Memorial: Has no known grave but is commemorated on the the Tower Hill Memorial, London.

BURNS, Martin: Rank: Private. Regiment or Service: Royal Irish Regiment. Unit: 6th Bn. Date of death: 16 August 1917. Service No. 1407. Born in Drombane. Enlisted in Thurles while living in Drombane. Killed in action. Age at death: 32.

Supplementary information: Son of Mrs Johanna Burns, of Roskeen, Drombane, Thurles. He has no known grave but is listed on Panels 51 and 52 on the Tyne Cot Memorial in Belgium.

BURNS, William: Rank: Private. Regiment or Service: Connaught Rangers. Unit: 2nd Bn. Date of death: 26 August 1914. Service No. 7719. Born in Nenagh. Enlisted in Birr while living in Nenagh. Killed in action. He has no known grave but is listed on the La Ferte-Sous-Jouarre-Memorial in France.

BURNS, William: Rank: Corporal. Regiment or Service: Kings Liverpool Regiment. Unit: 13th Bn. Date of death: 21 August 1918. Service No. 95105. Formerly he was with the Royal Irish Fusiliers where his number was 16545. Born in Tipperary. Enlisted in Clonmel, Munster while living in Tipperary. He won the Military Medal and is listed in the *London Gazette*. Killed in action. Grave or Memorial Reference: A. 45. Cemetery: Railway Cutting Cemetery, Courcelles-Le-Comte.

Killed at the Front.

News has reached Cloughjordan that Mr Martin Butler, son of Mr Edward Butler, of that town, has been killed in action in Flanders. Deceased with a number of young men from Cloughjordan enlisted in the 3rd Leinsters about twelve months ago, and when his battalion was under orders for the front got the option from his commanding officer of remaining in Ireland for a time, but he volunteered to go out with his comrades. It is stated that he was killed by a shell which struck the trench in which he was.

Martin Butler.

BUTLER, Hugh: Rank: Private. Regiment or Service: Labour Corps. Unit: 89th Coy. Date of death: 9 June 1918. Service No.478180. Formerly he was with the Leinster Regiment where his number was 3197. Born in Rathcabbin, Birr, Co. Tipperary. Enlisted in Birr Co. Tipperary. Killed in action. Grave or Memorial Reference: III. C. 2. Cemetery: Hershin Communal Cemetery Extension France.

BUTLER, James:. Rank: Private. Regiment or Service: Royal Dublin Fusiliers. Unit: 9th Bn. Date of death: 31 July 1916. Service No.17220. Born in Fethard and enlisted in Clonmel while living in Fethard. Killed in action.

Supplementary information: Son of James and Mary Butler, of The Green, Fethard, Co. Tipperary. Grave or Memorial Reference: III. K. 15. Cemetery:Vermelles British Cemetery in France.

BUTLER, James: Rank: Private. Regiment or Service: Royal Dublin Fusiliers. Unit: 2nd Bn. Secondary Regiment: South Irish Horse Secondary. Unit: formerly (2041). Date of death: 21 March 1918. Service No.27485. Born in Clonmel and enlisted there also.

Supplementary information: Husband of Florence Butler, of 7 Thomas Street, Clonmel, Co. Tipperary. Grave or Memorial Reference: Has no known grave but is commemorated on Panel 79 and 80. Memorial: Pozieres Memorial in France.

BUTLER, James: Rank: Private. Regiment or Service: Royal Irish Regiment. Unit: 'C' Coy. 2nd Bn. Age at death: 31. Date of death: 31 January 1917. Service No.9420. Born in Ballingarry in Tipperary and enlisted in Clonmel while livng in Ballycurry Co.Tipperary. Killed in action.

Supplementary information: Son of William Butler, of Ballincurry,Thurles, Co. Tipperary. Grave or Memorial Reference: M. 52. Cemetery: Kemmel

Grave of John Butler.

Chateau Military Cemetery in Belgium.

BUTLER, John: Rank: Private. Regiment or Service: Royal Irish Regiment. Unit: 3rd Bn. Date of death: 26 February 1916. Service No.9054. Born in Ballingarry. Enlisted in Clonmel while living in Thurles. Died at home. Age at death: 26.

Supplementary information: Son of William Butler, Ballincurry, Thurles. Grave or Memorial Reference: Near the south-east Corner. Cemetery: Ballingarry Old Graveyard in Tipperary.

BUTLER, Martin: Rank: Private. Regiment or Service: Royal Irish Regiment. Unit: 6th Bn. Age at death: 21. Date of death: 4 June 1916. Service No.7973. Born in Shinrone and enlisted in Cloughjordan. Killed in action.

Supplementary information: Son of Edward and Margaret Butler, of Knocknacree, Cloughjordan, Co. Tipperary. Grave or Memorial Reference: I. K. 18. Cemetery: Dud Corner Cemetery, Loos in France.

BUTLER, Michael: Rank: Private. Regiment or Service: Leinster Regiment. Unit: E Company, 5th Bn. Date of death: 26 December 1917. Service No.5778. Born in Tipperary. Emlisted in Limerick while living in Tipperary. Died at home. Age at death: 20.

Supplementary information: Son of Mrs Mary Butler, of Eatons Cottages, Tipperary. Grave or Memorial

Reference: None given. Cemetery: Glencorse New Cemetery, UK.

BUTLER, Patrick: Rank: Sergeant. Regiment or Service: Northumberland Fusiliers. Unit: 24th (Tyneside Irish) Bn. Age at death: 39. Date of death: 1 July 1916. Service No.24-348. Born in Clonmel and enlisted in Newcastle-on-Tyne. Killed in action on the first day of the battle of the Somme.

Supplementary information: Son of James and Bridget Butler: husband of Sarah Butler, of 5 Lambton Court, Newcastle-on-Tyne. Born in Co. Tipperary. Grave or Memorial Reference: V. J. 1. Cemetery: Ovillers Military Cemetery, France.

BUTLER, Peter: Rank: Private. Regiment or Service: East Lancashire Regiment. Unit: 2nd Bn. Date of death: 15 March 1915. Service No.11048. Born in Nenagh, Co. Tipperary. Enlisted in Preston in Lancs while living in Church, Lancs. Died of wounds. Grave or Memorial Reference: III. F. 2. Cemetery: Estaires Communal Cemetery and Extension in France.

BUTLER, Pierce: Rank: Private. Regiment or Service: Tank Corps. Unit: 14th Bn. Date of death: 9 August 1918. Service No.301846. Formerly he was with the Royal Field Artillery where his number was 99742. Born in Clonmel. Enlisted in Clonmel. Killed in action. Grave or Memorial Reference: I. B. 2. Rosiers Communal Cemetery Extension in France.

Grave of Thomas Butler-Stoney.

BUTLER, Richard: Rank: Sergeant. Regiment or Service: Canadian Cavalry Machine Gun Sqn. Age at death: 30. Date of death: 30 March 1918. Service No.116055. Son of the late Joseph and Ellen Butler, of Castle Street, Cahir, Co. Tipperary, Ireland. Age on Enlistment: 34 Years. 6 Months. Eye colour: Brown. Complexion: Dark. Hair colour: Black. Religion: R.C. Chest expansion: 1". Girth: 37". Date of Enlistment: 18 March 1915. Place of Enlistment:Vancouver.

Supplementary information: Brother of Mr John Butler, Victualler, Bridge Street, Tipperary. He has no known grave but is listed on Vimy Memorial, France. He is also commemorated on the Cahir War Memorial.

BUTLER-STONEY, Thomas. Rank: Lt. Regiment or Service: Irish Guards. Unit: 1st Bn. Age at death: 42. Died of wounds. Date of death: 30 September 1917. Lorrha, Cemetery, Tipperary. Grave location: In the family plot by the entrance

BUTLER, Thomas. Rank: Private. Regiment or Service: Royal Dublin Fusiliers. Unit: 1st Bn. Age at death: 25. Date of death: 10 October 1917. Service No.18631 He won the Military Medal. Born in Fethard and enlisted in Clonmel. Killed in action.

Supplementary information: Son of James and Mary Butler of Lower Green, Fethard, Co. Tipperary. Grave or Memorial Reference: Has no known grave but is commemorated on Panel 144 to 145. Memorial: Tyne Cot Memorial in Belgium.

BUTLER, Walter. Rank: Private. Regiment or Service: Royal Irish Regiment. Unit: 5th Bn and 2nd Bn.Age at death: 37. Date of death: 8 May 1915.

Service No.5885. Born in Monard in Tipperary and enlisted in Tipperary Town while living in Bohercrow Co. Tipperary. Killed in action.

Supplementary information: Son of Walter Butler, of Ballyhilip, Solohead, Tipperary. Brother of coachbuilder Mr P Butler of Bohercrowe. Grave or Memorial Reference: Has no known grave but is commemorated on Panel 33. Memorial: Ypres (Menin Gate) Memorial in Belgium.

BUTLER, Walter Paget: Rank: Private. Regiment or Service: Royal Fusiliers (City of London Regiment). Unit: 2nd Bn. Date of death: 1 July 1916, on the first day of the Battle of the Somme. Service No.L-12382. Born in Llandilo. Enlisted in Clonmel while living in Carrick-on-Suir, Co. Tipperary. Killed in action. He has no known grave but is listed on Pier and Face 8 C, 9 A and 16 A on the Thiepval Memorial in France.

BUTLER, William: Rank: Private. Regiment or Service: Irish Guards. Unit: 2nd Bn. Date of death: 15 September 1916. Service No.7404. Born in Ballingarry. Enlisted in Dublin. Killed in action.

Supplementary information: He has no known grave but is listed on Pier and Face 7 D on the Thiepval Memorial in France.

BYRNE, Edward: Rank: Private. Regiment or Service: Royal Irish Regiment. Unit: 2nd Bn. Date of death: 19 October 1914. Service No.10896. Born in St Mary's, Clonmel, Co.

Tipperary. Enlisted in Clonmel. Killed in action. Grave or Memorial Reference: IV. J. 3. Cemetery: Bailleul Communal Cemetery Extension (Nord) in France.

BYRNE, George Johnston: Rank: Lance Corporal. Regiment or Service: Auckland Infantry Regiment. Service No.30729. Born in Tipperary 12 August 1886. Religion, C.oE. Occupation on Enlistment: Driver. Next of Kin: Mrs M. Byrne (Mother), 28 Iona Road, Glasnevin, Dublin, Ireland, a widow with three children. Address at enlistment: Brown Street, Remuera, Auckland, New Zealand. Height: 5 feet 7 inches, Weight: 10 stone, Complexion: Fair, Hair colour: Fair. Date of enlistment 22 August 1916. Age on enlistment: 30. Embarked with 20th Reinforcements Auckland Infantry Battalion, A Company on the vessel 'Port Lyttelton' in Wellington heading for davenport and arrived there 18 September 1916. Illnesses during service: Admitted with pneumonia 26 May 1917. Discharged from dangerously ill list 11 June 1917. in 35th General Hospital. Transferred to Conv. Depot, Hornchurch 2 July 1917. Discharged Hornchurch 4 August. 1917. Killed in action in Havrincourt, France on 28 September 1918. Age at death 32.

Supplementary information: Son of John and the late Mary Byrne, husband of the late Janie Byrne. Born at Portland, Birr, Ireland. Husband to Ida Jane Byrne, died 27 October 1915. Father to George Johnston Byrne, born 12. August. 10 and John Edward

Byrne, born 8 March 1912. and Robert Leslie Byrne, born 20 May 1914. Grave or Memorial Reference: II. C. 7. Cemetery: Fifteen Ravine British Cemetery, Villers-Plouich, Nord, France.

BYRNE, Harry Benjamin Cyril: ank: Private. Regiment or Service; Royal Scots Fusiliers. Unit: 1st Bn. Date of death: 13 November 1914. Service No.8788. Born in Tipperary. Enlisted in London while living in Pimlico, London. Died of wounds. Age at death: 30.

Supplementary information: Son of Patrick and Mary Byrne, of 29A Bessborough Gardens, Grosvenor Rd, London. He has no known grave but is listed on Panel 19 and 33 on the Ypres (Menin Gate) Memorial in Belgium.

BYRNE, Henry Patrick. Rank: Lance Corporal. Regiment or Service: Leinster Regiment. Unit: 1st Bn. Age at death: 33. Date of death: 7 April 1917. Service No.8909. Born in Dublin and enlisted in Cahir. Died in Salonika.

Supplementary information: Son of Henry and Mary Ann Byrne, of Clonmel, Co. Tipperary, Ireland. Grave or Memorial Reference: 1. E. 10. Cemetery: Dar Es Salaam War Cemetery in Tanznia.

BYRNE, John M. Rank: Private. Regiment or Service: Irish Guards. Unit: 2nd Bn. Date of death: 28 September 1916. Service No.6374. Born in Tipperary. Enlisted in Dublin. Killed in action. He has no known grave but is listed on Pier and Face 7D on the Thiepval Memorial in France.

BYRNE, Patrick: Rank: Lance Corporal. Regiment or Service: Royal Irish Rifles. Unit: 1st Bn. Secondary. Unit: attd. 25th Light Trench Mortar Bty. Age at death: 21. Date of death: 30 August 1916. Service No.8638. Born in Thurles and enlisted in Dublin. Killed in action.

Supplementary information: Native of Tipperary. Grave or Memorial Reference: VI. E. 5. Cemetery: Vermelles British Cemetery in France.

BYRNE, Patrick: Served as **BEIRNE**. Rank: Sergeant. Regiment or Service: Connaught Rangers. Unit: 2nd Bn. Date of death: 19 September 1914. Service No.6574. Born in Castlerea, Co. Roscommon. Enlisted in Galway while living in Roscrea. Killed in action. Age at death: 34.

Supplementary information: Son of Thomas and Mary Beirne (née Murray), Furfield, Castlerea, Co. Roscommon, Served in South African War. He has no known grave but is listed on the La Ferte-Sous-Jouarre-Memorial in France.

BYRNE, Patrick: Rank: Private. Regiment or Service: Machine Gun Corps (Infantry). Unit: 152nd Coy. He was previously with the Royal Dublin Fusiliers where his number was 18883. Date of death: 9 July 1917. Service No.43219. Born in St Peter's and St Paul's Clonmel and enlisted in Clonmel. Died of wounds.

Supplementary information: Brother

of Thomas Byrne, of Raheen Cottage, Clonmel, Co. Tipperary. Grave or Memorial Reference: XIV. B. 20. Cemetery: Lijssenthoek Military Cemetary in Belgium.

BYRNE, Thomas: Rank: Private. Regiment or Service: Royal Irish Regiment. Unit: 2ND Bn. Age at death: 26. Date of death: 14 May 1915. Service No. 11008. Born in Cashel and enlisted in Cashel. Killed in action during the second battle of Ypres.

Supplementary information: Son of David and Catherine Byrne, of Lady's Well Street, Cashel, Co. Tipperary. Grave or Memorial Reference: Has no known grave but is commemorated on Panel 33. Memorial: Ypres (Menin Gate) Memorial in Belgium.

BYRNES, Denis: Rank: Private. No 4195, Irish Guards, 1st Bn, Died 6 November 14. Age at death: 26. Born: Cashel, Co. Tipperary and enlisted in Cork City. Killed in action during the first battle of Ypres. Has no known grave but is commemorated on the Ypres (Menin gate) Memorial on Panel 11.

C

CAHILL, Michael: Rank: Private. Regiment or Service: Connaught Rangers. Unit: 'A' Coy. 1st Bn. Age at death: 20. Date of death: 3 November 1914. Service No. 10210. Born in Nenagh and enlisted in Nenagh while living there also. Died of gunshot wounds.

Supplementary information: Son of Thomas and Norah Cahill, of Dublin Rd, Nenagh, Co. Tipperary. Michaels older brother Daniel who also served was wounded but survived the war. Grave or Memorial Reference: I. O. 1. Cemetery: La Gorgue Communal Cemetery in France.

CAHILL, Michael: Rank: Sergeant. Regiment or Service: Royal Irish Regiment. Unit: 2nd Bn. Age at death: 28. Date of death: 21 August 1918. Service No. 8993. Born in Gammensfield in Tipperary and enlisted in Clonmel. Killed in action.

Supplementary information: Son of Mr and Mrs Richard Cahill, of Killaloan, Tipperary husband of Mary Cahill, of Kilhefernan, Clonmel. Grave or Memorial Reference: Has no known grave but is commemorated on Panel 5. Vis-En-Artois Memorial in France.

CAHILL, Patrick J: Rank: Private. Regiment or Service: Irish Guards. Unit: 1st Bn. Age at death: 24. Date of death: 23 October 1915. Service No. 7714. Born in Clonmel and enlisted in Neath in Glamorganshire while living in Clonmel. Died of wounds in Gallipoli.

Supplementary information: Son of Bridget and Patrick Clancy, of Toomevara, Nenagh, Co. Tipperary. Grave or Memorial Reference: III. C. 9. Cemetery: Abbeyville Communal Cemetery in France.

Patrick Cahill (No, 437244).
Photograph courtesy of Bridgte Hayes, Holycross.

CAHILL, Patrick: Rank: Private. Regiment or Service: Manitoba Regiment, Canadian Infantry. Unit: 51st Bn and 78th Bn. Date of death: 9 April 1917. Service No.437244. Born in Holycross Co. Tipperary on 23 August 1894. Occupation on enlistment: automobile driver. Attested on 14 May 1915 in Edmonton in Canada. Age on enlistment: 20 years and 7 months. Height: 5' 5 ¾". Complexion: fair. Eyes: blue. Hair: brown. Religious Denomination: R.C. His will dated 2 June 16 states that all of his property is to be given to his sister Mary Cahill, Holycross, Co. Tipperary, Ireland. He list his next of Kin as Miss Bridget Hayes, Holycross, Tipperary. Circumstances of Casualty dated 9 April 1917. States: 'Killed in action during the attack on Vimy Ridge, and after reaching the German third line trench, he was shot through the head by an enemy machine gun bullet and instantly killed.' Cemetery: Cabaret Rouge British Cemetery, Souchez. Grave 1, Plot, 7 Row F.

Note: Thomas M Hayes (British Army) No 41758 Died in Mesopotamia, Patrick Hayes (British Army), No. 7079 died of wounds. John Quinane (Australian Army), No. 2225 Died of disease and Patrick Cahill (Canadian Army), (No. 437244) Killed at Vimy Ridge were all related.

CAIN, Thomas:. Rank: Private. Regiment or Service: Border Regiment. Unit: 2nd Bn. Date of death: 25 September 1915. Service No.19919. Born in Tipperary. Enlisted in Bolton while living in St Helen's. Killed in action. He has no known grave but is listed on Panel 68 and 69 on the Loos Memorial in France.

CAIRNS, James: Rank: Trooper. Regiment or Service: Household Cavalry and Cavalry of the line including the Yeomanry and Imperial Camel Corps. Unit: Household Battalion, C Company. Date of death: 9 May 1917. Service No.1924. Formerly he was with the Ayearshire Yeomanry where his number was 2753. Born in Ardfinnan. Enlisted in Saltcoats. Killed in action. Age at death: 32.

Supplementary information: Son of Thomas and Helen Bryan Cairns, of 84, Ran Street, Saltcoats. Husband of Henrietta McKie Cairns, of 14 Raise Street, Saltcoats, Ayrshire. He has no known grave but is listed in Bay 1 on the Arras Memorial in France.

CALLAGHAN, George: Rank: Private. Regiment or Service: Leicestershire Regiment. Unit: 7th Bn. Date of death: 14 July 1916. Service No.16882. Born in Knockeevin, Tipperary. Enlisted in Leicester. Killed in action. He has no known grave but is listed on Pier and Face 2C and 3A on the Thiepval Memorial in France.

CALLAGHAN, John: Rank: Private. Regiment or Service: Royal Irish Regiment. Unit: 2nd Bn. Date of death: 5 August 1917. Service No.9646. Born in Monard, Co. Tipperary. Enlisted in Tipperary. Killed in action. Grave or Memorial Reference: C.24. Cemetery: Potijze Chateau Lawn Cemetery in Belgium.

CALLAGHAN, Michael John: Rank: Sergeant. Regiment or Service: Machine Gun Corps (Infantry). Unit: 36th Coy. He was previously with the Royal Sussex regiment where his number was 459. Age at death: 23. Date of death: 16 February 1916. Service No.20301. Born in Grange in Tipperay and enlisted in Horesham in the UK while living in Clonmel. Killed in action.

Supplementary information: Son of Patrick and Mary Anne Callaghan, of Knocklofty, Demesne, Clonmel, Co. Tipperary. Grave or Memorial Reference: B. 26. Cemetery: Quarry Cemetery, Vermelles in France.

CALLAGHAN, William: Rank: Private. Regiment or Service: Kings Liver Pool Regiment. Unit: 8th Bn. Date of death: 1 July 1917. Service No.306618. Born in Scrageen Co. Tipperary. Enlisted in Liverpool while living in Tipperary. Killed in action. Grave or Memorial Reference: VIII. B. 24. Cemetery: Cite Bonjean Military Cemetery, Armentaires in France.

CANTWELL, Henry: Rank: Private. Regiment or Service: Irish Guards. Unit: 2nd Bn. Age at death: 36. Date of death: 9 October 1917. Service No.9438. Enlisted in Dublin. Killed in action.

Supplementary information: Son of William and Eliza Cantwell, of Newpark, The Commons, Thurles, Co. Tipperary. Grave or Memorial Reference. Has no known grave but is commemorated on Panel 10 to 11. Memorial: Tyne Cot Memorial in Belgium.

CARBERY, William: Rank: Private. Regiment or Service: Leinster Regiment. Unit: 'D' Coy. 6th Bn. Age at death: 26. Date of death: 20 June 1918. Service No.4385. Born in Carrick-on-Suir and enlisted in Clonmel while living in Clonmel. Died of wounds.

Supplementary information: Son of Philip and Ellen Carbery, of 25 Davis's Rd, Clonmel, Tipperary. Grave or Memorial Reference: III. D. 4. Cemetery: Aire Communal Cemetery in France.

CARDEN, Henry Charles: Rank: Major. Regiment or Service: Devonshire Regiment. Unit: 8th Bn. Age at death: 60. Date of death: 25 September 1915. He was a member of the peerage and previously fought in the Boer War. Awards: D S O.

Supplementary information: Son of Sir John Craven Carden, 4th Bart, of Templemore Abbey, Co. Tipperary: husband of Blanche Catherine Carden, (*née* Blanche Catherine Jones-Parry), daughter of Rear Admiral John Parry Jones-Parry, of Thelwall, Aylestone Hill, Hereford. Grave or Memorial Reference: Has no known grave but is commemorated on Panel 35 to 37. Memorial: Loos Memorial in France.

CAREW, J. M.: Rank: Wireless Operator. Regiment or Service: Mercantile Marine. Unit: S.S. *Clan Murray* (Glasgow) Age at death: 20. Date of death: 29 May 1917.

Supplementary information: Son of Mr Carew, of 9 The Square, Cahir, Co. Tipperary. Born at Cahir, Co. Tipperary. The S. S. *Clan Murray* was

Grave of Patrick Carrigan.

torpedoed by a German Submarine without warning in 1917. with a loss of 64 lives. Two of the ships officers were taken prisoner. Has no known grave but is commemorated on the Tower Hill Memorial, London. He is also commemorated on the Cahir War Memorial.

CAREY(CARRY), John: Rank: Private. Regiment or Service: Royal Irish Regiment. Unit: 2nd Bn. Age at death: 53. Date of death: 19 October 1914. Service No.6767. Born in Cashel and enlisted in Cashel. Killed in action.

Supplementary information: Son of the late Michael and Mary Carey: husband of Lizzie Carey, of The Green, Cashel, Co. Tipperary. Grave or Memorial Reference: Has no known grave but is commemorated on Panel 11 and 12. Memorial: Le Touret Memorial in France.

CAREY, Martin: Rank: Gunner. Regiment or Service: Royal Garrison Artillery. Date of death: 25 November 1916. Service No.7505. Enlisted in Llanelly while living in Carrick-on-Suir, Co. Tipperary. Died at home. Grave or Memorial Reference: C. 63. Cemetery: Fareham, Cemetery, UK.

CAREY, Patrick: Rank: Private. Regiment or Service: Royal Irish Regiment. Unit: 5th Bn. Date of death: 16 August 1915. Service No.2000. Born in St Mary's, Clonmel Co. Tipperary. Enlisted in while living in. Killed in action in Gallipoli. He has no known grave but is listed on Panel 55 on the Helles Memorial in Turkey.

CAREY, Thomas. Rank: Private. Regiment or Service: Yorkshire Regiment. Unit: 10th Bn. Date of death: 30 November 1915. Service No.12921. Born in Newport, Tipperary. Enlisted in West Hartlepool while living in Newport. Killed in action.

Grave of J. Carroll.

Grave or Memorial Reference: I A 22. Cemetery: Houplines Communal Cemetery Extension, France.

CARNEY, Thomas: Rank: Private. Regiment or Service: South Lancashire Regiment. Unit: 2nd Bn. Date of death: 3 June 1917. Service No.32045. Formerly he was with the D Gds where his number was 1708. Born in Roscrea. Enlisted in the Curragh. Killed in action. Grave or Memorial Reference: II. J. 8. Cemetery: St Quentin Cabaret Military Cemetery in Belgium.

CARR, Thomas. Rank: Private. Regiment or Service: Border Regiment. Unit: 3rd Bn. Date of death: 6 April 1916. Service No.24308. Born in Tipperary. Enlisted in Manchester while living in Hulme, Manchester. Died at home. Age at death: 22.
Supplementary information: Son of

Thomas Henry and Gertrude Carr, of 310, Ashton New Rd, Manchester. Grave or Memorial Reference: E. NG. 2346A. Cemetery: Bangor, (Glanadda) Cemetery, UK.

CARRIGAN, Patrick: Rank: Private. Regiment or Service: Coldstream Guards. Date of death: 2 November 1918. Age at death: 31. Service No.25083. Born in Tipperary. Enlisted in Leeds. Died at home.
Supplementary information: Son of James and Kate Carrigan, of Burnchurch, Killinauld: husband of Ellen Carrigan, of 15, Nowell Avenue, Harehills, Leeds. He served with the Leeds City Police before the War. Grave or Memorial Reference: south-west of the church. Cemetery: Moglass Catholic Churchyard, Tipperary.

CARROLL, David: Rank: Company Quartermaster Sergeant. Regiment or

Service: East-Lancashire Regiment. Unit: 2nd Bn. Age at death: 25. Date of death: 3 January 1918. Service No.9208. Born in Cashel and enlisted in Tipperary. Killed in action.

Supplementary information: Son of Daniel and Bridget Carroll, of Tipperary. Grave or Memorial Reference: II. E. 1. Cemetery: White House Cemetery, Jean-Les-Ypres in Belgium.

CARROLL, E: Rank: Private. Regiment or Service: Labour Corps. Date of death: 11 September 1917. Service No.200429. Born in Carrick-on-Suir, Co. Tipperary. Enlisted in Carrick-on-Suir, Co. Tipperary. Died at home. Age at death: 45.

Supplementary information: Husband of Anastatia Carroll, of Mill Street, Carrick-on-Suir. Grave or Memorial Reference: 603. Cemetery: Curragh Military Cemetery in Co. Kildare.

CARROLL, J.: Rank: Private. Regiment or Service: Connaught Rangers. Unit: 3rd Bn. Date of death: 18 January 1919. Service No.6683. Additional information: Husband of C. Carroll of Haymarket Street, Ballinasloe. Cemetery: Nenagh (Barrack Street) Old Graveyard. Grave location: In north-west part near the North wall.

CARROLL, Joseph: Rank: Private. Regiment or Service: Connaught Rangers. Unit: 2nd Bn. Date of death: 17 September 1914. Service No.6429. Born in Templemore. Enlisted in Birr while living in Templemore. Died of wounds. Grave or Memorial Reference: II. E. 6. Cemetery: Vailly British Cemetery in France.

CARROLL, Joseph: Rank: Sapper. Regiment or Service: Royal Engineers. Unit: 43rd Broad Gauge Railway Operating Coy. Age at death:

Grave of Matthew Carroll..

34. Date of death: 27 April 1918. Service No.249319. and WR-249319. Irelands Memorial Records say he was born in Cashel and enlisted in Tipperary Town while Soldiers died in the Great War say he was born in Roscrea, Co. Galway and enlisted in London. He was previously with the London Regiment (43rd B. G. O. Coy) where his number was 5079. Killed in action.

Supplementary information: Son of Wm. B. and A. Carroll, of 'Curregregue House', Templederry, Co. Tipperary. Grave or Memorial Reference: IV. A. 16. Cemetery: Abbeville Communal Cemetery Extension in France.

CARROLL, Martin: Rank: Lance Corporal. Regiment or Service: Royal Munster Fusiliers. Unit: 'D' Coy. 1st Bn. Age at death: 25. Date of death: 28 June 1915. Service No.9346. Born in Clonoulty and enlisted in Clonmel while living in Thurles. Killed in action in Gallipoli.

Supplementary information: Son of Thomas and Mary Carroll, of Cloneyharp, Drombane, Thurles, Co. Tipperary. Grave or Memorial Reference: Has no known grave but is commemorated on Panel 185 to 190. Memorial: Helles Memorial in Turkey.

CARROLL, Matthew: Rank: Sapper. Regiment or Service: Corps of Royal Engineers. Unit: Inland Water Transport and Inland Waterways and Docks. Date of death: 17 February 1918. Service No. WR-315439. Born in Templemore. Enlisted in Dublin while living in Templemore. Died at home. Age at death: 23. Grave or Memorial Reference: Plot 2. Cemetery: Templemore Catholic Cemetery, Tipperary.

CARROLL, Michael: Rank: Private. Regiment or Service: Royal Irish Regiment. Unit: 2nd Bn. Date of death: 21 October 1914. Service No.6627. Born in Nenagh. Enlisted in Nenagh. Killed in action. He has no known grave but is listed on Panels 11 and 12 on the Le Touret Memorial in France.

CARROLL, Patrick: Rank: Sergeant. Regiment or Service:

CARROLL, THOMAS, Private, No. 4449, 1st Battn. Irish Guards, s. of the late Martin Carroll, of Thurles, by his wife, Mary (Stradooner Street, Thurles, co. Tipperary), dau. of Joseph Pollard ; b. Thurles, 24 Aug. 1892 ; educ. Christian Brothers' School there ; enlisted 30 April, 1913 ; served with the Expeditionary Force in France and Flanders from Aug. 1914 ; was present at the Battles of Mons, of the Marne and Aisne, and was killed in action at Ypres, 1 Nov. following, by a sniper, after taking part in the First Battle of Ypres, and buried in a small wood near ; unm.

Thomas Carroll, From De Ruvigny's Roll of Honour.

61

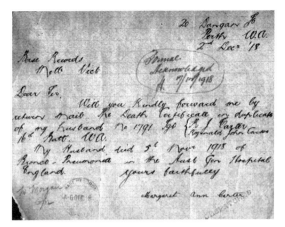

Letter written by the wife of Reginald John Carter.

Durham Light Infantry. Unit: 10th Bn. Date of death: 28 August 1916. Service No.9043. Born in Tipperary, Templemore, Tipperary. Enlisted in West Harltlepool while living in Templemore. Killed in action.

Supplementary information: Son of Daniel and Mary Carroll. He has no known grave but is listed on Pier and Face 14 A and 15 C on the Thiepval Memorial in France.

CARROLL, Thomas: Rank: Private. Regiment or Service: Manchester Regiment. Unit 1st Bn. Date of death: 8 March 1916. Service No.7716. Born in Roscrea. Enlisted in Manchester while living in Whitechurch, Salop. Killed in action in Mesopotamia. Age at death: 18.

Supplementary information: Son of Patrick and B Carroll. He has no known grave but is listed on panels 31 and 64 on the Basra Memorial in Iraq.

CARROLL, Thomas: Rank: Private. Regiment or Service: Irish Guards. Unit: 2nd Bn. Date of death: 1 November 1914. Service No.4449.

Born in Thurles. Enlisted in Clonmel. Killed in action. He has no known grave but is listed on Panel 11 on the Ypres (Menin Gate) Memorial in Belgium.

CARROLL, William: Rank: Gunner. Regiment or Service: Royal Garrison Artillery. Unit: 226th Siege Battery. Date of death: 28 May 1917. Service No.124729. Born in Tipperary. Enlisted in Tipperary. Killed in action. Grave or Memorial Reference: II. A. 8. Cemetery: Henin Communal Cemetery Extension in France.

CARTER, Reginald John: Rank: Sergeant. (CQMS). Regiment or Service: Australian Infantry, A. I. F. Service Number, 1791. Born in Clonmel. Husband of Mrs Margaret Anne. Carter, 17 Hooper Street, West Perth. Unit: 16th Bn. Age on enlistment: 30. Height 5' 7 ¾ ", weight 118lbs, brown eyes, sallow complexion, Brown hair and Religeon was C of E. Distinguishing marks: Devils head tattoo on left forearm. Occupation on enlistment: Railway Porter and

Christopher Casey's Victory medal purchased some years ago from the USA.

Cable boy. Enlistment date: 13 January 1915. Served in Mudros, Gallipoli, Alexandria, Sutton, Anzac, Portsmouth, Dartford, Hurdcott, Rouen, Camiers, Le Havre, Egypt, Folkstone, Abbeville, France and trained in the famous Bull Ring in Etaples. Age at death 34. Date of death: 15 November 1918. Admitted to hospital with influenza and died of Broncho Pneumonia due to exposure three days later. Enlisted in Perth, WA.

Supplementary information: Son of Thomas Bernard and Anna Carter and husband of Margaret Ann Carter, of 17, Hooper Street, Perth, Western Australia. Native of Ireland. Grave or Memorial Reference: V. A. 48. Cemetery: FRANCE 52 Abbeville Communal Cemetery Extension.

CARTHY, Thomas. Rank: Private. Regiment or Service: Royal Irish Regiment. Unit: 2nd Bn. Age at death: 47. Date of death: 24 May 1915. Service No.6566. Born: St Peter's and St Paul's in Clonmel and enlisted in Clonmel. Killed in action.

Supplementary information: Husband of Mary Carthy, of 34, River Street, Clonmel, Co. Tipperary. Grave or Memorial Reference: LVI. F. 7. Cemetery. Poelcapelle British Cemetery in Belgium. He is buried beside John Condon, the youngest

casualty of First World War, he was fourteen years old and it took seven years to find what was left of his body, some bones and a boot.

CARTY, John: Rank: CSM. Regiment or Service: Connaught Rangers. Unit: 1st Bn. Date of death: 18 April 1916. Service No.6083. Born in Thurles. Resided in Galway Woolwich. Killed in action in Mesopotamia. He has no known grave but is listed in Panels 40 and 64 of the Basra Memorial in Iraq.

CASEY, Christopher: Rank: Private. Regiment or Service: Royal Irish Regiment. Unit: 2nd Bn. Age at death: 20. Date of death: 19 October 1914. Service No.6123. Arrived in France only 12 days before he was killed in action. Born in Mitchelstown and enlisted in Tipperary.

A copy of the RIR War Diaries for that day states:

At 2.30 pm the battalion, under the command of Major E. H. E. Daniel, was ordered to attack the village of LE PILLIE (in conjunction with a French attack on the eastern side). At 3. 00 pm B company started the attack followed in succession by A, C and D companies. By 6. oo pm the western side of the village (including the railway station) had been captured but the French had been repulsed. The officer casualties during the attack were two second Lieutenants killed and three Captains wounded. The other rank casualties were about 150.

Supplementary information: Son of Martin and Ellen Casey, of Hannon's Cottages, Heary Street, Tipperary. Grave or Memorial Reference: Has no known grave but is commemorated on Panel 11 and 12. Memorial: Le Touret Memorial in France.

CASEY, Francis Dominick: Rank: Flight Commander. Regiment or Service: Royal Naval Air Service. Unit: 3rd Sqdn. Age at death: 25. Date of death: 10 August 1917.

Supplementary information: Son of Maurice J. and Agnes M. Casey, of Spring Garden, Clonmel, Co.

Tipperary. Awards: D S C. Killed on a test flight.

Citation from the *London Gazette* Suppliment 22 June 17:

Flt. Lieut. Francis Dominic Casey, R. N. A. S.
For conspicuous bravery and skill in attacking hostile aircraft on numerous occasions. On April 2[1st], 1917, he attacked a hostile two-seater machine at a range varying from 40 to 100 yards, and brought it down completely out of control. On 23 April, 1917, on four different occasions during one flight, he attacked hostile machines, one of which was driven down in a spinning nose dive and another turning over on its side went down completely out of control. This Officer has driven down four machines completely out of control, and forced many others down. Both Francis Casey and his brother (who also joined up) gained

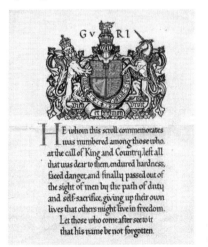

The scroll that always accompanied the Death Plaque , also known as 'The Widow's Penny'.

Distinguished Service Orders. Grave or Memorial Reference: G. 2. Cemetery: Adinkerke Military Cemetery. Belgium.

CASEY, John: Rank: Private. Regiment or Service: Irish Guards. Unit: 2nd Bn. Date of death: 3 July 1916. Service No.2810. Born in Templemore. Enlisted in Dublin. Died of wounds. Age at death: 37.

Supplementary information: Son of James Casey. Grave or Memorial Reference: VIII. B. 44. Cemetery: Lijssenthoek Military Cemetery in Belgium.

CASEY, Michael: Rank: Private. Regiment or Service: Royal Irish Regiment. Unit: 'C' Coy. 6th Bn. Age at death: 32. Date of death: 5 April 1917. Service No.5256. Born in Cahir and enlisted in Clonmel while living in Cahir. Killed in action.

Supplementary information: Son of the late John and Mary Casey, of Cahir, Co. Tipperary. Grave or Memorial Reference: N. 69. Cemetery: Kemmel Chateau Military Cemetery in Belgium. He is also commemorated on the Cahir War Memorial.

CASEY, Patrick: Rank: Private. Regiment or Service: Royal Irish Regiment. Unit: 'D' Coy. 2nd Bn. Age at death: 32. Date of death: 19 October 1914. Service No.4376. Born in Nenagh and enlisted in Tipperary while living in Nenagh. Killed in action.

Supplementary information: Son of Mary Casey, of William Street, Nenagh, and the late Michael Casey:

husband of Ann Casey, of William Street, Nenagh, Co. Tipperary. Served in the South African Campaign. Grave or Memorial Reference: Has no known grave but is commemorated on Panel 11 and 12. Memorial: Le Touret Memorial in France.

CASEY, William: Rank: Private. Irish Guards. Unit: 1st Bn. Date of death: 1 November 1914. Service No.1765. Born in Lochmore Co. Tipperary. Enlisted in Dublin. Killed in action. Age at death: 40.

Supplementary information: Son of the James and Bridget Casey. He has no known grave but is listed on Panel 11 on the Ypres (Menin Gate) Memorial in Belgium.

CASH, John: Rank: Private. Regiment or Service: Royal Irish Regiment. Unit: 2nd Bn. Age at death: 24. Date of death: 14 July 1916. Service No.5080. Born in Silvermines and enlisted in Nenagh while living in Silvermines. Killed in action.

Supplementary information: Son of John and Mary Cash, of Boultheeny, Silvermines, Nenagh, Co. Tipperary. Grave or Memorial Reference: Pier and Face 3 A. Memorial: Thiepval Memorial in France.

CASHIN, William: Rank: Private. Regiment or Service: Leinster Regiment. Unit: 6th Bn. Date of death: 9 April 1918. Service No.311. Born in Clonmel. Enlisted in Limerick. Killed in action in Egypt. Grave or Memorial Reference: U. 45. Cemetery: Ramleh War Cemetery in Israel.

CASSIDY, John: Rank: Private. Regiment or Service: Royal Dublin Fusiliers. Unit: 8th Bn. Date of death: 11 August 1917. Service No.22245. Born in Thurles. Enlisted in Dublin. ied of wounds. Grave or Memorial Reference: VI. B. 2. Cemetery: Brandhoek New Military Cemetery in Belgium.

CASSIDY, Nicholas: Rank: Sergeant. Regiment or Service: Leinster Regiment Unit: 'A' Coy. 2nd Bn. Age at death: 26. Date of death: 31 August 1916. Service No.9500. Born in Clonmel and enlisted there also. Killed in action.

Supplementary information: Son of Richard and Margaret Cassidy, of 15 Mitchell Street, Clonmel, Co. Tipperary. Grave or Memorial Reference: Pier and Face 16 C. MemoriaL: Thiepval Memorial in France.

CAVANAGH, John: Rank: Private. Regiment or Service: Irish Guards. Unit: 2nd Bn. Date of death: 15 September 1916. Service No.8159. Born in Tipperary. Enlisted in Tipperary. Killed in action. He has no known grave but is listed on Pier and Face 7D on the Thiepval Memorial in France.

CAWLEY, John: Rank: Private. Regiment or Service: Irish Guards. Unit: 2nd Bn. Age at death: 29. Date of death: 27 November 1917. Service No.3659. Won the Military Medal. Born in May Tipperary and enlisted in Templemore. Killed in action.

Supplementary information: Son of Julia Cawley, of 'Carraway', Toomevara, Nenagh, Co. Tipperary, and the late Michael Cawley. Grave or Memorial Reference: Has no known grave but is commemorated on Panel 2 and 3. Memorial: Cambrai Memorial in Louveral in France.

CAWLEY, Michael: Rank: Private. Regiment or Service: Irish Guards. Unit: 2nd Bn. Date of death: 27 March 1918. Service No.11266. Born in Bantis, Co. Tipperary. Enlisted in Nenagh, Co. Tipperary. Killed in action. Grave or Memorial Reference: He has no known grave but is listed in Bay 1 on the Arras Memorial in France.

CHAMBERS, Albert: Rank: Sergeant. Regiment or Service: Royal Irish Regiment. 19th Hussars. Date of death: 12 September 1914. Service No.4362. Born in Carrick-on-Suir, Co. Tipperary. Enlisted in Boyle while living in Sligo. Died at home. Grave or Memorial Reference: D4. Cemetery: Portsdown (Christ Church) Military Cemetery, UK.

CLANCY, David Francis: Rank: Pioneer. Regiment or Service: Royal Engineers. Unit: Signals. Age at death: 24. Date of death: 9 December 1918. Service No.267993.

Supplementary information: Son of David J. and Katharine Clancy. Born at Clonmel, Co. Tipperary. Grave or Memorial Reference: F. 105. Cemetery: Durban (Stellawood) Cemetery in South Africa.

CLANCY, Michael: Rank: Private. Regiment or Service: Royal Irish Regiment. Unit: 1st Bn. Date of death: 26 April 1915. Service No.3230. Born in Windgap, Co. Kilkenny. Enlisted in Tipperary while living in Carrick-on-Suir, Co. Tipperary. Killed in action. He has no known grave but is listed on Panel 33 on the Ypres (Menin Gate) Memorial in Belgium.

CLANCY, William: Rank: Private. Regiment or Service: Royal Irish Regiment. Unit: 2nd Bn. Date of death: 25 May 1915. Service No.5584. Born in Carrigmore, Co. Tipperary. Enlisted in Piltown, Co. Kilkenny while living in Carrigmore. Died of wounds. Grave or Memorial Reference: I. F. 70. Cemetery: Bailleul Communal Cemetery Extension (Nord) in France.

CLARKE, Daniel: Rank: Private and Drummer. Regiment or Service: Leinster Regiment. Unit: 2nd Bn. Date of death: 7 November 1914. Service No.9305. Born in Templemore. Enlisted in Dublin. Died of wounds. Grave or Memorial Reference: III. L. 9. Cemetery: Trois Arbres Cemetery, Steenerck in France.

CLARKE, James Arthur: Rank: Private. Regiment or Service: Royal Dublin Fusiliers. Unit: 'W' Coy. 1st Bn. Age at death: 19. Date of death: 4 September 1918. Service No.26984. Born in Castlemartyr in Co. Cork and enlisted in Nenagh while living in Cloughjordan. Killed in action.

Supplementary information: Son of

Samuel G. Clarke, of Moneygall, Cloughjordan, Co. Tipperary. Native of Rathcormac, Co. Cork. Grave or Memorial Reference: II. M. 14. Cemetery: Trois Arbres Cemetery, Steenerck in France.

CLARKE, Richard: Rank: Gunner. Regiment or Service: Royal Canadian Horse Artillery. Unit: A Battery. Date of death: 20 October 1916. Enlisted in Val Cartier on 25 August 1914 and was sworn in on 20 September 1914. Complexion: fair. Eyes: blue. Complexion: Fair. Born in Cloughjordan on 4 May 1879 and was a farmer by trade. Richard was in the RIC and the Imperial Yeomanry Irish Horse before he enlisted. Grave or Memorial Reference: W. 11. Cemetery: Carnoy Military Cemetery in France.

CLAVIN, John: Rank: Private. Regiment or Service: Leinster Regiment. Unit: 2nd Bn. Date of death: 12 April 1917. Service No.7198. Born in Nenagh, Co. Tipperary. Enlisted in Birr in Offaly. Killed in action. Grave or Memorial Reference: He has no known grave but is listed in Bay 1 on the Arras Memorial in France.

CLEARY, John: Rank: Private. Regiment or Service: Leinster Regiment. Unit: 6th Bn. Date of death: 11 October 1915. Service No.3055. Formerly he was with the Connaught Rangers where his number was 765. Born in Kilsheehan, Co. Tipperary. Enlisted in Naas. Died of wounds in Gallipoli. Age at death: 37.

Supplementary information: Son of

Mrs Mary Cleary. Grave or Memorial Reference: C. XIX. 3. Cemetery: Pieta Military Cemetery in Malta.

CLEARY, John: Rank: Private. Regiment or Service: Royal Irish Regiment. Unit: 2nd Bn. Date of death: 24 May 1915. Service No.9600. Born in Tipperary. Enlisted in Clonmel while living in Neath. Killed in action. He has no known grave but is listed on Panel 33 on the Ypres (Menin Gate) Memorial in Belgium.

CLEARY, Joseph: Private. Regiment or Service: Royal Irish Regiment, Unit: 6th Bn. Date of death: 31 May 1916. Service No.6415. Born in Thurles. Enlisted in Clonmel while living in Stradavoher. Died of wounds. Grave or Memorial Reference: V. D. 72. Cemetery: Bethune Town Cemetery in France.

CLEARY, Stephen: Rank: Private. Regiment or Service: Royal Irish Regiment. Unit: 6th Bn. Date of death: 9 September 1916. Service No.11508. Born in Barbaha, Co. Tipperary. Enlisted in Nenagh, Co. Tipperary while living in Barbaha. Killed in action. He has no known grave but is listed on Panel and Face 3A of the Thiepval memorial in France.

CLEARY, Thomas: Rank: Private. Regiment or Service: Leinster Regiment. Unit: 1st Bn. Date of death: 12 May 1915. Service No.3095. Born in Thurles. Enlisted in Thurles. Killed in action. Grave or Memorial Reference: XLIII. E. 17. Cemetery: Tyne Cot

Cemetery in Belgium.

CLEARY, Patrick: Rank: Private. Regiment or Service: Royal Irish Regiment. Unit: 2nd Bn. Date of death: 18 March 1918. Service No.7535. Born in Thurles. Enlisted in Thurles. Killed in action. Grave or Memorial Reference: III. F. 16. Cemetery: Villiers-Faucon Communal Cemetery Extension in France.

CLEER, John: Rank: Private. Regiment or Service: South Lancashire Regiment. Unit: 2nd Bn. Date of death: 20 September 1914. Service No.7490. Born in Ballingarry Co. Kilyenny. Enlisted in Ballingarry. Killed in action. La Ferte-Sous-Jouarre-Memorial in France.

CLOHESSY, David: Rank: Lance Corporal (promoted on 22 July 1917). Regiment or Service: Australian Infantry. Unit: 9th Bn. Date of death: 20 September 1918. Service No.599. Enlisted on 22 August 18 in Noggera, Maryborough, Queensland. He was 5'10" tall, 36 years' old, weighed 152 lbs, brown eyes, black hair, had a dark complexion and he was a Roman Catholic. He listed his occupation at the time of enlistment as a labourer. His Mother was Johanna Clohessy from Ballyhist, Ardfinnan. He had served five years with the Royal Irish Constabulary and three years with the Orange River Mounted Police. He spent time in Folkstone, before being sent to France where he trained in the Bull Ring in Etaples. He was hospitalised on 1 July 1915. when he was gassed. On 31 July

1915 he was shot in the left thigh in ANZAC Cove in Gallipoli. He was sent to hospital in Malta and onwards to Epsom, England where he recovered. He then went to musketry school and became proficient with the Lewis Gun. On 20 September 1918 he was standing at the entrance to a dugout when a shell burst alongside him. He was wounded in the stomach and arm and died about a minute later. His personal effects were returned to his Mother in Ballyhist. Born in Ballybacon, Co. Tipperary. Killed in action.

Supplementary information: Brother of Mr Michael Clohessy, of Ballyhist, Ardfinnan. Grave or Memorial Reference: II. H. 9. Bellicourt British Cemetery in France. He is also commemorated on the Cahir War Memorial.

COADY, Joseph: Rank: Private. Regiment or Service: Royal Irish Regiment. Unit: 2nd Bn. Age at death: 20. Date of death: 21 March 1918. Service No. 10701. Won the Military Medal. Born in thurles and enlisted in Clonmel while living in Thurles..

Supplementary information: Son of James Coady, of 11 Sarchfield Terrace, Thurles, Co. Tipperary. Grave or Memorial Reference: Has no known grave but is commemorated on Panel 30 and 31. Memorial: Pozieres Memorial in France.

COADY, Patrick: Rank: Bombardier. Regiment or Service: Royal Garrison Artillery. Unit: 255th Siege Bty. Date of death: 24 April 1918. Service No. 42300. Born in St Mary's in Clonmel and enlisted in Clonmel also.

Supplementary information: Son of Mr T. Coady, of 18 O'Neill Street, Clonmel, Co. Tipperary. Grave or Memorial Reference: C. 19. Cemetery: Boves West Communal Cemetery in France.

COADY, Richard: Rank: Private. Regiment or Service: Royal Irish Regiment. Unit: 5th Bn. Date of death: 18 January 1915. Service No. 1441. Born in Thurles and enlisted in Tipperary. Died in Gallipoli.

Supplementary information: Son of Mrs E. Kelly, of Cassestown, Thurles, Co. Tipperary. Grave or Memorial Reference: RC. 436. Cemetery: Grangegorman Military Cemetery in Dublin. Died in Gallipoli and buried in Dublin. This is very unusual.

COFFEY, Gerald Arthur: Rank: Private. Regiment or Service: Connaught Rangers. Unit: 5th Bn. Date of death: 7 September 1915. Service No. 770. Born in Clonmel. Enlisted in Liverpool while living in Dublin. Died of wounds in Gallipoli. Grave or Memorial Reference: R. C. C. 11099. Cemetery: Plymouth (Weston Hill) Cemetery, UK.

COFFEY, Michael: Rank: Private. Regiment or Service: Royal Munster Fusiliers. Unit: 3rd Bn. Date of death: 9 December 1914. Service No. 1928 and 4928. Born in Thurles. Enlisted in Cork while living in Cork. Died at home. Grave or Memorial Reference: Section 4. Cemetery: Cork (St Joseph's) Cemetery in Co. Cork.

PTE. D. P. G. COLE-BAKER,
of Onewhero, Military
Medal, Killed in action.

Douglas Patrick Cole-Baker.
Picture from Nominal Rolls of
New Zealand Expeditionary Force.

COFFEY, Stephen John: Rank: Private. Regiment or Service: Leinster Regiment. Unit: 'H' Coy. 2nd Bn. Age at death: 40. Date of death: 20 October 1914. Service No.7057. Born in Cloughbrior, Co. Tipperary and enlisted in Birr, Co. Offaly. Killed in action.

Supplementary information: Son of Stephen and Anne Coffey, of Carney, Borrisokane, Co. Tipperary. Grave or Memorial Reference: Has no known grave but is commemorated on Panel 10. Memorial: Ploegsteert Memorial in Belgium.

COFFEY, Thomas: Rank: Corporal. Regiment or Service: Manchester Regiment. Unit: 1st Bn. Date of death: 9 January 1917. Service No.2671. Born in Tipperary. Enlisted in Manchester. Killed in action in Mesopotamia. Grave or Memorial Reference: XVI. C 13. Amara War Cemetery in Iraq.

COLE-BAKER, Douglas Patrick Gordon: Rank: Private. Regiment or Service: New Zealand Expeditionary Force. Date of death: 4 or 5 October 1917.in France. Embarked on 26 June 1916 with J. Coy, 14th Reinforcements.

Service No.25197. Occupation before enlistment: farmer. Age at death 27 (also down as 28). Last unit served with Auckland Infantry Regiment. Won the Military Medal. Listed in the *London Gazette*: 16 August 1917, p8429, Rec No 1029: For conspicuous gallantry and devotion to duty. During the attack carried out by his Battalion on the morning of 7 June, near Warneton. This soldier was performing the duties of stretcher-bearer on that occasion. His commanding officer states in a letter that he went out several times by himself under heavy fire and each time brought in a wounded man. Killed in action in Ypres.

Supplementary information: Douglas Cole-Baker was the son of Mary Rachel Cole-Baker of 'Haunui', Onewhero, Tuakau, Auckland, New Zealand, and the late Mortimer O'Sullivan Cole-Baker. Native of Tipperary, Ireland. A landowner in New Zealand for ten years. Son of Mrs Mary Murray, of Chapel Street, Clogheen, Co. Tipperary. His Mothers identity in the records is listed as above. Grave or Memorial Reference: IV. D. 7. Cemetery: Tyne Cot Cemetery in Belgium.

COLEMAN, James: Rank: Private. No 25153, The Royal Irish Regiment, 7th Bn, Born: Cashel, Co. Tipperary. Enlisted in Cahir while living in Cashel. Killed in action in the Somme sector, France. These two Coleman men joined the Royal Irish Regiment on the same day even thought they enlisted at different recruiting centres. Has no known grave but is commemorated on the Thiepval Memorial Pier and Face 3 A.

COLEMAN, Michael: Rank: Driver. Regiment or Service: Royal Field Artillery. Unit: Base Details Age at death: 37. Date of death: 13 August 1917. Service No.4308. Born in Bruff in Limerick and enlisted in Clonmel.

Supplementary information: Husband of Catherine Coleman, of Greenrath, Tipperary. Grave or Memorial Reference: Div. 62. I. G. 10. Cemetery: Ste Marie, Cemetery, Le Havre in France.

COLEMAN, Patrick: Rank: Private. Regiment or Service: Royal Irish Regiment. Unit: 7th Bn. Born in Boherlahan, enlisted in Limerick while living in Goolds Cross. Date of death: 12 December 1917. Service No.25152.

Supplementary information: Son of Mr P. Coleman, of Friar Street, Cashel, Co. Tipperary. Grave or Memorial Reference: II. H. 32. Cemetery: Templeux-Le-Guerard British Cemetery in France.

COLEMAN, William: Rank: Private. Regiment or Service: Royal Lancaster Regiment. Unit: 8th Bn. Date of death: 16 August 1916. Service No.4600. Born in Tipperary. Enlisted in Manchester. Killed in action. He

Grave of Edmond Collins.

has no known grave but is listed on Pier and Face 5 D and 12 B on the Thiepval Memorial in France.

COLLEARY, James: Rank: Private. Regiment or Service: Royal Irish Regiment. Unit: 7th Bn. Date of death: 12 December 1917. Service No.25154. Formerly he was with the South Irish Horse where his number was 1534. Born in Clonmel. Enlisted in Dublin while living in Ballingarry, Co. Tipperary. Killed in action. Age at death: 22.

Supplementary information: Son of James and Julia Colleary, of Dromiskin, Castlebellingham, Co. Louth. Native of Clonmell. Grave or Memorial Reference: II. H. 35. Cemetery: Templeux-Le-Guerard British Cemetery in France.

COLLETON, Martin: Rank: Private. Regiment or Service: Connaught Rangers. Unit: 2nd Bn. Date of death: 2 November 1914. Age at death: 29. Born in Carrick-on-Suir. Enlisted in Carrick-on-Suir while living in Carrick-on-Suir. Killed in action.

Supplementary information: Son of Catherine Colleton, of Mill Street, Carrick-on-Suir, and Martin Colleton. He has no known grave but is listed on Panel 42n the Ypres (Menin Gate) Memorial in Belgium.

COLLINS, Daniel: Rank: Private. Regiment or Service: Munster Fusiliers. Unit: 2nd Bn. Date of death: 1 October 1916. Service No.6213. Born in Templederry, Co. Tipperary. Enlisted in Glasgow while living in Glasgow.

Killed in action. Grave or Memorial Reference: I. P. 3. Cemetery: Noeux-Les-Mines Communal Cemetery in France.

COLLINS, Edmond: Rank: Private. Regiment or Service: Royal Irish Regiment. Unit: 3rd Bn. Age at death: 32. Date of death: 7 November 1918. Service No.3426. Cemetery, St John's Famine Cemetery, Tipperary. Grave location: In the south-east part.

COLLINS, James: Rank: Private. Regiment or Service: Royal Irish Regiment. Unit: 2nd Bn. Age at death: 20. Date of death: 5 July 1916. Service No.5096. Born in Clerihan Co. Tipperary and enlisted in Clonmel while living in Knocklofty. Killed in action.

Supplementary information: Son of Bridget Collins, of Carriconeen, Knocklofty, Clonmel, Co. Tipperary, and Denis Collins. Grave or Memorial Reference: Pier and Face 3 A. Memorial: Thiepval Memorial in France.

COLLINS, John: Rank: Private. Regiment or Service: Leinster Regiment. Unit: 2nd Bn. Age at death: 38. Date of death: 20 November 1914. Service No.7066. Born in Kylegoona and enlisted in Birr in Offaly. Killed in action.

Supplementary information: Son of Michael and Nora Collins, of Kylenagoona, Borrisokane, Co. Tipperary. Brother-in-law to Mr James Shortt, Kylenagoona, Borrisokane. James was a member of the Borrisokane Volunteer Corps.

Grave or Memorial Reference: Has no known grave but is commemorated on Panel 10. Memorial: Ploegsteert Memorial in Belgium.

COLLINS, M: Rank: Drummer,. Regiment or Service: Royal Irish Fusiliers. Unit: 1st Garrison Bn. Age at death: 47. Date of death: 26 January 1919. Service No.25426.

Supplementary information: Husband of Elizabeth Collins (*née* Connor), of 27 Upper Abbey Street, Dublin. Served in the South African War. Born in Tipperary. Grave or Memorial Reference: 27. J. 22. Cemetery: Taukkyan War Cemetery in Burma.

COLLINS, Thomas: Rank: Rifleman. Regiment or Service: New Zealand Rifle Brigade. Last unit he served with was the New Zealand Rifle Brigade Reserve. Embarked with the 5th Re-inforcements 4th Bn, H Coy on 26 June 1916. Date of death: 27 December 1917. Service No.14785. Trade before enlistment: Labourer. Enlisted in while living in. He had one of his legs amputated a few months before he died of disease in the United Kingdom. Next of Kin details: Son of J Collins Carigataher, Nanagh, Co. Tipperary. Buried in Dolla old Graveyard near Nenagh on new years day. Also commemorated on Panel 10 (Screen Wall) in Grangegorman Cemetery in Dublin.

COLLINS, Thomas: Rank: Private. Regiment or Service: Leinster Regiment. Unit: 2nd Bn. Date of death: 21 March 1917. Service No.3395. Born in Puckawn, Co. Tipperary. Enlisted in Birr. Killed in action.

Supplementary information: Son of Mrs N Collins. Grave or Memorial Reference: I. C. 14. Cemetery: Aix-Noulette Communal Cemetery Extension in France.

COMAN, Michael: Rank: Private. Regiment or Service: Irish Guards. Unit: 2nd Bn. Age at death: 25. Date of death: 25 June 1917. Service No.10460. Brother of Connaught Rangers Mutineer William Coman, AKA Bill the Black. Born in Cashel and enlisted there also. Killed in action.

Supplementary information: Son of John and Mary Coman, of Windmill Cottage, Cashel, Co. Tipperary. Grave or Memorial Reference: VIII. A. 4. Cemetery: Duhallow A. D. S. Cemetery in Belgium. Duhallow Advanced Dressing Station was a front line casualty clearing station for soldiers wounded in this (Ypres) sector. It was named after a Southern Irish Hunt. Although Michael is now interred here he was originally buried in a temporary grave as this Cemetery did not exist until after he died.

COMAN, Michael: Rank: Corporal. No1929, Leinster Regt. 7th Bn, Died 22 March1918, Born in Cashel and enlisted in Dublin. Killed in action when the Allied 5th Army was driven back by overwhelming numbers across the former Somme battlefields on 22 March 1918. He has no known grave but is commemerated on the Poziers memorial on panel 78. Uncle of William Coman AKA, Bill the Black.

COMERFORD, Christopher:
Rank: Private. Regiment or Service:
Machine Gun Corps (Infantry). Unit:
86th Coy. Date of death: 28 February
1917. Service No.21022. He was formerly with the Royal Dublin Fusiliers
where his number was 11027. Born in
Menagh in Co.Tipperary and enlisted
there also. Killed in action.

Supplementary information: Son of
James and Mary Comerford, of Church
View, Nenagh, Co.Tipperary, Republic
of Ireland. Grave or Memorial
Reference: 9. A. 8. Cemetery: London
Cemetery and Extension, Longueval
in France.

CONDON, David: Rank: Private.
Regiment or Service: Irish Guards.
Unit: 1st Bn. Date of death: 15 March
1917. Service No.10076. Born in
Ballyporeen. Enlisted in Caerphilly,
Glamorganshire while living in
Kilbehenny, Co. Cork. Killed in action.
Grave or Memorial Reference: VI. F.
9. Cemetery: Sailly-Saillisel British
Cemetery in France.

CONDON, John: Rank: Private.
Regiment or Service: Royal Irish
Regiment. Unit: 2nd Bn. Date of death:
23 August 1914. Service No.7347. Born
in Bohercrowe, Co.Tipperary. Enlisted
in Swansea in Glamorganshire. Killed
in action. He has no known grave but
is listed on the La- Ferte-Sous-Jouarre
Memorial in France.

CONDON, Martin: Rank: Sapper.
Regiment or Service: Royal Engineers.
Unit: 54th Field Coy. Age at death: 22.
Date of death: 21 January 1917. Service

No.26168. Born in Nenagh and
enlisted there also. He was in two previous units the Royal Irish Regiment
where his number was 6231 and the
54th Field Company, Royal Engineers
where his number is not given.

Supplementary information: Son of
Thomas and Mary Condon, of Silver
Street, Menagh, Co. Tipperary. Grave
or Memorial Reference: XXI. C. 17.
Cemetery: Etaples Military Cemetery
in France.

CONDON, Thomas: Rank: Driver.
Regiment or Service: Army Service
Corps. Unit: 7th Div. H. Q. Age at death:
23. Date of death: 5 November 1914.
Service No.TS-45. Born in Clonmel
and enlisted in Southampton while
living in Clonmel. Killed in action.

Supplementary information: Son of
Michael and Mary Condon, of Market
Street, Clonmel, Co. Tipperary. Grave
or Memorial Reference: Has no
known grave but is commemorated
on Panel 56. Memorial: Ypres (Menin
Gate) Memorial in Belgium.

CONNELL, John: Rank: Private.
Regiment or Service: Leinster
Regiment. Unit: 1st Bn. Date of death:
14 February 1915. Service No.9596.
Born in Tipperary. Enlisted in
Limerick. Killed in action. He has no
known grave but is listed on Panel 44
on the Ypres (Menin Gate) Memorial
in Belgium.

CONNOR, John: Rank: Private.
Regiment or Service: East Lancashire
Regiment. Unit: 6th Bn. Age at
death: 40. Date of death: 10 April

1916. Service No. 18103. Born in Oswaldtwistle in Lancashire and enlisted in Accrington In Lancashire while living in Oswaldtwistle. Died in Mesopotamia.

Supplementary information: Son of Michael and Ann Connor, of John's Street, Nenagh, Co. Tipperary. Grave or Memorial Reference: XXI. L. 5. Cemetery: Amara War Cemetery in Iraq.

CONNOR/CONNORS, Henry: Private. No 1962, Royal Irish Regiment, 6th Bn. Date of death: 7 March 1915. Born St John's, Cashel Co. Tipperary. Enlisted in Clonmel while living in Cahir. Died at Home. Buried in an unspecified grave in Fermoy Military Cemetery. He is named on the Memorial on the Screen Wall therin.

CONNORS, J.: Rank: Private. Regiment or Service: Royal Irish Regiment. Date of death: 21 October 1918. Service No. 5746. Transferred to the Labour Corps where his number was 230836. Grave or Memorial Reference: E. H. 104. St Michael's New Cemetery, Tipperary.

CONNORS, James: Rank: Private. Regiment or Service: Royal Irish Regiment. Unit: 1st Bn. Date of death: 15 March 1915. Service No. 3593. Born in Clonmel. Enlisted in Tipperary while living in Kilkenny. Killed in action. He has no known grave but is listed on Panel 33 on the Ypres (Menin Gate) Memorial in Belgium.

CONNORS, Martin: Rank: Lance Corporal. Regiment or Service: Machine Gun Corps (Infantry). Unit: 182nd Coy. Age at death: 30. Date of death: 20 July 1916. Service No. 14236. He was formerly with the Liverpool Regiment where his number was 34775. Born Nenagh and enlisted in Nenagh. Killed in action.

Supplementary information: Son of Jeremiah and Maria Connors, of 14, St John's Terrace, Nenagh, Tipperary. Grave or Memorial Reference: Has no known grave but is commemorated on Panel 136. Memorial: Loos Memorial in France.

CONNORS, Michael: Rank: Private. Regiment or Service: Leinster Regiment. Unit: 2nd Bn. Date of death: 4 September 1918. Service No. 5664. Born in Roscrea. Enlisted in Roscrea while living in Brosna Co. Offaly. Killed in action. Age at death: 20.

Supplementary information: Son of Michael and Mary Connors, of Brosna, Roscrea, King's Co. Grave or Memorial Reference: Bristol. Castle Cem Mem 3. Messines Ridge British Cemetery in Belgium.

CONROY, Denis: Rank: Private. Regiment or Service: Royal Irish Regiment. Unit: 2nd Bn. Date of death: 7 August 1917. Service No. 18178. Born in Roscrea. Enlisted in Roscrea. Killed in action. Formerly he was with the Leinster Regiment where his number was 5358. He has no known grave but is listed on Panel 33 on the Ypres (Menin Gate) Memorial in Belgium.

CONROY, John: Rank: Corporal. Regiment or Service: Royal Garrison Artillery. Unit: 306th Siege Bty. Age at death: 29. Date of death: 2 August 1917. Service No.35865. Born in Clonmel and enlisted there also.

Supplementary information: Son of Thomas and Ellen Conroy, of Clonmel, Co. Tipperary and husband of Annie Conroy, of Church Bay Rd, Crosshaven, Cork. Grave or Memorial Reference: VII. D. 1. Cemetery: St Pierre Cemetery, Amiens in France.

CONROY, Michael: Rank: Private. Regiment or Service: Royal Irish Regiment. Unit: 2nd Bn. Date of death: 11 July 1918. Service No.11150. Born in Roscrea. Enlisted in Roscrea. Died. Grave or Memorial Reference: V. K. 12. Cemetery: Niederzwehren Cemetery in Germany.

CONWAY, Denis: Rank: Private. Regiment or Service: Royal Dublin Fusiliers. Unit: 8th Bn. Date of death: 29 April 1916. Service No.25732. Born in Thurles. Enlisted in Dublin while living in Thurles. Killed in action. He has no known grave but is listed on Panels 127 to 129 on the Loos Memorial in France.

CONWAY, George Henry: Rank: Private. Regiment or Service: Irish Guards. Unit: 1st Bn. Age at death: 24. Date of death: 27 December 1914. Service No.1688. Born in Clonbeg in Co. Tipperary and enlisted in Mullingar Co. Westmeath while living in Belfast Co. Antrim. Killed in action.

Supplementary information: Son of the late Thomas and Martha Conway, of Tipperary. Grave or Memorial Reference: I. C. 14. Cemetery: Le Touret Military Cemetery, Richebourg-L'Avoue in France.

COOKE, Henry Frederick: Rank: Second Lieutenant. Regiment or Service: Royal Sussex Regiment. Unit: 7th Bn. Age at death: 31. Date of death: 4 August 1916. Awards: Mentioned in Despatches.

Supplementary information: Son of the late Revd. C. S. Cooke, Rector of Thurles, and of Mrs C. S. Cooke, of Beakstown, Thurles, Co. Tipperary. Also served in German South West Africa. Grave or Memorial Reference: Pier and Face 7 C. on the Thiepval Memorial in France.

COOKE, Joseph. Rank: Corporal. Regiment or Service: Leinster Regiment. Unit: 1st Bn. Age at death: 24. Born in Ballinasloe and enlisted in Birr. Date of death: 10 March 1917. Died in Salonika.

Supplementary information: Son of Kate Cooke of Limerick Street Roscrea. Grave or Memorial Reference: VIII. E. 3. Cemetery: Strume Military Cemetery, Greece.

COOKE, John: Rank: Lance Corporal. Regiment or Service: Canadian Infantry (Manitoba Regiment) Unit: 27th Bn. Age at death: 24. Date of death: 6 November 1917. Service No.460079.

Supplementary information: Son of Henry and Lizzie Cooke, of Bonlea, The Commons, Thurles, Co. Tipperary,

COONEY, JOHN DANIEL, Private, No. 2486, 6th Battn. Manchester Regt. (T.F.), 2nd s. John Patrick Cooney, J.P., by his wife, Mary (Garranlea House, Cahir, co. Tipperary), dau. of Daniel Joseph Geary; b. Cahir, 20 Aug. 1889; educ. Rockwell College and Blackrock College, Ireland; enlisted in the Manchester Regt. on the outbreak of war, went with his battn. to the Dardanelles, and was killed in action at Gallipoli, 29 May, 1915. He had been nominated for a commission, against his express wishes, just before his death; *unm.* Private Cooney played Rugby football regularly for the Manchester City Club and Lancashire County. He was a good boxer and a first-rate athlete, winning many prizes at 440 and 880 yards.

John Daniel Cooney.

John Daniel Cooney.

Ireland. Grave or Memorial Reference: Panel 24 - 26 - 28 - 30. Memorial: Ypres (Menin Gate) Memorial in Belgium. Data from the reverse of the enlistment document:. Age on Enlistment: 21 Years. 3 Months. Height: 5' 9". Eye colour: Blue. Complexion: Dark. Hair colour: Black. Religion: COI. Chest expansion: 3". Girth: 37". Date of Enlistment: 14 June 1915. Place of Enlistment: Winnipeg.

COOLEY, Stephen: Rank: Private. Regiment or Service: Royal Irish Fusiliers. Unit: 6th Bn. Date of death: 11 September 1915. Service No. 12632. Born in Templemore. Enlisted in Stratford, East Sussex while living in Canning Town, East Sussex. Killed in action in Gallipoli. He has no known grave but is listed on Panel 178 to 180 on the Helles Memorial in Turkey.

COONAN, Edward: Rank: Private. Regiment or Service: Royal Irish Regiment. Unit: 2nd Bn. Date of death: 5 July 1916. Service No. 6405. Born in Cloughjordan, Co. Tipperary.

Enlisted in Nenagh while living in Cloughjordan. Killed in action. Age at death: 18.

Supplementary information: Son of John and Johanna Coonan, of 2, Park Street, St Peter Port, Guernsey. Born at Cloughgordon, Co. Tipperary. Grave or Memorial Reference: II. E. 12. Cemetery: Caterpillar Valley Cemetery, Longueval in France.

COONEY, David: See BEARY, David.

COONEY, John Daniel: Rank: Private. Regiment or Service: Manchester Regiment. Unit: 1st -6th Bn. Date of death: 29 May 1915. Service No. 2486. Born in Cahir. Enlisted in Manchester while living in New Inn. Killed in action in Gallipoli. Grave or Memorial Reference: He has no known grave but is listed on the Special Memorial in The Redoubt Cemetery, Helles in Gallipoli, Turkey. He is also commemorated on the Cahir War Memorial.

COONEY, John: Rank: Private.

Grave of John Cooney.

Regiment or Service: Royal Irish Regiment. Unit: 2nd Bn. Age at death: 35. Date of death: 21 April 1917. Service No. 7631.

Supplementary information: Husband of Mary Cooney of Church Rd. Nenagh Co. Tipperary Extract from the *Tipperary Star*, April, 1917: Private John Cooney of the Royal Irish Regiment, and a native of Lisboney, who died at the local infirmary on Saturday as a result of a wound received in action in France, was accorded a military funeral on Monday. The Leinster Regiment at Limerick supplied the band and firing party. The funeral to Lisboney was very large. Right Hon., Lord Dunalley, in the uniform of a Colonel of the Royal Irish Regiment, marched to and from the graveyard with the military. Buried in Lisbunny Cemetery. Grave location: North side of the cross-path.

CORBY, James: Rank: Rifleman. Regiment or Service: South Lancashire Regiment. Unit: 1st-5th Bn. Age at death: 20. Date of death: 20 September 1917. Service No. 39340. Born in Tipperary and enlisted in Widnes in Lancashire while living in Tipperary. Killed in action.

Supplementary information: Son of Edmond and Margaret Corby, of Kilfecale, Co. Tipperary. Grave or Memorial Reference: Has no known grave but is commemorated on Panel 92 to 93 and 162A. Memorial: Tyne Cot Memorial in Belgium.

CORCORAN, Michael: Rank: Private. Regiment or Service: Leinster Regiment. Unit: 'B' Coy. 4th Bn. Age at death: 22. Date of death: 16 March 1915. Service No. 3691. Born in Roscrea and enlisted in Birr Kings Co. Died of wounds.

Supplementary information: Son of Joseph and Margaret Corcoran: husband of Kate Corcoran, of Benamore, Roscrea, Co. Tipperary. Grave or Memorial Reference: J. 30. Cemetery: Bailleul Communal Cemetery Extension (Nord) in France.

CORCORAN, Richard: Rank: Private. Regiment or Service: Royal Irish Regiment. Unit: 6th Bn. Date of death: 29 May 1916. Service No.1694. Born in Clonmel. Enlisted in Cahir while living in Clonmel. Killed in action. Grave or Memorial Reference: I. J. 17. Cemetery: Dud Corner Cemetery, Loos in France.

CORCORAN, William: Rank: Private. Regiment or Service: Leinster Regiment. Unit: 2nd Bn. Date of death: 23 November 1917. Service No.3413. Born in Roscrea and enlisted in Birr, Kings Co. Killed in action.

Supplementary information: Son of Mr M. Corcoran, of Conville Lodge, Roscrea, Co. Tipperary. Grave or Memorial Reference: I. G. 15. Cemetery: Hargicourt British Cemetery, Aisne in France.

CORCORAN, William: Rank: Corporal. No 9576, Leinster Regt, 2nd Bn. Date of death: 6 November 17, Born: Cashel, Co. Tipperary. Enlisted in Cork City. Killed in action, France. Grave reference, IV. D. 5. Cemetery: Roisel Communal Cemetery Extension in France.

CORERI, Francis: Rank: Private. Regiment or Service: Royal Munster Fusiliers. Unit: 4th Bn: Born in Waterford. Enlisted in Cork while living in Cork. Died at home. Date of death: 27 December 1916. Service No.4/7334. Cemetery: St Michael's New Cemetery, Tipperary Town. Grave location: E. H. 98.

CORMACK, Michael: Rank: Private. Number 9902, 3rd Battalion, Royal Irish Regiment. Born in Holycross. Also listed as McCormack. Enlisted in Clonmel while living in Holycross (Other records say Waterford). Date of death: 20 January 1916. Age at death: 19. Son of William and Brigid McCormack of Holycross. Buried in Holycross Abbey and moved during renovations to the left of the path in the graveyard. Official records say he died at home but oral tradition indicate his remains were brought home for burial.

COSTELLO, J.: Rank: Fireman. Regiment or Service: Mercantile Marine. Unit: S.S. *Calypso* (Hull) Age at death: 38. Date of death: 11 July 1916.

Supplementary information: Born in Tipperary. Memorial: Has no known grave but is commemorated on the Tower Hill Memorial, London.

COSTELLO, Edward Martin: Rank: Private. Regiment or Service: Connaught Rangers. Unit: C Coy. 1st Bn. Age at death: 27. Date of death: 27 January 1916. Service No.10211. Born in Nenagh and enlisted in Nenagh while living there also. Died of wounds in Mesopotamia.

Supplementary information: Son of John and Mary Costello, of Silver

Killed In Action.

The sad news has reached Nenagh that Private Edward Costelloe, son of Mr John Costelloe, harness maker, Silver-street, Nenagh, was some weeks ago killed in action. Deceased was quite a young man, and what makes the death all the more sad is the fa t that only some months ago his brother gave his life for the same cause.

Edward Costello.

Street, Nenagh, Co. Tipperary. Grave or Memorial Reference: VII. H. 3. Cemetery: Amara War Cemetery in Iraq.

COSTELLO, Matthew: Rank: Private. Regiment or Service: Leinster Regiment. Unit: 2nd Bn. Age at death: 28. Date of death: 22 September 1914. Service No.6807. Born in Melford, Co. Tipperary and enlisted in Birr, Kings Co. Killed in action.

Supplementary information: Son of Matthew and Ann Costello. Born at Borrisokane, Co. Tipperary. Brother of Mr Thomas Costello, one of the instructors of the Borrisokane Volunteer Corps. Grave or Memorial Reference: II. B. 9. Cemetery: Vailly British Cemetery in France.

COTTER, Patrick: Rank: Corporal. Regiment or Service: Royal Irish Regiment. Unit: 2nd Bn. Age at death: 32. Date of death: 3 September 1916. Service No.10545. Born in Lisronagh, Co. Tipperary and enlisted in Clonmel while living in New Inn Co. Tipperary. Killed in action.

Supplementary information: Step-brother of Ellen Guidera, of Ballindoney, Cahir, Co. Tipperary. Grave or Memorial Reference: I. E. 7. Cemetery: Delville Wood Cemetery, Longueval in France. He is also commemorated on the Cahir War Memorial.

COUGHLIN/COUGHLAN, Edward: Rank: Private. Regiment or Service: Royal Dublin Fusiliers. Unit: 1st Bn. Age at death: 24. Date of death: 17 October 1914. Service No.10432. Born in Tipperary. Enlisted in Aldershot. Died in India.

Supplementary information: Son of Mary and John Coughlan. Grave or Memorial Reference: 10 95. Cemetery: Madras (St Mary's) Cemetery, Chennai, India.

COUGHLAN, John: Rank: Private. Regiment or Service: Royal Irish Regiment. Unit: 2nd Bn. Date of death: 19 October 1914. Service No.4803. Born in St John's Clonmel, Co. Tipperary. Enlisted in Tipperary while living in Kilmacuma, Co. Waterford. Killed in action. He has no known grave but is listed on Panels 11 and 12 on the Le Touret Memorial in France.

COUGHLAN, Patrick James: Rank: Private. Regiment or Service: Royal Munster Fusiliers. Unit: 2nd Bn.

Grave of Paul James Courteney.

Date of death: 22 March 1918. Service No.18191. Formerly he was with the Army Cyclist Coprs where his number was 7700. Born in Clonmel. Enlisted in Dublin while living in Clonmel. Killed in action. Age at death: 21.

Supplementary information: Son of Mrs Alice Coughlan, of 5, Clifton Mansions, Brixton, London. He has no known grave but is listed on Panel 78 and 79 on the Pozieres Memorial.

COURTNEY, Frederick J: Rank: Private. Regiment or Service: Leinster Regiment. Unit: 7th Bn. Age at death: 28. Date of death: 27 June 1916. Service No.3494. Born in Carrick-on-Suir and enlisted there also. Killed in action.

Supplementary information: Son of Mrs Sarah Anne Courtney, of 6, Park View Terrace, Carrick-on-Suir, Co. Tipperary. Grave or Memorial

Reference: III. N. 1. Cemetery: St Patrick's Cemetery, Loos in France.

COURTNEY, Paul James: Rank: Private. Royal Army Service Corps. Date of death: 26 July 1920. Service No.DM2/155419.

Supplementary information: Husband of Mrs Courtney of Ballina Killaloe. Buried in Ballina (Templehollow) Graveyard. Grave location: Near south-east corner.

COX, Nicholas: Rank: Gunner. Regiment or Service: Royal Field Artillery. Unit: C Bty. 74th Bde. Age at death: 22. Date of death: 14 November 1917. Service No.76438. Born in Clonmel and enlisted in Cahir. Died of wounds.

Supplementary information: Son of James and Annie Cox, of Clonmel, Co. Tipperary. Grave or Memorial

Reference: III. D. 26. Cemetery: Abbeville Communal Cemetery Extension in France.

CRAIG, Thomas: Rank: Battery Quartermaster Sergeant. Regiment or Service: Royal Field Artillery. Unit: 67th Bty. 232nd Bde. Born in Woolwich and enlisted in Liverpool. Died at home. Date of death: 2 January 1915. Service No.36156. Cemetery: Cahir Military Plot. Grave location: Between the main path and the west boundary.

CREAMER, James: Rank: Gunner. Regiment or Service: Royal Field Artillery. Unit: No. 5 Depot Age at death: 41. Date of death: 8 February 1915. Service No.76391. Born in Gastledown Co. Tipperary and enlisted in Nenagh. Died at home. *Supplementary information*: Husband of Bridget Creamer, of Ballycarrido,

Portroe, Nenagh, Co. Tipperary. Grave or Memorial Reference: G. 104. Cemetery: Cornamagh Cemetery in Westmeath.

CREED, Michael: Rank: Gunner. Regiment or Service: Royal Garrison Artillery. Unit: 19th Trench Mortar Battery. Date of death: 25 September 1915. Service No.19976. Born in Clougheen, Co. Tipperary. Enlisted in Wrexham while living in North Shields. Killed in action. He has no known grave but is listed on Panels 3 and 4 on the Loos Memorial in France.

CRERAND, Edward. Rank: Gunner. Regiment or Service: Royal Garrison Artillery. Unit: 1258th Siege Battery. Date of death: 26 October 1917. Service No.153525. Born in Templemore. Enlisted in Londinderry. Killed in action. Age at death: 22.

Grave of Thomas Craig.

Supplementary information: Son of Denis and Ellen Crerand, of 43, Rosville Street, Londonderry. Grave or Memorial Reference: I. B. 9. Cemetery: Divisional Collecting Post Cemetery and Extension in Belgium.

CROKE, Patrick: Rank: Private. Regiment or Service: Royal Dublin Fusiliers. Unit: 1ˢᵗ Bn. Age at death: 23. Date of death: 24 April 1917. Service No.43103. He was formerly with the Royal Irish Regiment where his number was 11478. Killed in action. Born in Killenaule and enlisted there also. Killed in action.

Supplementary information: Son of James Croke, of Manserghhill, Killenaule: Co. Tipperary. Grave or Memorial Reference: Bay 9. Memorial: Arras Memorial in France.

CRONIN, Daniel: Rank: Private. No 6184, Royal Irish Regiment, 2ⁿᵈ Bn, Died 24 May 1915, Born: Cashel, Co. Tipperary. Enlisted in Tipperary Town while living in Cashel. Killed in action during the second battle of Ypres. Has no known grave but is commemorated on Panel 33 on the Ypres (Menin Gate) Memorial in Belgium.

CRONYN, William Benn: Rank: Captain. Regiment or Service: Army Veterinary Corps. Unit: Indian Vet. Hosp. (Marseilles) Age at death: 55. Date of death: 1 February 1918. Vetinary Surgeon.

Supplementary information: Son of the late Dr. John and Caroline Cronyn, of Dromore, Newport, Co. Tipperary. Born at Dublin. Grave or Memorial Reference: Div. 62. I. O. 6. Cemetery: Ste Marie, Cemetery, Le Havre in France.

CROSSE, Patrick: Rank: Private. Regiment or Service: Australian Infantry. Unit: 26ᵗʰ Bn. Date of death: 5 November 1916. Service No.4113. Born in Tipperary, Ireland. Enlisted in Brisbane, Queensland on 27 September 1915. Occupation on enlistment: painter. Height: 5' 6". Hair: dark brown. Eyes: brown. Complexion: dark Weight: 9 st. Religious Denomination, R.C. In his records there is a letter from his Mother (dated twelve months after his death) stating that she wanted a devotional prayer book that he had in his possession and was not returned with his effects. It was given to him by a Church of England

Michael Creed's death Plaque was purchased from a Yorkshire dealer who in turn obtained it from a dealer in Glasgow.

Patrick Crosse.

Minister. Killed in action and buried 1 mile NE of Le Sars, 2 ½ miles SW of Bapaume, 6 ¾ miles ENE of Peronne. Age at death: 28. Served in Suez, Abbassia, Rollestone, England, France and the Bull Ring in Etaples. Mother, Mrs Mary Crosse, (Widow) Newstead Avenue, Brisbane. She moved to 322 Stanley Street, South Brisbane.

Supplementary information: Son of Michael (Died 26 January 1910) and Mary Crosse, William Street and Merton Rd, South Brisbane, Queensland. Native of Tipperary, Ireland. Grave or Memorial Reference: Plot 2, Row J. Grave, 30. Cemetery: Warlencourt British Cemetery.

CROTTY, Denis: Rank: Private. Regiment or Service: Machine Gun Corps. Unit: 12th Bn, Infantry. Formerly he was with the Royal Munster Fusiliers where his number was 7868. Date of death: 26 August 1918. Service No. 31438. Born in St Peter's and St Paul's, Clonmel, Co. Tipperary. Enlisted in Clonmel. Died of wounds. Grave or Memorial Reference: I. J. 2. Cemetery: Robemont Communal Cemetery Extension in France.

CROTTY, James: Rank: Lance Corporal. Regiment or Service: Royal Dublin Fusiliers. Unit: 8th Bn. Age at death: 24. Date of death: 9 April 1918. Service No. 17382. Born in Clonmel and enlisted there also. Died of wounds.

Supplementary information: Son of William and Catherine Crotty, of Coleman, Fethard Co. Tipperary. Grave or Memorial Reference: P. IX. C. 7A. Cemetery: St Sever Cemetery Extension, Rouen in France.

CROTTY, John: Rank: Private. Regiment or Service: Royal Irish Regiment. Unit: 6th Bn. Date of death: 7 June 1917. Service No. 11263. Born in Cahir. Enlisted in Cahir while living in Ballymacarberry, Co. Tipperary. Killed in action. Grave or Memorial Reference: B 12. Cemetery: Irish House Cemetery, Belgium.

CROTTY, William: Rank: Private. Regiment or Service: Leinster Regiment. Unit: 2nd Bn. Date of death: 3 September 1916. Service No. 4966. Born in Clonmel. Enlisted in Clonmel while living in Clonmel. Grave or Memorial Reference: I. B.

Grave of T. Crummey.

51. Cemetery: Danzig Alley British Cemetery Mametz in France.

CRUMMEY, T: Rank: Private. Regiment or Service: Northamptonshire Regiment. Unit: 1st Bn. Date of death: 28 October 1920. Service No.5875693. Cemetery: St Michael's New Cemetery, Tipperary Town. Grave location: E. H. 111.

CULLAGH, Timothy: Rank: Private. Regiment or Service: Durham Light Infantry. Unit: 19th Bn. Age at death: 20. Date of death: 15 July 1918. Service No.44994. Born in Cashel Co. Tipperary, enlisted in Mallow while living in Cashie. Killed in action attacking North Eastward beyond the Messines Ridge in rapidly deteriorating weather.

Supplementary information: Son of Denis and Catherine Cullagh, of Ballyfowloo, Cashel, Co. Tipperary. Grave or Memorial Reference: Has no known grave but is commemorated on Panel 128 to 131 and 162 and 162A. Memorial: Tyne Cot Memorial in Belgium.

CULLEN, James: Rank: Private. Regiment or Service: Royal Irish Regiment. Unit: 2nd Bn. Date of death: 19 October 1914. Service No.5775. Born in Nenagh, Co. Tipperary. Enlisted in Nenagh. Killed in action. He has no known grave but is listed on Panel 11 and 12 of the Le Touret memorial in France.

CULLEN, Michael: Rank: Private. Regiment or Service: Connaught Rangers. Unit: 5th Bn. Date of death:

10 October 1918. Service No. 15246. Formerly he was with the Leinster Regiment where his number was 3338. Born in Cahir. Enlisted in Dublin while living in Dublin. Killed in action. Age at death: 42.

Supplementary information: Husband of Margaret Cullen, Pembroke Road, Dublin. Grave or Memorial Reference: VII AC. 14. Cemetery: Terlincthun British Cemetery, Wimille, France.

CULLEN, Michael James. Rank: Lance Corporal. Regiment or Service: Middlesex Regiment. Unit: 4th Bn. Date of death: 2 July 1916 the second day of the battle of the Somme. Service No. L-15516. Born in Ballinacurra Co. Tipperary. Enlisted in Mill Hill in Middlesex. Killed in action. He has no known grave but is listed on Pier and Face 12D and 13B on the Thiepval Memorial in France.

CULLEN, Robert: Rank: Private. Regiment or Service: Royal Irish Regiment. Unit: 7th Bn. Date of death: 17 August 1917. Service No. 9104. Born in Tipperary. Enlisted in Tipperary. Killed in action. Grave or Memorial Reference: M. 3. Cemetery: Westoutre Military Cemetery in Belgium.

CUMMINGS, James. Rank: Sapper. Date of death: 6 November 1918. Service No. 91930. Formerly he was with the Royal Irish Rifles (181st Tunnelling Company Royal Engineers) where his number was 1422. Born in Clonmel. Enlisted in Swansea while living in Clydach in Glamorganshire. Killed in action.

Grave or Memorial Reference: I. B. 1. Cemetery: Cross Roads Cemetery, Fontaine-Au-Bois in France.

CUMMINGS/CUMMINS, G.: (Alias) See **FARRELL**, G, No 4805, Irish Guards.

CUMMINGS/CUMMINS John. Rank: Private. Regiment or Service: Connaught Rangers. Unit: 5th Bn. Date of death: 13 October 1918. Service No. 15182. Formerly he was with the Leinster Regiment where his number was 3860. Born in Fethard. Enlisted in Fethard while living in Fethard. Died of wounds. Grave or Memorial Reference: II. A. 12. Cemetery: Roisel Communal Cemetery Extension in France.

CUMMINS, John: Rank: Private. Regiment or Service: Royal Irish Regiment. Unit: 'C' Coy. 1st Bn. Age at death: 20. Date of death: 15 March 1915. Service No: 10291. Born in St Patrick's in Thurles and enlisted in Clonmel while living in Thurles. Killed in action.

Supplementary information: Son of James and Kate Cummins, of Annfield, Bouladuff, Thurles, Co. Tipperary. Grave or Memorial Reference: Has no known grave but is commemorated on Panel 33. Memorial: Ypres (Menin Gate) Memorial in Belgium.

CUMMINS, John: Rank: Private. Regiment or Service: Irish Guards. Unit: 2nd Bn. Date of death: 13 September 1916. Service No. 8139. Born in Fethard. Enlisted in St Paul's

Churchyard, Middlesex while living in Foulkstown Co. Tipperary. Killed in action. He has no known grave but is listed on Pier and Face 7D on the Thiepval Memorial in France.

CUMMINS, John Joseph: Rank: Private. Regiment or Service: Leinster Regiment. Unit: 1st Bn. Age at death: 25. Date of death: 9 May 1915. Service No.2636. Born in Roscrea and enlisted in Birr, King's Co. Killed in action.

Supplementary information: Son of John Joseph and Alicia Cummins, of 40, Railway Street, Roscrea, Co. Tipperary. Grave or Memorial Reference: Has no known grave but is commemorated on Panel 44. Memorial: Ypres (Menin Gate) Memorial in Belgium.

CUMMINS, Richard: Rank: Private. Regiment or Service: 4th (Queen's Own) Hussars Age at death: 37. Date of death: 5 June 1917. Service No.4680. Born St Mary's, Clonmel and enlisted in Cahir while living in Clonmel. Killed in action.

Supplementary information: Husband of Ellen Cummins, of 27, Rivers Street, Clonmel, Co. Tipperary. Grave or Memorial Reference: II. H. 9. Cemetery: Unicorn Cemetery, Vend'huile in France.

CUNNEEN, Michael: Rank: Sergeant. Regiment or Service: Leinster Regiment. Unit: 3rd Bn. Secondary Regiment: Gold Coast Regiment, R. W. A. F. F. Secondary. Unit: attd. Age at death: 27. Date of death: 18 October 1917. Service No.3396. Born in Puckaun, Co.

Tipperary and enlisted in Birr, King's Co. Killed in action in Egypt.

Supplementary information: Son of James Cunneen, of Lisduff, Puckane, Nenagh, Co. Tipperary, Ireland. Grave or Memorial Reference: 6. G. 18. Cemetery: Dar Es Salaam War Cemetery in Tanznia.

CUNNINGHAM, Arthur Joseph: Rank: Second Lieutenant. Regiment or Service: London Regiment (London Irish Rifles). Unit: 18th Bn. Age at death: 25. Date of death: 15 September 1916. Killed in action. Awards: D C M. He is listed in the *London Gazette* dated 11 March 1916. His citation reads: '1694 Sgt. (now 2nd Lt) A. J. Cunningham, 18th (County of London) London Irish Rifles, London Regt., TF. For conspicuous gallantry. During the attack he assumed command of his company when the officers became wounded, and led it with conspicuous bravery and skill until wounded himself'.

Supplementary information: Son of Patrick Tuhan Cunningham and Margaret Cunningham, of 43, Tavistock Rd, Westbourne Park, London. Born at Clonmel, Co. Tipperary. Grave or Memorial Reference: XII. B. 11. Cemetery: Caterpillar Valley Cemetery, Longueval in France.

CUNNINGHAM, J.: Rank: Private. Regiment or Service: Royal Irish Fusiliers. Age at death: 23. Date of death: 7 April 1919. Service No.40016. Transferred to the Labour Corps where his number was 670626. Grave or Memorial Reference: E.

H. 20. Cemetery: St Michael's New Cemetery, Tipperary.

CUNNINGHAM, James F.: Rank: Lance Corporal. Regiment or Service: Irish Guards. Unit: 1st Bn. Date of death: 20 November 1914. Service No.2114. Born in Clonmel. Enlisted in Dublin while living in Pimlico in Middlesex. Died of wounds at home. Grave or Memorial Reference: R. 291. Cemetery: Aldershot Military Cemetery, UK.

CUNNINGHAM, John: Rank: Corporal. Regiment or Service: Leinster Regiment. Unit: 4th Coy. 2nd Bn. Age at death: 29. Date of death: 16 April 1917. Service No.8916 Awards: V C. Born in Thurles in 1890 and enlisted there also. Died of wounds at Bois-En-Hache.

Supplementary information: Son of Johanna and Joseph Cunningham, of Stradavoher Street, Thurles, Co. Tipperary. The second son lost to a widowed mother in the war. Grave or Memorial Reference: I. A. 39. Cemetery: Barlin Communal Cemetery Extension.

An extract taken from The *London Gazette*, dated 8 June, 1917, records the following:

For most conspicuous bravery and devotion to duty when in command of a Lewis Gun section on the most exposed flank of the attack. His section came under heavy enfilade fire and suffered severly. Although wounded he succeeded almost alone in reaching his objective with his gun, which he got into action in spite of much oppositon. When counter-attacked by a party of twenty of the enemy he exhausted his ammuntion against them, then, standing in full view, he commenced throwing bombs. He was wounded again, and fell, but picked himself up and continued to fight single-handed with the enemy until his bombs were exhausted. He then made his way back to our lines with a fractured arm and other wounds. There is little doubt that the superb courage of this N. C. O. cleared up a most critical situation on the left flank of the attack. Corporal Cunningham died in hospital from the effects of his wounds.

CUNNINGHAM, John: Rank: Private. Regiment or Service: Royal

John Cunningham.

Grave of John Cunningham.

Irish Fusiliers. Unit: Transferred to the Labour Corps where his number was 670626. Date of death: 7 April 1919. Service No. 40016. Son of Patrick Cunningham who died in 1928. Grave or Memorial Reference: E. H. 104. Cemetery: St Michael's New Cemetery, Tipperary.

CUNNINGHAM, M: Rank: Private. Regiment or Service: Royal Irish Regiment Unit: transferred to the Labour Corps where his number was 230920. Date of death: 29 September 1919. Service No. 6766. Rock of Cashel Cemetery. Grave location: north-east of the Cathedral.

CUNNINGHAM, Patrick: Rank: Acting Corporal. Regiment or Service: Leinster Regiment. Unit: 1st Bn. Date of death: 4 June 1915. Service No. 10181. Formerly he was with the Royal Irish Regiment where his number was 10381. Born in Thurles. Enlisted in Templemore. Died of Wounds at home.

Supplementary information: Brother of John Cunningham V.C. (see John's information above). Grave or Memorial Reference: South of the west end of the church. Cemetery: Thurles (St Mary's) Church of Ireland Churchyard.

CUNNINGHAM, Patrick: Rank: Private. Regiment or Service: Connaught Rangers. Unit: 1st Bn. Age at death: 29. Date of death: 30 November 1914. Service No. 10232. Born in Roscrea and enlisted in Templemore while living in Roscrea.

Grave of M. Cunningham.

Died of wounds.

Supplementary information: Son of Sarah Cunningham, of 43, Railway View, Roscrea, Co. Tipperary. Grave or Memorial Reference: III. A. 61. Cemetery: Bethune Town Cemetery in France.

CURRAN, Michael: Rank: Private. Regiment or Service: Royal Dublin Fusiliers. Unit: 9th Bn. Age at death: 21. Date of death: 9 September 1916. Service No.26028. Born in Fethard and enlisted there also. Killed in action.

Supplementary information: Son of Mr and Mrs Thomas Curran, of Watergate, Fethard, Co. Tipperary. Grave or Memorial Reference: XVII. G. 3. Cemetery: Delville Wood Cemetery, Longueval in France.

CUSACK, Oliver: Rank: Sapper. Regiment or Service: Corps of Royal Engineers. 11th Field Company, Royal Engineers. Date of death: 28 May 1915. Service No.26169. Born in Thurles. Enlisted in Ennis Co. Clare. Died of wounds at home. Age at death: 20.

Supplementary information: Son of Thomas and Margaret Cusack of Clarecastle Co. Clare. Grave or Memorial Reference: Gen 7377 (Screen Wall). Cemetery: Tottenham Cemetery, UK.

CUSACK, Patrick: Rank: Private. Regiment or Service: Australian Infantry. Unit: 35th Bn. Date of death: 9 June 1917. Age at death: 34. Service No.1792. Born in Tipperary. Enlisted in Sydney, NSW on 14 April 1916. Occupation on enlistment: labourer, Age: 33, Height 9' 8 ¼", Complexion:

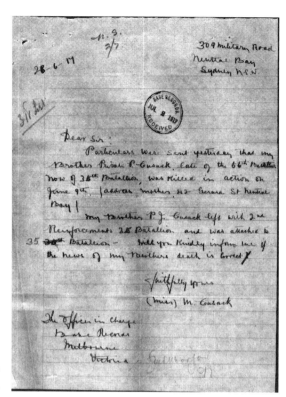

Letter written by
Oliver Cusack's sister.

ruddy. Eyes: blue, Hair: light, Religious Denomination: R.C. Sister: Miss M Cusack, 309 Military Road, Neutral Bay. Sydney, NSW. Killed in action.

Supplementary information: Son of Michael and Ellen Cusack, of 95, Gerard Street, Neutral Bay, New South Wales. Native of Tipperary, Ireland. Originally he was buried in a shell hole East of a mine crater in the German Reserve, 1 miles East of Messines. Burial took place on 27 July 1917 by Revd J. E. N. Osbourne. Re-interred in the Strand Military Cemetery 7 ½ miles from Ypres. Grave or Memorial Reference: VIII. L. 6. Cemetery: Strand Military Cemetery, Ploegsteert near Ypres, Belgium.

CUSACK, Patrick Joseph: Rank: Private. Number 10220, 2nd Bn, Irish Guards. Born in Ballycahill, enlisted in Melton Mowbay in Leicester while living in Castlefogerty. Died of wounds in one of the Medical Unit Hospitals in Wimereux on Wednesday, 17 October 1917. Buried in Grave Reference-VI. D. 25A.

CUSSEN, William: Rank: Private. Regiment or Service: Royal Irish Regiment. Unit: 1st Bn. Date of death: 22 December 1917. Service No. 8084. Born in Templemore. Enlisted in Templemore. Died of wounds in Palestine. Grave or Memorial Reference: G. 60. Cemetery: Ramleh War Cemetery in Israel.

D

DAGG, George: Rank: Private. Regiment or Service: Canadian Infantry (Central Ontario Regiment) Unit: 3rd Bn. Age at death: 23. Date of death: 8 October 1916. Service No.172435.

Supplementary information: Son of John E. and Rebecca Dagg of The Orchard, Templederry, Co. Tipperary, Ireland. Memorial: Vimy Memorial, France. Data from the reverse of the enlistment document: Age on enlistment: 26 Years. 1 Months. Height: 5' 10". Eye colour: blue. Complexion: fair. Hair colour: light brown. Religion: C.o E. Chest expansion: 3" Girth: 40". Scar of left leg and mole on back. Date of enlistment: 4 February 1916. Place of enlistment: Toronto, Ontario.

DAGG, Michael: Rank: Private. Regiment or Service: Irish Guards. Unit: 1st Bn. Date of death: 17 October 1914. Service No.4338. Born in Fethard. Enlisted in Clonmel. Killed in action. Age at death: 19.

Supplementary information: Son of Patrick Dagg. He has no known grave but is listed on Panel 11 on the Ypres (Menin Gate) Memorial in Belgium.

DALTON, Charles: Rank: Lieutenant Colonel. Regiment or Service: Royal Army Medical Corps Age at death: 48. Date of death: 18 September 1914.

Supplementary information: Son of the late John Edward and Katherine M. Dalton, of Ballygriffin, Co. Tipperary. Grave or Memorial Reference: In the East quarter. Cemetery: Vieil-Arcy Communal Cemetery in France.

DALTON, Edward: Rank: Private. Regiment or Service: Royal Irish Regiment. Unit: 2nd Bn. Date of death: 3 May 1915. Service No.4321. Born in St Nichoas, Carrick-on-Suir, Co. Tipperary. Enlisted in Carrick-on-Suir while living in Carrickbeg, Co. Waterford. Died of wounds. Grave or Memorial Reference: V. C. 14. Cemetery: Klein-Vierstraat British Cemetery in Belgium.

DALTON, James: Rank: Private. Regiment or Service: Middlesex Regiment. Unit: 16th Bn. Age at death: 33. Date of death: 31 May 1917. Service No.G-40356. He was previously in the Royal Sussex Regiment where his number was G-12299. Born in Carrick-on-Suir and enlisted there also. Killed in action.

Supplementary information: Brother of Peter Dalton, Upper Ballyrichard Rd, Carrick-on-Suir, Co. Tipperary. Grave or Memorial Reference: Bay 7. Memorial: Arras Memorial in France.

DALTON, John: Rank: Sergeant. Regiment or Service: Cheshire Regiment. Unit: 2nd Bn. Date of death: 15 October 1915. Service

Alfred Daly.

No. 7212. Born in Carrick-on-Suir, Co. Tipperary. Enlisted in Stockport in Cheshire. Died of wounds. Age at death: 30.

Supplementary information: Brother of Josephine York, of 309, Leeds Rd, Bradford, Yorks. Grave or Memorial Reference: III. O. 13. l. Cemetery: Etaples Military Cemetery in France.

DALTON, John. Rank: Private. Regiment or Service: Royal Irish Regiment. Unit: 1st Bn. Age at death: 17. Date of death: 12 March 1915. Service No. 4558. Born in Carrick-on-Suir and enlisted there also. Killed in action.

Supplementary information: Son of John and Margaret Dalton, of Ballyrichard Rd, Carrick-on-Suir, Co. Tipperary. Grave or Memorial Reference: II. A. 5. Cemetery: Voormezeele Enclosures No. 1 and No. 2 in Belgium.

DALTON, Maurice: Rank: Private. Regiment or Service: Royal Munster Fusiliers. Unit: 8th Bn. Age at death: 36. Date of death: 9 September 1916. Service No. 7898. Born in Cluen in Tipperary and enlisted in Dublin while

living in Cluen. Killed in action.

Supplementary information: Son of Jeremiah and Johanna Dalton, of Cluen, Bansha, Tipperary. Grave or Memorial Reference: XV. D. 29. Cemetery: A. I. F. Burial Ground, Fleurs in France.

DALTON, Michael Patrick: Rank: Gunner. Regiment or Service: Royal Garrison Artillery. Unit: 250th Siege Battery. Date of death: 27 August 1917. Service No. 59799. Born in Carrick-on-Suir, Co. Tipperary. Enlisted in Marleybone in Middlesex while living in Kilburn. Died of wounds.

Supplementary information: Grave or Memorial Reference: I. G. 11. Cemetery: Kandahar Farm Cemetery in Belgium.

DALTON, Patrick: Rank: Driver. Regiment or Service: Royal Field Artillery. Unit: 61st (South Midland). Age at death: 20. Date of death: 20 July 1917. Service No. 119709. Born in Carrick-on-Suir and enlisted in Clonmel. Died of wounds.

Supplementary information: Son of Patrick and Margaret Dalton, of Kickham Street, Carrick-on-Suir, Co. Tipperary. Grave or Memorial

Reference: XVI. D. 13A. Cemetery: Lijssenthoek Military Cemetary in Belgium.

DALTON, Patrick: Rank: Corporal. Regiment or Service: Royal Dublin Fusiliers. Unit: 9th Bn. Date of death: 16 August 1917. Service No. 16101. Born in Carrick, Co. Tipperary. Enlisted in Perth while living in Methven in Perth. Killed in action.

Supplementary information: Husband of Jemima Dalton, of Culdeesland, Methven, Perthshire. He has no known grave but is listed on Panels 14 and 145 on the Tyne Cot Memorial in Belgium.

DALY, Alfred: Rank: Rifleman. Regiment or Service: Rifle Brigade. Unit: 2nd Bn. Date of death: 17 March 1916. Service No. S-11335. Formerly he was with the Royal Field Artillery where his number was 86421. Born in Nenagh. Enlisted in Lemington, Warwick while living in Nenagh. Killed in action. Grave or Memorial Reference: I. B. 22. Cemetery: Rue-Du-Bois Military Cemetery, Fleurbaix in France.

DALY, Jeremiah: Rank: Private. Regiment or Service: Leinster Regiment. Unit: 2nd Bn. Age at death: 32. Date of death: 20 October 1914. Service No. 5918. Born in Tipperary and enlisted in Nenagh. Killed in action.

Supplementary information: Husband of Mary Daly (*née* O'Donnell), of 11, Mountain View, Tipperary. Grave or Memorial Reference: Has no known grave but is commemorated on Panel 10. Memorial: Ploegsteert Memorial in Belgium.

DALY, John: Rank: Corporal. Regiment or Service: Machine Gun Corps (Infantry). Unit: 40th Coy. Age at death: 27. Date of death: Thursday 21 March 1918. Service No. 27699. Formerly 1383, Leinster Regiment (Birr Bks). Born in Holycross. Enlisted in Cahir while living in Clonmel.

Supplementary information: Son of the late William and Alice Daly, of 8 Cross Street, Clonmel, Co. Tipperary. He has no known grave but is commemorated on the Arras Memorial in France on Bay 10.

DALY, Michael: Rank: Private. Regiment or Service: Cameronains (Scottish Rifles). Unit: 10th Bn. Date of death: 31 August 1916. Service No. 21438. Born in Nenagh. Enlisted in Glasgow. Died of wounds. Grave or Memorial Reference: IV. B. 9. Heilly Station Cemetery, Mericourt-l'Abbe in France.

DALY, Michael: Rank: Private. Regiment or Service: Royal Irish Regiment. Unit: 6th Bn. Date of death: 4 August 1917. Service No. 9800. Born in Tipperary. Enlisted in Tipperary. Killed in action. He has no known grave but is listed on Panel 33 on the Ypres (Menin Gate) Memorial in Belgium.

DALY, Michael: Rank: Private. Regiment or Service: Irish Guards. Unit: 1st Bn. Age at death: 25. Date of death: 1 November 1914. Service No.4471. Born in Latten Co. Tipperary and enlisted in Newport in Monday while living in Latten. Killed in action.

Supplementary information: Son of Michael and Margaret Daly, of Lattin Cottage, Tipperary. Grave or Memorial Reference: Has no known grave but is commemorated on Panel 11. Memorial: Ypres (Menin Gate) Memorial in Belgium.

DANAGHER, Patrick: Rank: Sergeant. Regiment or Service: Connaught Rangers. Unit: 5th Bn. Date of death: 23 August 1915. Service No.8545. Born in Templemore. Enlisted in Ahmednagar, India while living in Portsmouth. Died of wounds in Gallipoli. Age at death: 28.

Supplementary information: Son of Serjt. John Danagher, Victoria Cross Winner (late Connaught Rangers), and Mrs John Danagher, of 115, Fratton Rd, Portsmouth. Grave or Memorial Reference: SP Mem, B. 2. Cemetery: 7th Field Ambulance Cemetery in Turkey.

DANAHER, Patrick: Rank: Sergeant. Regiment or Service: Royal Irish Regiment. Unit: 2nd Bn. Date of death: 5 July 1916. Service No.3258. Born in Nenagh, Co. Tipperary. Enlisted in Tipperary while living in Killaloe, Co. Clare. Killed in action. Age at death: 35.

Supplementary information: Son of Dan and Catherine Danaher: husband of Bridget Danaher, of New Street, Killaloe, Co. Clare. He has no known

grave but is listed on Pier and Face 3A of the Thiepval memorial in France.

DANIELS, Jeremiah: Rank: Private. Regiment or Service: Connaught Rangers. Unit: 5th Bn. Date of death: 26 August 1915. Service No.4453. Formerly he was with the Royal Irish Regiment, where his number was 172. Born in Clonmel. Enlisted in Clonmel while living in Clonmel. Died of wounds in Gallipoli. He has no known grave but is listed on Panel 181 to 183 on the Helle's Memorial in Turkey.

DANIELS, Thomas:. Rank: Private. Regiment or Service: Connaught Rangers. Unit: 5th Bn. Age at death: 22. Date of death: 11 October 1918. Service No.15251. He was formerly in the Leinster Regiment where his number was 10350. Born in Boston, Mass. and enlisted in Clonmel while living in Clonmel.

Supplementary information: Son of James and Johanna Daniels, of Strand House, Old Bridge, Clonmel, Co. Tipperary. Grave or Memorial Reference: I. A. 4. Cemetery: Roisel Communal Cemetery Extension in France.

DARMODY, Edward: Rank: Private. Regiment or Service: Royal Irish Regiment. Unit: 2nd Bn. Date of death: 4 July 1916. Service No.4675. Born in St Nicholas's, Carrick-on-Suir, Co. Tipperary. Enlisted in Waterford while living in Carrick-on-Suir, Co. Tipperary. Died of wounds. Age at death: 19.

Supplementary information: Son of Patrick and Bridget Darmody, of Villa Factory, Carrick-on-Suir. Grave or Memorial Reference: A 12. Cemetery: Morlancourt British Cemetery No. 1 in France.

DARMODY, Jeremiah: Rank: Lance Sergeant. Regiment or Service: Irish Guards. Unit: 2nd Bn. Date of death: 13 September 1916. Service No.7329. Born in Tipperary. Enlisted in Dublin while living in Bansha. Killed in action.

Extract from the *Tipperary Star*, 1916:
Gallant Tipperary Man.

In the battle of the Somme, on Sept 13th, Sergt, Jeremiah Darmody, 2nd Battalion, Irish Guards, son of Mr John Darmody, Tipperary, lost his life in a gallant but fruitless attempt to recover the body of his Officer, Capt, Montgomery. Darmody, who was a young man of 24 years and of powerful physique, was in agricultural employment in the Bansha district at the outbreak of the war, and was a member of the National Volunteers and of the bansha Pipe Band. On the occasion of the great review of the national Volunteers in the Phoenix Park on Easter Sunday, 1915, Darmody went up to Dublin along with his comerades of the Bansha War Pipers, all of whom were attired in the picturesque costume of the band. After the review he, with a number of other young fellows from Tipperary Town and district, joined the Irish Guards. In the fol-

lowing September he was reported killed in action but this proved to be incorrect. Last September, in one of the fierce engagements in the battle of the Somme, in which the Irish Guards, along with several other Irish regiments, took such a memorable part, darmody's officer, Capt Montgomery, was killed. Shells were bursting all round his body, but heedless of this hurricane of death, Darmody ran forward to take it away. In the effort to do so he paid the penalty of his own life. For this heroic deed of the young Tipperary Man Capt, Montgomery's mother, a wealthy English lady, is not ungrateful, and this week she forwarded to Mr Brownrigg, District Inspector of Police in Tipperary, to be given to Darmody's father, a very handsome monetary gift, accompanied by an appreciative sympathetic letter, in which reference was made to their mutual sorrow. When Mr Darmody opened the letter the first thing that met his hand was a cheque for £5, but great was his astonishment when he also discovered in the enclosure an Exchequer Bond for £100. The following is the letter addressed by Mrs Montgomery to Mr Darmody:-
"70 Harley House, Regency Park, N. W. Nov. 7th, 1916. Dear Sir:-I am told that your son lost his life in a gallant attempt to recover the body of my son, who was killed whilst leading his company. I could'nt tell you how sorry I feel for you in your great loss, and that

such a brave act should have cost him his life. Still, we feel so proud to think that the country has given us such men, and you and I can feel that our sons have not lived in vain if they died so bravely, as mine was killed, I am told in an attempt to carry a point he knew to be almost hopeless when undertaking it. Please accept enclosed note and Exchequer Bond for £100. I have sent it to you by the District-Inspector of the R. I. C. as some slight token of sympathy in the loss you have sustained. I congratulate you on having had such a son, and trust time may help to soften your sorrow, - Yours Truly, Grace Montgomery.

Jeremiah has no known grave but is listed on Pier and Face 7D on the Thiepval Memorial in France.

DARMODY, John Parnell: Rank: Private. Regiment or Service: Australian Infantry A. I. F. Unit: 26th Bn. Died of wounds. Date of death: 24 August 1916. Service No. 1673. Additional information: Son of John and Catherine Darmody of Willoon Ipswich Queensland. Cemetery: Powerstown (St John's) Catholic Cemetery. Grave location: East of the church near the East boundary. Tipperary.

DARMODY, Patrick: Rank: Private. Regiment or Service: Royal Irish Regiment. Unit: 2nd Bn. Date of death: 21 March 1918. Service No. 6402. Born in Emly. Age at death: 20. Enlisted in Cork while living in Emly Co. Tipperary. Killed in action.

Supplementary information: Son of Patrick and Bridget Darmody (*née* Ryan), of Ballycurrane, Emly, Co. Tipperary. He has no known grave but is listed on Panels 30 and 31 on the Pozieres Memorial in France.

DAUGHTON, Richard: Rank: Private. Regiment or Service: Irish Guards. Unit: 1st Bn. Date of death: 31 October 1914. Service No. 1478. Born in Killenaule. Enlisted in Clonmel while living in Ballynonty. Killed in action. Age at death: 28.

Supplementary information: Before

Grave of John Parnell Darmody.

Grave of Frederick William Day.

enlisting he was a Constable in the R. I. C. Son of Michael and Harriet Daughton. He has no known grave but is listed on Panel 11 on the Ypres (Menin Gate). Memorial in Belgium.

DAVIES, J.: Rank: Private. Regiment or Service: Royal Welsh Fusiliers, transferred to the Labour Corps where his number was 268063. No. 12569. Unit: 9th Bn. Date of death: 15 November 1918, four days after the war ended. Service No. 12569.

Supplementary information: Cemetery, Clonmel, St Patrick's Cemetery. Grave location: 8. MC. 9.

DAVIN, John Jerome: Rank: Private. Regiment or Service: Royal Dublin Fusiliers. Unit: 2nd Bn. Date of death: 28 July 1918. Service No. 28103. Born in Clonmel. Enlisted in Clonmel. Died.

Supplementary information: Son of Mrs M Davin. Grave or Memorial Reference: 3. EC. 101. Cemetery: Clonmel (St Patrick's) Cemetery.

DAVIN, Thomas Joseph: Rank: Private. Regiment or Service: Irish Guards. Unit: 2nd Bn. Age at death: 26. Date of death: 31 July 1917. Service No. 10568. Born in Barrickbeg, Co. Waterford and enlisted in Clonmel. Killed in action.

Supplementary information: Son of Thomas Davin and Mrs Davin, of Carrick Beg, Carrick-on-Suir, Co. Tipperary. Grave or Memorial Reference: Has no known grave but is commemorated on Panel 11. Memorial: Ypres (Menin Gate) Memorial in Belgium.

DAY, Frederick William: Rank: Private. Regiment or Service: Royal Army Medical Corps. Unit: 16th Coy Age at death: 62. Date of death: 24

Grave of Timothy Deane.

December 1916. Service No. 104005. Born in Peterborough and enlisted in Nenagh.

Supplementary information: Husband of Matilda Day, of Peter Street, Nenagh, Co. Tipperary. Grave or Memorial Reference: In south-east corner. Cemetery: Nenagh (Barrack Street) Old Graveyard.

DAY, John Edward: Rank: Captain. Regiment or Service: Royal Irish Regiment. Unit: 'A' Coy. 6ᵗʰ Bn. Age at death: 22. Date of death: 6 April 1917.

Supplementary information: Son of the Very Revd Maurice W. Day and Katherine L.F. Day, Or Culloden, Bray, Co. Wicklow. Born at Newport, Co. Tipperary. Grave or Memorial Reference: III. B. 60. Cemetery: Bailleul Communal Cemetery Extension (Nord) in France.

DEA, Patrick: Rank: Private. Number H-73751. 19ᵗʰ (Queen Alexandra's Own Royal) Hussars. Born in Ballycahill. Enlisted in Thurles while living in Thurles. Died in one of the seven hospitals in Rouen, France on Thursday 11 November 1918. the last day of the War. He is buried in St Sever Cemetery Extension, Seine-Maritime, France. Grave Reference-S. II. GG. 25.

DEANE, Timothy: Rank: Private. Regiment or Service: Royal Irish Regiment. Unit: 3ʳᵈ Bn. Date of death: 7 April 1917. Service No. 3/4595. Cemetery: Nenagh (Barrack Street) Old Graveyard. Grave location: In the south-west part near the South wall.

DEASY, E.: Rank: Company Sergeant Major. Regiment or Service: Royal Munster Fusiliers. Transferred

Grave of E. Deasy.

to the Labour Corps where his number was 427006. Unit: 1st Bn. Age at death: Date of death: 31 March 1920. Service No. 5936. Cemetery: St Michael's New Cemetery, Tipperary Town. Grave location: E. H. 110.

DEEGAN, William: Rank: Private. Regiment or Service: Leinster Regiment. Unit: 2nd Bn. Date of death: 16 January 1915. Service No. 8122. Born in Roscrea. Enlisted in Birr. Killed in action. He has no known grave but is listed on Panel 10 on the Ploegsteert Memorial in Belgium.

DEERING, Charles: Rank: Private. Regiment or Service: Royal Irish Regiment. Unit: 2nd Bn. Age at death: 30. Date of death: 5 July 1916. Service No. 9765. Born in Tipperary and enlisted there also. Killed in action.

Supplementary information: Son of William and Margaret Deering, of Tipperary Grave or Memorial Reference: IV. H. 4. Cemetery: Danzig Alley British Cemetery Mametz in France.

DEEVES, John Henderson: Rank: Private. Regiment or Service: Canadian Infantry (Central Ontario Regiment) Unit: 20th Bn. Age at death: 22. Date of death: 11 November 1917. Service No. 404819

Supplementary information: Son of Matthew and Margaret Deeves, of Grange, Kilcooley, Thurles, Co. Tipperary, Ireland. Grave or Memorial Reference: Panel 18 24 26

John Henderson Deeves.

30. Memorial: Ypres (Menin Gate) Memorial in Belgium. Data from the reverse of the enlistment document: Age on enlistment: 20 Years. 1 Month. Height: 5' 9 ½". Eye colour: brown. Complexion: dark. Hair colour: dark brown. Religion: C. of E. Chest expansion: 2 ½" Girth: 33". Scar on left knee. Date of Enlistment: 12 April 1915. Place of Enlistment: Toronto.

DELAHUNTY, James: Rank: Private. Regiment or Service: Connaught Rangers. Unit: 1st Bn. Age at death: 42. Date of death: 31 May 1916. Service No. 5459. Born in Clonkenny Co. Tipperary and enlisted in Manchester while living in Manchester. Died in Mesopotamia.

Supplementary information: Son of Mr and Mrs Delahunty, of Roscrea, Co. Tipperary. Grave or Memorial Reference: XXI. B. 14. Cemetery: Amara War Cemetery in Iraq.

DELANEY, Michael: Rank: Private. Regiment or Service: Royal Munster Fusiliers. Unit: 1st Bn. Date of death: 22 September 1916. Service No. 14048. Formerly he was with the Royal Field Artillery where his number was 75278. Born in Drum, Clonismullen, Co. Tipperary. Enlisted in Kildare while living in Nenagh. Killed in action. Age at death: 22.

Supplementary information: Son of William and Nora Delaney. He has no known grave but is listed on Panel 44 on the Ypres (Menin Gate) Memorial in Belgium.

DELANEY, Patrick: Rank: Private. Regiment or Service: Royal Dublin Fusiliers. Unit: 2nd Bn. Date of death: 1 July 1916, the first day of the battle of the Somme. Service No. 5569. Born in Ballinagrry, Co. Tipperary. Enlisted in Carlow while living in Kilkenny. Killed in action.

Supplementary information: Son of John Delaney of Maudlin Street, Kilkenny. Grave or Memorial Reference: I.D.94. Cemetery: Sucrerie Military Cemetery, Colinclamps in France.

DELMEGE, Edwin: Rank: Private. Regiment or Service: Royal Munster Fusiliers. Unit: 1st Bn. Date of death: 1 May 1915. Service No.9569. Born in Tipperary. Enlisted in Limerick while living in Lucan, Co. Dublin. Killed in action in Gallipoli. He has no known grave but is listed on Panel 185 to 190 on the Helles Memorial in Turkey.

DELMEGE, Eyre Bolton Massy: Rank: Captain. Regiment or Service: East Lancashire Regiment. Unit: 2nd Bn. Age at death: 25. Date of death: 23 October 1916. Was awarded the Military Cross and Mentioned in despatches.

Supplementary information: Son of Stafford Delmege, of Ballymore, Tipperary. Native of Gadesby, Leicestershire. Grave or Memorial Reference: V. G. 12. Cemetery: Bancourt British Cemetery in France.

DEMPSEY, Joseph: Rank: Private. Regiment or Service: Royal Irish Regiment. Unit: 2nd Bn. Date of death: 19 October 1914. Service No.10766. Born in Templemore. Enlisted in Thurles while living in Templemore. Killed in action. Grave or Memorial Reference: I. J. 5. Cemetery: Rue-Petillon Military Cemetery, Fleurbaix in France.

DENNEY, Frederick: Rank: Private. Regiment or Service: Hampshire Regiment. Unit: 1st Bn. Date of death: 2 March 1918. Service No.26471. Formerly he was with the Essex Regiment where his number was 28122. Born in Borrisoleigh. Enlisted in Norwich, Norfolk. Killed in action. Age at death: 22.

Supplementary information: Son of Ernest Claude and Helen Mary Denney, of Costessey, Norfolk. He has no known grave but is listed in Bay 6 on the Arras Memorial in France.

DENNY, Michael: Rank: Private. Regiment or Service: Royal Irish Regiment. Unit: 2nd Bn. Date of death: 19 October 1914. Service No.9363. Born in Moyglass Co. Tipperary. Enlisted in Clonmel while living in Fethard. Killed in action. He has no known grave but is listed on Panels 11 and 12 on the Le Touret Memorial in France

DEVAN, J.: Rank: Private. Regiment or Service: Scots Guards. Unit: 2nd Bn. Age at death: 35. Date of death: 4 October 1914. Service No.6032.

Supplementary information: Son of Michael and Catharine Devan: husband of Mary Byrne (formerly Devan), of William Street, Cashel, Co. Tipperary. Grave or Memorial Reference: J.R.C. 608. Cemetery: Lyndhurst Cemetery, Hampshire.

DIGNAM/DIGNUM/DIGNAN, Robert: Rank: Private. Regiment or Service: Leinster Regiment. Unit: A Coy, 1st Bn. Date of death: 12 May 1915.

Service No.3199. Born in Roscrea. Enlisted in Birr. Killed in action. Age at death: 34.

Supplementary information: Husband of Mary K. Dignum, of 45 Abbey Street, Milby Arcade, Nuneaton, Warwickshire. He has no known grave but is listed on Panel 44 on the Ypres (Menin Gate) Memorial in Belgium.

DILLON, James: Rank: Gunner. Regiment or Service: Royal Garrison Artillery. Unit: 38th Siege Battery. Date of death: 9 August 1917. Service No.279840. Born in Roscrea. Enlisted in Birr while living in Roscrea. Killed in action. Age at death: 38.

Supplementary information: Husband of Katie Dillon, of 5 Grove Street, Roscrea, Co. Tipperary. Grave or Memorial Reference: XIX. D. 20. Cemetery: Loos British Cemetery in France.

DILLON, Michael: Rank: Private. Regiment or Service: Royal Irish Regiment. Unit: 2nd Bn. Age at death: 36. Date of death: 27 September 1918. Service No.9990. Born in Grange Co. Tipperary and enlisted in Clonmel while living in Lisnamuck Co. Tipperary. Killed in action.

Supplementary information: Son of Mrs Mary Dillon, of Lisnamuck, Cahir, Co. Tipperary. Grave or Memorial Reference: A. 22. Cemetery: Sucrerie Military Cemetery, Colinclamps in France. He is also commemorated on the Cahir War Memorial.

DILLON, Patrick: Rank: Private. Regiment or Service: Kings (Liverpool Regiment). Unit: 1st Bn. Date of death: 14 September 1915. Service No.12295. Born in Clobmell, Tipperary. Enlisted in Warrington while living in Dublin. Killed in action.

Supplementary information: Son of John and Ellen Dillon Husband of Mary Dillon of Kathrea Street, Dublin. Grave or Memorial Reference: A. 5. Cemetery: Cambrin Military Cemetery, France.

DODDS, John Carrick: Rank: Private. Regiment or Service: Royal Sussex Regiment. Unit: 9th Bn. Date of death: 4 November 1914. Age at death: 21. Service No.G-3761. Born in Tipperary. Enlisted in Guildford. Died at home.

Supplementary information: Son of Charlotte Clark Dodds, of 89, Goldstone Villas, Hove, and the late Charles Thomas Dodds. Born at Sunderland. Grave or Memorial Reference: ZHN. 15. Cemetery: Brighton (Bear Road) Cemetery, UK.

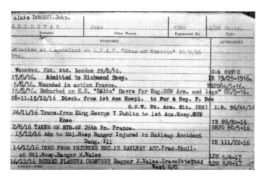

John Doheny.

DOHENY, John: Served as **SULLIVAN**. Rank: Private. Regiment or Service: Australian Infantry. Unit: 26th Bn. Date of death: 14 December 1916. Service No.4586. Age at death: 32. Enlisted in Brisbane Queensland. Wounded in France on 5 August 1916. Gunshot wounds to the arms and legs. After treatment he was discharged on 13 December 1916. He died the day after. Cause of death: Fracture of skull (accident on Railway line). He felt sick during a train journey and put his head out of a window to vomit and his head struck a tunnel or bridge. His enlistment document states he was born in Tipperary. His Mother lived in Ballingarry in Tipperary and he was a twenty-nine-year-old labourer when he joined up. This conflicts with information from other sources.

Supplementary information: Son of John and Alice Doheny, of Callow, Co. Kilkenny. Born at Harley Park, Callow,. Documentary evidence was produced and his name of the official recordsGrave or Memorial Reference: W. OG. 704A. Cemetery: Bangor, Flandva (Glanadda) Cemetery in Wales.

DOHENY, John: Rank: Private. Regiment or Service: Royal Irish Regiment. Unit: 1st Bn. Date of death: 14 October 1914. Service No.8580. Born in Ballingarry, Co. Tipperary. Enlisted in Thurles. Died in Colaba in India. He has no known grave but is listed on Face C of the Kirkee 1914-18 Memorial in India.

DOHENY, Thomas: Rank: Private. Regiment or Service: Royal Irish Regiment. Unit: 2nd Bn. Date of death: 24 April 1915. Service No.8385. Born in St Mary's Clonmel. Enlisted in Clonmel. Killed in action. He has no known grave but is listed on Panel 4 on the Ploegsteert Memorial in Belgium

DOLAN, Robert: Rank: Regimental Sergeant Major. Regiment or Service: Royal Inniskilling Fusiliers. Unit: 'C' Coy. 7th-8th Bn. Age at death: 36. Date of death: 27 March 1918. Service No.13133. Born in Newtownstewart, Co. Tyrone and enlisted in Glasgow. Killed in action.

Supplementary information: Husband of Mary Bridget Dolan of 8 Dillon Street, Tipperary. Grave or Memorial Reference: Has no known grave but is commemorated on Panel 38 to 40. Memorial: Pozieres Memorial in France.

DONEGAN, Thomas: Rank: Private. Regiment or Service: Royal Welsh Fusiliers. Unit: 2nd Bn. Date of death: 20 March 1918. Service No.33254. Born in Clonmel. Enlisted in Dolgelly, Merioneth. Died at home. Grave or Memorial Reference: A. 1632. Cemetery: Paisley(Hawkhead) Cemetery. UK.

DONNELLAN, James: Rank: Sergeant. Regiment or Service: Lancashire Fusiliers. Unit: 10th Bn. Date of death: 3 November 1915. Service No.8814. Born in Clonmel. Enlisted in Cardiff. Killed in action. Grave or

Memorial Reference: XXVII. F. 20. Cemetery: New Irish Farm Cemetery in Belgium.

DONOHOE, Patrick: Rank: Private. Regiment or Service: Royal Irish Regiment. Unit: 2nd Bn. Date of death: 8 May 1915. Service No.6714. Born in Borrisokane. Enlisted in Nenagh while living in Borrisokane. Killed in action. Age at death: 38.

Supplementary information: Son of Partick and Birdget Donohoe. He has no known grave but is listed on Panel 33 on the Ypres (Menin Gate) Memorial in Belgium.

DONOHUE/DONOHOE, Patrick: Rank: Private. Regiment or Service: Royal Irish Regiment. Unit: 2nd Bn. Age at death: 25. Date of death: 26 September 1914. Service No.10885. Born in Nenagh and enlisted there also. Died of wounds received at the battle of Aisne on 16 September 1914.

Supplementary information: Son of Patrick and Mary Donohue, of Birr Rd, Nenagh, Co. Tipperary. Grave or Memorial Reference: A. 5. (Sp. Mem.). Cemetery: Braine Communal Cemetery in France.

DONOHUE, John: Alias, correct name is **O'DONOHUE**. Rank: Private. Regiment or Service: Age at death: 52. Date of death: 11 January 1917. Service No.15012. Formerly he was in the Royal Irish Regiment where his number was 5590. Born in Cashel and enlisted in Cashel while living in Cashel. Died.

Supplementary information: See **O'DONOHUE** the true family name. Cemetery: Rock of Cashel Graveyard in Tipperary.

DONOHUE, William: Rank: Private. Regiment or Service: Royal Irish Regiment. Unit: 6th Bn. Age at death: 30. Date of death: 9 September 1916. Service No.5577. Formerly he was in the Royal Munster Fusiliers where his number was 6538. Killed in action. Born in Nenagh and enlisted there also. Killed in action.

Supplementary information: Son of Mrs Mary Donohue, of Birr Rd, Nenagh, Co. Tipperary. Grave or Memorial Reference: Pier and Face 3 A. Memorial: Thiepval Memorial in France.

DONOVAN, Thomas: Rank: Private. Regiment or Service: Royal Irish Regiment. Unit: E Company, 2nd Bn. Date of death: 19 October 1914. Service No.5928. Born in Fermoy, Co. Cork. Enlisted in Clonmel while living in Golden, Co. Tipperary. Killed in action. Age at death: 19.

Supplementary information: Son of Mary Donovan, of Golden, Cashel, Co. Tipperary, and Thomas Donovan. He has no known grave but is listed on Panels 11 and 12 on the Le Touret Memorial in France.

DOOLEY, Matthew: Rank: Private. Regiment or Service: Leinster Regiment. Unit: 1st Bn. Date of death: 4 February 1915. Service No.3142. Born in Fethard. Enlisted in Birr. Killed in action. Grave or Memorial Reference: LVI.V. I. Cemetery: Poelcapelle British Cemetery in Belgium.

DOOLEY, Thomas: Rank: Private. Regiment or Service: Leinster Regiment. Unit: 3rd Bn. Date of death: 1 August 1915. Service No.8737. Born in Templemore. Enlisted in Coatbridge in Lanarkshire. Died at home. Age at death: 25.

Supplementary information: Son of Thomas and Elizabeth Dooley. Grave or Memorial Reference: MD, 282. Cemetery: Londonderry City Cemetery.

DORAN, John: Rank: Private. Regiment or Service: Loyal North Lancashire Regiment. Unit: 10th Bn. Date of death: 17 July 1916. Service No.13369. Born in Tipperary. Enlisted in Blackburn while living in Kilkenny. Killed in action. Age at death: 28.

Supplementary information: Son of Ellen Doran, of Green's Hill, Kilkenny, and James Doran. Grave or Memorial Reference: III. G. 31. Cemetery: Pozieres British Cemetery, Ovillers–La Boiselle in France.

DORNEY, Patrick: Rank: Corporal. Regiment or Service: Royal Irish Regiment. Unit: 6th Bn. Date of death: 9 September 1916. Service No.1701. Born in Grangemockler, Co. Tipperary. Enlisted in Clonmel while living in Carrick-on-Suir, Co. Tipperary. Killed in action. He has no known grave but is listed on Face 3 A on the Thiepval Memorial in France.

DOUGHERTY, Timothy: Rank: Rifleman. Regiment or Service: Royal Irish Rifles. Unit: 2nd Bn. Date of death: 4 May 1918. Service No.5480. Born in Tipperary. Enlisted in Ballykinlar, Co. Down while living in Belfast. Died at the Military Hospital, Clifton Street. Cause of death, Gun Shot Wound, 5 months, Septicaemia. Age at death: 35.

Supplementary information: Son of Daniel Doherty whose address on his marriage certificate was Tipperary Barracks. His father married Johanna Flynn (from Spittal, Co. Tipperary) on 20 January 1881 and gave his address as 48th Regt, Tipperary Barracks. Timothy was married to Mary Dougherty, of 12 (death cert says 13) Cairns Street, Belfast. Grave or Memorial Reference: B. NE. 11. Cemetery: Belfast (Milltown) Roman Catholic Cemetery.

DOWD, J.: Rank: Sergeant. Regiment or Service: Lincolnshire Regiment. Unit: 2nd Bn. Age at death: 36. Date of death: 5 April 1921 Service No.4793158 He was awarded the Military Medal.

Supplementary information: Son of James and Julia Dowd, of Tipperary, Republic of Ireland. Grave or Memorial Reference: Face 3. Memorial: Kirkree 1914- 1918 Memorial.

DOWD, Thomas Richard: Rank: Sergeant. Regiment or Service: Leinster Regiment. Unit: 5th Bn. Secondary Regiment: King's African Rifles Secondary. Unit: attd. 1st-2nd. He was also previously in the Lincolnshire Regiment where his number was 6238. Age at death: 30. Date of death: 20

March 1918. Service No.10251. Born in Roscrea and enlisted in Dublin. Died in Egypt.

Supplementary information: Son of James and Julia Dowd (*née* McNally), of Knock, Roscrea, Co. Tipperary. Grave or Memorial Reference: R.C.V.A. 1. Cemetery: Mombasa (MBARAKI) Cemetery in Kenya.

DOWLING, John: Rank: Sapper. Regiment or Service: Corps of Royal Engineers. Unit: 254th Tunnelling Company. Date of death: 7 August 1917. Service No.91935. Formerly he was with the Royal Irish Regiment where his number was 10905. Born in Ballingarry. Enlisted in Clonmel. Died of wounds. Grave or Memorial Reference: IV. F. 6. Cemetery: Brandhoek New Military Cemetery in Belgium.

DOYLE, Andrew: Rank: Acting Corporal. Regiment or Service: Leinster Regiment. Unit: 7th Bn. Date of death: 24 June 1916. Service No.1377. Born in Carrick-on-Suir, Co. Tipperary. Enlisted in Merthyr, Glam. Killed in action. Age at death: 32.

Supplementary information: Husband of Margaret Doyle, of 297, Crumlin Rd, Belfast. Grave or Memorial Reference: III. N. 4. Cemetery: St Patrick's Cemetery, Loos in France.

DOYLE, Joseph: Rank: Private. Regiment or Service: Royal Irish Regiment. Unit: 2nd Bn. Date of death: 4 May 1915. Service No.5059. Born in Carrick-on-Suir, Co. Tipperary. Enlisted in Carrick-on-Suir, Co.

Tipperary. Killed in action. He has no known grave but is listed on Panel 11 on the Ypres (Menin Gate) Memorial in Belgium

DOYLE, Peter: Rank: Private. Regiment or Service: York and Lancaster Regiment. Unit: 16th (Transport Workers) Regiment. Date of death: 31 March 1917. Service No.27086. Formerly he was with the Liverpool Regiment where his number was 22854. Born in St Mary's, Clonmel, Co. Tipperary. Enlisted in Liverpool. Died at home. Grave or Memorial Reference: W. U. 390. Cemetery: Newcastle-Upon-Tyne (St Andrew's and Jesmond) Cemetery, UK.

DROHAN, Edward: Rank: Private. Regiment or Service: Royal Dublin Fusiliers. Unit: 1st Bn. Age at death: 39. Date of death: 7 August 1915. Service No.19020. Born in Carrick-on-Suir and enlisted in Waterford while living in Carrick-on-Suir. Killed in action.

Supplementary information: Son of David Drohan and Mary Connors, his wife: husband of Johanna Drohan (*née* Meaney), of John Street, Carrick-on-Suir, Go. Tipperary. Grave or Memorial Reference: Has no known grave but is commemorated on Panel 190 to 196. Memorial: Helles Memorial in Turkey.

DROHAN, Michael: Rank: Private. Regiment or Service: Royal Irish Regiment. Unit: 1st Bn. Date of death: 15 March 1915. Service No.4082. Born in Carrickbeg, Co. Waterford. Enlisted in Clonmel while living in Carrick-on-Suir, Co. Tipperary. Killed in action. Age at death: 19.

Supplementary information: Son of David and Bridget Drohan. He has no known grave but is listed on Panel 33 on the Ypres (Menin Gate) Memorial in Belgium.

DRUDY, Edmund James: Rank: Private. Regiment or Service: Connaught Rangers. Unit: 3rd Bn. Age at death: 41. Date of death: 22 May 1917. Service No. 35416 and 5416. Died at home.

Supplementary information: Son of John and Mary Drudy, of Cashel, Co. Tipperary and husband of Kate Drudy, of 26 Coliston Rd, Southfields, London. Born in Cashel, Co. Tipperary, enlisted in Wandsworth while living in Wandsworth. He is commemorated on the Grangegorman (Cork) Memorial. He is buried in Cork Military Cemetery but his headstone is in Grangegorman Military Cemetery before the Grangegorman memorial in Blackhorse Avenue in Dublin. Died. At home.

DUFFILL, George: Rank: Private. Regiment or Service: Royal West Kent Regiment. Unit: 7th Bn. Date of death: 12 October 1917. Service No. G-19495. Formerly he was with the Sherwood Foresters where his number was 82152. Born in Tipperary, Cork. Enlisted in Lincoln while living in Lincoln, Lancs. Killed in action. Age at death: 22.

Supplementary information: Son of Fred and Fanny Duffill, of White

House, Worlaby, Brigg, Lincs. He has no known grave but is listed on Panels 106 to 108 on the Tyne Cot Memorial in Belgium.

DUGGAN, Thomas: Rank: Rifleman. Regiment or Service: Royal Irish Rifles. Unit: 1st-8th London Regiment. Date of death: 7 April 1918. Service No. 20438. Formerly he was with the Royal Army Service Corps where his number was T-28834. Born in Ballypatrick Clonmel, Co. Tipperary. Enlisted in Aldershot in Hants. while living in Farnborough in Hants.. Killed in action. Grave or Memorial Reference: I. D. 5. Cemetery: Senlis Communal Cemetery Extension in France.

DUGGAN, William: Rank: Rifleman. Regiment or Service: Royal Irish Rifles. Unit: 2nd Bn. Date of death: 24 March 1918. Service No. 10532. Enlisted in Belfast while living in Clonmel. Killed in action. He has no known grave but is listed on Panel 74 to 76 on the Pozieres Memorial in France.

DUNLEA, John: Rank: Private. Regiment or Service: Irish Guards. Unit: 2nd Bn. Date of death: 28 March 1918. Service No. 8531. Born in Ballyporeen. Enlisted in Newport, Monmouthshire while living in Coolentallagh, Co. Tipperary. Killed in action. Age at death: 42.

Supplementary information: Son of Thomas and Katherine Dunlea. He has no known grave but is listed in Bay 1

on the Arras Memorial in France. He is also commemorated on the Cahir War Memorial.

DUNNE, Denis: Rank: Ship's Cook. Regiment or Service: Mercantile Marine Reserve Unit: R. F. A. *Hughli.* Age at death: 36. Date of death: 26 April 1919. Service No.998261.

Supplementary information: Son of John and Mary Dunne, of Templemore, Co. Tipperary: husband of L. Dunne, of 38, Chapel Place, Dover. Grave or Memorial Reference: 32. Memorial: Plymouth Naval Memorial, UK.

DUNNE, John: Rank: Corporal. Regiment or Service: Royal Irish Regiment. Unit: 7th Bn. Formerly he was with the South Irish Horse where his number was 855. Date of death: 21 March 1918. Service No.25244. Born in Roscrea. Enlisted in Fancroft, Kings County while living in Roscrea. Killed in action. He has no known grave but is listed on Panel 30 and 31 on the Pozieres Memorial in France.

DUNNE, John: Rank: Private. Regiment or Service: Royal Dublin Fusiliers. Unit: 2nd Bn. Secondary Regiment: Royal Army Medical Corps Secondary. Unit: formerly (His number was 11849) Age at death: 23. Date of death: 21 March 1918. Service No.21859. Awarded the Military Medal. Born in Dublin and enlisted there also. Killed in action.

Supplementary information: Son of Frank and Mary Dunne, of Pike Street, Thurles, Co. Tipperary. Grave or Memorial Reference: Has no known grave but is commemorated on Panel 79 and 80. Memorial: Pozieres Memorial in France.

DUNNE, John: Rank: Driver. Regiment or Service: Royal Horse Artillery and Royal Field Artillery. Date of death: 28 July 1917. Service No.31735. Born in Newcastle, Tipperary. Age at death 19. Enlisted in Clonmel. Died of wounds.

Supplementary information: Son of Margaret and William Dunne of Middle Quarter, Clonmel, Co. Tipperary. Grave or Memorial Reference: I. H. 12. Cemetery: Dozinghem Military Cemetery in Belgium.

DUNNE, John James (Jack): Rank: Corporal. Regiment or Service: Royal Irish Regiment. Unit: 7th Bn. Date of death: 21 March 1918. Service No.25244. Formerly he was with the South Irish Horse where his number was 855. Born in Roscrea. Enlisted in Fancroft in Co. Offaly while living in Roscrea. He has no known grave but is listed on Panel 30 and 31 on the Pozieres Memorial.

DUNNE, Philip: Rank: Private. Regiment or Service: Royal Dublin Fusiliers. Unit: 1st Bn. Date of death: 25 April 1915. Service No.10894. Born in Roscrea. Enlisted in Cork. Killed in action in Gallipoli. He has no known grave but is listed on Panel 190 to 196 on the Helles Memorial in Turkey.

Grave of Michael Dwyer.

DUNNE, Timothy: Rank: Private. Regiment or Service: Leinster Regiment. Unit: 6ᵗʰ Bn. Date of death: 12 August 1915. Service No.827 and 6-827. Born in Roscrea. Enlisted in Roscrea. Died of wounds in Gallipoli. Grave or Memorial Reference: Sp Mem B. 12. Cemetery: Embarkation Pier Cemetery in Turkey.

DUNNE, William: Rank: Private. Regiment or Service: Leinster Regiment. Unit: 2ⁿᵈ Bn. Date of death: 20 October 1914. Service No.8753. Born in lisduff Co. Tipperary. Enlisted in Templemore. Killed in action. He has no known grave but is listed on Panel 10 on the Ploegsteert Memorial in Belgium.

DURANT, George Hugo: Rank: Private. Regiment or Service: Cheshire Regiment. Unit: 10ᵗʰ Bn. Date of death: 16 July 1916. Service No.25138. Born in Carrick-on-Suir, Co. Tipperary. Enlisted in Crewe in Cheshire. Died of wounds. Age at death: 43.

Supplementary information: Son of James Hugo Durant, husband of Mary Durant of Marley Green, Whitchurch, Salop. Grave or Memorial Reference: Thilloy German Mil. Cem. Mem. Cemetery: Valley Cemetery, Vis-En-Artois in France.

DWANE, Michael: Rank: Private. Regiment or Service: Royal Irish Regiment. Unit: 1ˢᵗ Bn. Age at death: 24. Date of death: 10 March 1918. Service No.3-8916. Born in Nenagh and enlisted there also. Killed in action.

Supplementary information: Son of Thomas and Norah Dwane, of Mount Pleasant, Nenagh, Co. Tipperary. Grave or Memorial Reference: J. 93. Cemetery: Jerusalem War Cemetery, Israel.

DWYER, Charles: Rank: Private. Regiment or Service: Leinster Regiment. Unit: 2nd Bn. Age at death: 33. Date of death: 20 October 1914. Service No.6768. Born in Tipperary and enlisted in Waterford. Killed in action.

Supplementary information: Son of Hannah Dwyer, of Old Rd, Tipperary, and the late Charles Dwyer. Grave or Memorial Reference: Has no known grave but is commemorated on Panel 10. Memorial: Ploegsteert Memorial in Belgium.

DWYER, Cornelius: Rank: Gunner. Regiment or Service: Royal Garrison Artillery. Unit: 86th Trench Mortar Battery. Date of death: 4 March 1916. Service No.3560. Born in Thurles. Enlisted in Cork while living in Cashel. Died of wounds. Grave or Memorial Reference: C. 11. Cemetery: Villiers-Bocage Communal Cemetery Extension in France.

DWYER, John: Rank: Private. No 7037, Royal Irish Regiment, 2nd Bn, These two men seem to be brothers and joined the Royal Irish Regiment at the same time. Died 24 August 1914, Born: Cashel, Co. Tipperary. Enlisted in Clonmel while living in Cashel. Killed in action during the battle of Mons. Grave reference II. B. 18. Cemetery: St Symphrien Military Cemetery in Belgium

DWYER, John: Also listed in the records as **O'DWYER, John**. Rank: 2 Lt (TP). Regiment or Service: General List, New Armies and Royal Irish Fusiliers. Unit: 7th Bn. Secondary Unit: Trench Mortar Battery. Date of death: 10 September 1916. Residence: Barrack Street, Thurles. Enlisted in London. Died of wounds. Grave or Memorial Reference: II. C. 61. Cemetery: La-Neuville British Cemetery, Corbie in France.

DWYER, Michael: Rank: Private. No 6092, Royal Irish Regiment, Unit: 3rd Bn and 2nd Bn. Date of death: 9 March 1915, Born: Cashel, Co. Tipperary. Enlisted in Clonmel while living in Cashel. Died of wounds at home. Age at death: 37.

Supplementary information: Died in the County Infirmary on 9 March 1915. Michael, a trusted employee of Cashel Urban District Council and fought in the Boer war with his old Regiment until he retired into the reserve. At the battles of Lille and Le Basse he was wounded by a shrapnel splinter which tore his abdomen and lacerated his arteries. He was not expected to live very long but he battled through and made it to the American Womens Hospital in Devonshire where he was treated for seven weeks and sent home for further treatment. His condition deteriorated here and he had to be removed to the County Infirmary under the care of Dr G. H. Russell and his staff. For two months he battled his injuries until he finally passed away. Last rites were administered by Revd T. Dunne. Soldiers from his Regiment were at the front and were not available to attend his funeral however it was represented by Major Murdock and several of his wounded comrades who were invalided during the war. The large funeral was presided over by Revd W. Condon and Revd T. Dunne. Michael left behind a young wife and five small children. Buried in the south-west part of Hore Abbey ruins just outside Cashel. Grave location: In the south-west part.

DWYER, Michael: Rank: Private. Regiment or Service: Royal Irish Regiment. Unit: 1st Bn. Age at death: 35. Date of death: 17 October 1916. Died in Salonika. Serial Number: 7286. Enlisted in Clonmel while living in Kilmacoma, Co. Waterford.

Supplementary information: Son of John and Bridget Dwyer of Kilmacomma, Clonmel. Grave or Memorial Reference: 595. Cemetery: Salonika (Lambet Road) Military Cemetery in Greece.

DWYER/O'DWYER, Thomas: Rank: Private. Regiment or Service: Royal Army Medical Corps. Unit: 1st Malt Company. Date of death: 4 July 1916. Service No. 30436. Born in Bansha and enlisted in Clonmel. Died in Malta. Age at death: 29.

Supplementary information: Son of Thomas and Mary O'Dwyer of Upper Abbey Street, Cahir. Grave or Memorial Reference: E. EA. A. 688. Cemetery: Addolorata Cemetery in Malta.

DWYER, Michael: Rank: Trooper. Regiment or Service: Australian Light Horse. Previously served three years with the 8th Hussars. Unit: 10th. Service No. 794. Killed in action. Enlisted in Blackboy Hill, Kalgoorlie, Western Australia on 8 January 1915. Born in Nenagh. Married to Mrs Sarah Dwyer(died 1927) 227 Piccadilly

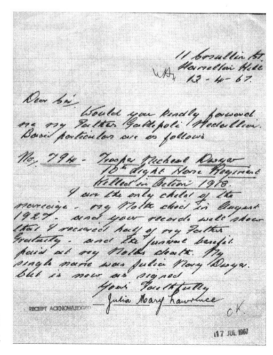

Letter written by Michael Dwyer's daughter.

Street, Kalgoorlie, WA. Occupation on enlistment: Coachman. Daughters name, Julia Mary Lawrence. Date of death: 31 July 1918. Age on enlistment: 30 years and 5 months. Height: 5' 8". Weight: 161lbs. Complexion: dark. Eyes: brown. Hair: dark brown. Religion: RC. Distinctive marks: tattoos on both arms. Served in Anzac, Alexandria, Mudros, Heliopolis, Shellal, Sueilma, El Arish, Abbassia, Mosaid, Tel El Kebir, Moascar Cairo and Gallipoli.

Extract from a Court of Inquiry held at Tellul:

On the morning of the 31st ulto at about 1000 No 1271 Trooper McCormick, who had been firing the gun on previous days asked permission to range in front of Vaux Post where outposts had exchanged shots the previous night. Permission was granted. One shot was successfully fired. The second shot exploded prematurely in the gun, bursting the barrel, breaking a recoil spring and fatally wounding No 1721 Tpr McCormick and also No 794 Tpr Dwyer, who was standing by the gun.

Finding of the Court:

The court finds that No 794 Trooper Dwyer was killed in action on 31st July 1918, whilst registering ranges with a salved Trench Howitzer and that no blame is attached to anyone.

Grave or Memorial Reference: H. 63. Jerusalem War Cemetery

DWYER, William: Rank: Private. Regiment or Service: Royal Irish Regiment. Unit: 2nd Bn. Age at death: 21. Date of death: 21 March 1918. Service No.11398. Born in Fethard and enlisted in Clonmel while living in Fethard. Killed in action.

Supplementary information: Son of William and Ellen Dwyer, of Lower Valley, Fethard, Co. Tipperary. Grave or Memorial Reference: Has no known grave but is commemorated on Panel 30 and 31. Memorial: Pozieres Memorial in France.

DWYER, William: Rank: Private. Regiment or Service: Royal Irish Regiment. Unit: 2nd Bn. Date of death: 22 October 1914. Service No.6725. Born in Tipperary. Enlisted in Clonmel while living in Tipperary. Died of wounds.

Supplementary information: Son of Tipperary Town Newsagent Mr William Dwyer. Before enlisting William was a tinsmith by trade. He left behind a wife and six children. Grave or Memorial Reference: III. C. 38. Cemetery: Boulogne Eastern Cemetery in France

Extract from the *Tipperary Star*, 14 November 1914:

From the War Office that his second Son, William Dwyer, who was a member of the reserves of the 18th Royal Irish Regiment, had died in France and was buried there on the 22nd of last Mr William Dwyer, Newsagent, Eaton's Cottages, received an official notification on Sunday morning. The deceased, who was a tinsmith by trade leaves a wife and six children. Much sympathy is felt with them and with the father who is a most popular and respected native of the town, and also with his brother, Thomas O'Dwyer. Deceased was a member of the Confraternity of the Holy Family whose prayers will be offered for the repose of his soul.

E

EGAN, Martin: Rank: Private. Regiment or Service: Royal Irish Regiment. Unit: 2nd Bn. Age at death: 27. Date of death: 3 September 1916. Service No.6012. Born in Thurles and enlisted in templemore while living in Thurles. Killed in action.

Supplementary information: Son of Patrick and Mary Egan, of Mitchell Street, Thurles, Co. Tipperary. Grave or Memorial Reference: Pier and Face 3 A. on the Thiepval Memorial in France.

EGAN, Thomas: Rank: Private. Regiment or Service: Royal Welsh Fusiliers. Unit: 5th Bn. Date of death: 1 February 1918. Service No.59946. Formerly he was with the Cheshire Regiment where his number was 54979. Born in Cahir. Enlisted in Chester while living in Cahir. Killed in action in Egypt. Grave or Memorial Reference: O. 109. Cemetery: Jerusalem War Cemetery, Israel.

ELLIS, Henry David: Rank: Company Sergeant Major. Regiment or Service: Labour Corps. Date of death: 18 October 1918. Service No.161809. Formerly he was with the Essex Regiment where his number was 2945. Born in Templemore. Enlisted in London while living in Peckham in Surrey. Died at home. Grave or Memorial Reference: B. 185A. Cemetery: Epsom Cemetery, UK.

ENGLISH, Edward: Rank: Private. Regiment or Service: Royal Irish Regiment. Unit: 2nd Bn. Age at death: 35. Date of death: 21 March 1918. Service No.7489. Born in St Peter's in Clonmel and enlisted in Cahir while living in Clonmel. Killed in action.

Supplementary information: Son of Patrick and Bridget English, of Clonmel: husband of Ellen English, of 33, River Street, Clonmel, Co. Tipperary. Grave or Memorial Reference: Has no known grave but

John Joseph Esmonde.

is commemorated on Panel 30 and 31. Memorial: Pozieres Memorial in France.

ENGLISH, George:. Rank: Private. Regiment or Service: Royal Dublin Fusiliers. Unit: 8th Bn. Date of death: 6 September 1916. Service No.16771. Born in Roscrea, King's Co. Enlisted in Manchester. Killed in action. He has no known grave but is listed on Pier and Face 16 C on the Thiepval Memorial in France.

ENGLISH, John: Rank: Leading Stoker. Regiment or Service: Royal Navy. Unit: HMS *Monmouth*. Date of death: 1 November 1914. Service No.234610.

Supplementary information: Husband of Alice English, of Convent Rd, Clogheen, Co. Tipperary. Grave or Memorial Reference: 3. Memorial: Plymouth Naval Memorial, UK. During the Battle of Coronel in Chile on the day John English died H.M.S *Monmouth* received a 8.2

inch shell from the S.M.S. *Gneisenau* which almost blew her to pieces. She limped away and later that day was sent to the bottom by S.S. *Nurnberg*. There were no survivors. He is also commemorated on the Cahir War Memorial.

ENGLISH, Joseph: Rank: Sergeant. Regiment or Service: Guards Machine Gun Regiment. Unit: 4th Bn. Date of death: 23 October 1918. Service No.1072. Formerly he was with the Irish Guards where his number was 6465. Born in Nenagh, Co. Tipperary. Enlisted in Dublin. Died of wounds. Grave or Memorial Reference: II. C. 5. Cemetery: Delsaux Farm Cemetery, Beugny in France.

ENGLISH, Theobald F.: Rank: Private. Regiment or Service: Irish Guards. Unit: 1st Bn. Date of death: 3 November 1917. Service No.5618. Born in Tipperary. Enlisted in Clonmel. Killed in action. He has no known grave but is listed on Panel 2

John Joseph Esmonde,

117

and 3 on the Cambrai Memorial in Louveral in France.

ESMONDE, John Joseph: Rank: Captain. Regiment or Service: Royal Army Medical Corps Age at death: 53. Died from pneumonia and heart failure consequent on the strain of overwork. Date of death: 17 April 1915. Born in Drominagh, Borrisokane. He was a Nationalist MP for North Tipperary 1910-1915.

Supplementary information: His son Eugene Esmonde won a VC in 1942. Member of Parliament for North Tipperary. Son of James Esmonde. Note the reference to Geoffrey on the bottom of the memorial. He was 2nd Lt Geoffrey Esmonde, 26th Bn Northumberland Fusiliers who was killed in action on 7 October 1917. Grave or Memorial Reference: In family vault behind church. Cemetery: Terryglass (St Columba) Catholic Churchyard in Tipperary.

EUSTACE, Thomas: Rank: Gunner. No 30213, 23rd Res. Bty. Royal Field Artillery, Aged 50. Date of death: 5 October 1915, Born: Cashel, Co. Tipperary and enlisted in Cashel while living in Cashel. Died at home. Grave reference G. 106. Buried in Cornamagh Cemetery outside Athlone, Westmeath.

F

FAHEY, John: Rank: Chaplain. Date of death: 1915. Supposedly killed in action. Extract from the *Nenagh Guardian*, 1915:

A Gallant Tipperary Chaplain
An Appreciation of the Revd John Fahey, a gallant Tipperary Chaplain, who lost his life at the Dardinelles, appeared in the Australian "Sunday Times". It is told of him that when all the Officers had been potted off he called on the remnants of a Company to 'Follow him' and ' Deal it out to the bounders'. He had a genial, unaffected manner, and he was an all round athlete. At a Perth sports meeting he won a State championship for putting the stone (Irish style). He was a "topnotcher" at football, a capital tennis player, a fine wrestler, and set to lead in the horizontal bar and trapeze. He was also enthusiastic at rifle practice, and held that it was the duty of every man to make himself proficient in the use of the weapon.

From the Australian Dictionary of Biography:

FAHEY, John: Catholic priest and military chaplain, was born on 3 October 1883 at Glenough, Tipperary, Ireland, son of Michael Fahey, farmer, and his wife, Catherine, *née* Ryan. Educated by the Cistercians at Mount Melleray and at the Brignole Sale Seminary, Genoa, Italy, he was ordained priest in May 1907. Leaving almost immediately for the Australian mission he worked briefly in Perth at the cathedral and was then appointed to the parish of York and of Yarloop-Pinjarra in the south-east. Fahey was a manly type of priest will suited to the timberworkers he served. He was an excellent sportsman, a fine shot and lived a rough unconventional life. Bush experience provided him with an excellent preparation for the Australian Imperial Force which he joined on 8 September 1914 as a chaplain, 4th class (captain). He was assigned to the 11th Battalion.

Fahey reached Gallipoli on 25 April 1915 and although chaplains were ordered not to disembark because every available space was reserved for combatants, he disregarded this, asserting his duty to go with his men. His work, consoling the wounded, burying the dead and encouraging the living, was widely appreciated and he became a very popular figure: he typified the active, robust priesthood so admired in Australia. From Gallipoli he wrote that he 'was shot twice through my overcoat without the skin being touched. I had a book shot out of my hands, the jam tin I was eating out of was shot through'. Evacuated sick in July, he resumed

Michael Fahy from New Inn on the right. On the left is Thomas O'Grady from Clashamhadra, Tipperary. Thoams survived the war but was wounded in the foot. (Photograph courtesy of Frank Fahy).

duty in September and remained at Gallipoli until 7 November. He was mentioned in dispatches and awarded the Distinguished Service Order for 'gallantry under fire'.

Rejoining the 11th Battalion in March 1916 Fahey left for France in April. Here a new battle experience awaited him: to the horrors of Gallipoli were added the might of heavy artillery. 'For an hour or so', he wrote, 'shells of all calibres, mostly high explosive, simply rain on a small sector of the front ... It is appalling, it is diabolical, and it is wonderful how anyone escapes'. He remained in France until 14 November 1917, becoming the longest-serving frontline chaplain of any denomination, although he only won promotion to chaplain 3rd class (major). He left for Australia on 16 March 1918. Against his wishes, he was fêted on his return to Perth. War service had aroused in

him a deep admiration for Australian soldiers: he explained that 'the more I knew them the more I loved and admired them ... Their bravery has been written in deeds that will live to the end of the world'.

Revd Fahey was stationed at Cottesloe in 1919-32, at Kellerberrin in 1932-36 and at various Perth parishes in 1936-39, after which he was parish priest at Cottesloe until his death. He was a faithful pastor, kept up his A. I. F. and sporting contacts and occupied a number of minor diocesan positions. He died at the St John of God Hospital, Subiaco, on 28 April 1959 and was buried in Karrakatta cemetery. About 2000 people attended his funeral. The newspaper article concerning his death in the Dardinelles should have been about Fr Finn (see **FINN, William Joseph**)

FAHEY, Patrick: Rank: Private. Regiment or Service: Royal Irish Regiment. Unit: 2nd Bn. Date of death: 19 October 1914. Service No.5917. Born in Carrick-on-Suir, Co. Tipperary. Enlisted in Clonmel while living in Carrick-on-Suir, Co. Tipperary. Killed in action. He has no known grave but is listed on Panels 11 and 12 on the Le Touret Memorial in France.

FAHEY, Richard: Rank: Private. Regiment or Service: Royal Irish Regiment. Unit: 2nd Bn. Age at death: 18. Date of death: 19 October 1914. Service No.4555. Born in St Nicholas's in Carrick-on-Suir and enlisted in Carrick-on-Suir. Killed in action.
Supplementary information: Son of James and Margaret Fahey, of Cook Street, Carrick-on-Suir, Co. Tipperary. Grave or Memorial Reference: Has no known grave but is commemorated on Panel 11 and 12. Memorial: Le Touret Memorial in France.

FAHY, Michael: Rank: Private. Regiment or Service: Royal Irish Regiment. Unit: 2nd Bn. Date of death: 21 August 1918. Service No.5587. Born in Lisronagh. Enlisted in Cashel while living in New Inn. Killed in action. Grave or Memorial Reference: X. J. 3. Cemetery: A. I. F Burial Ground, Flers in France. He is also commemorated on the Cahir War Memorial.

FAHY/FAHEY, Philip: Rank: Rifleman. Regiment or Service: London Regiment (London Irish Rifles). Unit: 18th Bn. Age at death: 33.

Date of death: 29 May 1917. Service No.592337. Born in Tipperary and enlisted in Caxton Hall while living in Westminster. Enlisted twelve months before his death. Killed in action.
Supplementary information: Son of Mary Fahy, of Main Street, Cappawhite, Co. Tipperary, and the late John Fahy. Grave or Memorial Reference: Enclosure No. 4 II. C. 16. Cemetery: Bedford House Cemetery in Belgium.

FALCONER, John: Rank: Private. Regiment or Service: Welsh Regiment. Unit: 2nd Bn. Date of death: 25 January 1915. Service No.12539. Born in St Michael's, Tipperary. Enlisted in Merthyr while living in Tipperary. Killed in action. He has no known grave but is listed on Panels 23 and 24 on the Le Touret Memorial in France.

FALLON, Thomas: Rank: Bandsman. East Lancashire Regiment. Unit: 2nd Bn. Date of death: 7 November 1914. Service No.9354. Born in Clonmel. Enlisted in London while living in Walsall. Killed in action. He has no known grave but is listed on Panel 18 on the Le Touret Memorial in France.

FALVEY, Daniel: Rank: Ordinary Seaman. Regiment or Service: Royal Navy. Unit: *HMS Tipperary*. Age at death: 20. Date of death: 27 December 1915. Service No.J-43999.
Supplementary information: Son of Michael and Mary Falvey, of Murgasty Cottages, Tipperary. Grave

or Memorial Reference: General L. 8. 0. Cemetery: Ford Park Cemetery (Formerly Plymouth Old Cemetery) HMS *Pennycomequick*. Tipperary was one of the casualties of the battle of Jutland but Daniel died six months before she sank.

FANNING, Anthony: Rank: Corporal. Regiment or Service: Worcestershire Regiment. Unit: 1st Bn. Age at death: 32. Date of death: 13 March 1915. Service No. 4799. Born in Workington in Cumberland and enlisted in Carlisle while living in Workington. Killed in action.

Supplementary information: Husband of Bridget Fanning, of 2 Brodeen Cottages, Carhil Rd, Tipperary. Grave or Memorial Reference: Has no known grave but is commemorated on Panel 17 and 18. Memorial: Le Touret Memorial in France.

FANNING, John: Rank: Private. Regiment or Service: Connaught Rangers Unit: 6th Bn. Age at death: 30. Date of death: 3 July 1917. Service No. 1-7957. Born in Cahir and enlisted in Cahir while living in Cahir. Enlisted into the Royal Irish Regiment in 1905. Served in India and went with the 1st Bn Connaught Rangers to France in 1914. Died at No 10 Stationary Hospital in St Omer of Gastitis. As well as his WWI medals he was entitled to the 1911 Durbar Medal.

Supplementary information: Son of Michael and M. Fanning, of Cahir, Co. Tipperary: husband of Mary Josephine Kellett (formerly Fanning), of 43 Priolo Rd, Charlton, London. John had only one son John Richard Patrick Fanning. Grave or Memorial Reference: IV. C. 43. Cemetery: Longuenesse (St Omer) Souvenir Cemetery in France. He is also commemorated on the Cahir War Memorial.

FARNDEN, George: Rank: Private. Regiment or Service: Royal Fusiliers, (City of London Regiment). Unit: 8th Bn. Date of death: 28 June 1917. Service No. 2525. Born in Tipperary. Enlisted in Hounslow while living in Chiswick. Died of wounds. Grave or Memorial Reference: I. V. J12. Cemetery: Faubourg D'Amiens Cemetery, Arras, France.

FARRELL, Alexander: Rank: Private. Regiment or Service: Royal Irish Regiment. Unit: 4th Bn. Date of death: 12 February 1916. Service No. 5436. Born in Ballylooby, Co. Tipperary. Enlisted in Clonmel. Died at home. There is no burial information for this man.

FARRELL, Edward: Rank: Private. Regiment or Service: Royal Irish Regiment. Unit: 2nd Bn. Date of death: 8 September 1914. Service No. 8879. Born in Carlow and enlisted there also. Killed in action.

Supplementary information: Husband of Mary Farrell, of Cappadeen, Ballinahinch, Newport, Co. Tipperary. Cemetery: Orly-Sur-Morin Communal Cemetery in France.

FARRELL, G.: Alias, correct name is **CUMMINGS**. Rank: Private. Regiment or Service: Irish Guards.

Date of death: 20 October 1918. Service No.4805.

Supplementary information: Son of Mrs M. Farrell of 46 Albert Street, Clonmel. Cemetery, Clonmel, St Patrick's Cemetery. Grave location: 5. M. 135.

FARRELL, P: Rank: Private. Regiment or Service: Royal Inniskilling Fusiliers. Unit: 4th Bn. Date of death: 16 May 1917. Service No.11552.

Supplementary information: Husband of M. Farrell. Cemetery, Clonmel, St Patrick's Cemetery. Grave location: 4. CA. 114.

FEEHAN, John: Rank: Lance Corporal. Regiment or Service: Leinster Regiment. Unit: 2nd Bn. Date of death: 27 March 1918. Service No.9848. Born in Roscrea. Enlisted in Birr. Killed in action. He has no known grave but is listed on Panel 78 on the Pozieres Memorial in France.

FEEHAN, Martin: Rank: Private. Regiment or Service: Leinster Regiment. Unit: 1st Bn. Age at death: 30. Date of death: 12 May 1915. Service No.2926. Born in Birr, Kings Co. and enlisted in Dublin. Killed in action.

Supplementary information: Husband of Julia Feehan, of Cloughjordan, Co. Tipperary. Grave or Memorial Reference: Has no known grave but is commemorated on Panel 44. Memorial: Ypres (Menin Gate) Memorial in Belgium.

FENNESSY, William: Rank: Private.

Regiment or Service: Irish Guards. Unit: 1st Bn. Age at death: 21. Date of death: 27 June 1916. Service No.4694. Born in Ballyhickey Co. Tipperary and enlisted in Clonmel. Killed in action.

Supplementary information: Son of William Fennessy, of Ballyhickie, Cahir, Co. Tipperary. Grave or Memorial Reference: I. P. 14. Cemetery: Essex Farm Cemetery in Belgium. He is also commemorated on the Cahir War Memorial.

FERMOYLE, Patrick: Rank: Stoker, Regiment or Service: Royal Naval Reserve. Unit: HMS *Roberts*. Age at death: 20. Date of death: 17 September 1916. Service No.2969/S.

Supplementary information: Son of the late Catherine Fermoyle of Graffin Clonmore Templemore. Cemetery: Templemore Catholic Cemetery. Grave location: Plot 2.

FIELDS, John: Rank: Private. Regiment or Service: Royal Dublin Fusiliers. Unit: 1st Bn. Date of death: 19 July 1917. Service No.4093. Formerly he was with the Leinster Regiment where his number was 3530. Born in Mullalaghan, Co. Monaghan. Enlisted in Belfast while living in Moneygall, Co. Tipperary. Died of wounds. Age at death: 22.

Supplementary information: Son of Patrick and Teresa Fields, of Mullaloughan, Co. Monaghan: husband of Margaret Fields, of Springfield, Moneygall, King's Co. Grave or Memorial Reference: II. F. 3. Cemetery: Mendingham Military Cemetery in Belgium.

Claud Gibney Finch-Davies.

FINCH-DAVIES, Claude Gibney: Rank: Lieutenant. Regiment or Service: South African Mounted Rifles. Unit: 1st. Age at death: 44. Date of death: 3 August 1920. He was born in India and was awarded the Order of the Star of India. Not only was he an Ornitologist but an accomplished artist. He enlisted as a private just before the first Boer war and worked his way up through the ranks. He died from Angina Pectoris.

Supplementary information: Son of Maj. Gen. Sir William Davies, K.C.B, K. C. S. I: Husband of Aileen Finch-Davies, of Kilcoleman, Nenagh, Co. Tipperary, Ireland. Grave or Memorial Reference: Sec. 4. 97325C. Sp. Mem. Cape Town (Maitland) Cemetery in South Africa.

FINGLETON, Thomas: Rank: Private. Regiment or Service: Irish Guards. Unit: 1st Bn. Date of death: 29 December 1914. Service No.3408. Born in Monasterevan, Co. Kildare.

Enlisted in Maryborough, Queens County while living in Roscrea. Killed in action. Age at death: 25.

Supplementary information: Son of Patrick and Elizabeth Fingleton, of 10, Green Street, Roscrea, Co. Tipperary. Grave or Memorial Reference: I. D. 14. Cemetery: Le Touret Military Cemetery, Richebourg-L'Avoue in France.

FINLAY, Owen M.: Rank: Lance Corporal. Regiment or Service: Irish Guards. Unit: 2nd Bn. Date of death: 13 April 1918. Service No.10182. Born in Carrick-on-Suir, Co. Tipperary. Enlisted in Dublin. Killed in action. He has no known grave but is listed on Panel 1 on the Ploegsteert Memorial in Belgium.

FINN, Michael: Rank: Sergeant. Regiment or Service: Royal Garrison Artillery. Unit: 83rd Siege Bty. Age at death: 27. Date of death: 19 February 1918. Service No.40718. Born in

William Joseph Finn.

Rathgormack in Wexford and enlisted in Merthyr Tydfil in Wales while living in Waterford.

Supplementary information: Son of Thomas and Mary Finn, of Ballynock, Carrick-on-Suir, Co. Tipperary. Grave or Memorial Reference: XIII. E. 20. Cemetery: Poelcapelle British Cemetery in Belgium.

FINN, Thomas: Rank: Private. Regiment or Service: Royal Irish Regiment. Unit: 'D' Coy. 1ˢᵗ Bn. Age at death: 32. Date of death: 10 March 1918. Service No.10110. Born in Nenagh and enlisted there also. Killed in action in Palestine.

Supplementary information: Son of Michael Finn, of Nenagh, Co. Tipperary. Grave or Memorial Reference: J. 89. Cemetery: Jerusalem War Cemetery, Israel.

FINN, William Joseph: Rank: Chaplain 4ᵗʰ Class. Regiment or Service: Army Chaplains Department. Date of death: 25 April 1915. Grave or Memorial Reference: Joint Grave V. 4. Cemetery, V Beach Cemetery in Turkey. David Charles Verrent, Daniel Lynch and Philip Dunne, were all Tipperary men died with him on the beach that day.

Extract from the *Nenagh Guardian*, July 1915:

How the Gallant Tipperary Chaplain Fell

The *Daily Telegraph* says,

> The Revd H. C. Foster, Church of England Chaplain, attached to the 2nd Royal Naval Brigade, describes the death of Father Finn, attached to the 1ˢᵗ Bn of the Royal Dublin Fusiliers, during the landing of the troops at the Gallipoli Peninsula as follows: 'Many of the gallant Dublins fell wounded and bleeding

into the water, and when Father Finn saw it he jumped in and tried his utmost to rescue them. He succeeded in assisting several men, but suddenly several bullets entered his own body, and he fell just short of the waters edge. He was carried by some of the men to whom he had ministered so faithfully, and he lived only a few minutes. His last words are said to have been: "Are our fellows winning?" and then, amid the thunder of the guns on sea and land, he passed away.' Father Finn, who was a Tipperary Man, was the first Chaplain killed in the operations.

From the Diary of John F. Goate, Machine Gun Section, 5th Royal Scots, 29th Division

Our turn now came to land. The Essex and two companies of the [sth] R. S. with machine-gun Section transferred to gun-boat which took us closer in. All had to huddle down before as Turks were sweeping decks with rifle fire and machine-gun fire. Each man had his rifle equipment, five-days rations, bundle of firewood. In addition we had all the machine-gun stuff. Transferred to small boats rowed by sailors – a very risky proceeding. Many of the sailors killed before we got ashore. Now we saw what we took to be a line of skirmishers lining the shore. Had to jump waist-deep into the sea and wade ashore. Our skirmishers proved to be a line of dead Fusiliers. R. C. priest [Revd Father William J. Finn] did neat work tending the wounded until he was killed himself. Rushed across the narrow strip of shore and commenced to scale the cliff – a very difficult task – being heavily laden and under fierce fire.

A poem written about him by Bertrand Shadwell:

He was down among the lees
Of the blood-encrimsoned seas:
But he struggled to his knees,
Father Finn.
With a bullet through his breast,
He raised his hand and us he blest:
'And I pardon all your sin,'
Said Father Finn.

Sure, there never was a priest
Like Father Finn.
Other Priests were not the least
Like Father Finn

O! the boys are all in tears
In the Dublin Fusiliers–

They have lost the friend of years,
Father Finn.

His old Scholl, Urshaw College carried his obituary in the 1915 edition and the
following poem:

He did not turn his ears from that high call,
Nor parley with himself, nor hesitate.
Men would have held him: but he did not wait,
Albeit the air was thick with shell and ball.

He saw with tears his gallant Dublins fall:
His place was with them. Like a mountain spate,
His spirit o'leaped its banks and laughed at Fate,
Knowing God's Providence that ruleth all.

O Alma Mater, bind your brows with laurel!
Your sons have flocked to wield their Country's sword,
And take up arms in Honour's latest quarrel.
But this one seized the javelin of the Lord,
And hurled it flashing, all to brief a star,
High up the bloody steeps of Sedd-ul-Bahr.

Poem by an unknown Author:
We were in the Dardanelles, just the same as history tells,
It was raining red-hot shells like sin,
For the men were feeling grand, for they knew they had to land,
But the keenest of the band, was Father Finn.
'Go in, my boys, begin!' said Father Finn,
'And I'll come and see ye win,' said Father Finn.

He was kind and he was mild, was Father Finn,
He was gentle as a child, he was brave among the brave,
Where the battle standards wave,
And Gallipoli's the grave of Father Finn.

The cannon of the fleet, drowned the tramp of forming feet
And our engines steady beat, steaming in,
The boats were hanging low, and the screws were turning slow,
When the order came from below for Father Finn.
That the priest was 'not to go', that's Father Finn.

Oh, an angry Father then was Father Finn,
'I must go and shrive my men,' said Father Finn,
"There's a message in my mind, from the Saviour of mankind,
'Would he wave stayed behind' said Father Finn.
'Who died to shrive our sins', said Father Finn.

The shells began to skip, as we started on our trip,
But the first to leave the ship was Father Finn,
With a smile upon his face and a joke, he took his place,
'Now boys, we'll have to race', said Father Finn,
Oh! a happy saggarth then, was Father Finn.

He was laughing as the men came pulling in,
But the shots poured from the crest, and down among the rest
Fell the bravest and the best, Father Finn,
With a bullet through his breast, Father Finn.

He was down among the lees, of the blood-crimsoned seas,
But he struggled to his knees, Father Finn,
With a bullet through his breast, he raised his hand and blest,
'And I pardon all their sin', said Father Finn,
'Go in my boys, and win', gasped Father Finn.

Faithful comrade, pious, brave, Father Finn,
Gave his life our souls to save, did Father Finn,
Sure the boys were all in tears, in the Dublin Fusiliers,
When they lost the friend of years, Father Finn,
And their hearts are in the grave of Father Finn.

Also from Myles Dungan's Book, *They shall not grow old*:

A total of 172 padres were killed in the Great War, 16 of whom were Irish. Among the best known Irish chaplains to die were. Fr Finn, the first padre of the war to be killed, who died at Gallipoli having ignored an order not to go ashore with the troops. He was a Tipperary man serving with the 1st Dublin Fusiliers. Before the V beach landing he had asked to be allowed to accompany the Dublins into what became an infamous massacre. He is reputed to have said, 'The priest's place is beside the dying soldier: I must go'. He certainly spent a considerable part of the day beside dying soldiers as there was an abundance of them at V Beach. He attempted to save a number of drowning and wounded men before being hit himself, in the right arm. He managed to get ashore and crawled around the beach offering help or consolation to the wounded and dying Dublins and Munsters. In order to give absolution he had to hold up an injured right arm with his left. While he was blessing one of the men in this fashion, there was a shrapnel burst above him which blew part of his skull away. He was buried on the beach and his grave marked with a cross made out of an ammunition box 'To the Memory of the Revd Capt. Finn'.

(In the book *Mayo Comrades of the Great War* by Patrick J Clarke and Michael Feeney it is stated that Fr Finn's Parents were from Aghamore, Ballyhaunis in County Mayo and not from Tipperary.)

Grave or Memorial Reference: Joint Grave V. 4. Cemetery, V Beach Cemetery in Turkey.

FISHER, John: Rank: Private. Regiment or Service: Manchester Regiment. Unit: 12th Bn. Date of death: 8 February 1917. Service No.2696. Born in Tipperary, Ireland. Enlisted in Ashton-Under-Lyne, Lancs while living in Oldham, Lancs. Killed in action. Grave or Memorial Reference: IV. G. 9. Cemetery: Sailly-Saillisel British Cemetery in France.

FITZGERALD, Edward: Rank: Corporal. Regiment or Service: Royal Munster Fusiliers. Unit: 1st Bn. Date of death: 1 May 1915. Service No.8877. Born in Roscrea. Enlisted in Tralee. Killed in action in Gallipoli. Age at death: 26.

Supplementary information: Son of Margaret Fitzgerald and the late Thomas Fitzgerald. He has no known grave but is listed on Panel 185 to 190 on the Helles Memorial in Turkey.

FITZGERALD, James: Private. Regiment or Service: Royal Irish Regiment. Unit: 6th Bn. Date of death: 16 December 1916. Service No.9987. Born in Ss Peter, Clonmel and enlisted in Clonmel also. Killed in action.

Supplementary information: Husband of Mrs T. Fitzgerald, of 1 Suir Island, Old Bridge, Clonmel, Co. Tipperary. Grave or Memorial Reference: G. 11. Cemetery: Pond Farm Cemetery in Belgium.

FITZGERALD, Jeremiah: Rank: Private. Regiment or Service: Royal Irish Regiment. Unit: 2nd Bn. Date of death: 30 December 1917. Service No.11879. Formerly he was with the Royal Field Artillery where his number was 120056. Born in St Mary's Clonmel. Enlisted in Waterford. Died at sea. Age at death: 19.

Supplementary information: Son of William and Ellen Fitzgerald, of 23, Emmet Place, Waterford. He has no known grave but is listed on the Chatby Memorial in Egypt.

FITZGERALD, John: Rank: Sergeant. Regiment or Service: Argyll and Southern Highlanders. Unit: 11th Bn. Date of death: 20 April 1918. Service No.S-4677. Born in Tipperary. Enlisted in Cathcart, Lanarkshire while living in Glasgow in Lanarkshire. Killed in action. Grave or Memorial Reference: III. G. 6. Cemetery: Feuchy Chapel British Cemetery, Wancourt in France.

FITZGERALD, Patrick: Rank: W. O. CL, 11 (CSM). Regiment or Service: Royal Irish Regiment. Unit: 6th Bn. Date of death: 3 May 1917. Service No.1170. Born in Roscrea. Enlisted in Westminster while living in Clonmel. Died. Grave or Memorial Reference: IV. C. 17. Cemetery: Longuenesse (St Omer) Souvenir Cemetery in France.

FITZGERALD, Robert Maurice: Rank: Private. Regiment or Service: Princess Patricia's Canadian Light Infantry (Eastern Ontario Regiment) Age at death: 26. Date of death: 16 November 1917. Service No.2193344.

Supplementary information: Youngest son of Charles Ball Fitzgerald and Mary Ellen Fitzgerald of 25 Summer Hill, Nenagh, Co. Tipperary. Born in

Ballina, Co. Mayo. Grave or Memorial Reference: II. C. 7. Cemetery: Duhallow A. D. S. Cemetery in Belgium. Data from the reverse of the enlistment document: Age on Enlistment: 25 Years. Height: 5' 5''. Eye colour: grey. Complexion: fair. Hair colour: fair. Religion: COI. Chest expansion: 2 ½''. Girth: 38''. Vision: R. E. 20-30, L. E. 20-40. Hearing: Normal. Date of Enlistment: 2 May 1917. Place of Enlistment: Saskatoon.

FITZGIBBON, Patrick: Rank: Private. Regiment or Service: Irish Guards. Unit: 1st Bn. Date of death: 15 September 1916. Service No.6419. Born in Ballyporeen, Co. Cork. Enlisted in Cork. Killed in action.

Supplementary information: Son of Robert and Bridget Fitzgibbon, of Barnahown, Araglin, Kilworth, Co. Cork. He has no known grave but is listed on Pier and Face 7 D on the Thiepval Memorial in France He is also commemorated on the Cahir War Memorial.

FITZPATRICK, Daniel: Rank: Private. Regiment or Service: East Lancashire Regiment. Unit: 1st Bn. Date of death: 29 June 1918. Service No.7654. Born in Nenagh, Co. Tipperary. Enlisted in Accrington in Lancashire. Died at home. Grave or Memorial Reference: C. F. 432. Cemetery: Accrington Cemetery, UK.

FITZPATRICK, James: Rank: Private. Regiment or Service: Royal Irish Regiment. Unit: 6th Bn. Date of death: 10 September 1916. Service No.1963. Born in Fethard. Enlisted in Waterford while living in Fethard. Killed in action. Grave or Memorial Reference: II. B. 51. Cemetery: Bronfay Farm Military Cemetery, Bray-Sur-Somme in France.

FITZPATRICK, Joseph: Rank: Private. Regiment or Service: Leinster Regiment. Unit: 2nd Bn. Age at death: 26. Date of death: 17 November 1915. Service No.8213. Born in Thurles and enlisted there also. Died of wounds.

Supplementary information: Son of Alice Fitzpatrick, of Quarry Street, Thurles, Co. Tipperary. Grave or Memorial Reference: IV. A. 4A. Cemetery: Lijssenthoek Military Cemetary in Belgium.

Letter from his Chaplain, Chas O'C. Higgins, R. C. Chaplain, 2nd Leinsters, B. E. F. France, November 19, 1915:

Dear Mrs Fitzpatrick,

I have to fulfil a most unpleasant task in this letter. Your son, John, was seriously wounded on the night of the 15th of November. He was hit by a bullet in the head and as he was speedily removed to the Field Ambulance I cannot say how he has got on since I last saw him. His wound was very serious but you will have consolation in the thought that your son was a brave man, and if it should please God to take him to Himself you will be brave and courageous too. I was quickly by his side, and for you and all Irish Mothers the greatest consolation will be in the thought that your boy received all the last Sacraments of our Holy Church. I shall remember him always in my Masses. I hope and pray that he will be spared to you. He is safely prepared in any case to appear before his God and in His mercy He will decide whether 'tis best to take him to Himself or return him to health. I hope you will be brave under this great trial and be proud of your boy, who fell like an Irishman and this indeed is all that an Irish Priest can say. I remain, in deepest sympathy, yours very sincerely,

Chas, O'C. Higgins. R. C. Chaplain.

FITZPATRICK, Patrick Joseph: Rank: Private. Regiment or Service: Royal Irish Fusiliers. Unit: 1st Bn. Age at death: 25. Date of death: 21 March 1918. Service No. 17259. Born in Templemore and enlisted in Glasgow while living in Templemore. Killed in action.

Supplementary information: Son of Patrick and Alice Fitzpatrick, of Mitchell Street, Thurles, Co. Tipperary. Grave or Memorial Reference: Has no known grave but is commemorated on Panel 76 and 77. Memorial: Pozieres Memorial in France.

FITZPATRICK, Thomas: Rank: Private. Regiment or Service: Royal Irish Regiment. Unit: 6th Bn. Date of death: 31 August 1917. Service No. 11036. Born in Foyle Co. Tipperary. Enlisted in Clonmel while living in Foyle. Died of wounds. Grave or Memorial Reference: XXII. R. 5. Cemetery: Etaples Military Cemetery in France.

FITZPATRICK, William: Rank: Private. Regiment or Service: Royal Irish Regiment. Unit: 2nd Bn. Date of death: 20 June 1917. Service No. 7671. Born in Mainstown, Tipperary. Enlisted in Carrick-on-Suir. Died of wounds. Grave or Memorial Reference: III. D. 63. Cemetery: Bailleul Communal Cemetery Extension (Nord) in France.

FLANAGAN/FLANIGAN, James: Rank: Pioneer. Regiment or Service: Royal Engineers. Unit: 12th Labour Bn. Age at death: 46. Date of death: 5 October 1916. Service No. 163362. Born in Ballybricken Co. Cork and enlisted in Waterford. Died in Salonika.

Supplementary information: Son of John and Mary Flanagan, of Carrick-on-Suir, Co. Tipperary: husband of Margaret Flanagan, of 3 Pump Lane, Waterford. Grave or Memorial Reference: 522. Cemetery: Salonika (Lembet Road) Military Cemetery in Greece.

FLANNERY, Michael: Rank: Private. Regiment or Service: Connaught Rangers. Unit: 1st Bn. Date of death: 23 November 1914. Service No. 10125. Born in Nenagh. Enlisted in Birr while living in Birr. Killed in action.

Supplementary information: Son of John and Margaret Flannery, of Pound

Grave of J. Fleming.

Street, Birr, Offaly. He has no known grave but is listed on panel 43 on the Le Touret Memorial in France.

FLANNERY, Robert: Rank: Private. Regiment or Service: Household Cavalry and Cavalry of the line. Unit: 2nd Dragoon Guards, (Queens Bays). Date of death: 21 May 1917. Service No.6482. Born in Clonmel. Enlisted in Dublin. Died at home. Grave or Memorial Reference: IX. 347. Glasgow (St Kentigern's) Roman Catholic Cemetery.

FLEMING, J.: Rank: Private. Regiment or Service: Connaught Rangers Unit: Depot. Date of death: 23 November 1918. Service No.1614.

Grave or Memorial Reference: E. H. 107. Cemetery: St Michael's New Cemetery, Tipperary.

FLOOD, Thomas: Rank: Private. Regiment or Service: Scottish Rifles. Unit: 10th Bn. Date of death: 25 September 1915. Service No.13406. Born in Newport Co. Tipperary. Enlisted in Shotts while living in Lisnagry. Killed in action. Age at death: 36.

Supplementary information: Son of Matthew and C. Mary Maher Flood. He has no known grave but is listed on Panels 57 to 59 on the Loos Memorial in France.

FLYNN, Edmund: Rank: Private. Regiment or Service: Royal Irish

133

Regiment. Unit: Depot. Born in Coolnamuck, Co. Waterford. Enlisted in Carrick-on-Suir, Co. Tipperary while living in Coolnamuck. Date of death: 6 November 1918. Service No.7381. Cemetery, Clonmel, St Patrick's Cemetery. Grave location: 4. E. 119.

FLYNN, Edward: Rank: Private. Regiment or Service: Irish Guards. Unit: 1st Bn. Date of death: 1 November 1914. Service No.3425. Born in Grange, Co. Tipperary. Enlisted in Clonmel. Killed in action. He has no known grave but is listed on Panel 11 on the Ypres (Menin Gate) Memorial in Belgium.

FLYNN, James: Rank: Private. Regiment or Service: Leinster Regiment. Unit: 2nd Bn. Date of death: 8 September 1915. Service No.2581. Born in Nenagh. Enlisted in Birr. Died of wounds. Age at death: 44.

Supplementary information: Son of the late Michael and Margaret Flynn, of 3 Waterside, Waterford: husband of Johanne Flynn, of 2, The Manor, Waterford. Grave or Memorial Reference: III. B. 36. Cemetery: Lijssenthoek Military Cemetery in Belgium.

FLYNN, John: Rank: Private. Regiment or Service: Royal Irish Regiment. Unit: 2nd Garrison Battalion. Date of death: 2 June 1916. Service No.8786. Born in St John's, Carrick-on-Suir. Enlisted in Carrick-on-Suir. Died of wounds at home. Grave or Memorial Reference: Near the South East boundary. Cemetery: Owning Cemetery, near Piltown Co. Kilkenny.

FLYNN, Martin: Rank: Private. Regiment or Service: Royal Irish Regiment. Unit: 1st Bn. Age at death: 23. Date of death: 11 January 1916. Service No.7438. Born in Carrigbeg Co. Waterford and enlisted in Carrick-on-Suir. Died in Salonkia.

Supplementary information: Son of Mr and Mrs Martin Flynn, of Carrick-on-Suir, Co. Tipperary. Grave or Memorial Reference: 47. Cemetery: Salonika (Lembet Road) Military Cemetery in Greece.

FLYNN, Michael: Rank: Private. Regiment or Service: Irish Guards. Unit: 1st Bn. Date of death: 18 May 1915. Service No.5372. Born in Ballygrage, Co. Tipperary. Enlisted in Lancaster in Lancashire. Died of wounds. Killed in action. He has no known grave but is listed on Panel 4 on the Le Touret Memorial in France.

FLYNN, Patrick: Rank: Private. Regiment or Service: Royal Irish Regiment. Unit: 2nd Bn. Age at death: 18. Date of death: 21 March 1918. Service No.11467. Born in Tipperary and enlisted in Clonmel while living in Tipperary. Killed in action.

Supplementary information: Son of Thomas and Johanna Flynn, of Upper Dillon Street, Tipperary. Grave or Memorial Reference: Has no known grave but is commemorated on Panel 30 and 31. Memorial: Pozieres Memorial in France.

FLYNN, Patrick: Rank: Private. Regiment or Service: Royal Irish Regiment. Unit: 6th Bn. Date of death: 11 August 1916. Service No.2086. Born in Moyearkey, Co. Tipperary. Enlisted in Thurles while living in Ballycurrane, Co. Tipperary. Killed in action. Grave or Memorial Reference: I. A. 20. Cemetery: St Patrick's Cemetery, Loos in France.

FLYNN, Patrick: Rank: Rifleman. Regiment or Service: London Regiment (Post Office Rifles). Unit: 1st-8th Bn. Age at death: 20. Date of death: 27 August 1917. Service No.371401. Enlisted in London while living in Knocklofty, Co. Tipperary. Killed in action.

Supplementary information: Son of Mary Flynn, of Domey's Well, Knocklofty, Co. Tipperary, and Patrick Flynn. Grave or Memorial Reference: Has no known grave but is commemorated on Panel 54. Memorial: Ypres (Menin Gate) Memorial in Belgium.

FLYNN, Patrick. Rank: Private. Regiment or Service: Loyal: North Lancashire Regiment. Unit: 6th Bn. Date of death: 12 January 1917. Service No.10874. Born in Fethard. Enlisted in Preston while living in Dublin. Killed in action in Mesopotamia. He has no known grave but is listed on Panel 27 on the Basra Memorial in Iraq.

FOGARTY, C.: Rank: Corporal. Regiment or Service: South African Medical Corps. Age at death: 39. Date of death: 12 January 1917. Service No.1387.

Supplementary information: Son of Michael and Margaret Fogarty, of Rossaguile, Newport, Co. Tipperary, Ireland. Grave or Memorial Reference: III. B. 8. Cemetery: Morogoro Cemetery in Tanzania.

FOGARTY, James: Rank: Private. Regiment or Service: Connaught Rangers. Unit: 5th Bn. Date of death: 8 October 1918. Service No.15188. Formerly he was with the Leinster Regiment where his number was 4247. Born in Clonmel. Enlisted in Clonmel while living in Clonmel. Killed in action. Grave or Memorial Reference: A. 7. Cemetery: Serain Communal Cemetery Extension in France.

FOGARTY, Patrick: Rank: Private. Regiment or Service: Royal Munster Fusiliers. Unit: 2nd Bn. Age at death: 22. Date of death: 27 April 1916. Service No.6217. Born in Templemore and enlisted in Maryhill, Glasgow while living in Maryhill. Killed in action.

Supplementary information: Son of Ellen Fogarty, of Dispensary House, Barrack Street, Templemore, Co. Tipperary, and the late Patrick Fogarty. Grave or Memorial Reference: A. 80. Cemetery: Bully-Grenay Communal Cemetery, French Extension in France.

FOGARTY, Philip: Rank: Private. Regiment or Service: Royal Munster Fusiliers. Unit: 2nd Bn. Date of death: 10 November 1917. Service No.6216. Born in Templemore. Enlisted in Maryhill in Glasgow while living in

Maryhill. Killed in action. He has no known grave but is listed on Panels 143 to 144 on the Tyne Cot Memorial in Belgium.

FOGARTY, Thomas: Rank: Private. Regiment or Service: Leinster Regiment. Unit: 2nd Bn. Date of death: 20 October 1914. Service No.9763. Born in Templemore. Enlisted in Birr. Killed in action. Age at death: 19.

Supplementary information: Son of James Fogarty, of Ashbury, Roscrea, and the late Mary Fogarty. He has no known grave but is listed on Panel 10 on the Ploegsteert Memorial in Belgium.

FOLEY, William: Rank: Private. Regiment or Service: Royal Irish Regiment. Unit: 1st Bn. Age at death: 23. Date of death: 26 August 1918. Service No.4497. Born in Carrick-on-Suir and enlisted in Waterford while living in Carrick-on-Suir. Died in Egypt.

Supplementary information: Son of Laurence and Mary Foley, of Sir John's Rd, Carrick-on-Suir, Co. Tipperary. Grave or Memorial Reference: C. 89. Cemetery: Alexandria (Hadra) War Memorial Cemetery in Egypt. He is also commemorated on the Cahir War Memorial.

FOLEY, William: Rank: Private. Regiment or Service: Royal Irish Regiment. Unit: 7th (South Irish Horse) Bn. Age at death: 22. Date of death: 21 March 1918. Service No.11271. Born in Ardfinnan Co. Tipperary and enlisted in Clonmel while living in Ardfinnan. Killed in action.

Supplementary information: Son of Margaret Foley (*née* Morgan), of Gortralour, Ardfinnan, Cahir, Co. Tipperary, and the late William Foley. Grave or Memorial Reference: Has no known grave but is commemorated on Panel 30 and 31. Memorial: Pozieres Memorial in France.

FORBES, John: Rank: Lance Corporal. Regiment or Service: Sherwood Foresters (Notts and Derby Regiment). Unit: 9th Bn. Age at death: 23. Date of death: 26 September 1916. Service No.13106. Born in Castle Pollard in Co. Meath and enlisted in Derby while living in Ballymacarberry, Co. Cork. Killed in action.

Supplementary information: Son of Mr and Mrs Archibald Forbes, of Newcastle, Clonmel, Co. Tipperary. Grave or Memorial Reference: Pier and Face 10 C 10 D and 11 A. Memorial: Thiepval Memorial in France.

FORD, Henry Thomas: Rank: Air Mechanic 3rd Class. Regiment or Service: Royal Air Force. Unit: 19th Sqdn. Age at death: 19. Date of death: 15 January 1919. Service No.193292.

Supplementary information: Son of Thomas and Martha Ford, of The Elms, Cahir, Co. Tipperary. Grave or Memorial Reference: IV. M. 4. Cemetery: Tournai Communal Cemetery Allied Extension in Belgium. He is also commemorated on the Cahir War Memorial.

FORD, James William: Also recorded as William JAMES. Rank: Corporal. Royal Irish Regiment. Unit: 5ᵗʰ Bn. Age at death: 18. Born in Cahir, Co. Tipperary and enlisted in Clonmel. Died in Egypt. Date of death: 20 November 1917. Service No. 5142.

Supplementary information: Son of Thomas and Martha Ford, of The Elms, Cahir, Co. Tipperary. Native of Cork. Grave or Memorial Reference: D. 222. Cemetery: Alexandria (Hadra) War Memorial Cemetery in Egypt. He is also commemorated on the Cahir War Memorial.

FORESTER, Martin: Rank: Private. Regiment or Service: Royal Irish Regiment. Unit: 6ᵗʰ Bn. Age at death: 22. Date of death: 20 August 1917. Service No. 10010. Died of injuries from the advance of the Germans as they drove the Allies out of Bologne. Born in Golden, enlisted in Cashel while living in Golden.

Supplementary information: Son of Ellen Holden (formerly Forester) of Golden Cashel, Tipperary, and Patrick Forester. Grave or Memorial Reference: VIII. I. 10. Cemetery: Boulogne Eastern Cemetery in France.

FOULDS, John Robertson: Rank: Private. Regiment or Service: London Regiment. Unit: 15ᵗʰ (County of London) Bn. P. W. O. Civil Service Rifles. Date of death: 4 May 1918. Service No. 535270. Born in Tipperary. Enlisted in Merthyr. Killed in action. Age at death: 19.

Supplementary information: Son of William Mason Foulds and Mary Foulds of Cromlix Gardens, Dunblane, Perthshire. Grave or Memorial Reference: X. A. 14. Cemetery: Dernancourt Communal Cemetery Extension in France.

FOUNTAIN, Charles: Rank: Private. Regiment or Service: Royal West Surrey Regiment. Unit: 2ⁿᵈ Bn. Date of death: 5 July 1916. Service No. G-3953 and 3953. Born in Templemore in Tipperary. Enlisted in Guildford in Surrey while living in Templemore. Grave or Memorial Reference: VIII. C. 93. Cemetery: Boulogne Eastern Cemetery in France.

FRANKLIN, William: Rank: Private. Regiment or Service: Royal Irish Regiment. Unit: 6ᵗʰ Bn. Date of death: 11 August 1916. Service No. 2067. Born in Fethard, Co. Tipperary. Enlisted in Cashel, Co. Tipperary while living in Rathoran, Co. Tipperary. Killed in action. Grave or Memorial Reference: I. A. 19. Cemetery: St Patrick's Cemetery, Loos, France.

FREEMAN, John: Rank: Private. Regiment or Service: Leinster Regiment. Unit: 2ⁿᵈ Bn. Age at death: 22. Date of death: 17 March 1917. Service No. 4738. Another mystery man here, records differ. Born in Borris-in-Ossory in Queen's Co. and enlisted in Donaghmore in Tyrone while living in Ballybrophy in Queen's Co. Killed in action.

Supplementary information: Son

Neville Nicholas Fryday.

of John and Alice Freeman, of The Bungalow, Ross, Herefordshire. Born at Templemore, Co. Tipperary. Grave or Memorial Reference: I. C. 12. Cemetery: Aix-Noulette Communal Cemetery Extension in France.

FRY, CHARLES AUGUSTUS: Rank: Captain. Regiment or Service: Essex Regiment. Unit: 6th Bn. Secondary Regiment: Suffolk Regiment Secondary. Unit: attd. 2nd Garr. Bn. Age at death: 58. Date of death: 2 April 1918.

Supplementary information: Son of the late Revd Canon Charles and Mrs Fry, of Holy Cross, Thurles, Co. Tipperary. Husband of Elsie M. Fry, of Church Manor, Bishop's Stortford, Herts. Grave or Memorial Reference: III. A. 2. Cemetery: Les Baraques Military Cemetery, Sangatte in France.

FRYDAY, Neville Nicholas: Rank: Private. Regiment or Service: Canadian Infantry (Central Ontario Regiment) Unit: 75th Bn. Age at death: 17. Date of death: 30 April 1916. Service No. 140229. His enlistment document above states in his own hand that he was born in Upperchurch in Tipperary on 4 September 1893.

Supplementary information: Born at Ballydough Milestone, Thurles, Co. Tipperary. Son of William and Elizabeth A. Fryday, of Mill House, Shankill, Co. Dublin. Grave or Memorial Reference: 276. 2101. Cemetery: Mount Jerome Cemetery in Dublin. Data from the reverse of the enlistment document: Age on Enlistment: 21 Years 10 Months. Height: 5' 9". Eye colour: Brown. Complexion: Dark. Hair colour: Brown. Religion: C. of E.. Chest expansion: 4". Girth:

36". Date of Enlistment: 20 July 1915. Place of Enlistment: Toronto. He was shot by Irish Rebels during the 1916 Rebellion.

G

GALLIGAN, John: Rank: Rifleman. Regiment or Service: Royal Irish Rifles. Unit: 1st Bn. Age at death: 21. Date of death: 9 February 1918. Service No.20646. Born in Clonmel and enlisted in Widnes in Lancashire while living in Clonmel. Killed in action.

Supplementary information: Son of Thomas and Bridget Galligan, of 10 Peter Street, Clonmel, Co. Tipperary. Grave or Memorial Reference: I. A. 5. Cemetery: Grand-Seraucourt British Cemetery in France.

GARDINER, Thomas: Rank: Private. Regiment or Service: Irish Guards. Unit: 1st Bn. Age at death: 25. Date of death: 12 July 1916. Service No.3812. Born in Ennis, Co. Clare and enlisted in Dublin while living in Cloughjordan, Co. Tipperary. Killed in action.

Supplementary information: Son of Patrick and Anne Gardiner, of Northland, Cloughjordan, Co. Tipperary. Grave or Memorial Reference: I. X. 5. Cemetery: La Brique Military Cemetery, No. 2 in Belgium.

GAUGHAN, Thomas: Rank: Private. Regiment or Service: King's Shropshire Light Infantry. Unit: 3rd Bn. Secondary Regiment: Labour Corps Secondary. Unit: transf. to (242936) 424th Coy. Age at death: 40. Date of death: 24 November 1917. Service No.7263. Born in Whitechurch in Salop and enlisted in Clitheroe in Lancashire while living in Whitechurch in Salop. Died at home.

Supplementary information: Son of Mr and Mrs Gaughan: husband of Bridget Gaughan, of 8 Meeting Street, Tipperary. Born at Whitchurch, Salop. Grave or Memorial Reference: 191. Cemetery: Claines (St John the Baptist) Churchyard, UK.

GAVIN, Michael: Rank: Sergeant. Regiment or Service: Leinster Regiment. Unit: 2nd Bn. Age at death: 44. Date of death: 26 March 1915. Service No.1334. Born in Borrisokane and enlisted in Birr. Killed in action.

Supplementary information: Husband of Anne Gavin, of Tower Hill, Borrisokane, Co. Tipperary. Grave or Memorial Reference: B. 4. Cemetery: Ferme Buterne Military Cemetery, Houplines in France.

GIBSON, David: Rank: Private. Regiment or Service: Royal Irish Regiment. Unit: 2nd Bn. Age at death: 35. Date of death: 16 August 1918. Service No.9922. Born in Tipperary and enlisted in Roscrea.

Supplementary information: Son of John and Selina Gibson, of Ballybritt, Roscrea, Co. Tipperary. Grave or Memorial Reference: V. F. 25. Cemetery: Valenciennes (St Roch) Communal Cemetery in France.

GILBERT, Henry Nicholas: Rank: Lance Corporal. Regiment or Service: Irish Guards. Unit: 2nd Bn. Age at death: 30. Date of death: 16 April 1918. Service No.9763. Born in Fethard and enlisted in Cork while living in Farranaleen, Co. Tipperary. Died of injuries.

Supplementary information: Son of Henry Gilbert and Joanna M. Mannix, of Moyglass, Fethard, Co. Tipperary. Grave or Memorial Reference: XXIX. E. 5A. Cemetery: Etaples Military Cemetery in France.

GILBERT, Thomas: Rank: Private. Regiment or Service: Leinster Regiment. Unit: A Coy, 2nd Bn. Date of death: 12 December 1914. Service No.9793. Born in Roscrea. Enlisted in Maryborough (Portlaoise). Killed in action. Age at death: 23.

Supplementary information: Son of Thomas and Bridget Gilbert, of Patrick Street, Durrow, Queen's Co. Grave or Memorial Reference: IX. F. 2. Cemetery: Strand Military Cemetery in Belgium.

GILL, Noel Brendan: Rank: Captain. Regiment or Service: Manchester Regiment. Unit: 18th Bn. Age at death: 20. Date of death: 23 April 1917.

Supplementary information: Son of Robert Paul and Margaret Mary Gill, of Fattheen House, Nenagh, Co. Tipperary. A member of O.T.C. Royal College of Surgeons, Ireland. Gazetted

July, 1915, proceeded to France. Grave or Memorial Reference: Bay 7. Memorial: Arras Memorial in France.

GILMAN, William: Rank: Private. Regiment or Service: Connaught Rangers. Unit: 1st Bn. Date of death: 21 January 1916. Service No.7518. Born in Clonmel. Enlisted in Clonmel while living in Clonmel. Killed in action in Mesopotamia. He has no known grave but is listed on Panels 40 and 64 on the Basra Memorial in Iraq.

GLANCY, Michael John: Rank: Corporal. Regiment or Service: Machine Gun Corps (Infantry). Unit: 17th Coy, formerly 2nd Bn. Date of death: 16 March 1916. Service No.20589. Formerly he was with the Leinster Regiment where his number was 9650. Born in Roscrea. Enlisted in Drogheda while living in Dublin. Killed in action. Age at death: 20. He won the Military Medal and is listed in the *London Gazette*.

Supplementary information: Son of Michael Patrick and Mary Jane Glancy, of 22 Allingham Street, Dublin. He has no known grave but is listed on the Santuary Wood Cemetery Special Memorial in Belgium.

GLEESON, James: Rank: Private. Regiment or Service: Royal Irish Fusiliers. Unit: 1st Garrison Bn. Date of death: 14 April 1916. Service No.673 and G-673. Formerly he was with the Connaught Rangers where his number was 4123. Born in Carrick-on-Suir, Co. Tipperary. Enlisted in Cardiff in Glam while living in Carrick-on-Suir,

Frank R. Gorbey.

Francis Rueben Gorbey.

Co. Tipperary. Died in India. Age at death: 40.

Supplementary information: Son of James and Elizabeth Gleeson (née Hammett). Grave or Memorial Reference: He has no known grave but is listed on Face E of the Kirkee 1914-18 Memorial in India.

GLEESON, John: Rank: Rifleman. Regiment or Service: Royal Irish Rifles. Unit: 1st Garrison Bn. He was previously in the Royal Irish Regiment, where his number was 1965. Age at death: 27. Date of death: 6 November 1918. Service No. 1156. Born in Fethard and enlisted in Clonmel while living in Fethard. Died in India.

Supplementary information: Son of William and Johanna Gleeson, of Knockelly, Fethard, Co. Tipperary, Republic of Ireland. Buried in Cawnpore Cantonment New Cemetery. Grave or Memorial Reference: Face 23. Memorial: Madras 1914-1918 War Memorial, Chennai, India.

GLEESON, Thomas: Rank: Private. Regiment or Service: Irish Guards. Unit: 1st Bn. Age at death: 24. Date of death: 17 September 1916. Service No. 7679. Born in Nenagh and enlisted there also. Died of injuries.

Supplementary information: Son of John and Bridget Gleeson, of Rathnaleen, Nenagh, Co. Tipperary. Grave or Memorial Reference: Pier and Face 7D. Memorial: Thiepval Memorial in France.

GLEESON, William: Rank: Lance Sergeant. Regiment or Service: York and Lancaster Regiment. Unit: 13th (Service) (1st Barnsley) Bn. Date of death: 1 July 1916, the first day of the battle of the Somme. Service No. 13-391. Born in Tipperary. Enlisted in Barnsley. Killed in action. He has no known grave but is listed on Pier and Face 14A and 14B on the Thiepval Memorial in France.

GLENNON, Thomas: Rank: Private. Regiment or Service: Royal Inniskilling Fusiliers. Unit: 7th Bn. Date of death: 27 April 1916. Service No.27719. He was previously with the Royal Irish Regiment where his number was 9101. Killed in action. Born in Cloughjordan and enlisted in Nenagh while living in Cloughjordan.

Supplementary information: Son of Margaret Glennon, of Glenahilly, Cloughjordon, Co. Tipperary. Grave or Memorial Reference: I. E. 15. Cemetery: Philosophe British Cemetery, Mazingarbe in France.

GONLEY, Dominic: Rank: Lance Corporal. Regiment or Service: New Zealand Rifle Brigade. Unit: 4th Bn. 3rd. Age at death: 23. Date of death: 12 October 1917. Service No.26/561.

Supplementary information: Son of Patrick and M. A. Gonley, of 26, Church Hill, Sligo, Ireland. Educated at Rockwell College, Co. Tipperary, and Fermoy College, Co. Cork. Has no known grave but is commemorated on the Tyne Cot Memorial N. Z. Apse, in Belgium. on Panel 7.

GORBEY, Francis Rueben: Rank: Private. (Lance Corporal). Regiment or Service: Royal Irish Regiment. Unit: 1st Bn. Date of death: 23 April 1915. Service No.8930. Born in Villierstown, Co. Waterford. Enlisted in Aldershot, Hants while living in Carrick-on-Suir, Co. Tipperary. Killed

in action. Age at death: 25.

Supplementary information: Son of Mrs E. Gorbey, of 9, The Terrace, Tranmore, Co. Waterford, and the late Mr J. W. Gorbey. He has no known grave but is listed on Panel 33 on the Ypres (Menin Gate) Memorial in Belgium.

GORMAN John: Alias, correct name is O'Brien. Rank: Private. Regiment or Service: Royal Irish Regiment. Unit: 2nd Bn. Age at death: 30. Date of death: 19 October 1914. Killed in action on the 4th Day of the Battle of Aisne during the retreat from Mons. After enlistment and training he first entered the Theatre of War on 26th of August 1914. Service No.4438.

Supplementary information:Husband of Bridget O'Brien of 33, River Street, Clonmel, Co. Tipperary. Grave or Memorial Reference: Has no known grave but is commemorated on Panel 11 and 12. Memorial: Le Touret Memorial in France.

GORMAN, Peter: Rank: Private. Regiment or Service: Welsh Regiment. Unit: 2nd Bn. Date of death: 26 July 1916. Service No.1763. Born in Waterford. Enlisted in Merthyr Tydfil while living in Kilshellan, Tipperary. Killed in action. He has no known grave but is listed on Pier 7 A and Face 10 A on the Thiepval Memorial in France.

GORMAN, Patrick: Sapper, No 2499831. Canadian Railway Troops, Died 19 October 1918. Age at death: 29, Has no known grave but is listed on the Jerusalem Memorial, Addenda Panel. Son of John Gorman, of Gort McElles, Cashel, Co. Tipperary. Born 6-April-1889.

Supplementary information: Data from the reverse of the enlistment document: Age on Enlistment: 28 Years. 10 Months. Height: 5' 9". Eye colour: blue. Complexion: medium. Hair colour: brown. Religion: R.C. Chest expansion: 4". Girth: 37". Vision: OK. Hearing: OK. Scar right thigh, scar on second finger on the left hand. Date of Enlistment: 15 February 1918. Place of Enlistment: Toronto.

GOSS, Patrick: Rank: Private. Regiment or Service: Royal Irish Regiment. Unit: 1st Bn. Date of death: 14 January 1916. Service No.9143. Born in Killenaule. Enlisted in Kilkenny while living in Maryborough (Portlaoise). Died of wounds in Mesopotamia. Grave or Memorial Reference: VI. D. 6. Cemetery: Basra War Cemetery in Iraq.

GOTT, John: Rank: Private. Regiment or Service: Royal Irish Regiment. Unit: 2nd Bn. Age at death: 22. Date of death: 20 July 1918. Service No: 11438. Born in Newbridge and enlisted in Clonmel while living in Templemore. Killed in action.

Supplementary information: Son of the late William James and Annie Gott, of Barrack Street, Templemore, Co. Tipperary. Grave or Memorial Reference: Has no known grave but is commemorated on Panel 30 and 31. Memorial: Pozieres Memorial in France.

GOULD, A.: Rank: Warrant Officer Class II (B. S. M.). Regiment or Service: Royal Field Artillery. Unit: 2nd Highland Bde. Age at death: Date of death: 14 May 1920. Service No.43106. Grave location: 4. BB. 115.

GOULDSBOROUGH, Patrick: Rank: Private. Regiment or Service: Leinster Regiment. Unit: 2nd Bn. Date of death: 15 August 1915. Service No.7415. Born in Thurles. Enlisted in Thurles. Killed in action. He has no known grave but is listed on the Union Street Graveyard No. 1 Cem. Mem. 13 in Birr Cross Roads Cemetery in Belgium.

GRACE, Simon: Rank: Private. Regiment or Service: Irish Guards. Unit: 1st Bn. Date of death: 27 November 1915. Service No.7918. Born in Drangan Co. Tipperary. Enlisted in Tipperary. Killed in action. Grave or Memorial Reference: I. E. 9. Cemetery: Rue-Du-Bacquerot No. 1 Military Cemetery, Laventie in France.

GRACE, Thomas: Rank: Private. Regiment or Service: Leinster Regiment. Unit: 2nd Bn. Date of death: 20 October 1914. Service No.7375. Born in Silvermines, Co. Tipperary. Enlisted in Nenagh. Killed in action.

Supplementary information: Son of Thomas Grace: husband of the late Bridget Grace. He has no known grave but is listed on Panel 10 on the Ploegsteert Memorial in Belgium.

GRAHAM, Douglas: Rank: Private. Regiment or Service: Royal Inniskilling Fusiliers. Unit: 1st Date of death: 1 July 1916, the first day of the battle of the Somme. Service No. 10477. Born in Tipperary. Enlisted in Swinford while living in Wicklow. Killed in action. He has no known grave but is listed on Pier and Face 4 D and 5 B on the Thiepval Memorial in France.

GRANT, Thomas: Rank: Private. Regiment or Service: Scottish Rifles. Unit: A Company, 5th Bn. Date of death: 6 July 1915. Service No. 6277. Born in Tipperary, Ireland. Enlisted in Glasgow. Killed in action. Age at death: 22.

Supplementary information: Son of Mr and Mrs Alexander Grant, of 33 Agnes Street, Maryhill, Glasgow. Grave or Memorial Reference: I. C. 29. Cemetery: Houplines Communal Cemetery Extension in France.

GREEN, David: Rank: Private. Regiment or Service: Welsh Regiment. Unit: 2nd Bn. Date of death: 9 May 1915. Service No. 1748. Born in Carrick-on-Sea, Co. Tipperary. Enlisted in Carmarthen while living in Carrick-on-Sea, Co. Tipperary. Killed in action. He has no known grave but is listed on Panels 23 and 24 on the Le Touret Memorial in France.

GREENE, Edward: Rank: Private. Regiment or Service: Manchester Regiment. Unit: 2nd Bn. Date of death: 10 July 1916. Service No. 5647. Born in Clonmel. Enlisted in Tralee while living in Clonmel. Killed in action. Age at death: 30.

Supplementary information: Son of

W and Bridget Greene. He has no known grave but is listed on Pier and Face 13A and 14C on the Thiepval Memorial in France.

GREEN/GREENE, Joseph: Rank: Private. Regiment or Service: Leinster Regiment. Unit: 2nd Bn. Age at death: 30. Date of death: 3 June 1918. Service No. 1866. Born in Fethard and enlisted in Clonmel while living in Fethard. Killed in action.

Supplementary information: Son of William and Margaret Green, of Burke Street, Fethard, Co. Tipperary. Grave or Memorial Reference: F. 26. Cemetery: Cinq Rues British Cemetery, Hazebrouck in France.

GRIFFIN/GRIFFEN Thomas: Rank: Private. Regiment or Service: Leinster Regiment. Unit: 2nd Bn. Date of death: 17 June 1917. Service No. 10485. Formerly he was with the Royal Army Medical Corps where his number was 11931. Born in Kilsheelan, Co. Tipperary. Enlisted in Clonmel. Killed in action. He has no known grave but is listed on Panel 44 on the Ypres (Menin Gate) Memorial in Belgium.

GRIFFIN, Thomas: Rank: Private. Regiment or Service: Connaught Rangers. Unit: 1st Bn. Date of death: 20 June 1915. Service No. 4638. Born in Thurles. Enlisted in Longford while living in Christchurch, Surrey. Killed in action. He has no known grave but is listed on Panel 43 of the Le Touret Memorial in France.

Grave of Patrick Gunnell.

GRIFFITHS, William: Rank: Private. Regiment or Service: Household Cavalry and Cavalry of the line including the Yeomanry and Imperial Camel Corps. Unit: Royal Irish Lancers. Date of death: 31 October 1914. Service No.4200. Born in Clonmel. Enlisted in Clonmel. Killed in action. He has no known grave but is listed on Panel 5 on the Ypres(Menin Gate) Memorial in Belgium.

GROGAN, John: Rank: Private. Regiment or Service: Leinster Regiment. Unit: 6th Bn. Age at death: 27. Date of death: 30 December 1917. Service No.4610. Born in Bansha and enlisted in Limerick while living in Bansha. Died at sea.

Supplementary information: Son of John and Bridget Grogan, of Foxfort, Bansha, Co. Tipperary. Memorial: Alexandria (Chatby) Military and War memorial Cemetery in Egypt.

GUILFOYLE, John: Rank: Private. Regiment or Service: Irish Guards. Unit: 2nd Bn. Date of death: 27 September 1915. Service No.6691. Born in Nenagh. Enlisted in Nenagh. Killed in action. He has no known grave but is listed on Panels 9 and 10 on the Loos Memorial in France.

GUILFOYLE, Michael: Rank: Regimental Sergeant Major. Regiment or Service: Royal Dublin Fusiliers. Unit: 7th Bn. Age at death: 42. Date of death: 9 October 1916. Service No.7-16972. Born in Dublin and enlisted in London. Died of wounds in the Balkans.

Supplementary information: Son

of William and Sarah Guilfoyle, of 5 Whitworth Rd, Drumcondra, Dublin: husband of Norah Guilfoyle, of 42, O'Connell Street, Clonmel, Co. Tipperary. Grave or Memorial Reference: 1592. Cemetery: Mikra British Cemetery, Kalamaria in Greece.

GULLY, Thomas: Rank: Private. Regiment or Service: East Lancashire Regiment. Unit: 'B' Coy. 1st Bn. Age at death: 26. Date of death: 14 May 1915. Service No.9033. and 9333. Born in Carrick-on-Suir and enlisted there also. Died of wounds.

Supplementary information: Son of James and Bridget Gully, of Sir John's Rd, Carrick-on-Suir, Co. Tipperary. Grave or Memorial Reference: I. A. 104. Cemetery: Bailleul Communal Cemetery Extension (Nord) in France.

GUNNELL, Patrick: Served as **KENNEDY, Michael** . Rank: Private. Regiment or Service: Middlesex Regiment. Unit: 3rd Bn. Age at death: 29. Date of death: 20 June 1915. Service No.L-15291. Born in Nevagh Co. Tipperary and enlisted in Cork. Died of wounds to the head and eye. He was only in the army a few months when he was fatally wounded on active service.

Supplementary information: Husband of Bridget Butler (formerly Gunnell), of Silver Street, Nenagh, Co. Tipperary. Grave or Memorial Reference: Near middle of South wall. Cemetery: Nenagh (Barrack Street) Old Graveyard.

H

HACKETT, Edward Francis: Rank: Private. Regiment or Service: Machine Gun Corps (Infantry). Unit: 44th Coy. He was previously in the Royal Irish Regiment where his number was 19511. Age at death: 18. Date of death: 9 September 1916. Service No.43308. Born in Clonmel and enlisted in Cahir while living in Clonmel. Died of wounds.

Supplementary information: Son of Daniel and the late Ellen Hackett, of 33, Thomas Street, Clonmel, Co.Tipperary. Grave or Memorial Reference: I. A. 12. Cemetery: Contalmaison Chateau Cemetery in France.

HACKETT, John: Rank: Private. Regiment or Service: Leinster Regiment. Unit: 4th Bn. Age at death: 23. Date of death: 30 December 1917. Service No.4606. He was previously in the Royal Field Artillery where his number was 205748. Born in Fethard and enlisted in Clonmel while living in Clonmel. Died at sea.

Supplementary information: Husband of Kate Dwyer (formerly Hackett), of 4, Thomas Street Clonmel, Co.Tipperary. Grave or Memorial Reference: C. 49. Cemetery: Alexandria(Hadra) War Memorial Cemetery in Egypt.

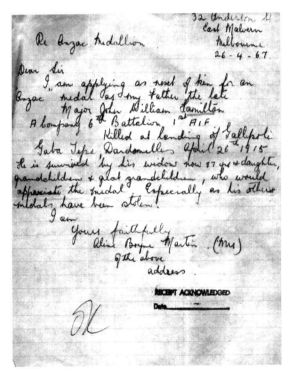

John William Hamilton.

HACKETT, Martin: Rank: Private. Regiment or Service: Royal Munster Fusiliers. Unit: 2nd Bn. Age at death: 18. Date of death: 21 August 1916. Service No.4307. Born in Borrisleigh and enlisted in Templemore while living in Thurles. Killed in action.

Supplementary information: Son of John and Mary Hackett, of Summerhill, Borrisoleigh, Co. Tipperary. Grave or Memorial Reference: Pier and Face 16 C. Memorial: Thiepval Memorial in France.

HAIGH, Thomas: Served as **GLANCEY**. Rank: Sergeant. Regiment or Service: Royal Field Artillery. Unit: 140th Bty. Secondary Regiment: Labour Corps Secondary. Unit: transf. to (616260) Age at death: 32. Date of death: 26 November 1918. Service No.47104.

Supplementary information: Son of Thomas and Hannah Haigh: husband of Margaret Glancey, of Abbey Street, Cahir, Co. Tipperary. Grave or Memorial Reference: Screen Wall. N. 15. Cemetery: Leeds Roman Catholic Cemetery, UK.

HALLORAN, William: Rank: Private. Regiment or Service: Royal Irish Regiment. Unit: 2nd Bn. Date of death: 9 October 1914. Service No.5079. Born in Galbally, Co. Tipperary. Enlisted in Tipperary. Killed in action. He has no known grave but is listed on Panels 11 and 12 on the Le Touret Memorial in France.

HALLY, James: Rank: Private. Regiment or Service: Royal Irish Regiment. Unit: 2nd Bn. Age at death: 19. Date of death: 24 May 1915. Service No.10558. Born in St James' in Clonmel and enlisted in Clonmel. Died of wounds.

Supplementary information: Son of Patrick and Mary Hally, of Clonmel, Co. Tipperary. Grave or Memorial Reference: III. B. 7. Cemetery: Vlamertinghe Military Cemetery in Belgium.

HALLEY/HALLY Michael: Rank: Private. Regiment or Service: Royal Irish Regiment. Unit: 2nd Bn. Date of death: 19 October 1914. Service No.6682. Born in St Mary's, Clonmel, Co. Tipperary. Enlisted in Cahir while living in Clonmel. Killed in action. He has no known grave but is listed on Panels 11 and 12 on the Le Touret Memorial in France.

HALLY, Patrick: Rank: Private. Regiment or Service: Royal Irish Regiment. Unit: 2nd Bn. Age at death: 25. Date of death: 8 November 1918. Service No.5585. Born in New Inn and enlisted in Cashel while living in New Inn. Killed in action.

Supplementary information: Son of Timothy and Hanoria Hally: husband of Ellen Hally, of the New Inn, Cahir, Co. Tipperary. Grave or Memorial Reference: IV. D. 11. Cemetery: Belgrade Cemetery in Belgium. He is also commemorated on the Cahir War Memorial.

HAMILTON, John William: Rank: Major. Regiment or Service: Australian Infantry, A. I. F. Unit: 6ᵗʰ Bn. Age at death: 45. Born in Clonmel. Occupation prior to enlistment Patients Examiner. Killed in Acvtion at Lone Pine in Turkey. Date of death: 25 April 1915.

Supplementary information: Son of William and Anne Mellefont: Husband of Una Hamilton of 'Rosedale' Kerferd Street, East Malvern, Victoria. Hamilton. Grave or Memorial Reference: 25. Cemetery: Lone Pine Memorial in Turkey.

HANLEY, James: Rank: Private. Regiment or Service: Leinster Regiment. Unit: 2ⁿᵈ Bn. Date of death: 26 August 1916. Service No. 8113. Born in Roscrea. Enlisted in Templemore. Killed in action. He has no known grave but is listed on Pier and Face 16C on the Thiepval Memorial in France.

HANLEY/HANLY, Patrick: Rank: Private. Regiment or Service: Royal Irish Regiment. Unit: 6ᵗʰ Bn. Age at death: 28. Date of death: 6 September 1916. Service No. 8940. Born in Cashel and enlisted there also. Co. Tipperary. Died of wounds.

Supplementary information: Native of Cashel, Co. Tipperary. Grave or Memorial Reference: Plot 2. Row C. Grave 30. Cemetery: Corbie Communal Cemetery Extension in France.

HANLEY, William: Rank: Private. Regiment or Service: Leinster Regiment. Unit: 1ˢᵗ Bn. Date of death: 12 May 1915. Service No. 3183. Born in Roscrea. Enlisted in Birr. Killed in action. He has no known grave but is listed on Panel 44 on the Ypres (Menin Gate) Memorial in Belgium.

HANNIGAN, Robert: Rank: Gunner. Regiment or Service: Royal Field Artillery. Unit: 14ᵗʰ Bty. 4ᵗʰ Bde. Date of death: 18 July 1916. Service No. 5652. Born in Waterford and enlisted there also. Died in Mesopotamia.

Supplementary information: Husband of Annie Hannigan, of Town Wall,

Grave of John Hanrahan.

Grave of M. Harrigan.

Carrick-on-Suir, Co. Tipperary. Grave or Memorial Reference: VII. C. 7. Cemetery: Amara War Cemetery in Iraq.

HANNIGAN, John Thomas: Rank: Private. Regiment or Service: Royal Army Service Corps. Unit: 3rd Base Remount Depot Age at death: 43. Date of death: 24 December 1918. Service No.R April 06796.

Supplementary information: Son of Michael and Elizabeth Hannigan, of Cashel, Co. Tipperary. Grave or Memorial Reference: II. B. 5. Cemetery: Janval Cemetery, Dieppe in France.

HANRAHAN, Daniel: Rank: Private. Regiment or Service: Royal Irish Regiment. Unit: 'C' Coy. 2nd Bn. Age at death: 26. Date of death: 26 August 1914. Service No.9197. Born in Thurles and enlisted there also.

Supplementary information: Son of Patrick Hanrahan, of Ballingarry, Thurles: husband of Johanna Hayden Martin Ryan (formerly Hanrahan), of Hall Street, Thurles, Co. Tipperary.

Memorial: La Ferte-Sous-Jouarre-Memorial in France.

HANRAHAN, John: Rank: Private. Regiment or Service: Army Cyclist Corp. Date of death: 30 December 1917. Service No.6917. Formerly he was with the Royal Munster Fusiliers where his number was 2390. Born in Turbrid, Co. Tipperary. and enlisted in Burnley in Lancs. Died in Mesopotamia.

Supplementary information: Son of Patrick and Mary Fagin Flannery: husband of Mary Ann Monagle Flannery. Grave or Memorial Reference: XIX. F. 5. Baghdad (North Gate) War Cemetery in Iraq. He is also commemorated on the Cahir War Memorial.

HANRAHAN, John: Rank: Private. Regiment or Service: Royal Irish Regiment. Unit: 6th Bn. Date of death: 30 January 1917. Service No.2032. Born in Ballingarry. Enlisted in Clonmel while living in Ballingarry. Died of wounds at home. Age at death: 22. Grave or Memorial Reference: On the East Boundary. Cemetery:

NENAGH OFFICER'S DEATH.—Sec.-Lieut. Wilfred Harty, R.D.F., son of the late Mr. John Harty, J.P., Nenagh, has been killed in action. He was 20 years of age, and was educated at Clongowes Wood College. He had passed his first medical examination when he joined the army as a private. Prior to his departure for the Front his friends and school companions presented him with a wristlet watch.

Wilfred A. Harty.

Ballingarry Old Graveyard, Tipperary.

HARKNESS, Charles Henry: Rank: Rifleman. Regiment or Service: Kings Royal Rifle Corps. Unit: 16th Bn. Date of death: 22 June 1916. Service No. C-738. Born in Tipperary. Enlisted in Cork while living in Tipperary. Died of wounds at home. He has been accepted for inclusion on the Brookwood (United Kingdom 1914-18) Memorial, 30 Miles from London but this has not yet been done.

HARNETT, William: Rank: Private. Regiment or Service: Connaught Rangers. Unit: 5th Bn. Age at death: 23. Date of death: 24 September 1917. Service No. 7617. Born in Tipperary and enlisted in Galway while living in Carrick-on-Suir. Died in Salonika.

Supplementary information: Son of William and Catherine Harnett, of William Street, Carrick-on-Suir, Co. Tipperary. Grave or Memorial Reference: A. 36. Cemetery: Ismailia War Memorial Cemetery in Egypt.

HARRAHER, Michael: Rank: Private. Regiment or Service: Machine Gun Corps (Infantry). Unit: 97th Coy. Date of death: 18 November 1916. Service No. 9427. Previously he was in the Royal Irish Regiment where his number was 5090. Born in St Nicholas in Carrick-on-Suir and enlisted in Clonmel while living in Carrick-on-Suir. Killed in action.

Supplementary information: Son of Mrs M. Harraher, of New Lane, Carrick-on-Suir, Co. Tipperary. Grave or Memorial Reference: VII. A. 12. Cemetery: Serre Road Cemetery No. 1 in France.

HARRIGAN, M.: Rank: Private. Regiment or Service: Royal Irish Regiment. Unit: 2nd Bn. Age at death: 22. Date of death: 7 April 1917. Service No. 10622. Additional information: Mrs Bridget Harrigan of Ballyrichard Rd. Carrick-on-Suir. Cemetery: Carrick-on-Suir New Cemetery. Grave location: R. 1.

HARRIS, Patrick Joseph: Rank: Sapper. Regiment or Service: Royal Engineers. Unit: 26th Field Coy. Age at death: 22. Date of death: 23 August 1916. Service No.25888. Born in Cahir and enlisted in Manchester. Killed in action.

Supplementary information: Born at Tipperary. Son of Richard and Johannah Harris, of 1155, Eleventh Street, Trafford Park, Manchester. Grave or Memorial Reference: XXX. L. 10. Cemetery: Delville Wood Cemetery, Longueval in France.

HARTE-MAXWELL, Albert Herbert: Rank: Corporal. Regiment or Service: Black Watch (Royal Highlanders). Unit: 9th Bn. Age at death: 36. Date of death: 1 September 1919. Service No.S-6328.

Supplementary information: Son of the late Samuel Maxwell Harte-Maxwell and E. Harte-Maxwell, of Glen Albert, Roscrea, Co. Tipperary. Twice wounded. Grave or Memorial Reference: CE. 790. Cemetery: Grangegorman Military Cemetery in Dublin.

HARTY, J.J.: Rank: Second Lieutenant. Regiment or Service: Royal Munster Fusiliers. Unit: 1st Bn. Secondary Regiment: Royal Irish Rifles and the Royal Irish Fusiliers. Secondary. Unit: attd. 10th Bn. Age at death: 18. Date of death: 27 September 1916. Age at death: 18.

Supplementary information: Studied in Newbridge College. Entered the Military College, Sandhurst on 14 May, 1915. Youngest son of the late John J.

Harty, (General Merchant and Army Contractor) of View House, Cahir, Co. Tipperary. Grave or Memorial Reference: II. F. 63. Cemetery: Bailleul Communal Cemetery Extension (Nord) in France.

HARTY, Wilfred A:. Rank: 2 Lt. Regiment or Service: Royal Dublin Fusiliers. Unit: 11th Bn. Date of death: 8 August 1917. Killed in action.

Supplementary information: Son of the late Mr John Harty, J. P. Nenagh. Grave or Memorial Reference: VIII. B. 16. Cemetery: Perth Cemetery (China Wall) in Belgium.

HAVREY, Victor Albert: Rank: Lance Corporal. Regiment or Service: Royal Dublin Fusiliers. Unit: 8th Bn. Date of death: 3 June 1916. Service No.17442. Born in Clonmel and enlisted in Exeter while living in Clonmel. Killed in action.

Supplementary information: Son of R. Havrey, of Clonmel, Co. Tipperary. Grave or Memorial Reference: III. H. 3. Cemetery: St Patrick's Cemetery, Loos in France.

HAVREY, William: Rank: Private. Regiment or Service: Royal Lancaster Regiment. Unit: 2nd-5th Bn. Date of death: 8 October 1918. Service No.240282. Born in Tipperary. Enlisted in Lancaster. Killed in action. Grave or Memorial Reference: I. E. 11. Cemetery: Marcoing British Cemetery in France.

HASSETT, John: Rank: Gunner. Regiment or Service: Royal Garrison

Artillery. Unit: 305th Siege Bty. Age at death: 24. Date of death: 31 August 1918. Service No.41966. Born in St Peter's and St Paul's in Clonmel and enlisted in Clonmel also. Died of wounds.

Supplementary information: Son of Peter and Mary Hassett, of 12, Storyes Lane, Old Bridge, Clonmel, Co. Tipperary. Grave or Memorial Reference: B. 16. Cemetery: Ligny-Sur-Canche British Cemetery in France.

HASSETT, Michael: Rank: Private. Regiment or Service: Royal Irish Regiment. Unit: 6th Bn. Date of death: 9 September 1916. Service No.9064. Born in Nenagh. Enlisted in Cashel while living in Nenagh. Killed in action. Grave or Memorial Reference: XXV. G. 2. Cemetery: Delville Wood Cemetery, Longueval in France.

HAY, Charles Gordon: Rank: Gunner. Regiment or Service: Royal Horse Artillery and Royal Field Artillery. Unit: B Battery, 83rd Brigade. Date of death: 3 November 1917. Service No.L-12221. Born in Tipperary, Ireland. Enlisted in York. Killed in action. Age at death: 30.

Supplementary information: Son of Peter and Mary Hay, of Stirling: husband of Lizzie May Hay, of 26, West Lea Avenue, Harlow Hill, Harrogate. Grave or Memorial Reference: V. C. 28. Cemetery: Bard Cottage Cemetery in Belgium.

HAYDEN, William: Rank: Private. Regiment or Service: Irish Guards. Unit:. 1st Bn. Date of death: 13 April 1915. Service No.4479. Born in Clonmel. Enlisted in Clonmel. Killed in action. Grave or Memorial Reference: I. F. 17. Cemetery: Guards Cemetery, Windy Corner, Cuinchy in France.

HAYES, Daniel:. Rank: Private. Regiment or Service: Royal Irish Regiment. Unit: 5th Bn. Date of death: 16 August 1915. Service No.2248. Born in Thurles. Enlisted in Templemore while living in Thurles. Killed in action in Gallipoli. He has no known grave but is listed on Panel 55 on the Helles Memorial in Turkey.

Grave of Patrick Hayes.

154

HAYES, John: Rank: Private. Regiment or Service: Machine Gun Corps (Infantry) Age at death: 23. Date of death: 10 October 1918. Service No.60831. Boorn in Aheeny Co. Tipperary and enlisted in Carrick-on-Suir while living in Aheeny. Died at sea.

Supplementary information: Son of Patrick and Johanna Hayes, of Ahenny, Carrick-on-Suir, Co. Tipperary. Memorial: Hollybrook Memorial, in Southampton, UK.

HAYES, John: Rank: Private. Regiment or Service: Royal Munster Fusiliers. Unit: 1st Bn. Date of death: 8 May 1915. Service No.9789. Born in Newport Co. Tipperary. Enlisted in Limerick while living in Lisnagry. Killed in action in Gallipoli. Age at death: 20.

Supplementary information: Son of Mrs Johanna Hayes, of Rivers Annacothy, Lisnagry, Co. Limerick. He has no known grave but is listed on Panel 185 to 190 on the Helles Memorial in Turkey.

HAYES, Michael Joseph: Rank: Private. Regiment or Service: Royal Munster Fusiliers. Unit: 1st Bn. He was previously with the Royal Irish Regiment where his number was 5031. Age at death: 22. Date of death: 18 April 1917. Service No.3769.

Supplementary information: Son of John and Margaret Hayes, of Ballymackeogh, Newport, Co. Tipperary. Grave or Memorial Reference: IV. C. 9. Cemetery: Boulogne Eastern Cemetery in France.

HAYES, Patrick: Rank: Guardsman. Number 7079. 3rd Reserve Battalion, Irish Guards. Date of death: 27 May 1917. Age at death: 21. Died of wounds received in SePrivatember 1916. in the Battle of Flers-Courcelette or Marval in France. Son of John Hayes, Post Office, Holycross. Thomas M Hayes (British Army) No 41758 Died in Mesopotamia, Patrick Hayes (British Army) No 7079. Died of wounds. John Quinane (Australian Army) No 2225 Died of disease and Patrick Cahill (Canadian Army) (No 437244) Killed at Vimy Ridge were all related. Buried in the Church of Ireland Graveyard (in front of Bill the Black) in Holycross. Extract from the *Tipperary Star*, 9 June 1917:

Holycross Guardsman's death.

We regret to chronicle the death on Sunday, 27th, ult. At Portland Road Hospital, Hove, Sussex, of Private Patrick Hayes, –Battalion Irish Guards, resulting from wounds received in action in the Battle of the Loos Last September. He was the fourth son of Mr John Hayes, the Post office, Holycross, and was in the firing line in France for eighteen months: he took part in the engagements at hill 60, Loos, (where he was previously wounded), and the advance on the Somme. Many of his comrades-in-arms, who returned from time to time, spoke of his high charac-ter, good fellowship, and coolness in danger. The funeral procession from Thurles Station to the family burial ground at Holycross testified to the high esteem in which he was held and the great sympathy which is felt for his bereaved people. The chief mourners at the graveyard were- Mr John Hayes (Father), Marain(?) (G. P. O. Queenstown,), John and Conor (brothers): Miss Nell Hayes (sister): Patrick, Cornelius, James, Denis, and William Hayes (Uncles): Mrs Skelly and Miss Catherne Hayes (Aunts): Thos. M Skelly, Patrick Ryan, Miss Bab Skelly, Miss Alice Ryan, John Hayes (Junior), Misses Nan, Kitty and Bridget Hayes and Jas Skehan (Cousins). The wreaths placed on the grave were- "Deepest sympathy from Mr and Mrs Cooke, Brian and Ellia, Newtown House", "With heartfelt sympathy from Mrs Bayly and family Killough Castle" "Deepest sympathy from Sister K. Hall, The Hospital, Brighton", "With loving remembrance from Nan and Bab", "Deepest sympathy from Nan and Sarah, Cardiff" "With fond remembrance from Mary and Bridgie Ryan" The funeral arrangements were carried out by Mr Leahy, Main Street Thurles in his usual capable manner. The utmost sympathy is felt for Mr Hayes and Family whose eldest son, Thos Hayes, Royal Engineers and late of the Ordinance Survey who, after encountering the dangers and hardships of Gallipoli and Mesopotamia, died last August in Basra on the Persian Gulf.

Thomas M Hayes (British Army) No 41758 Died in Mesopotamia, John Quinane (Australian Army) No 2225 Died of disease and Patrick Cahill (Canadian Army) were all related.

HAYES, Timothy: Rank: Private. Regiment or Service: Royal Munster Fusiliers. Unit: 1st Bn. Date of death: 28 August 1918. Service No.8076. Born in Tipperary. Enlisted in Whitehall, Middlesex while living in Islington, Middlesex. Killed in action. Age at death: 36.

Supplementary information: Son of William and Julia Hayes, of 5 Baileys New Street, Waterford. Grave or Memorial Reference: II. A. 30. Cemetery: St Martin Calvaire British Cemetery, St Martin-Sur-Cojeu.

HAYES, Thomas M.: Rank: Sapper. Regiment or Service: Royal Engineers. Unit: 71st Field Coy. (formerly 71st Field Company, R. E.). No 41758. Enlisted in Ammanford in Carmarthenshire. Died on Friday 11 August 1916. in Mesopotamia. Born in Thurles. He was a son of Mr John Hayes, Post Office, Holycross. He is buried in the Basra War emetery in Iraq. Grave Reference-V. P. 11. Sapper Hayes is also commemorated on the First World War Memorial Wall in St Mary's Churchyard, Thurles. (Thomas was one of over 200 people who attended and helped out at the coming of age celebrations for Marcus Beresford Armstrong's son William (Pat) at the all night singing, dancing and celebrations held in Moyaliffe house in September 1910.) Thomas M Hayes (British Army) No 41758 Died in Mesopotamia, Patrick Hayes (British Army) No 7079 died of wounds. John Quinane (Australian Army) No 2225 Died of disease and Patrick Cahill (Canadian Army) (No 437244) Killed at Vimy Ridge were all related.

HEALEY, Maurice Kevin: Rank: Corporal. Regiment or Service: Machine Gun Corps (Infantry). Unit: 177th Coy. He was previously with the Duke of Cornwalls Light Infantry where his number was 18687. Died of wounds. Age at death: 28. Enlisted in Tipperary. Date of death: 28 September 1917. Service No.83381. Died of wounds.

Supplementary information: Son of Tom and Kathleen Healey, of Wexford: husband of Marjorie E. Healey, of Peter Street, Nenagh, Co. Tipperary. Grave or Memorial Reference: VI. F. 18. Cemetery: Mendingham Military Cemetery in Belgium.

HEALY, Michael: Rank: Private. Regiment or Service: Royal Irish Regiment. Unit: 6th Bn. Date of death: 4 August 1917. Service No.7613. Born in Killenaule. Enlisted in Clonmel while living in Killenaule. Killed in action. He has no known grave but is listed on Panel 33 on the Ypres (Menin Gate) Memorial in Belgium.

HEALY, Thomas: Rank: Private. Regiment or Service: Leinster Regiment. Unit: 2nd Bn. Formerly No 8206 of the Connaught Rangers. Born in Bellygar Co. Galway, enlisted

in New York USA while living in Bellygar. Died of wounds. Date of death: 3 June 1918. Service No.18147.

Supplementary information: Husband of Mrs M. Healy, of Cashel, Co. Tipperary. Grave or Memorial Reference: I. F. 22. Cemetery: Ebblinghem Military Cemetery in France.

HEAPHEY, Patrick: Rank: Private. Regiment or Service: Royal Dublin Fusiliers. Unit: 2nd Bn. He was previously with the Royal Irish Regiment where his number was 5022. Age at death: 18. Date of death: 16 October 1916. Service No.43020. Born in Gurtnahoe and enlisted in Fethard while living in Killenaule. Killed in action.

Supplementary information: Son of Patrick and Catherine Heaphey, of Knockinglass, Fethard, Co. Tipperary. Grave or Memorial Reference: Pier and Face 16 C. Memorial: Thiepval Memorial in France.

HEDGES, Arthur: Rank: Private. Regiment or Service: Wiltshire Regiment. Unit: Depot. Date of death: 2 December 1914. Service No.3-258. Born in Carrick-on-Suir, Co. Tipperary. Enlisted in Salisbury while living in St Alban's in Hertfordshire. Died at home. Grave or Memorial Reference: Church. P.34. Cemetery: Devizes Cemetery, UK.

HEENAN, Martin: Rank: Private. Regiment or Service: Irish Guards. Unit: 1st Bn. Age at death: 33. Date of death: 1 December 1917. Service

No. 12055. Born in Tipperary Town and enlisted in Liverpool while living in Lissadona in Tipperary. Killed in action.

Supplementary information: Son of the late John and Mary Heenan, of Lissadona, Cloughjordan, Co. Tipperary. Grave or Memorial Reference: Has no known grave but is commemorated on Panel 2 and 3. Memorial: Cambrai Memorial in Louveral in France.

HEFFERNAN, Francis Joseph Christopher: Rank: Lieutenant Colonel. Regiment or Service: Royal Army Medical Corps Age at death: 42. Date of death: 16 July 1917.

Supplementary information: Son of Mortimer Heffernan, of Lowesgreen, Fethard, Co. Tipperary, husband of Edith Heffernan, of 7, Brunswick Rd, Hove, Brighton. Grave or Memorial Reference: XIII. J. 12. Cemetery: Amara War Cemetery in Iraq.

HEFFERNAN, James: Rank: Private. Regiment or Service: Machine Gun Corps (Infantry). Unit: 101st Coy. He was previously with the Royal Irish Regiment where his number was 11400. Age at death: 18. Date of death: 1 July 1916. Killed in action on the first day of the battle of the Somme. Service No. 13679. Born in Gortnahoe and enlisted in Killenaule while living in New Bermingham.

Supplementary information: Son of Denis and K. Heffernan, of Paynstown, New Birmingham, Thurles, Co. Tipperary. Grave or Memorial Reference: Pier and Face 5 C and 12

C. Memorial: Thiepval Memorial in France.

HEFFERNAN, James: Rank: Company Quartermaster Sergeant. Regiment or Service: Lancashire Fusiliers Unit: 1st Bn. Age at death: 30. Date of death: 27 April 1915. Service No. 9794. Born in St Helen's in Lancashire and enlisted in Warrington in Lancashire while living in Tipperary. Died of wounds in Gallipoli.

Supplementary information: Son of the late Patrick and Eliza Heffernan: husband of Elizabeth Heffernan, of 11, Nelson Street, Tipperary. Grave or Memorial Reference: Has no known grave but is commemorated on Panel 58 to 72 or 218 to 219. Memorial: Helles Memorial in Turkey.

HEFFERNAN, James: Rank: Private. Regiment or Service: Royal Irish Regiment. Unit: 2nd Bn. Date of death: 1 June 1915. Service No. 5877. Born in St Michael's, Tipperary. Enlisted in Tipperary. Died of wounds. Age at death: 22. Grave or Memorial Reference: VIII. A. 60. Cemetery: Boulogne Eastern Cemetery in France.

HEFFERNAN, Michael: Rank: Private. Regiment or Service: Royal Irish Regiment. Unit: 2nd Bn. Date of death: 21 January 1915. Service No. 6686. Born in Tipperary. Enlisted in Tipperary while living in Askeaton, Co. Limerick. Grave or Memorial Reference: III. L. 12. Cemetery: Niederzwehren Cemetery in Germany.

HEFFERNAN, Patrick: Rank: Private. Regiment or Service: Irish Guards. Unit: 1st Bn. Age at death: 17. Date of death: 9 October 1917. Service No.11743. Born in Windgap in Kilkenny and enlisted in Carrick-on-Suir. Killed in action.

Supplementary information: Son of Michael and Mary Heffernan, of Cussane Lodge, Carrick-on-Suir, Co. Tipperary. Grave or Memorial Reference: Has no known grave but is commemorated on Panel 10 to 11. Memorial: Tyne Cot Memorial in Belgium.

HEFFERNAN, Stephen: Rank: Private. Regiment or Service: Leinster Regiment. Unit: 'C' Coy. 2nd Bn. Age at death: 34. Date of death: 12 April 1917. Service No.163. Born in Tipperary and enlisted in Clonmel. Killed in action by a shell splinter.

Supplementary information: Son of Mrs Margaret Heffernan, of 25, Spittle Street, Tipperary. His brother had been a prisoner in Germany since October 1914. Grave or Memorial Reference: Bay 9. Memorial: Arras Memorial in France.

HEFFERNAN, William Patrick: Rank: Second Lieutenant. Regiment or Service: Royal Irish Regiment. Unit: 3rd Bn. Secondary Regiment: Gloucestershire Regiment Secondary. Unit: attd. 1st Bn. Age at death: 28. Born in Killenaule 10 December 1885. Date of death: 9 May 1915. Educated Dublin University (prize winner at boxing and running). Had been wounded at La Bassee February 1915, and was killed at Festubert leading his company.

Supplementary information: Son of Dr. W. K. Heffernan, J. P. of Riverdale, Killenaule, Co. Tipperary, and of Mary Heslop, his wife. Two exhibitions in Mathematics, Trinity College, Dublin. Volunteered for service at the outbreak of the war and joined the Gloucestershire Regiment in which he obtained a Commission as Second Lieutennant. Grave or Memorial Reference: Has no known grave but is commemorated on Panel 11 and 12. Memorial: Le Touret Memorial in France.

HEGARTY, Edward: Rank: Captain. Regiment or Service: Royal Irish Regiment. Unit: 3rd Bn. attd. 2nd Bn. Age at death: 35. Date of death: 3 September 1916. Service No.5432. This is the first Officer I ever found that had a service number. He was awarded the Military Cross and is listed in the *London Gazette*.

Supplementary information: Son of Nicholas and Catherine Hegarty, of Limerick: husband of Bridget Hegarty, of 22, Queen Street, Clonmel, Co. Tipperary. Grave or Memorial Reference: V. K. 2. Cemetery: Delville Wood Cemetery, Longueval in France.

HEGARTY, Patrick: Rank: Private. Regiment or Service: Royal Army Ordnance Corps. Formerly he was with the Leinster Regiment. Date of death: 21 July 1919. Service No.S/9485. Born in Roscrea, Co. Tipperary. Enlisted in Whitehall, London while

Martin Hennessy.

living in Birr, Kings County. Died in North Russia. Buried in Maselskaya Burial Ground and Commemorated on the Archangel Memorial in the Russian Federation.

HEGNEY, Christopher Stephen: Rank: Private. No 3-10111, West Riding Regiment, 2ⁿᵈ Bn, Died 14 December 1914. Born: Cashel, Co. Tipperary. Born in Cashel, enlisted in Halifax, UK while living in Cashel. Killed in action defending the Ypres Salient. Has no known grave but is comemmorated on the Ypres (Menin Gate) memorial on Panel 20.

HEGNEY, James: Rank: Rifleman. Regiment or Service: Royal Irish Rifles. Unit: 1ˢᵗ Garrison Bn. Age at death: 32. Date of death: The records give two dates of death 8 July 1918, and 25 May 1916. Service No.G-784 and 784. Born: Cashel, Co. Tipperary and enlisted in Cashel while living in Cashel. Died at home.

Supplementary information: Son of Thomas and Mary Hegney: husband of Johanna Hegney, of Killenaule, Thurles, Co. Tipperary Republic of Ireland. Buried in Chakrata Cemetery. Grave or Memorial Reference: Face 23. Memorial: Madras 1914-1918 War Memorial, Chennai, India. The Madras 1914-1918 War Memorial is situated at the rear of the cemetery. It bears the names of more than 1, 000 servicemen who died during the First World War who lie in many civil and cantonment cemeteries in various parts of India where it is not possible to maintain their graves in perpetuity. Died at home and buried in India. With two different dates of death, this mans records raise more questions than it answers.

HEMSLEY, Dudley Staunton: Rank: Private. Regiment or Service: Household Cavalry and Cavalry of the Line (Including Yeomanry and Imperial Camel Corps). Unit: 18ᵗʰ (Queen Marys own Royal) Hussars and the 3ʳᵈ Kings Own Hussars. Date of death: 26 March 1918. Service No.9411. Born in Tipperary. Enlisted in Bedford while living in Bedford. Died of wounds. Age at death: 21.

Supplementary information: Son of Henry and Isabella Hemsley, of 39 London Rd, Bedford. Grave or Memorial Reference: VII. AA. 16, Cemetery: Dernancourt Communal Cemetery Extension in France.

HENDERSON, William: Rank: Sergeant. Regiment or Service: Royal Irish Rifles. Unit: 13th Bn. Date of death: 25 August 1917. Service No.19881. Born in Templemore. Enlisted in Belfast. Died of wounds. Age at death: 54.

Supplementary information: Son of James and Jane Henderson, of Belfast: husband of Annie Henderson, of 44, Warkworth Street, Belfast. Grave or Memorial Reference: I. E. 11. Cemetery: Rocquigny-Equancourt Road British Cemetery, Equancourt in France.

HENDY, Edward George: Rank: Private. Regiment or Service: Royal Fusiliers(City of London Regiment). Unit: 2nd Bn. Date of death: 1 July 16, first day of the battle of the Somme. Service No.PS. 7823 and PS-7823. Born in Clonmel. Enlisted in Manchester while living in Oldham. Killed in action. Age at death: 26.

Supplementary information: Son of the late Mr and Mrs A. W Hendy, of 32, Avon Rd, Southport. He has no known grave but is listed on Pier and Face 8 C and 9 A and 16 A on the Thiepval Memorial in France.

HENNESSY, James: Rank: Private. Regiment or Service: Royal Dublin Fusiliers. Unit: 2nd Bn. Date of death: 23 December 1914. Service No.8922. Born in Tipperary. Enlisted in Carlow while living in Graigue, Carlow. Killed in action. Grave or Memorial Reference: I. C. 4. Cemetery: Prowse Point Military Cemetery in Belgium.

HENNESSY, James C.: Rank: Private First Class. 61st Infantry Regiment, 5th Division. U. S. Army. Born Cashel on the 15 September 1876. Enlisted in Caldwell, New Jersey while living in Humboldt New York. Killed in action 3 November 1918. Buried Plot B Row 14, Grave 6 Meuse-Argonne American Cemetery, Romagne, France.

HENNESSEY/HENNESSY, Martin: Rank: Private. Regiment or Service: Aukland Infantry Regiment, Embarked with the 31st Reinforcements Aukland Infantry Regiment, A Company on the Vessel 'Tahiti' on 16 November 1917. Date of death: 1 October 1918. Service No.63871. Age at death: 35. Martin Hennessy is down as Mr W Hennessy in an article in the Tipperary Star in October 1918. A requiem Mass was held in Toomevara one Monday in October 1918 for the repose of his soul. The celebrants were Revd T Dooley, CC, assisted by Revd M O'Connor, CC and the Revd Fr Flynn, PP. Son of Philip and Mary Hennessy of Kilnafinch, Latteragh, Thurles, Ireland. Fathers address is also down as Grennanstown, Toomevara. Killed in action in Le Chateau in

France. Grave or Memorial Reference: V. A. 2. Cemetery: Flesquieres British Cemetery in France.

HENNESSEY/HENNESSY, THOMAS: Rank: Private. Regiment or Service: Royal Munster Fusiliers. Unit: 8th Bn. Date of death: 7 September 1916. Service No.4881. Born in Thurles. Enlisted in Templemore while living in Thurles. Died of wounds. Grave or Memorial Reference: Plot 2, Row C, Grave 39. Cemetery: Corbie Communal Cemetery Extension in France.

HENNESSY/HENESSEY, William: Rank: Gunner. Regiment or Service: Royal Horse Artillery and Royal Field Artillery. Unit: 12th Battery. Date of death: 12 March 1915. Service No.28957. Born in Templemore. Enlisted in Exeter. Killed in action. Grave or Memorial Reference: III. G. 5. Cemetery: Royal Irish Rifles Graveyard Laventie in France.

HERLIHAN, John: Rank: Private. Regiment or Service: Royal Inniskilling Fusiliers. Unit: 2nd Bn. Date of death: 26 October 1918. Service No.27697. Formerly he was with the Royal Irish Regiment where his number was 11388. Born in Bansha Co. Tipperary. Enlisted in Clonmel while living in Tipperary. Killed in action.
Supplementary information: Son of the late David and Ann Herlihan. Grave or Memorial Reference: IV. C. 3. Cemetery: Harlebeke New British Cemetery in Belgium.

HERLIHY, John D.: Rank: Sapper. Regiment or Service: Royal Engineers. Unit: 10th Railway Coy. Age at death: 30. Date of death: 12 January 1915. Service No.16697. Born in Kilvamon Co. Tipperary and enlisted in Enniskillen Co. Fermanagh. Died.
Supplementary information: Son of Daniel and Marie Herlihy, of Mullinahone, Co. Tipperary. Grave or Memorial Reference: Plot 3. Row A. Grave 14. Cemetery: Le Grand Hasard Military Cemetery, Morbecque in France.

HETHERINGTON, Arthur Sherbrooke: Rank: Guardsman. Regiment or Service: Grenadier Guards. Unit: 2nd Company, 1st Bn. Date of death: 27 September 1916. Service No.17852. Born in Tipperary. Enlisted in Limerick. Died of wounds. Age at death: 25.
Supplementary information: Son of Richard George and Margaret Anna Hetherington, of 7, Verona Esplanade, Limerick. Grave or Memorial Reference: XI. B. 10A. Cemetery: Etaples Military Cemetery in France.

HEWITT, Robert: Rank: Private. Regiment or Service: Royal Irish Regiment. Unit: 2nd Bn. Date of death: 26 May 1915. Service No.7094. Born in Nenagh. Enlisted in Nenagh. Died of wounds. Grave or Memorial Reference: VII.A.49. Cemetery: Boulogne Eastern Cemetery in France.

HICKEY, Edward: Rank: Private. Regiment or Service: Argyll and

Sutherland Highlanders. Unit: 2nd Bn. Age at death: 27. Date of death: 26 July 1916. Service No.4-9763. Born in Waterford and enlisted in Glasgow. Died of wounds.

Supplementary information: Son of Ellen and the late Serjt. John Hickey, of Tipperary: husband of Bridget Hickey, of 12 Portugal Street, Glasgow. Grave or Memorial Reference: A. 38. 1. Cemetery: St Sever Cemetery Extension, Rouen in France.

HICKEY, James: Rank: Driver. Regiment or Service: Royal Horse Artillery and Royal Field Artillery. Unit: 'X' 14th Trench Mortar Battery. Date of death: 28 February 1917. Service No.100619. Born in Clonmel. Enlisted in Clonmel. Killed in action. He has no known grave but is listed on Pier and Face 1 A and 8 A on the Thiepval Memorial in France.

HICKEY, John: Rank: Private. Regiment or Service: Royal Irish Regiment. Unit: 7th (South Irish Horse) Bn, formerly the Royal Army Medical Corps where his number was 79771. Age at death: 21. Date of death: 21 March 1918. Service No.10359. Born in Newcastle Co. Tipperary and enlisted in Clonmel while living in Knocklofty. Died of wounds.

Supplementary information: Son of Michael and Ellen Hickey, of Rathokelly, Clonmel, Co. Tipperary. Grave or Memorial Reference: Has no known grave but is commemorated on Panel 30 and 31. Memorial: Pozieres Memorial in France.

HICKEY, William: Rank: Lance Corporal. Regiment or Service: Royal Dublin Fusiliers. Unit: 10th Bn. Date of death: 26 August 1918. Service No.26226. Born Grammorsfield Co. Tipperary and enlisted in Dublin while living in Clonmel. Died of wounds.

Supplementary information: Son of John and Kate Hickey (*née* Maher), of Ballyknockane, Clonmel, Co. Tipperary. Grave or Memorial Reference: XI. D. 9. Cemetery: Berlin South-Western Cemetery in Germany.

HICKEY, Michael: Rank: Corporal. Regiment or Service: Leinster Regiment. Unit: 7th Bn. Age at death: 22. Date of death: 8 March 1917. Service No.5147. Born in Clonmel and enlisted in Clonmel while living in Clonmel. Killed in action.

Supplementary information: Son of John and Johanna Hickey, of 7 St Mary's Place, Clonmel, Co. Tipperary. Grave or Memorial Reference: K. 10. Cemetery: Pond Farm Cemetery in Belgium.

HIGGINS, William: Rank: Private. Regiment or Service: Royal Munster Fusiliers. Unit: 9th Bn. Date of death: 27 March 1916. Service No.3350. Born in St Mary's, Cahir, Co. Tipperary. Enlisted in Limerick while living in Cahir. Died of wounds. He has no known grave but is listed on Panel 127 on the Loos Memorial in France.

HIRONS, Francis John: Rank: Rifleman. Regiment or Service: Rifle Brigade. Unit: 3rd Bn. Date of death: 16

James Henry
Hogan..

August 1915. Service No.3049. Born In Bicester and enlisted in Bicester while living in Bicester, Oxon. Died of wounds.

Supplementary information: Husband of Catherine Mary Hirons, of 10, Cashel Rd, Tipperary. Grave or Memorial Reference: III. D. 34A. Cemetery: Lijssenthoek Military Cemetary in Belgium.

HODGINS, Richard: Rank: Private. Regiment or Service: Australian Infantry. Unit: 48th Bn. Date of death: 12 October 1917. Service No.3159. Age at death 27. Born in Tipperary, Ireland. Enlisted in Southern Cross, Western Australia 1 October 1916 while living in Bondai, Western Australia aged 26 years and 5 months. Height: 6' ½". Weight: 179 lbs. Complexion: ruddy. Eyes: hazel. Hair: brown. Religious Denomination: C. of E. Occupation on enlistment: Repairer. Originally reported as missing on 12 October 1917 but later changed to 'Killed in

action' after a Court of Inquiry held on 8 November 1918.

Supplementary information: Son of Margaret Hodgins, of Garravally, Ballymackey, Nenagh, Co. Tipperary, Ireland. Grave or Memorial Reference: VI. A. 15. Cemetery: Buttes New British Cemetery Polygon Wood Zonnebeke, Belgium.

HOGAN, J.: Rank: Private. Regiment or Service: Royal Irish Regiment. Unit: 2nd Bn. Age at death: 32. Date of death: 12 November 1918. just one day after the end of the war. Service No.8424.

Supplementary information: Son of James and Catherine Hogan: husband of Mary Hogan, of Sir John's Rd, Carrick-on-Suir, Co. Tipperary. Grave or Memorial Reference: XV. C. 7. Cemetery: Berlin South-Western Cemetery in Germany.

HOGAN, James: Rank: Private. Regiment or Service: Irish Guards.

Grave of M. Hogan,

Unit: 1st Bn. Age at death: 24. Date of death: 9 October 1917. Service No.8447. Born in Shanrahan Co. Tipperary and enlisted in Waterford, Killed in action.

Supplementary information: Son of Michael and Mary Hogan, of Shanrahan, Clogheen, Cahir, Co. Tipperary. Grave or Memorial Reference: Has no known grave but is commemorated on Panel 10 to 11. Memorial: Tyne Cot Memorial in Belgium. He is also commemorated on the Cahir War Memorial.

HOGAN, James Henry: Rank: Private. Regiment or Service: Australian Imperial Force. Unit: 1st Bn. Date of death: 2 May 1915. Repoted missing on 2 May 1915 and declared Killed in action after a Court of Inquiry on 11 May 1915. Body not recovered. Service No.1367. Born in Arkloney, Borris Okane, Tipperary. Enlisted in Sydney, NSW on 10 November 1914. Age on enlistment: 28 Years 7 Months. Height,

5'8". Weight: 9st 7lbs. Eyes: blue. Hair: brown, Complexion: Med. Religious Denomination: C of E. Occupation on enlistment: Carpenter-Joiner. Next of Kin: Father, Mr Samuel Hogan, Congor Cottage, Borrisokane, Co. Tipperary. Killed in action. He has no known grave but is listed on the Lone Pine Memorial, Gallipoli. Memorial Reference: 14

HOGAN, John: Rank: Driver. Regiment or Service: Army Service Corps. Unit: 16th Div. Train H. Q. Date of death: 6 October 1916. Service No.T4-089417. Born in Cappawhite and enlisted in Clonmel.

Supplementary information: Father of Miss Mary Hogan, of 24 Davis Rd, Clomnel, Co. Tipperary. Grave or Memorial Reference: A. 18. Cemetery: Allonville Communal Cemetery in France.

HOGAN, John: Rank: Private. Regiment or Service: Middlesex Regiment. Unit: 5th Bn. Age at death:

19. Date of death: 10 October 1918. Service No.G-95753. Born in Grawn Co. Tipperary and enlisted in Nenagh while living in Nenagh. Died at sea.

Supplementary information: Son of Michael and Johanna Hogan, of Sally Park, Latteragh, Thurles, Co. Tipperary. Memorial: Hollybrook Memorial, in Southampton, UK.

HOGAN, Joseph: Rank: Private. Regiment or Service: Royal Irish Regiment. Unit: 5th Bn. Date of death: 18 September 1915. Service No.4888. Born in Killen Co. Tipperary. Enlisted in Naas while living in Birr. Died in Salonika. Age at death: 24.

Supplementary information: Son of Thomas and Mary Hogan, of Killimore, Co. Galway. He has no known grave but is listed on the Doiran Memorial in Greece.

HOGAN, M.: Rank: Private. Regiment or Service: Royal Irish Regiment. Unit: Depot. Date of death: 31 May 1917. Service No.6026. Grave or Memorial Reference: E. H. 100. Cemetery, St Michael's New Cemetery, Tipperary.

HOGAN, Matthew: Rank: Private. Regiment or Service: Leinster Regiment. Unit: 7th Bn. Date of death: 3 September 1916. Service No.3489. Born in Nenagh. Enlisted in Accrington while living in Accrington in Lancashire. Killed in action. He has no known grave but is listed on Pier and Face 16C on the Thiepval Memorial in France.

HOGAN, Michael: Rank: Stoker First Class. Regiment or Service: Royal Navy. Ship: HMS *Jason*. Date of death: 3 April 1917. Service No.K/26064. Died at Sea. Age at death: 24. His Naval records say he was born on 24 January 1885 which disagrees with the Commonwealth War Graves information. HMS *Jason* was a Torpedo Gunboat and sank after hitting a mine near Coll Island, Scotland. He has no known grave but is listed on Chatham Naval Memorial In England.

HOGAN, Patrick: Rank: Private. Regiment or Service: Leinster Regiment. Unit: 'D' Coy. 2nd Bn. Age at death: 33. Date of death: 16 June 1917. Service No.4774. Born in Nenagh and enlisted there also. Killed in action.

Supplementary information: Son of John and Sarah Hogan, of 15, Pound Street, Nenagh, Co. Tipperary. Grave or Memorial Reference: Has no known grave but is commemorated on Panel 44. Memorial: Ypres (Menin Gate) Memorial in Belgium.

HOGAN, Patrick: Rank: Private. Regiment or Service: Royal Irish Regiment. Unit: 6th Bn. Date of death: 20 June 1916. Service No.9736. Born in Borrisokane and enlisted in Nenagh while living in Borrisokane. Killed in action.

Supplementary information: Born Borrisokane, near Nenagh, Co. Tipperary. Grave or Memorial Reference: I. J. 16. Cemetery: Dud Corner Cemetery, Loos in France. Is this the P Hogan of the RIR commemorated on the Cahir Memorial.

Grave of F. Hollingsworth.

HOGAN, Philip: Rank: Corporal. Regiment or Service: Machine Gun Corps (Infantry). Unit: 82nd Coy. Age at death: 27. Date of death: 5 September 1918. Service No.49046. Born: Cashel, Co. Tipperary, enlisted in Cashel while living in Cashel.

Supplementary information: Son of John and Bridget Hogan, of Clonmel Poulmucka, Co. Tipperary. Grave or Memorial Reference: D. 855. Cemetery: Karasouli Military Cemetary. This Cemetery was 'fed' from casualty clearing stations on the Doiran front.

HOGAN, Stephen: Rank: Private. Regiment or Service: Royal Irish Regiment. Unit: 2nd Bn. Date of death: 24 August 1914. Service No.7309. Born in St Nicholas, Carrick-on-Suir, Co. Tipperary. Enlisted in Piltown, Co. Kilkenny while living in Carrick-on-Suir, Co. Tipperary. Died of wounds. He has no known grave but is listed on the Obourg Chyd Memorial 4 in St Symphrien Military Cemetery in Belgium.

HOGAN, William: Rank: Private. Regiment or Service: Irish Guards. Unit: 2nd Bn. Date of death: 27 November 1917. Service No.10396. Born in Puckane. Enlisted in Nenagh. Killed in action. He has no known grave but is listed on Panel 2 and 3 on the Cambrai Memorial in Louveral in France.

HOGAN, William: Rank: Gunner. Regiment or Service: Royal Garrison Artillery. Unit: 1st Mountain Battery. Date of death: 13 January 1916. Service No.25388. Born in Borrisokane. Enlisted in Nenagh while living in Borrisokane. Died in India. Age at death: 35.

Supplementary information: Son of the late Rody and Bridget Hogan. Grave or Memorial Reference: 2. D. 14. Cemetery: Rawalpindi War Cemetery in Pakistan.

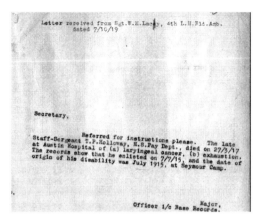

Letter received from Sgt. W.H. Lacey, 4th L.H. Fld. Amb. dated 7/10/19

Secretary,

Referred for instructions please. The late Staff-Sergeant T.P. Holloway, H.S. Pay Dept., died on 27/3/17 at Austin Hospital of (a) laryingeal cancer, (b) exhaustion. The records show that he enlisted on 7/7/15, and the date of origin of his disability was July 1915, at Seymour Camp.

Officer i/c Base Records. Major,

Thomas Patrick Holloway.

HOLDEN, James: Rank: Private. Regiment or Service: Royal Irish Regiment. Unit: 2nd Bn. Age at death: 50. Date of death: 9 May 1915. Service No. 6505. Born in St Mary's Clonmel and enlisted in Clonmel. Killed in action.

Supplementary information: Son of Edward and Mary Holden: husband of Mary Holden, of 30, College Street, Clonmel, Co. Tipperary. Grave or Memorial Reference: Has no known grave but is commemorated on Panel 33. Memorial: Ypres (Menin Gate) Memorial in Belgium.

HOLLAND, Stephen: Rank: Corporal. Regiment or Service: Royal Garrison Artillery. Unit: 108th Heavy Battery. Date of death: 5 July 1916. Service No. 26065. Born in Templemore. Enlisted in Templemore. Died of wounds. Grave or Memorial Reference: VIII. C. 96. Cemetery: Boulogne Eastern Cemetery in France.

HOLLAND, Thomas: Rank: Private. Regiment or Service: Royal Munster Fusiliers. Unit: 1st Bn. Date of death: 3 May 1915. Service No. 3959. Born in Nenagh. Enlisted in Limerick. Died of wounds in Gallipoli. He has no known grave but is listed on Panel 185 to 190 on the Helles Memorial in Turkey.

HOLLINGSWORTH, F.: Rank: Sergeant, Regiment or Service: Lincolnshire Regiment. Unit: 1st Bn. Age at death: Date of death: 24 June 1920. Service No. 5757. Cemetery: Mary's Churchyard, Tipperary. Grave location: The old military plot to the west of the church.

HOLLOWAY, Thomas Patrick: Rank: Staff Sergeant. Regiment or Service: Australian Infantry Base Depot. Unit: Pay Dept. Born in Cahir, Co. Tipperary. Next of kin listed as Nan Holloway of Cahir, Co. Tipperary. Date of death: 27 March 1917. Died of Laryingeal Cancer and Exhaustion in Austin Hospital in Melbourne. Spent four years in Dublin serving an apprenticeship. When thirty-two he was enlisted on 7 July 1915 in Melbourne, Australia. Height: 5'11". Weight: 11st 7lbs, Eyes: brown. Hair: dark brown. Complexion: fresh. Grave

Robert Howard.

or Memorial Reference: R.C. E. 675. (GRM/3★). Cemetery: Pine Ridge Memorial Park, Australia. He is also commemorated on the Cahir War Memorial.

HOOKWAY, James William: Rank: Private. Regiment or Service: Lancashire Fusiliers. Unit: 17th Bn. Date of death: 23 July 1916. Service No.14020. Born in Templemore. Enlisted in Salford in Lancashire. Killed in action. He has no known grave but is listed on Pier and Face 3 C and 3 D on the Thiepval Memorial in France.

HOPE, William Robert: Rank: Gunner. Regiment or Service: Royal Horse Artillery and Royal Field Artillery. Unit: 60th Battery. Date of death: 22 September 1914. Service No.50327. Born in Templemore. Enlisted in London. Died of wounds. Age at death: 19.

Supplementary information: Son of John and Annie Hope, of 125, Childeric Rd, Clifton Hill, New Cross, London. Grave or Memorial Reference: Military Row South Boundary. Cemetery: Maintenon Communal Cemetery in France.

HORAN, Joseph: Rank:

Private. Regiment or Service: Northamptonshire Regiment. Unit: 1st Bn. Date of death: 23 October 1914. Service No.5778. Born in Thurles. Enlisted in Seaforth in Lancashire. Died of wounds. Killed in action. He has no known grave but is listed on Panels 43 and 45 on the Ypres (Menin Gate) Memorial in Belgium.

HORGAN, John: Rank: Sergeant. Regiment or Service: Royal Irish Regiment. Unit: Depot. Born in Kenneigh, Co. Cork. Enlisted in Cork while living in Youghal, Co. Cork. Died at home. Date of death: 31 December 1915. Service No.1968. Cemetery, Clonmel, St Patrick's Cemetery. Grave location: 4. E. 114.

HOULIHAN. Thomas: Rank: Private. Regiment or Service: Canterbury regiment NZEF. Unit: 2nd Bn. Age at death: 27 Date of death: 5 October 1918. Service No.62321. Brother of O'**HOULIHAN, Patrick** who died with the Australians.

Supplementary information: Son of John Houlihan, of Abbeyville, Lorrha, Birr, Co.Tipperary. Grave or Memorial Reference: I. B. 30. Cemetery: Honnechy British Cemetery in the little village of Honnechy eight kilometres south-west of Le Cateau, in France.

HOURIGAN, William: Rank: Regimental Sergeant Major. Regiment or Service: 18th (Queen Mary's Own) Hussars. Date of death: 1 October 1918 or 2 October 1918. Service No.47638. Born in Tipperary and enlisted in Tipperary while living there also. Died in Tidworth, UK. Age at death: 40.

Supplementary information: Son of Richard and Johanna Hourigan, of 3, O'Connell Rd, Tipperary and also of Henry Street Tipperary. 24 years service. He was the nephew of William O'Meara, Henry Street, Tipperary and cousin of Mr Rafferty, Acraboy and Mr R Donovan, Brensha. Grave or Memorial Reference: About 28 yards north-east of gate. Cemetery: Shronnel Old Graveyard in Tipperary.

HOWARD, Robert: Rank: Private. Regiment or Service: Australian Pioneers. Unit: 2nd Pioneer Bn. Previous service with the Australian Colonial Forces, six years. Enlisted in Blackbutt, Queensland while living in Blackbutt. Occupation on enlistment: Storekeeper. Age 39 Complexion: fair. Eyes: blue. Hair: fair. Religious Denomination, C. of E. Served in Southampton, Havre, Portsmouth, Perham Downs, Fovant, Boulogne, Mosscar, and Belgium. Date of death: 14 October 1917. Service No.3541. Age at death: 41. Received multiple shrapnel wounds (left hand, right shoulder and legs) 12 August 1916 in France, hospitalised and rejoined his unit on 13 October 1917. Died of wounds received in action the next day. Buried in a temporary grave and re-buried in Hooge Crater cemetery in the presence of a Chaplain on 13 January 1920. Born in Dundrum, Tipperary, Ireland. Enlisted in Blackbutt, Queensland while living in Blackbutt. Died of wounds received in action.

Supplementary information: Son of John and Eliza Howard: husband of Barbara S. Howard, of Blackbutt, Queensland. Born at Dundrum, Co. Tipperary, Ireland. Grave or Memorial Reference: XIV, F. 3. Hooge Crater Cemetery Zillebeke, Belgium.

HOWSON, Samuel: Rank: Sergeant. Regiment or Service: Household Cavalry and Cavalry of the line including the Yeomanry and Imperial Camel Corps. Unit: 3rd Dragoon Guards, A Squadron. Date of death: 13 May 1915. Service No.3607. Age at death 36. Born in Cloghela, Tipperary. Enlisted in Canterbury while living in Poplur, E. . Killed in action.

Supplementary information: Son of the late Thomas Howson: husband of the late Emily Amelia Howson. Served in the South African Campaign. He has no known grave but is listed on Panel 3 on the Ypres (Menin Gate) Memorial in Belgium.

HUDSON, Albert Edward: Rank: Sergeant. Regiment or Service: Lancashire Fusiliers. Unit: C Company, 11th Bn. Date of death: 15 April 1918. Service No.19433. Born in Tipperary.

Enlisted in Bury, Lancsashire while living in Nottingham. Died of wounds. Age at death: 29.

Supplementary information: Husband of Lily Hudson, of 5, Standhill Cottages, Sneinton Hill, Nottingham. Grave or Memorial Reference: I. A. 24. Cemetery: Ebblinghem Military Cemetery in France.

HUGHES, Matthew: Rank: Rifleman. Regiment or Service: New Zealand Rifle Brigade. 4th Bn. 3rd. Age at death: 29. Date of death: 6 April 1918. Service No.62573. Embarked with the 30th Reinforcments H Company, 13 October 17 aboard the *Corinthic*. Killed in action on the Somme.

Supplementary information: Son of James and Susan Hughes, of Ballybeg, Littleton, Thurles, Co. Tipperary, Ireland. Grave or Memorial Reference: V. B. 4. Euston Road Cemetery, Colincamps in France.

HUMPHREYS, John William: Rank: Corporal. Regiment or Service: Royal Dublin Fusiliers. Unit: 'A' Coy. 5th Bn. Age at death: 29. Date of death: 25 April 1916. Service No.19222. Soldiers died in the Great War disagrees with the Commonwealth Commission on this one. It says he was born in Dublin and enlisted there also. Died at home.

Supplementary information: Born in Clonmel, Co. Tipperary. Son of Marguerite Elizabeth Warfield (formerly Humphreys), of 13, Swanage Rd, Wandsworth, London, and the late Robert Humphreys. Grave or Memorial Reference: RC. 484.

Cemetery: Grangegorman Military Cemetery in Dublin.

HUMPHRIES, Thomas Francis: Rank: Private. Regiment or Service: Royal Dublin Fusiliers. Unit: 1st Bn. He was previously with the Royal Munster Fusiliers where his number was 10021. Age at death: 20. Date of death: 26 March 1918. Service No.40905. Born in Castleconnell in Limerick and enlisted in Cork while living in Dublin. Died of wounds.

Supplementary information: Son of William and Bridget Humphries, of Tipperary: husband of Philomena Humphries, of 45, Synge Street, Dublin. Native of Tipperary. Grave or Memorial Reference: XXXI. J. 25. Cemetery: Etaples Military Cemetery in France.

HUNT, John: Rank: Private. Regiment or Service: Royal Irish Regiment. Unit: 'C' Coy. 6th Bn. Age at death: 27. Date of death: 20 November 1917. Service No.2621. Born in Moyglass in Tipperary and enlisted in Clonmel while living in Moyglass. Killed in action.

Supplementary information: Son of James and Johanna Hunt, of Grangebarry, Fethard, Co. Tipperary. Grave or Memorial Reference: I. C. 23. Cemetery: Croisilles Railway Cemetery in France.

Thomas
HUNT, T.: Rank: Private. Regiment or Service: Royal Irish Fusiliers. Unit: 8th Bn. Age at death: 23. Date of death: 1 January 1919. Service No.17052.

Supplementary information: Son of

The Late Lieutenant Ireland.

Regarding the deaths of Commander Usborne and Lieutenant Commander Ireland it is only permissible to say that they were killed in an accident. One may add that such an accident could never have taken place but for some unforgivable blunder on the part of someone concerned, and that one can hardly imagine anyone with mechanical knowledge making such a mistake.

Lieutenant-Commander de Courcy Wyndor Plunkett Ireland, R.N, was born at Clonmel on January 18th, 1885. He was promoted to Lieutenant-Commander, R.N, in February, 1914, and was appointed Squadron-Commander, R.N.A.S, in May, 1916. He was originally a specialist in wireless and joined the R.N.A.S. for wireless duties. He took his certificate, No 676 on a Bristol biplane at Eastchurch on November 1st, 1913, and soon became a daring pilot. At first he showed more daring than skill, as became the hasty Irish nature, but he acquired skill also, and became in time one of the finest pilots in the service. In his early days he was the hero of the famous upside down descent from 4,000 feet at Eastchurch. When war broke out he went to Flanders and did much gallant work. Later he commanded a coast defence station with conspicuous vigour and effectiveness, considering the material doled out to him. In him the service has lost a very gallant and energetic officer, and his striking personality will be greatly missed by all who have had to do with him.—"The Aeroplane".

De Courcy Wyndor Plunkett Ireland.sy of Karen Black, USA.

James Hunt of Grangebarry Fethard. Moglass Catholic Churchyard, Tipperary. Grave location: south–west of the church.

HUTCHINGS/HUTCHINS, Thomas Patrick:

Rank: Sergeant and Temporary Sergeant. Regiment or Service: Royal Army Veterinary Corps. Unit: Depot. Date of death: 31 January 1916. Service No.SE-429. Born in Tipperary, Ireland. Enlisted in Woolwich. Died at home. Age at death: 42.

Supplementary information: Son of Thomas and Johanna Hutchins, of 4, Albion Rd, Easton, Bristol. Grave or Memorial Reference: Screen Wall, 3 Gen. B. 205. Cemetery: Greenwich Cemetery, UK.

HUTTON, Peter:

Rank: Private. Regiment or Service: Northumberland Fusiliers. Unit: 2nd Garrison Bn. Date of death: 3 June 1917. Service No.50375. Formerly he was with the Royal Irish Rifles where his number was 1137. Born in Temple Moor, Co. Tipperary. Enlisted in Londonderry. Died in Mesopotamia. Grave or Memorial Reference: VI. N. 9. Cemetery: Basra War Cemetery in Iraq.

HYLAND, John:

Rank: Sergeant. Regiment or Service: Leinster Regiment. Unit: 1st Bn. Date of death: 13 March 1915. Service No.7399. Born in Clonmel. Enlisted in Clonmel. Killed in action. Age at death: 32.

Supplementary information: Son of James and Mary Hyland: husband of Freda Ernestine Hyland, of 35, Cremyll Street, Stonehouse, Plymouth. He has no known grave but is listed on

172

Panel 44 on the Ypres (Menin Gate) Memorial in Belgium.

HYNES, Philip: Rank: Private. Regiment or Service: Leinster Regiment. Unit: 2nd Bn. Age at death: 33. Date of death: 15 August 1915. Age at death: 33. Service No.4084. Born in Ballywilliam in Tipperary and enlisted in Nenagh. Killed in action.

Supplementary information: Son of P. and Margaret Hynes, of Capparoe, Nenagh, Co. Tipperary. Philip was the third son of a Crimean veteran and was at the taking of Armentieres on the 18 and 19 October 1914. His brother who also served with him fought side by side in many a bloody engagement was seriously wounded but survived the war. An extract of a letter sent to his Mother by Captain Daly, 2nd Bn Leinster Regt states:

> As regards Private Hynes, he was killed instantly by a shell on 20 August at Hooge, and he was buried at the Battalion Dressing Station on the right of the menin Road, about a mile before you reach Hooge. Father Maloney buried him in my presence, and that of about 10 men of the Company. A cross has been put over his grave, and the grave registration people will keep a record for his people. He was a very fine soldier, and it was a great grief to me and to B. Company to lose him. You can tell his mother so, and how much I sympathise with her. He was my best bomb thrower, and would have been mentioned in dispatches if only opportunity had come his way.

Dated 26 November 1915.

Grave or Memorial Reference: III. C. 20. Cemetery: Birr Cross Roads Cemetery in Belgium.

HYNES, Thomas: Rank: Rifleman. Regiment or Service: Royal Irish Rifles. Unit: 6th Bn. Age at death: 25. Date of death: 16 May 1917. Service No.2289. Born in Roscrea and enlisted in Birr Co. Offaly while living in Roscrea. Killed in action in Gallipoli.

Supplementary information: Son of John and Mary Ann Hynes, of Ballygurteen, Roscrea, Co. Tipperary. Grave or Memorial Reference: VII. B. 8. Cemetery: Struma Military Cemetery in Greece.

I

IRELAND, De Courcy Wyndor Plunkett: Rank: Squadron Commander. Regiment or Service: Royal Naval Air Service Age at death: 31. Date of death: 21 February 1916.

Supplementary information: Son of de Courcy Ireland, of Merton Hall, Borrisokane, Co. Tipperary: husband of Myrtle Ireland, of East Burnham House, Farnham Royal, Slough, Bucks. Grave or Memorial Reference: Naval. 23. 1191. Cemetery: Gillingham (Woodlands) Cemetery, UK.

IRELAND, Herbert Richard Hall: Rank: Lieutenant Colonel. Regiment or Service: Leinster Regiment. Unit: 3rd Bn. Secondary Regiment: Royal Munster Fusiliers Secondary. Unit: attd. 2nd Bn. Age at death: 39. Date of death: 28 March 1918. Awards: M C.

Supplementary information: Son of Mr and Mrs de Courcy Plunkett Ireland, of Merton Hall, Borrisokane, Co. Tipperary. Native of Clonmel, Co. Tipperary. Grave or Memorial Reference: Officers, B. 6. 15. Cemetery: St Sever Cemetery, Rouen in France.

IVERS, Patrick Joseph: Rank: Private. Regiment or Service: Royal Munster Fusiliers. Unit: 1st Bn. Age at death: 20. Date of death: 9 September 1916. Service No.6369. Born In Ballingarry Co. Tipperary and enlisted in Limerick while living in the Commons Tipperary. Killed in action.

Supplementary information: Son of Mrs Johanna Ivers, of Lisnamrock, Coalbrook, Thurles, Co. Tipperary. Grave or Memorial Reference: Pier and Face 16 C. Memorial: Thiepval Memorial in France.

J

JACKSON, Edward: Rank: Corporal. Regiment or Service: Royal Dublin Fusiliers. Unit: D Coy, 10th Bn. Date of death: 15 April 1917. Service No.27623. Formerly he was with the South Irish Horse where his number was 1307. Born in Aghancon, Roscrea, Co. Tipperary. Enlisted in Dublin while living in Fortwilliam, Roscrea. Killed in action. Age at death: 19.

Supplementary information: Son of Edward Jackson, of Crowthers, Yate, Bristol, late of Fortwilliam, Roscrea. He has no known grave but is listed in Bay 9 on the Arras Memorial in France.

JENNINGS, William Cornelius: Rank: Lieutenant. Regiment or Service: Australian Infantry, A. I. F. Unit: 53rd Bn. Age at death: 46. Date of death: 25 September 1917.

Supplementary information: Son of Patrick and Bridget Jennings: husband of Mrs N. M. Jennings, of 115, High Holborn, London, England. Native of Shanakill, Co. Tipperary, Ireland. Grave or Memorial Reference: XLIV. B. 16. Cemetery: Tyne Cot Cemetery in Belgium. He was mentioned in dispatches and was listed in the *London Gazette* on 4 January 1917, page 256, position 34 and also in the *Commonwealth of Australia Gazette* on 29 June 1917, page 1393, position 96.

JOBE, Patrick John:. Rank: Private-Lance Corporal. Regiment or Service: Royal Irish Regiment. Unit: 2nd Bn. Date of death: 21 October 1914.

Grave of William Johnston.

Service No.8398. Born in St Mary's, Clonmel, Co. Tipperary. Enlisted in Clonmel. Died of wounds at home. Age at death: 29.

Supplementary information: Husband of E. E. Jobe, of 48, George Road, Guildford. Grave or Memorial Reference: Between the Road and the Prysbytery. (This is the only Wargrave in this Cemetery). Cemetery: Oldcoates-Oldcoats (St Helen's) Roman Catholic Cemetery

JOHNSON, Frederick: Rank: Shoeing Smith. Regiment or Service: Household Cavalry and Cavalry of the line including the Yeomanry and Imperial Camel Corps. Unit: 6th Dragoons (Inniskillings). Date of death: 6 April 1915. Service No.3935. Born in Clonmell. Enlisted in Nenagh while living in Clonmel.

Supplementary information: Brother of Mr A Johnson, 41 Barrack Street, Waterford. Grave or Memorial Reference: 1. A. 75. Cemetery: Longuenesse (St Omer) Souvenir Cemetery in France.

JOHNSON, George: Rank: Private. Regiment or Service: Leinster Regiment. Unit: 'F' Coy. 1st Bn. Age at death: 24. Date of death: 8 April 1915. Service No.3259. Born in Roscrea and enlisted in Borris in Ossory. Killed in action.

Supplementary information: Son of George and Anne Johnson, of 43, Bunkers Hill, Roscrea, Co. Tipperary. Grave or Memorial Reference: Has no known grave but is commemorated on Panel 44. Memorial: Ypres (Menin Gate) Memorial in Belgium.

JOHNSON, Joseph: Rank: Private. Regiment or Service: Hampshire Regiment. Unit: 1st-4th(T. F) Bn. Date of death: 24 January 1916. Service No.2581. Born in Tipperary. Enlisted in Aldershot. Died of wounds in Mesopotamia. Age at death: 18.

Supplementary information: Son of Henry William and Margaret Johnson, of 63, Edward Street, Aldershot. Grave or Memorial Reference: I. C. 27. Cemetery: Amara War Cemetery in Iraq.

L/C. WILLIAM JOHNSTON, R.I.R., Died from pneumonia on 24th October, 1918. Son of Mr. Wm. John Johnston, Katesbridge.

William Johnston.

JOHNSTON, William: Rank: Lance Corporal. Regiment or Service: Royal Irish Rifles. Unit: 11th Bn. Age at death: 20. Born in Shanaghan Co. Down. Enlisted in Banbridge, Co. Down. Died of Pneumonia at home. Date of death: 24 October 1918. Service No.315. The image newspaper above is from the Banbridge Household Almanac 1919. Additional information: Son of William John and Bridget Johnston of Katesbridge Banbridge Co. Down. Cemetery, Marys Churchyard, Tipperary. Grave location: The old military plot to the west of the church.

JONES, Andrew: Rank: Pioneer. Regiment or Service: Corps of Royal Engineers. Date of death: 24 June 1916. Service No.163584. Formerly he was with the 12th Labour Battalion of the Royal Engineers. Born in Cahir. Enlisted in Ennis Co. Clare. Died at home.

Supplementary information: Brother of P Jones, Upper Jail Street, Ennis, Co. Clare. Grave or Memorial Reference: near the South boundary. Cemetery: Ennis (Clare Abbey) Cemetery.

JONES, Francis: Rank: Rifleman. Regiment or Service: London Regiment (Post Office Rifles). Unit: 8th Bn. Age at death: 21. Date of death: 30 January 1918. Service No.372261.

Supplementary information: Son of Mrs Margaret Jones of 7 Cashel Street, Clonmel. Cemetery, Clonmel, St Patrick's Cemetery. Grave location: 4. BB. 117.

JONES, Ludlow Norman: Rank: Lieutenant. Regiment or Service: Royal Air Force. Unit: 48th Sqdn. Age at death: 21. Date of death: 3 October 1918. His plane (F2b E2523) went down in flames near Ingelmunster at 6.30pm and he was missing in action with the pilot Lt J. B. Cowan. Lt Jones was the observer on that mission. Mentioned in the *London Gazette* 22 September 1914.

Supplementary information: Son of Ludlow Mainwaring Jones, of Moyroe Nanagh, Co. Tipperary, and Georgina Jones. Grave or Memorial Reference: XI. B. 13. Cemetery: Harlebeke New British Cemetery in Belgium.

JORDAN, Denis/Dennis: Rank: Lance Corporal. Regiment or Service: Royal Irish Regiment. Unit: 'B' Coy. 2nd Bn. Age at death: 24. Date of death: 28 June 1916. Service No.9789. Born in Thurles and enlisted in Templemore while living in Thurles. Killed in action.

Supplementary information: Son of John Jordan, of Pike Street, Thurles, Co. Tipperary. Grave or Memorial Reference: II. B. 2. Cemetery: Citadel New Military Cemetery, Fricourt in France.

JOY, James: Rank: Private. Regiment or Service: South Wales Borderers Unit: 1st Bn. Age at death: 27. Date of death: 9 June 1915. Service No.13064. Born in Carrickbog in Waterford and enlisted in Tonypandy in Wales. Killed in action.

Supplementary information: Brother of John Joy, of Friary Hill, Carrickbeg,

Carrick-on-Suir, Co. Tipperary. Grave or Memorial Reference: Has no known grave but is commemorated on Panel 14 and 15. Memorial: Le Touret Memorial in France.

K

KANE, J.F.: Rank: Sergeant. Regiment or Service: Highland Light Infantry. Date of death: 11 July 1920. Service No. TR/2128. Cemetery, Clonmel, St Patrick's Cemetery. Grave location: 4. C. 120.

KAVANAGH, Eugene: Rank: Sapper. Regiment or Service: Corps of Royal Engineers. Unit: 181st Tunnelling Company. Date of death: 28 November 1916. Service No. 139487. Formerly No 1396 Leic Regt, (181st Tunnelling Company, Royal Engineers). Born in Roscrea, King's Co. Enlisted in Birr. Died of wounds. Age at death: 43.

Supplementary information: Son of Kate Kavanagh, of Grove Street, Roscrea, Co. Tipperary, and the late Gilbert Kavanagh. Grave or Memorial Reference: XX. D. 1. Cemetery: Etaples Military Cemetery in France.

KAVANAGH, Thomas: Rank: Private. Regiment or Service: Leinster Regiment. Unit: 2nd Bn. Age at death: 21. Date of death: 3 September 1917. Service No. 3539. Born in Roscrea and enlisted in Birr. Died of wounds.

Supplementary information: Son of Gilbert and Kate Kavanagh, of Roscrea, Co. Tipperary. Grave or Memorial Reference: IV. M. 2A. Cemetery: Mont Huon Military Cemetery, Le-Treport in France.

Grave of George Kells.

KEANE, Michael: Rank: Private. Regiment or Service: Royal Irish Regiment. Unit: 2nd Bn. Date of death: 15 September 1914. Service No.7733. Born in Bansha Co. Tipperary. Enlisted in Clonmel while living in Bansha. Killed in action. He has no known grave but is listed on the La-Ferte-Sous-Jouarre-Memorial in France.

KEARNEY, Frank Michael: Rank: Private. Regiment or Service: Royal Munster Fusiliers. Unit: 2nd Bn. Date of death: 10 November 1917. Service No.18029. Formerly he was with the Leinster Regiment where his number was 1983. Born in Carrick-on-Suir, Co. Tipperary. Enlisted in Fermoy while living in Carrick-on-Suir, Co. Tipperary. Killed in action. He has no known grave but is listed on Panels 143 and 144 on the Tyne Cot Memorial in Belgium.

KEARNS, John: Rank: Private. No 4640, Leinster Regiment, 2nd Bn. Died 1 September 1916, Born: Cashel, Co. Tipperary, enlisted in Cork while living in Cashel. Killed in action in France during the Battle of the Somme trying to regain Thiepval Village from the Germans. Has no known grave but is commemorated on Pier and Face 3 A on the Thiepval Memorial in France.

KEATING, James: Rank: Private. Regiment or Service: Royal Irish Regiment. Unit: 2nd Bn. Date of death: 25 April 1914. Service No.6224. Born in Fethard. Enlisted in Clonmel while living in Fethard. Killed in action. Grave or Memorial Reference: XII.D. 16. Cemetery: Cabaret-Rouge British Cemetery, Souchez in France.

KEATING, John: Rank: Private. Regiment or Service: Irish Guards. Unit: 2nd Bn. Date of death: 30 September 1915. Service No.6316. Born in Cahir. Enlisted in Liverpool while living in Chelsea, Mass, USA. Killed in action. He has no known grave but is listed on Panels 9 and 10 on the Loos Memorial in France.

KEATING, Lawrence: Rank: Private. Regiment or Service: Loyal North Lancashire Regiment. Unit: 2nd-5th Bn (Territorial Force). Date of death: 26 October 1917. Service No.28585. Formerly he was with the Army Service Corps where his number was 25900. Born in Clonmel. Enlisted in Cahir while living in Westpool Co. Mayo. Killed in action.
Supplementary information: Son of Thomas and Mary Keating. He has no known grave but is listed on Panels 102 to 104 on the Tyne Cot Memorial in Belgium.

KEATING, Patrick: Rank: Private. Regiment or Service: Royal Dublin Fusiliers. Unit: 9th Bn. Age at death: 25. Date of death: 5 August 1917. Service No.23733. Born in Fethard and enlisted in Clonmel. Killed in action.
Supplementary information: Son of Mrs Bridget Keating, of Abbey Street, Fethard, Co. Tipperary. Grave or Memorial Reference: Has no known grave but is commemorated on Panel

44 and 46. Memorial: Ypres (Menin Gate) Memorial in Belgium.

KEATING, William: Rank: Private. Regiment or Service: Royal Irish Regiment. Unit: 2nd Bn. Date of death: 8 May 1915. Service No. 7477. Born in Powerstown Co. Tipperary. Enlisted in Clonmel while living in Barne Co. Tipperary. Killed in action. He has no known grave but is listed on Panel 33 on the Ypres (Menin Gate) Memorial in Belgium.

KEEFE, John: Rank: Private. Regiment or Service: Royal Irish Regiment. Unit: 6th Bn. Date of death: 3 September 1916. Service No. 11070. Born in Ahenny Co. Tipperary. Enlisted in Carrick-on-Suir while living in Ahenny. Killed in action. He has no known grave but is listed on Pier and Face 3A on the Thiepval Memorial in France.

KEENAN, John: Rank: Private. Regiment or Service: Leinster Regiment. Unit: 6th Bn. Date of death: 21 August 1915. Service No. 3006 and 6-3006. Formerly he was with the Connaught Rangers where his number was 16663. Born in Tipperary. Enlisted in Tipperary while living in Wishaw, Lanarks. Killed in action in Gallipoli. He has no known grave but is listed on the Special Memorial, B 79. Cemetery: Embarkation Pier Cemetery in Turkey.

KEHOE, Patrick: Rank: Rifleman. Kings Royal Rifle Corps. Unit: 11th Bn. Date of death: 3 September 1916. Service No. R-15491. Born in Mullinahone. Enlisted in Fithard while living in Waterford. Killed in action. He has no known grave but is listed on Pier and Face 13 A and 13 B on the Thiepval Memorial in France

KELLETT, Richard Henry Villiers: Rank: Lieutenant. Regiment or Service: Royal Field Artillery. Unit: 'B' Bty. 74th Bde. Age at death: 20. Date of death: 21 August 1916.

Supplementary information: Son of Maj. Gen. R. O. and Mrs Kellett, of Clonacody, Fethard, Co. Tipperary. Grave or Memorial Reference: II. C. 17. Cemetery: Couin British Cemetery in France.

KELLS, George: Rank: Private. Regiment or Service: Royal Inniskilling Fusiliers. Unit: 7th Bn. Born in Tashinney, Co. Longford. Enlisted in Belfast. Died of wounds at home. Date of death: 14 June 1915. Service No. 16747. Cemetery, Marys Churchyard, Tipperary. Grave location: Son of Mary Jane Kells of 54 Hillman St. Belfast. The old military plot to the west of the church.

KELLY, Denis: Rank: Private. Regiment or Service: Royal Irish Regiment. Unit: 2nd Bn. Date of death: 16 October 1914. Service No. 10712. Born in St Mary's, Clonmel, Co. Tipperary. Enlisted in Clonmel. Died of wounds. Grave or Memorial Reference: I. D. 9. Cemetery: Bethune Town Cemetery in France.

KELLY, James: Rank: Rifleman. Regiment or Service: Royal Irish Rifles. Unit: 7th Bn. Age at death: 25. Date of death: 16 August 1917. Service No.6133. Born in Thurles and enlisted in Thurles. Killed in action.

Supplementary information: Son of Richard and Julia Kelly, of Reiska, Kilcommon, Thurles, Co. Tipperary. Grave or Memorial Reference: Has no known grave but is commemorated on Panel 138 to 140 and 162 to 162A and 163A. Memorial: Tyne Cot Memorial in Belgium.

KELLY, John: Rank: Lance Corporal. Regiment or Service: Leinster Regiment. Unit: 2nd Bn. He was previously with the Roayl Irish Regiment where his number was 10443. Age at death: 22. Date of death: 12 April 1917. Service No.10738. Born in Ballingarry and enlisted in Kilkenny. Killed in action.

Supplementary information: Son of Martin and Mary Kelly, of Ballintaggart, Ballingarry, Thurles, Co. Tipperary. Grave or Memorial Reference: Bay 9. Memorial: Arras Memorial in France.

KELLY, John: Rank: Private. Regiment or Service: Royal Munster Fusiliers. Unit: 1st Bn. Date of death: 21 August 1915. Service No.5708. Formerly he was with the Lancers of the line where his number was 16037. Born in Ballyhale Co. Kilkenny. Enlisted in Dublin while living in Carrick-on-Suir, Co. Tipperary. Age at death 25. Killed in action in Gallipoli.

Supplementary information: Son of Mrs Hanoria Kelly, of Jamestown, Piltown, Co. Kilkenny, and the late Constable J. Kelly, (Royal Irish Constabulary). He has no known grave but is listed on the Helles Memorial on panel 185 to 190.

KELLY, Martin: Rank: Private. Regiment or Service: Irish Guards. Unit: 2nd Bn. Age at death: 22. Date of death: 27 November 1917. Service No.8905. Born in Emly and enlisted in Cashel. Killed in action.

Supplementary information: Son of Edward and Hannah Kelly, of Goldscross, Co. Tipperary. Grave or Memorial Reference: Has no known grave but is commemorated on Panel 2 and 3. Memorial: Cambrai Memorial in Louveral in France.

KELLY, Martin: Rank: Private. Regiment or Service: Leinster Regiment. Unit: 1st Bn. He was previously with the Irish Guards where his number was 3703. Age at death: 24. Date of death: 19 April 1915. Service No.9558. Born in Kilcommon and enlisted in Nenagh. Killed in action.

Supplementary information: Son of Anne Kelly, of 77 Silver Street, Nenagh, Co. Tipperary, and the late Timothy Kelly also of Silver Street. Grave or Memorial Reference: II. G. 40. Cemetery: Ypres Town Cemetery Extension in Belgium.

KELLY, Michael: Rank: Private. Regiment or Service: Royal Irish Regiment. Unit: 2nd Bn. Age at death: 26. Date of death: 19 October 1914. Service No.5177. Born in Carrick-on-Suir and enlisted in Tipperary while living in Carrick-on-Suir.

Killed in action. Michael was an old Contemptable, meaning he was a regular soldier at the outbreak of war and was stationed in India at that time. On the day his parents received the news of his death they were also informed of the death of his sister.

Supplementary information: Son of Michael and Nora Kelly (*née* Norris), of Long Lane, Carrick-on-Suir: husband of Ellen Kelly, of Rackham Street, Carrick-on-Suir, Co. Tipperary. His brother, Sergeant Kelly received the following letter from Sergeant Major Shaw dated 21 April, 1915:

Dear Sergeant Kelly,
I am writing to inform you of the death of your brother Martin, 'B' Company, who was killed by shell-fire in his billet on the 19th inst. I know you will feel his loss keenly, as he was a model soldier in every way, and a credit to his Company and Regiment in peace and war. I can add little else to lessen your grief, but as I had the opportunity of seeing him in hospital you will be pleased to know he was not disfigured in any way, and died peacefully in a war torn town in B---. I shall be pleased to hear from you at any time, as I would like if possible to keep in touch with all the old 'B' Company's N. C. O. As for myself I am keeping fit and doing my best,
Yours sincerely,
P Shaw, Sergeant Major.

He has no known grave but is com-

memorated on Panel 11 and 12. Memorial: Le Touret Memorial in France.

KELLY, Patrick: Rank: Private. Regiment or Service: Leinster Regiment. Unit: 2nd Bn. Date of death: 31 August 1916. Service No.6674. Born in Clonmel. Enlisted in Manchester. Killed in action. He has no known grave but is listed on Pier and Face 16C on the Thiepval Memorial in France.

KELLY, Thomas: Rank: Private. Regiment or Service: Royal Irish Regiment. Unit: 5th Bn. Age at death: 29. Date of death: 23 October 1915. Service No.2138. Born in Nenagh and enlisted there also. Died in Salonika.

Supplementary information: Son of Thomas and Norah Kelly: husband of Julia Kelly, of Chapel Street, Nenagh, Co. Tipperary. He died on his way back from the the front on the ship *Aquitania* just two days of landing and was buried at sea. He was a rural postman before he enlisted. He left behind a wife and child. He has no known grave but is listed on the Doiran Memorial in Greece.

KELLY, William:. Rank: Sergeant. Regiment or Service: Royal Irish Regiment. Unit: 2nd Bn. Date of death: 25 August 1918. Service No.5984. Born in Ballingarry. Enlisted in Templemore while living in Thurles. Killed in action. He has no known grave but is listed on Panel 5 on the Vis-En-Artois Memorial in France. Memorial.

KEMP, Joseph Ernest: Rank: Private. Regiment or Service: West Riding Regiment. Unit: 2nd Bn. Date of death: 24 August 1914. Service No.9096. Born in Tipperary. Enlisted in Leeds while living in Bradford,Yorks. Killed in action. Age at death: 31.

Supplementary information: Husband of Mrs Kemp, of 10 Snowden Street, Manningham Lane, Bradford, Yorks. Grave or Memorial Reference: II. E. 5. Cemetery: Hautrage Military Cemetery in Belgium

KENNA, Philip: Rank: Private. Regiment or Service: Leinster Regiment. Unit: 2nd Bn. Date of death: 18 July 1916. Service No.4009. Born in Lorrha, Co. Tipperary. Enlisted in Birr. Died of wounds. Grave or Memorial Reference: II. B. 48. Cemetery: Heilly Station Cemetery, Mericourt–l'Abbe in France.

KENNEDY, Edward: Rank: Trooper. Regiment or Service: Australian Light Horse. Unit: 10th. (4th Reinforcements). Previously served twelve years with the Queens Own Hussars an completed his service. Occupation on enlistment :soldier. Aged: 39 years 5 months. Height: 5' 7 ½". Weight: 143 lbs. Complexion: fresh. Eyes: blue. Hair: dark. Religious Denomination: RC. Date of death: 19 April 1917. Service No.876. Born in Clonniele also spelled Clownille, Co. Tipperary. Enlisted in West Perth, Western Australia. Next of Kin listed as niece Miss E Kennedy, West Perth, Florence Sh, W.A. (He was the Uncle of **McLOUGHLIN John Joseph**. Rank Gunner, No 323, KIA

16 November 1916). Killed in action in El Nunkheilah, Palestine. Served in Alexandria, Anzac, Heliopolis, The kit he signed for when he enlisted is as follows: Rifle: 1. Bayonet: 1. Boots brown: 2 pairs. Braces pairs: 1. Breeches pairs: 2. Field service cap: 1. Greatcoat: 1. Felt Hat: 1. White Hat: 1. Dungaree jacket:1. Jacket service dress: 2. Laces pairs: 2. Leggings C. P. brown: 1. Straps, chin,: 1. Bag kit universal: 1. Belts abdominal: 2. Brush hair: 1. Brush tooth: 1. Brush shaving: 1. Cap comforter: 1. Comb: 1. Disc identity with cord: 1. Drawers cotton pairs: 2. Fork: 1. Holdall: 1. Housewife(sewing kit): 1. Jersey: 1. Knife: 1. Razor (in case): 1. Shirts flannel: 2. Singlets: 2. Soap, piece: 1. Socks, pairs: 5. Spoon: 1. Towels: 2. Web equipment: 1. Tins mess: 1. Tins covers: 1, Field dressing, 1. His unburied body was last seen El Nunkheileh, Ref Beersheeba Map 1–86009 (A) (5) and 1–125000 Enemy Territory. Grave or Memorial Reference: He has no known grave but is listed on the Jerusalem Memorial on panel 58.

KENNEDY, James: Rank: Private. Regiment or Service: Royal Irish Regiment. Unit: 2nd Bn. Age at death: 28. Date of death: 6 September 1914. Service No.8334. Born in Ss Peter and Paul, Clonmel and enlisted in Clonmel. *Supplementary information*: Son of Patrick and Mary McCarthy Kennedy, of 34, River Street, Clonmel. Co. Tipperary. Memorial: La Ferte-Sous-Jouarre-Memorial in France.

Grave of P. Kennelly.

KENNEDY, James Patrick: Rank: Second Lieutenant. Regiment or Service: London Regiment (London Irish Rifles). Unit: 18th Bn. Secondary Regiment: Machine Gun Corps Secondary. Unit: attd. Age at death: 24. Date of death: 19 June 1918.

Supplementary information: Son of James P. and Ida M. Kennedy, of New Street, Carrick-on-Suir, Co. Tipperary. Grave or Memorial Reference: Has no known grave but is commemorated on Panel 11. Memorial: Ploegsteert Memorial in Belgium.

KENNEDY, John: Rank: Private. Regiment or Service: Royal Lancaster Regiment. Unit: 1st Bn. Date of death: 4 February 1917. Service No. 10342. Born in Tipperary. Enlisted in Blackburn. Killed in action. He has no known grave but is listed on Pier and Face 5D and 12B on the Thiepval Memorial in France.

KENNEDY, Laurence: Rank: Rifleman. Regiment or Service: Royal Irish Rifles. Unit: 6th Bn. He was previously with the Roayl Field Artillery where his number was 100327. Age at death: 18. Date of death: 27 October 1915. Service No. 7763. Born in Clonmel and enlisted in Clonmel while living in Kilganny Co. Waterford. Died in Gallipoli.

Supplementary information: Son of Martin and Mary Kennedy, of Upper Croan, Clonmel, Co. Tipperary. Grave or Memorial Reference: III. C. 70. Cemetery: East Mudros Military Cemetery in Greece.

KENNEDY, Matthew:. Rank: Private. Regiment or Service: Royal Irish Regiment. Unit: 1st Bn. Age at death: 21. Date of death: 16 March 1915. Service No. 10213. Born in Cormackstown and enlisted in Clonmel while living in Thurles.

Killed in action.

Supplementary information: Son of Johanna Kennedy, of The Heath, Cormackstown,Thurles, Co.Tipperary. Grave or Memorial Reference: Has no known grave but is commemorated on Panel 33. Memorial:Ypres (Menin Gate) Memorial in Belgium.

KENNEDY, Michael: Rank: Private. Regiment or Service: Royal Irish Regiment. Unit: 2nd Bn. Age at death: 39. Date of death: 24 May 1915. Service No.7108. Born in Cashel, enlisted in Clonmel while living in Killenaule Enlisted in Clonmel while living in Thurles. Killed in action defending the Ypres salient. According to the 1901 census he was one of a family of eight living in a two roomed cottage.

Supplementary information: Son of Michael and Bridget Kennedy, of Ladywell Street, Cashel, Co. Tipperary: husband of Mary Anne Kennedy, of Cashel Rd, Killenaule, Thurles, Co. Tipperary. Grave or Memorial Reference: Has no known grave but is commemorated on Panel 33. Memorial:Ypres (Menin Gate) Memorial in Belgium.

KENNEDY, Michael: Rank: Private. Regiment or Service: Royal Dublin Fusiliers. Unit: 10th Bn. Date of death: 11 October 1916. Service No.26298. Born in Tipperary. Enlisted in Manchester while living in Bansha, Co.Tipperary. Killed in action. He has no known grave but is listed on Pier and Face 5D and 12B on the Thiepval Memorial in France.

KENNEDY, Patrick: Rank: Private. Regiment or Service: Border Regiment. Unit: 1st Bn. Date of death: 15 October 1918. Service No.11964. Born in Cory Co. Sligo and enlisted in Wigan in Lancashire. Killed in action.

KENNY, CECIL JOHN, Lieut., 3rd (Reserve) Battn. The Royal Irish Regt., attd. Machine Gun Corps, 3rd *s*. of Harry Briscoe Kenny, of Clyduffe House, Roscrea, co. Tipperary, by his wife, Elizabeth, dau. of the late John Wallace, of Ballincor, Shinrone, King's County ; *b*. 8 May, 1895 ; educ. The Grammar School, Tipperary ; subsequently held an appointment in the Queenstown branch of the Bank of Ireland ; enlisted as a Motor Despatch Rider on the outbreak of war ; gazetted 2nd Lieut. in Jan. 1915, Lieut. in Sept. 1917 ; served with the Expeditionary Force in France and Flanders from Jan. 1916 ; was wounded at Mametz Wood the following July ; on recovery was attached to the Machine Gun Corps, and was killed in action at Ham, during the retreat from St. Quentin, 24 March, 1918. An officer wrote : " Your son Cecil, who was universally loved by his brother officers and men, died fighting in an endeavour to save his gun. For two days he had bluffed the Boche and held their attack, persuading the infantry to hold the line with him. Even when the Boche came to handgrips, he could have got away, but scorned to do so without his gun," and another : " Lieut. Kenny is sadly missed by his brother officers and men. He was always so good-humoured, a thorough gentleman and an all-round sportsman." *Unm.*

Cecil John Kenny.

Cecil John Kenny.

Supplementary information: Son of Martin and Mary Kennedy, of Drombane, Thurles, Co. Tipperary: husband of Ann Kennedy, of 26 Linney Street, Platt Lane Wigan. Grave or Memorial Reference: I. C. 5. Cemetery: Dadizeele New British Cemetery in Belgium.

KENNEDY, Patrick: Rank: Lance Corporal. Regiment or Service: Leinster Regiment. Unit: 2nd Bn. Date of death: 10 January 1917. Service No.4755. Born in Ballinaclough, Co. Tipperary. Enlisted in Nenagh while living in Nenagh. Killed in action. He has no known grave but is listed on Panel 127 on the Loos Memorial in France.

KENNEDY, Thomas: Rank: Private. Regiment or Service: Kings Royal Irish Hussars. Unit: 8th Bn. Date of death: 22 March 1918. Service No.11618. Born in Scrouthea, Co. Tipperary. Enlisted in Clonmel while living in Clonmel. Killed in action. He has no known grave but is listed on Panel 3 and 4 on the Pozieres Memorial in France.

KENNEFICK, Edward Hamerton: Rank: Captain. Regiment or Service: Essex Regiment. Unit: 9th Bn. Date of death: 8 July 1916.

Supplementary information: Son of the late Dr. Kennefick, of Auburn, Clonmel, Co. Tipperary. His brother, Capt. J.G.H. Kennefick also fell. Grave or Memorial Reference: Pier and Face 10 D. Memorial: Thiepval Memorial in France.

KENNEFICK, John George Hamerton: Rank: Captain. Regiment or Service: Essex Regiment. Unit: 3rd Bn. attd. 2nd Bn. Age at death: 34. Date of death: 20 April 1918.

Supplementary information: Son of the late Dr Kennefick and Mrs Kennefick (*née* Hamerton), of Auburn, Clomnel, Co. Tipperary. His brother, Capt. Edward Hamerton Kennefick, also fell. Grave or Memorial Reference: B. 5. Cemetery: Gonnehem British Cemetery in France.

KENNELLY, Michael: Rank: Sergeant. Regiment or Service: Irish Guards. Unit: 1st Bn. Date of death: 3 September 1917. Service No.6640. Born in Clogheen, Co. Tipperary. Enlisted in Dublin while living in Clogheen. Killed in action. Age at death: 27.

Supplementary information: Son of Alexander and Elizabeth Kennelly. Grave or Memorial Reference: I. H. 36. Cemetery: Bluet Farm Cemetery in Belgium. He is also commemorated on the

KENNELLY, P.: Rank: Private. Regiment or Service: Leinster Regiment. Date of death: 3 November 1918. Service No.5665. Age at death: 42. Grave or Memorial Reference: 5. M. A. 134. Cemetery: St Patrick's Cemetery, Tipperary.

KENNY, Cecil John: Rank: Lieutenant. Regiment or Service: Royal Irish Regiment. Unit: 3rd Bn. Secondary Regiment: Machine Gun Corps (Infantry) Secondary. Unit: attd.

Age at death: 25. Date of death: 24 March 1918. He worked for the Bank of Ireland.

Supplementary information: Son of Harry Briscoe Kenny and Elizabeth Kenny, of Clyduffe House, Roscrea, Co. Tipperary. Grave or Memorial Reference: II. C. 7. Cemetery: Ham British Cemetery, Muille-Villette in France. He is also listed on the 1914-1918. Bronze War Memorial in the Bank of Ireland in College Green, Dublin 2.

KENT, John: Rank: Private. Regiment or Service: Leinster Regiment. Unit: 1st Bn. Date of death: Two different given: 4 February 1915. and 14 February 1915. Service No.9323. Born in Borrisoleague, Co. Tipperary and enlisted in Birr. Killed in action.

Supplementary information: Son of Mrs Ellen Lawlor (formerly Kent), of 4, Sarsfield St, Thurles, Co. Tipperary. Grave or Memorial Reference: Has no known grave but is commemorated on Panel 44. Memorial: Ypres (Menin Gate) Memorial in Belgium.

KEOGH, Christopher: Rank: Private. Regiment or Service: Royal Irish Regiment. Unit: 2nd Bn. Date of death: 17 July 1918. Service No.5923. Born in Augrim Street, Dublin. Enlisted in Clonmel while living in Fethard. Died of wounds. Grave or Memorial Reference: II. N. 3. Cemetery: Gezaincourt Communal Cemetery Extension in France.

KEOGH, Denis: Rank: Private. Regiment or Service: The King's (Liverpool Regiment). Unit: 29th Bn. Age at death: 46. Date of death: 24 October 1919. Service No.100484.

Supplementary information: Husband of Mary Keogh, of 2 John St, Tipperary. Served in the South African campaign. Grave or Memorial Reference: XIX.A. 11A. Cemetery: Les Baraques Military Cemetery, Sangatte in France.

KEOGH, James: Rank: Private. Regiment or Service: Royal Munster Fusiliers. Unit: 2nd Bn. Age at death: 18. Date of death: 21 March 1918. Service No.18219. Born in Cashel, enlisted in Cashel while living in Cashel. He was previously with the Royal Dublin Fusiliers where his Number was 28044. Killed in action.

Supplementary information: Son of Thomas and Mary Keogh, of Carron, Cashel, Tipperary. Grave or Memorial Reference: Has no known grave but is commemorated on Panel 78 and 79. Memorial: Pozieres Memorial in France. This man is also on the Cahir Memorial.

KERR, Arthur: Rank: Private. Regiment or Service: Duke of Cornwalls Light Infantry. Unit: 1st Bn. Date of death: 2 October 1917. Service No.14586. Born in Tipperary. Enlisted in London while living in Walworth in London. Killed in action. Age at death: 22.

Supplementary information: Son of Mr and Mrs Kerr, of 175, Merrow Street Walworth, London. He has no known grave but is listed on Panels 80 to 82

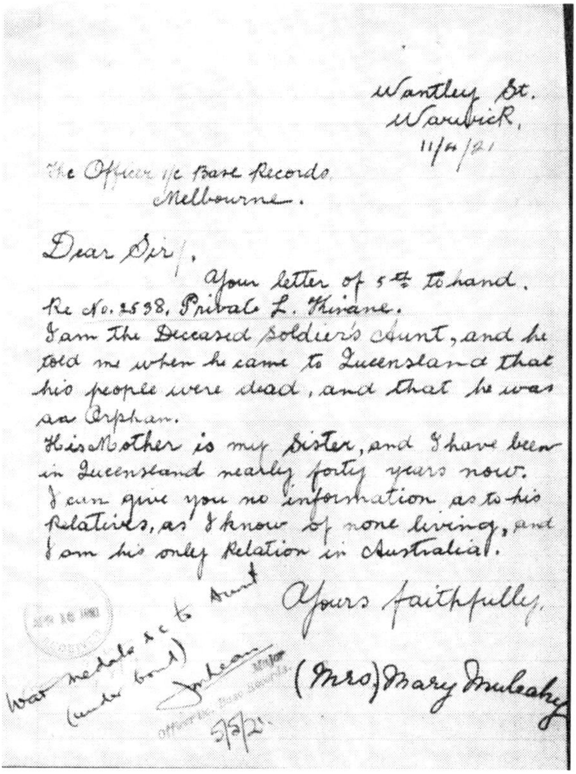

Wantley St.
Warwick,
11/4/21

The Officer i/c Base Records.
Melbourne.

Dear Sir/,

Your letter of 5th to hand.
Re No. 2538, Private L. Kinane.
I am the Deceased Soldier's Aunt, and he told me when he came to Queensland that his people were dead, and that he was an Orphan.
His Mother is my Sister, and I have been in Queensland nearly forty years now.
I can give you no information as to his relatives, as I know of none living, and I am his only Relation in Australia.

Yours faithfully,

(Mrs) Mary Mulcahy

War medals &c to Aunt (under bond)

Letter written by Lawrence Kinane's aunt.

and 163A on the Tyne Cot Memorial in Belgium.

KERR, Henry: Rank: Private. Regiment or Service: Seaforth Highlanders. Unit: B Company, 9th Bn. Date of death: 1 August 1917. Service No.S-11576. Born in Tipperary. Enlisted in Edinburgh, Midlothian. Died of wounds. Age at death: 23.

Supplementary information: Son of William Alexander Kerr (late Col. Sergeant. Seaforth Highlanders), of 6, Waverley Park, Edinburgh. Grave or Memorial Reference: IV. L. 12B. Cemetery: Mont Huon Military Cemetery, Le-Treport in France.

KIELY, John: Rank: Petty Officer. Regiment or Service: Royal Navy. Unit: Coast Guard Station (Southampton) Age at death: 45. Date of death: 11 March 1918. Service No.145087.

Supplementary information: Son of Nicholas and Emily Kiely: husband of Susan Kiely, of 10, Ebrington St, Kingsbridge, Devon. Born at Clonmel, Co. Tipperary. Grave or Memorial Reference: E. 121. Cemetery: Hove Old Cemetery, UK.

KIELY, Matthew: Rank: Private. Regiment or Service: Royal Irish Regiment. Unit: 2nd Bn. Date of death: 6 October 1916. Service No.9670. Born in St Marys Clonmel, Co. Tipperary. Enlisted in Clonmel while living in Knocklofty, Co. Tipperary. Died of Wounds. Grave or Memorial

Reference: I. I. 18. Cemetery: Berks Cemetery Extension in Belgium.

KIELY, Owen: Rank: Private. Regiment or Service: Royal Irish Regiment. Unit: 6th Bn. Date of death: 9 September 1916. Service No.9708. Killed in action. Age at death: 21.

Supplementary information: Son of Patrick Kiely of Hall Street Thurles. Grave or Memorial Reference: XXV. G. 1. Cemetery: Delville Wood Cemetery, Longueval in France.

KIELY/KIELLY, Thomas: Rank: Private. Regiment or Service: Australian Imperial Force. Unit: 3rd Bn. Date of death: 17 August 1916. Service No.3118. Born in Templemore. Attested in Holdsworthy, NSW 23 August 1915. Enlisted in Dawes Point, NSW. Aged: 26 ½. Height: 5'6 ½". Weight: 8st 3. Eyes: grey. Hair: ginger. Complexion: fair. Religious Denomination: R.C. Occupation on enlistment: Coal Lumper. Served in Marseilles, France, Alexandria, Tel-El-Kabir. Recipient of his personal effects listed as Miss May Johnston, 69 Tower Fort Street, Dawes Point, Sydney, NSW.

Supplementary information: Father. Mr T Kiely, Town Clerk, Main Street Templemore. Co. Tipperary. Cousin: Miss E Donohoe, 39 Lower North Street, Dawes Point, Sydney, NSW. Killed in action. He has no known grave but is listed on the Villiers-Bretonneux Memorial in France.

KIELY, William: Rank: Lance Corporal. Regiment or Service: Irish Guards. Unit: 1st Bn. Age at death: 26. Date of death: 6 November 1914. Service No.3541. Born in Gammonsfield Co. Tipperary and enlisted in Clonmel. Killed in action.

Supplementary information: Son of Richard and Mary Kiely, of Ballynavin, Kilsheelan, Co. Tipperary: husband of Mary Kiely, of Ballynavin, Kilsheelan, Co. Tipperary. Grave or Memorial Reference: Has no known grave but is commemorated on Panel 11. Memorial: Ypres (Menin Gate) Memorial in Belgium.

KINANE, Lawrence: Rank: Private. Regiment or Service: Australian Infantry. Unit: 5th Reinforcements, 49th Bn. Date of death: 6 January 1917. Service No.2538. Enlisted in Warwick in Queensland on 10 June 1916. Born in Tipperary. Enlistment details: Age: 19. Weight: 147 lbs. Height: 5'7". Complexion: medium. Eyes: grey. Hair: dark brown. Religious denomination: R.C. Died of broncho-pneumonia at No 3 New Zealand Hospital Codford. Age at death: 19.

Supplementary information: Son of Daniel and Catherine Kinane. Records also say he was born in Co. Cork, Ireland. He had no relatives alive and his medals were sent to his aunt: Mrs Mary Mulcahy on 3 August 1922. Grave or Memorial Reference: 42. Cemetery: Wiltshire. Codford Street, Mary (St Mary) New Churchyard. Wiltshire, UK.

KINANE, Michael: Rank: Private.

I join with my grateful people
in sending you this memorial
of a brave life given for others
in the Great War.

George R.I.

Letter of commiseration from the King of England.

Regiment or Service: Royal Dublin Fusiliers. Unit: 2nd Bn. Secondary Regiment: Royal Irish Regiment Secondary. Unit: formerly (4887) Age at death: 28. Date of death: 23 October 1916. Service No.43024. Born in Tipperary and enlisted in Clonmel while living in Newtown Co. Tipperary.

Supplementary information: Brother of John Kinane, of Newtown, Cappawhite, Co. Tipperary. Grave or Memorial Reference: Pier and Face 16 C. Memorial: Thiepval Memorial in France.

KING, Albert: Rank: Private. Regiment or Service: 8th (King's Royal Irish) Hussars Age at death: 34. Date of death: 24 July 1918. Service No.45465. Born in Bryansford and enlisted in Cahir while living in Clonmel. Died.

Supplementary information: Son of John King, of 14, Stanton Row, Clonmel, Co. Tipperary: husband of Margaret King, of 28, North Main St, Cork. Grave or Memorial Reference:

V. D. 10. Cemetery: Valenciennes (St Roch) Communal Cemetery in France.

KINNARNEY, William: Rank: Private. Regiment or Service: Leinster Regiment. Unit: 'A' Coy. 2nd Bn. Age at death: 37. Date of death: 9 June 1917. Service No.6853. Born Balltcommon King's County and enlisted in Tullamore. Died.

Supplementary information: Son of John Kinnarney. Husband of Annie Pender (formerly Kinnarney), of Dublin Rd, Roscrea, Co. Tipperary. Grave or Memorial Reference: VI. F. 8. Cemetery: Wytschaete Military Cemetery in Belgium.

KINNEAR, Robert Patrick: Rank: Sergeant. Regiment or Service: Corps of Royal Engineers. Unit: 57th Field Company, Royal Engineers. Date of death: 14 September 1914. Service No.995. Born in Templemore. Enlisted in Chatham in Kent. Killed in action. Age at death: 32.

Supplementary information: Son of

Miles and Mary Kinnear: husband of Eleanor Margaret Kinnear, of 22 Paget Street, Gillingham, Kent. Born at Chatham. He has no known grave but is listed on SP Mem 34 on the Vailly British Cemetery Memorial in France.

KINSELLA, James: Rank: Private. Regiment or Service: Irish Guards. Unit: 1st Bn. Date of death: 15 March 1917. Service No.2469. Born in Clonmel. Enlisted in Waterford while living in Pimlico in Middlesex. Killed in action. Grave or Memorial Reference: II. E. 3. Cemetery: Sailly-Saillisel British Cemetery in France.

KINSELLA, Patrick: Rank: Acting Sergeant Major. Regiment or Service: Leinster Regiment. Unit: 2nd Bn. Date of death: 3 September 1916. Service No.1335. Born in Clonmel. Enlisted in Clonmel. Killed in action. He has no known grave but is listed on Pier and Face 16C on the Thiepval Memorial in France.

KIRBY, Patrick: Rank: Private. Regiment or Service: Royal Irish Regiment. Unit: 2nd Bn. Age at death: 26. Date of death: 29 January 1916. Service No.4832. and 4812. Born in Golden, enlisted in Tipperary Town while living in Golden.
Supplementary information: Brother of Mr J. Kirby, of Thomastown, Golden, Co. Tipperary. Grave or Memorial Reference: I.A.1. Cemetery: Auchonvillers Military Cemetery in France.

KIRWAN, Patrick: Rank: Private. Regiment or Service: Royal Dublin Fusiliers. Unit: 2nd Bn. Age at death: 20. Date of death: 21 March 1918. Service No.25760. Born in Clonmel and enlisted there also. Killed in action.
Supplementary information: Son of Patrick and Ellen Kirwan, of Knocklofty, Clonmel, Co. Tipperary. Grave or Memorial Reference: Has no known grave but is commemorated on Panel 79 and 80. Memorial: Pozieres Memorial in France.

KIRWAN, William: Rank: Private. No 10797, Royal Irish Regiment, 2nd Bn. Died 8 December 1918. Born in Cashel, enlisted in Clonmel while living in Cashel. Buried in Charmes Military Cemetery, Essegney in France. Grave reference I. G. 18. Died four weeks after the war ended.

KNIGHT, Bertie: Rank: Drummer. Regiment or Service: Royal Berkshire Regiment. Unit: 2nd Bn. Date of death: 25 September 1915. Service No.7868. Born in Tipperary. Enlisted in London while living in Portsmouth. Killed in action. Age at death: 25.
Supplementary information: Son of Martha Tallyn (formerly Knight), of 88, Ranelagh Rd, Stamshaw, Portsmouth, and the late Serjt. J. Knight (2nd Bn. Royal Berkshire Regt). He has no known grave but is listed on Panel 7 and 8 on the Ploegsteert Memorial in Belgium.

KNOX, Hubert: Rank: Lieutenant Colonel. Regiment or Service: Manchester Regiment. Unit: 16th Bn.

Date of death: 13 October 1916.

Supplementary information: Son of Fitzroy Knox, D. L, of Brittas Castle, Thurles, Tipperary. Husband of Eleanor Alice Hector House (formerly Knox, of The Lyceum Club, 138, Piccadilly, London. Grave or Memorial Reference: VIII. B. 11. Cemetery: Caterpillar Valley Cemetery, Longueval in France.

L

LAMBE, Patrick: Rank: Private. Regiment or Service: Leinster Regiment. Unit: 2nd Bn. Age at death: 21. Date of death: 5 February 1918. Service No. 10357. Born in Clonmel and enlisted in Clonmel. Killed in action.

Supplementary information: Son of Patrick and Ellen Lambe, of 6, Cascade, Old Bridge, Clonmel, Co. Tipperary. Grave or Memorial Reference: II. F. 20. Cemetery: Unicorn Cemetery, Vend'huile in France.

LAVELLE, Garrett: Rank: Lance Corporal. Regiment or Service: Leinster Regiment. Unit: 2nd Bn. Date of death: 1 September 1916. Service No. 5172. Born in Carrigatroy, Co. Tipperary. Enlisted in Borrisokane while living in Birr. Killed in action. He has no known grave but is listed on Pier and Face 16C on the Thiepval Memorial in France.

LAWLER/LAWYER, Joseph: Rank: Private. Regiment or Service: Royal Irish Regiment. Unit: 6th Bn. Age at death: 29. Date of death: 7 June 1917. Service No. 8822. Born in Thurles and enlisted there also.

Supplementary information: Son of Michael Lawler, of College Lane, Thurles, Co. Tipperary. Grave or Memorial Reference: X. 76. Cemetery: Kemmel Chateau Military Cemetery in Belgium.

LAWLESS, George: Rank: Private. Regiment or Service: Irish Guards. Unit: 1st Bn. Date of death: 15 September 1916. Service No. 5451. Born in Tipperary. Enlisted in Clonmel. Killed in action. He has no

Joseph Loftus. Photograph courtesy of Bridget Brennan.

known grave but is listed on Pier and Face 7D on the Thiepval Memorial in France.

LAWLESS, William: Rank: Private. Regiment or Service: Suffolk Regiment. Unit: 7th Bn. Age at death: 39. Date of death: 26 February 1916. Service No.9084. Born in Tipperary and enlisted in Wisbech. Killed in action.

Supplementary information: Son of Edward and Bridget Lawless, of Ballynavin, Kilsheelan, Clonmel, Co. Tipperary. Grave or Memorial Reference: II. G. 9. Cemetery: Vermelles British Cemetery in France.

LEAHY, Henry Charles: Rank: 2nd Corporal. Regiment or Service: Royal Engineers. Unit: 54th Field Coy. Age at death: 28. Date of death: 30 October 1914. Service No.20008. Born in Clonmel and enlisted in Wrexham in Denbigshire. Killed in action.

Supplementary information: Son of Charles W. Leahy, of 4, Tivoli Terrace, Clonmel, Co. Tipperary. Grave or Memorial Reference: XVII. A. 8. Cemetery: Harlebeke New British Cemetery in Belgium.

LEAHY, John: Rank: Private. Regiment or Service: Irish Guards. Unit: 1st Bn. (Formerly Number 1383 Leinster Regiment, Birr Barracks). A member of the original British Expeditionary Force (known as the Old Contemptables) Age at death: 28. Died of wounds on Tuesday, 15 September 1914. Service No.2699. Born in Holycross in the tin roofed house beside Crokes shop. Enlisted in Templemore while living in Newbridge Co. Kildare.

Supplementary information: Son of the late Mr and Mrs Patrick Leahy, of Holy Cross, Thurles, Co. Tipperary: husband of Mary Leahy, of Old Connell, Newbridge, Co. Kildare. Grave or Memorial Reference: A. 5. Cemetery: St Nazaire (Toutes-Aides) Cemetery in France.

LEAHY, Patrick: Rank: Private. Regiment or Service: Royal Irish Fusiliers. Unit: 5th Bn. He was previously with the Royal Irish Regiment where his number was 300. Date of death: 31 August 1915. Service No.16227. Born in Tipperary and enlisted in Clonmel while living in Tipperary. Died of wounds at sea.

Supplementary information: Husband of Mary Anne Leahy, of 2 Dawson's Villa, Tipperary. Grave or Memorial Reference: Has no known grave but is commemorated on Panel 178 to 180. Memorial: Helles Memorial in Turkey.

LEAHY, Thomas: Rank: Private. Regiment or Service: Royal Irish Regiment. Unit: 1st Bn. Date of death: 24 April 1915. Service No.7199. Born in Killenaule. Enlisted in Clonmel. Killed in action. Age at death: 34.

Supplementary information: Son of Mr and Mrs Leahy. He has no known grave but is listed on Panel 11 on the Ypres (Menin Gate) Memorial in Belgium.

LEECH, James Michael:. Rank: Rifleman. Regiment or Service:

James Lonergan.

London Regiment. 18th Bn (London Irish Rifles). Date of death: 7 April 1917. Service No.593541. Born in Templemore. Enlisted in Marlebone while living in Exeter. Died of wounds. Age at death: 32.

Supplementary information: Son of Richard and Kate Leech, of Templemore, Co. Tipperary: husband of Mary C. H. Leech, of 773, Fulham Rd, London. Grave or Memorial Reference: XI. C. 28. Cemetery: Lijssenthoek Military Cemetery in Belgium.

LENIHAN, Michael: Rank: Private. Regiment or Service: Royal Munster Fusiliers. Unit: 2nd Bn. Age at death: 22. Date of death: 10 July 1917. Service No.6061. Born in Newport Co. Tipperary and enlisted in Limerick while living in Newport. Killed in action.

Supplementary information: Son of William and Mary Lenihan, of Killeen, Newport, Co. Tipperary. Grave or Memorial Reference: I. E. 29. Cemetery: Coxyde Military Cemetery in Belgium.

LEONARD, William: Rank: Private. Regiment or Service: Leinster Regiment. Unit: 1st Bn. Date of death: 27 October 1914. Service No.9441. Born in Cloughjordan, Co. Tipperary. Enlisted in Birr. Died at sea. He has no known grave but is listed on the Hollybrook Memorial, in Southampton, UK.

LILLY, Denis: Rank: Corporal. Regiment or Service: Leinster Regiment. Unit: 2nd Bn. Age at death: 35. Date of death: 27 June 1915. Service No.1680. Born in Roscrea and enlisted in Birr. Killed in action.

Supplementary information: Son of Mary Lilly, of Grove St, Roscrea: husband of Ellen Lilly, of Green St, Roscrea, Co. Tipperary. Grave or Memorial Reference: I. C. 7. Cemetery: Brandhoek New Military Cemetery in Belgium.

LINDEN, Michael: Rank: Private/ Driver. Regiment or Service: Royal Army Service Corps. Unit: 4th Base Remount Depot. Date of death: 11 January 1916. Service No.R4/062906. Born in Ballynahinch. Enlisted in Lathom Park while living in Blackpool. Died.

Supplementary Information: Husband of Amy Linden, of 5, Freckleton Street. Blackpool. Grave or Memorial Reference: VIII.C.80. Cemetery:

John Long.

Boulogne Eastern Cemetery in France. He is also commemorated on the Cahir War Memorial.

LOFTUS, Joseph: Rank: Private. Regiment or Service: Argyll and Sutherland Highlanders. Unit: 10th Bn. Age at death: 23. Date of death: 9 May 1917. Service No.S-10249. Born in Tipperary and enlisted in Glasgow while living in Tipperary. Killed in action. Patrick Loftus below was a cousin to Joseph. Two of Joe's elder brothers also served in First World War, Martin in the Royal Field Artillery and William in the Royal Munster Fusiliers.

Supplementary information: Son of James and Mary Loftus, of Borrisokane, Co. Tipperary. Grave or Memorial Reference: Bay 9. Memorial: Arras Memorial in France.

LOFTUS, Patrick: Rank: Private. Regiment or Service: Royal Irish Fusiliers. Unit: 'B' Coy. 8th Bn. Age at death: 27. Date of death: 27 April 1916. Service No.16673. Born in Galway and enlisted in Tipperary.

Supplementary information: Patrick and Joseph above were cousins. Son of Patrick and Ellen Loftus, of 10 Panton St, Belfast: husband of Margaret Loftus,

of 17 Spittal Street, Tipperary. Grave or Memorial Reference: Has no known grave but is commemorated on Panel 124. Memorial: Loos Memorial in France.

LONERGAN, Edward: Rank: Private. Regiment or Service: Irish Guards. Unit: 1st Bn. Date of death: 1 April 1915. Service No.4853. Born in Fethard. Enlisted in Seaford in Lancashire while living in Waterford City. Killed in action. Grave or Memorial Reference: I. E. 20. Cemetery: Guards Cemetery, Windy Corner, Cuinchy in France.

LONERGAN, James: Rank: Private. Regiment or Service: Australian Infantry. Unit: 48th Bn. Date of death: 12 October 1917. Service No.1693. Next of Kin Details: Mother, (died 6 June 18) Mrs Mary Lonergan. Served in Alexandria, Plymouth, Perham Downs, le Havre, Boulogne, Wimereux, Anzac, Belgium and the Bull Ring in Etaples. Born in Cahir, Tipperary. Enlisted in Adelaide, South Australia while he was a twenty-year-old labourer. Killed in action. Grave or Memorial Reference: Panel 7 - 17 - 23 - 25 - 27 - 29 - 31. He has no known grave but is listed on the Ypres (Menin

Gate) Memorial Belgium. He is also commemorated on the Cahir War Memorial.

LONERGAN, Jeremiah: Rank: Private. Regiment or Service: Irish Guards. Unit: 1ˢᵗ Bn. Date of death: 10 January 1915. Service No.4774. Born in Fethard. Enlisted in Clonmel. Killed in action. Grave or Memorial Reference: I. A. 6. Cemetery: Rue-Des Berceaux Military Cemetery, Richebourg-L'Avoue in France.

LONERGAN, Matthew: Rank: Scullion. Regiment or Service: Mercantile Marine Reserve. Unit: HMS *Princess Alberta*. Age at death: 17. Date of death: 21 February 1917.

Supplementary information: Son of John and Mary Lonergan, of Sherwood Street, Liverpool. Native of Co. Tipperary. Grave or Memorial Reference: 26. Memorial: Plymouth Naval Memorial, UK. The HMS *Princess Alberta* was on duty as a messenger and was travelling from Stavros to Mudros in the Aegean Sea. She hit a mine and sank just off the island of Lemnos.

LONERGAN, Patrick:. Rank: Private. Regiment or Service: Royal Irish Regiment. Unit: 1ˢᵗ Bn. Date of death: 1 December 1917. Service No.8775. Born in Clogheen Co. Tipperary and enlisted in Cahir. Died in Salonika.

Supplementary information: Son of Pat and Ellen Lonergan, of Chapel Row, Clogheen, Co. Tipperary. Grave or Memorial Reference: 166. Cemetery: Mikra British Cemetery, Kalamaria in Greece. He is also commemorated on the Cahir War Memorial.

LONERGAN, Patrick Rank: Private. Regiment or Service: Royal Irish Regiment. Unit: 1ˢᵗ Bn. Age at death: 40. Date of death: 16 March 1915. Service No.4690. Born in Fethard and enlisted in Clonmel while living in Clogheen. Killed in action.

Supplementary information: Son of John and Mary Lonergan: husband of

Edward Looby.

Margaret Lonergan, of 55, Thomas St, Clonmel, Co. Tipperary. Served on the North-West Frontier, 1897-8. Grave or Memorial Reference: Has no known grave but is commemorated on Panel 33. Memorial: Ypres (Menin Gate) Memorial in Belgium.

LONERGAN, Richard: Rank: Corporal. Regiment or Service: London Regiment. Unit: 8th Bn, (Post Office Rifles). Date of death: 20 September 1917. Service No. 371381. Born in Fethard. Enlisted in Clonmel while living in Fethard. Killed in action. He has no known grave but is listed on Panel 54 on the Ypres (Menin Gate) Memorial in Belgium.

LONERGAN, Richard: Rank: Private. Regiment or Service: Royal Irish Regiment. Unit: 6th Bn. Date of death: 7 June 1917. Service No. 5585. Born in Cahir. Enlisted in Cahir. Killed in action. Grave or Memorial Reference: B. 10. Cemetery: Irish House Cemetery in Belgium. He is also commemorated on the Cahir War Memorial.

LONG, John: Rank: Trooper. Regiment or Service: Australian Pioneers. Unit: 4th Bn. John left Rathcannon and sailed for Australia where he enlisted in Brisbane on 24 February 1916. Age: 33 Occupation: labourer. Weight: 136 lbs. Hair: brown. Eyes: black. Height: 5'8 ½". Complexion: dark. Religious denomination: R.C. He was aboard the *Seang Choon* from Brisbane to Plymouth and then to Folkstone to prepare for the trenches. Left Folkstone and sailed on the *Princess Clementine* for France and there trained in the famous Bull Ring in Etaples on 25 January 1917.

Supplementary information: Lists his sister Mary A Long, Rathcannon, Holycross to receive his estate in the case of his death. On 24 June 1917 he was wounded in action when he was hit by shrapnel from a high explosive shell. He suffered severe lacerations to his back and right leg. He was taken by field ambulance to the 53rd Casualty Clearing Station when he died the next day. Service No. 2662. Born in Rathcannon, Holycross, Tipperary. Enlisted in Brisbane, Queensland. Grave or Memorial Reference: III. D. 98. Cemetery: Bailleul Communal Cemetery Extension, (Nord), France.

LOOBEY, Edward: Rank: Private. Regiment or Service: Irish Guards. Unit: 1st Bn. Date of death: 26 September 1916. Service No. 6191. Enlisted in Dublin while living in Templemore. Killed in action.

Supplementary information: Brother of Mrs A. Fogarty, of Graique Cottage, Drom, Thurles, Co. Tipperary. Grave or Memorial Reference: Pier and Face 7 D. Memorial: Thiepval Memorial in France.

LOOBY, Edward: Rank: Private. Regiment or Service: Royal Army Service Corps. Date of death: 30 October 1918. Service No. S4-094598. Born in Clonmel. Enlisted in Clonmel while living in Clonmel. Died at Home. Age at death: 50.

Supplementary information:

Husband of Annie Looby of King Street, Clonmel. Grave or Memorial Reference: On the East boundary of the site of the old church. Cemetery: Newcastle Old Catholic Graveyard in Tipperary.

LOOBY, Patrick: (Also known as **LUBY, Patrick**). Rank: Commissioned as Chaplain to the Forces 4th Class on 22 August 1915. Regiment or Service: Army Chaplains Department. Date of death: 26 October 17.

Supplementary information The son of Denis and Alice Looby. Born in Cahir, Co. Tipperary on the 23 February 1889. Studied at St John's Waterford and the Irish College, in Paris. Ordained by Bishop Sheehan on the 21 June 1914. He was Curate of St Alphonsus in the Liverpool R C Diocese. Became a Chaplain to the forces in 1915 and was killed in action at the Battle of Passchendaele, Belgium. Grave or Memorial Reference: VI.E.13. Cemetery: Poelcapelle British Cemetery in Belgium. He is also remembered on the Aldershot Memorial. He is also commemorated on the Cahir War Memorial.

LOUGHNANE, Patrick: Rank: Lance Corporal. Regiment or Service: Royal Irish Regiment. Unit: 'B' Coy. 2nd Bn. Age at death: 28. Date of death: 8 May 1915. Service No. 5049. Born in Roscrea and enlisted in Tipperary while living in Roscrea. Killed in action.

Supplementary information: Son of Henry Loughnane, of Green St, Roscrea, Co. Tipperary, and Winifred Loughnane. Grave or Memorial Reference: Has no known grave but is commemorated on Panel 33. Memorial: Ypres (Menin Gate) Memorial in Belgium.

LOURY/LOWRY, Timothy: Rank: Lance Corporal. Regiment or Service: Royal Dublin Fusiliers. Unit: 2nd Bn. Date of death: 21 March 1918. Service No. 27487. Born in Tipperary. Enlisted in Limerick while living in Fanagown, Co. Tipperary. Died of wounds. Killed in action. He has no known grave but is listed on Panel 79 and 80 on the Pozieres Memorial in France.

LOVELL, Frank: Rank: Lance Sergeant. Regiment or Service: Royal Berkshire Regiment. Unit: 1st Bn. Date of death: 25 August 1914. Service No. 7708. Born in Templemore. Enlisted in Dublin while living in Penryn in Cornwall. Killed in action. Age at death: 24.

Supplementary information: Son of Fred and Annie Lovell, of Comford, Mylor Bridge, Cornwall. Born in Royal Berks Regt. Templemore. Maroilles Communal Cemetery in France.

LUCAS, George: Rank: Lance Sergeant. Regiment or Service: Royal Irish Rifles. Unit: 1st Bn. Age at death: 22. Date of death: 2 October 1918. Service No. 16800. He was awarded the Military Medal and mentioned in the *London Gazette*. Born in Roscrea and enlisted in Birr while living in Roscrea. Killed in action.

Grave of Patrick Lyons.

Supplementary information: Son of Robert Lucas, of 54 South Richmond Street, Dublin, and late Jane Mary Lucas. Born at Glasseloone, Roscrea, Co. Tipperary. Grave or Memorial Reference: IV. D. 21. Cemetery: Dadizeele New British Cemetery in Belgium.

LUCAS, Robert: Rank: Corporal. Regiment or Service: London Regiment. Unit: 2nd (City of London) Bn (Royal Fusiliers). Date of death: 16 August 1917. Service No.230748. Born in Tipperary. Enlisted in London while living in Westminster. Killed in action. Age at death: 20.

Supplementary information: Son of William and Margaret Lucas, of 64 Collin's Road, Southsea, Hants. He has no known grave but is listed on Panel 52 on the Ypres (Menin Gate) Memorial in Belgium.

LUCY/LUCEY, John: Rank: Private. Regiment or Service: Royal Irish Regiment. Unit: 2nd Bn. Age at death: 20. Date of death: 14 July 1916.

Service No.5088. Born in Moyne Co. Tipperary and enlisted in Thurles while living in Moyne. Killed in action.

Supplementary information: Son of Cornelius and Mary Lucy, of Lisheen, Moyne, Templemore, Co. Tipperary. Grave or Memorial Reference: Pier and Face 3 A. Memorial: Thiepval Memorial in France.

LUDDY, John: Rank: Private. Regiment or Service: Machine Gun Corps (Infantry). Unit: 101st Bn. Previously he was with the Royal Irish regiment where his number was 9890. Age at death: 30. Date of death: 1 August 1916. Service No.36405. Born in Ballybacon Co. Tipperary and enlisted in Clonmel while living in Ballybacon. Died of wounds.

Supplementary information: Son of Mrs M. Foley (formerly Luddy), of Gortnacour, Ardfinnan, Cahir, Co. Tipperary, and the late John Luddy. Grave or Memorial Reference: J. 37. Cemetery: Dernancourt Communal Cemetery Extension in France. He is also commemorated on the Cahir War Memorial.

LUKEMAN, Michael: Rank: Private. Regiment or Service: Royal Irish Regiment. Unit: 2nd Bn. Age at death: 28. Date of death: 19 October 1914. Service No. 5940. Born in Cashel, enlisted in Clonmel while living in Cashel, Killed in action.

Supplementary information: Son of Michael and Mary Lukeman, of Moon Lane, Cashel, Co. Tipperary. Grave or Memorial Reference: Has no known grave but is commemorated on Panel 11 and 12. Memorial: Le Touret Memorial in France.

LYNCH, Daniel: Rank: Private. Regiment or Service: Royal Munster Fusiliers. Unit: 1st Bn. Date of death: 25 April 1915. Service No. 9248. Born in Lattan Co. Tipperary and enlisted in Limerick while living in Limerick. Killed in action in Gallipoli. Grave or Memorial Reference: He has no known grave but is listed on the Helles Memorial on Panel 185 to Panel 190.

LYNCH, Edward: Rank: Private. Regiment or Service: Irish Guards. Unit: 1st Bn. Date of death: 5 November 1916. Service No. 10953. Born in Clonmel. Enlisted in Rochdale in Lancashire while living in Clonmel. Killed in action. Grave or Memorial Reference: X. O. 5. Cemetery: Guards Cemetery, Lesboeufs in France.

LYNCH, Patrick: Rank: Private. Regiment or Service: Royal Dublin Fusiliers. Unit: 2nd Bn. Age at death:

45. Date of death: 24 May 1915. Service No. 6696. Born in Newport Co. Tipperary and enlisted in Dublin while living in Tipperary. Killed in action

Supplementary information: Son of Thomas and Mary Lynch, of Cork Rd, Newport, Co. Tipperary. Husband of Ellen Lynch. Grave or Memorial Reference: Has no known grave but is commemorated on Panel 44 and 46. Memorial: Ypres (Menin Gate) Memorial in Belgium.

LYNCH, Philip: Rank: Private. Regiment or Service: Royal Irish Regiment. Unit: 1st Bn. Date of death: 3 April 1918. Service No. 10214. Born in Carrick-on-Suir, Co. Tipperary. Enlisted in Clonmel while living in Carrick-on-Suir, Co. Tipperary. Died in Egypt. Grave or Memorial Reference: M. 164. Cemetery: Cairo War Cemetery in Egypt.

LYONS, John: Rank: Private. Regiment or Service: Royal Irish Regiment. Unit: 2nd Bn. Date of death: 6 September 1914. Service No. 8534. Born in Kilsheelan Co. Tipperary. Enlisted in Waterford. Killed in action. He has no known grave but is listed on the La Ferte-Sous-Jouarre-Memorial in France

LYONS, John: Rank: Corporal. Regiment or Service: Royal Dublin Fusiliers. Unit: 1st Bn. Date of death: 4 June 1915. Service No. 10846. Born in Tipperary. Enlisted in Naas. Killed in action in Gallipoli. He has no known grave but is listed on Panel 190 to 196 on the Helles Memorial in Turkey.

LYONS, Michael: Rank: Private. Regiment or Service: East Lancashire Regiment. Unit: 6th Bn. Date of death: 14 August 1915. Service No.6167. Born in Clonmel. Enlisted in Blackburn in Lancashire. Died of wounds in Gallipoli. Age at death: 40. Grave or Memorial Reference: Sp Mem, A. 40. Cemetery: 7th Field Ambulance Cemetery in Turkey.

LYONS, Patrick: Rank: Private. Regiment or Service: Royal Irish Regiment. Unit: Depot. Date of death: 26 October 1914. Service No.1524. Born in Ballingarry. Enlisted in Thurles while living in Killenaule. Died at home. Age at death: 32. Grave or Memorial Reference: In the North East Part. Cemetery: Cemetery: Ballingarry Old Graveyard, Tipperary.

LYONS, William: Rank: Private. Regiment or Service: Leinster Regiment. Unit: 2nd Bn. Secondary Regiment: Labour Corps Secondary. Unit: transf. to (386936) 255 Area Employment Coy. Age at death: 27. Date of death: 20 October 1918. Service No.9804. Born in Boherlahan and enlisted in Clowmel. Died of wounds.

Supplementary information: Son of Thomas and Mary Lyons, of Kilshinane, Cashel, Co. Tipperary. Grave or Memorial Reference: IV. H. 30. Cemetery: Duhallow A. D. S. Cemetery in Belgium.

LYONS, William Rank: Private. Regiment or Service: Royal Irish Regiment. Unit: 2nd Bn. Date of death: 20 October 1918. Service No.10436. Formerly he was with the Dorset Regiment where his number was 25278. Born in Tipperary. Enlisted in Tonypandy, Glam. Grave or Memorial Reference: VII. D 5. Cemetery: Niederzwehren Cemetery in Germany.

M

MABER, Christopher: Rank: Private. Regiment or Service: Hampshire Regiment. Unit: 'Z' Coy, 2nd Bn. Date of death: 17 July 1916. Service No.3-4267. Born in Clonmel. Enlisted in Christchurch. Killed in action. Age at death: 18.

Supplementary information: Son of Charles and Barbara Maber, of 2 St Catherine's, Boscombe, Hampshire. II. F. 9. Cemetery: Auchonvillers Military Cemetery in France.

MACDONALD, Ronald Francis Keith: Rank: Private. Regiment or Service: London Regiment. Unit: 28th (County of London) Battalion (Artists Rifles). Date of death: 25 December 1917. Service No.767182. Born in Newport Co. Tipperary. Enlisted in Gower Street, W. C. while living in London. Age at death: 25.

Supplementary information: Son of A. Le Clare Macdonald and Kathleen Macdonald: husband of Mary Ravenscroft (formerly Macdonald), of 86 Burford Lane, Lymm, Warrington. Grave or Memorial Reference: C. of E. 2070. Cemetery: Knutsford Cemetery, Cheshire.

MACKEY, Denis: Rank: Private. Regiment or Service: Royal Irish Regiment. Unit: 7th (South Irish Horse) Bn. Age at death: 29. Date of death: 21 March 1918. Service No.25578. Born in Fethard and enlisted in Limerick while living in Fethard. Killed in action.

Supplementary information: Son of Mr and Mrs James Mackey, of Moonroe, Fethard, Co. Tipperary. Grave or Memorial Reference: Has no known grave but is commemorated on Panel 30 and 31. Memorial: Pozieres Memorial in France.

MACKEY, Michael: Rank: Private. Regiment or Service: Royal Irish Regiment. Unit: 1st Garrison Bn. Age at death: 53. Date of death: 22 May 1917 Service No.9276. Information on this casualty is sketchy as he was only accepted for inclusion in the Commonwealth Wargraves Commission Database in February, 2006. He is not mentioned in Soldiers who died in the Great War publication for the Royal Irish Regiment.

Supplementary information: Son of James and Annie Mackey and husband of Teresa Mackey of Nenagh, Co. Tipperary. Grave or Memorial Reference: Nenagh (Barrack Street) Graveyard, Co. Tipperary.

MACKEY, William: Rank: Private. Regiment or Service: Royal Irish

Regiment. Unit: 2nd Bn. Age at death: 29. Date of death: 14 July 1916. Service No.7449. Born in Fethard and enlisted in Limerick while living in Fethard. Killed in action.

Supplementary information: Son of Mrs Hannah Murphy, of Coolmoyne, Fethard, Co. Tipperary. Grave or Memorial Reference: Pier and Face 3 A. Memorial: Thiepval Memorial in France.

MACKIN, James: Rank: Private. Regiment or Service: Corps of Royal Engineers. Date of death: 22 October 1916. Service No.46359. Formerly he was with the 130th Field Company, Royal Engineers. Born in Cahir. Enlisted in Cahir. Killed in action. Grave or Memorial Reference: IX. B. 1. 3. Cemetery: Regina Trench Cemetery, Grandcourt in France. He is also commemorated on the Cahir War Memorial.

MADDEN, David: Rank: Private. Regiment or Service: Royal Munster Fusiliers. Unit: 2nd Bn. Date of death: 11 January 1916. Service No.7347. Born in Cloneen Co. Tipperary. Enlisted in Newcastle West while living in Newcastle West. Died of wounds.

Supplementary information: III. L. 2. Cemetery: Niederzwehren Cemetery in Germany.

MADDEN, Frederick: Rank: Private. Regiment or Service: Canadian Infantry (Central Ontario Regiment) Unit: 3rd Bn. Age at death: 23. Date of death: 8 October 1916. Service No.A-4146

Supplementary information: Son of John and Alicia Madden, of Rackethall, Roscrea, Co. Tipperary, Ireland. Memorial: Vimy Memorial, France. Data from the reverse of the enlistment document: Age on Enlistment: 21 Years. 4 Months. Height: 5' 10". Eye colour: blue. Complexion: dark. Hair colour: dark brown. Religion: C. of E.. Chest expansion: 2". Girth: 36. Date of Enlistment: 5 April 1915. Place of Enlistment: Toronto.

MAGUIRE, Dominic:. Rank: Private. Regiment or Service: Irish Guards. Unit: 2nd Bn. Date of death: 12 September 1917. Service No.9358. Born in Tipperary. Enlisted in Portarlington. Killed in action.

Supplementary information: Brother of Miss Kate Maguire. of Spa Street, Portarlington, Queen's Co. Grave or Memorial Reference: VIII. E. 7. Cemetery: Artillery Wood Cemetery in Belgium.

MAHER, Daniel: Rank: Private. Regiment or Service: Leinster Regiment. Unit: 2nd Bn. Previously he was with the Royal Irish regiment where his number was 5466. Age at death: 36. Date of death: 24 January 1917. Service No.15034. Born in Tipperary and enlisted there also. Killed in action.

Supplementary information: Son of Thomas and Mary Maher, of Ballingarry, Co. Tipperary. Husband of Ellen Maher, of 2, Lower Mayfield, Cork. Grave or Memorial Reference: I. M. 34. Cemetery: Maroc British Cemetery, Grenay in France.

MAHER, Denis: Rank: Private. Regiment or Service: Leinster Regiment. Unit: 2nd Bn. Date of death: 23 August 1916. Service No.3591. Born in Nenagh. Enlisted in Birr Co. Offaly. Killed in action.

Supplementary information: Son of Mr Denis Maher of Silver Street. Denis had six brothers all of whom served in wwi. He has no known grave but is listed on Pier and Face 16C on the Thiepval Memorial in France.

MAHER, Denis: Rank: Private. Regiment or Service: Irish Guards. Unit: 1st Bn. Date of death: 1 November 1914. Service No.870. Born in Roscrea. Enlisted in Glasgow while living in Glentara Co. Tipperary. Killed in action. He has no known grave but is listed on Panel 11 on the Ypres (Menin Gate) Memorial in Belgium.

MAHER, Denis: Rank: Lance Corporal. Regiment or Service: Lancashire Fusiliers. Unit: 20th Bn. Date of death: 23 July 1916. Service No.21838. Born in Tipperary, Co. Tipperary. Enlisted in Salford in Lancashire. Killed in action. He has no known grave but is listed on Pier and Face 3C and 3D on the Thiepval Memorial in France.

MAHER, Edward: Rank: Lance Corporal. Regiment or Service: Leinster Regiment. Unit: 1st Bn. Date of death: 7 February 1915. Age at death: 20. Service No.3485. Born in Roscrea. Enlisted in Birr. Killed in action.

Supplementary information: Son of Mrs A Maher. Grave or Memorial Reference: II. C. 1. Cemetery: Voormezeele Enclosures No.1 and No.2 in Belgium.

MAHER, Edward: Rank: Private. Regiment or Service: Royal army Medical Corps. Date of death: 1 November 1916. Service No.66429. Born in Tipperary. Enlisted in Southampton. Killed in action. He has no known grave but is listed on Pier and Face 4C on the Thiepval Memorial in France.

MAHER, Edward: Rank: Private. Regiment or Service: Connaught Rangers. Unit: 2nd Bn. Age at death: 27. Date of death: 10 December 1918. Service No.9668. Born in Templemore.

Supplementary information: Son of Patrick and Johanna Maher, of Church Street, Templemore, Co. Tipperary. Grave or Memorial Reference: In the South-west corner. Cemetery: Thionville (Diedenhofen) French National (Mixed) Cemetery in France.

MAHER, Frank: Rank: Private. Regiment or Service: Royal Sussex Regiment. Unit: 7th Bn. Date of death: 7 October 1916. Service No.G-18128. Born in Thurles. Enlisted in London. Killed in action. He has no known grave but is listed on Pier and Face 7C on the Thiepval Memorial in France.

MAHER, John: Rank: Sergeant. Regiment or Service: Border Regiment. Unit: 7th Bn. Age at death:

Joseph Maher (9242) and his mother Catherine. Photogragh courtesy of Carmel Lee, Middlesex.

42. Date of death: 25 August 1918. Service No. 18788. He was awarded the Military Medal and mentioned in the *London Gazette*. Born in Munninahod Co. Tipperary and enlisted in Whitehaven in Cumberland. Killed in action.

Supplementary information: Son of Daniel Maher, of Mullinahone, Co. Tipperary: husband of Margaret Maher. Grave or Memorial Reference: VI. F. 35. Cemetery: Adanac Military Cemetery, Miraumont in France.

MAHER, John: Rank: Private. Regiment or Service: Royal Irish Regiment. Unit: 2nd Bn. Date of death: 14 July 1916. Service No. 7604. Born in Thurles. Enlisted in Thurles while living in Moyne. Killed in action. Age at death: 32.

Supplementary information: Son of John Maher and husband of Bridget Maher. He has no known grave but is listed on Pier and Face 3A on the Thiepval Memorial in France.

MAHER, John: Rank: Private. Regiment or Service: Royal Munster Fusiliers. Unit: 1st Bn. Date of death: 26 May 1915. Service No. 6308. Born in Templemore. Enlisted in Naas while living in Templemore. Killed in action in Gallipoli. He has no known grave but is listed on the Special Memorial 63 in Pink Farm Cemetery, Helles in Turkey

MAHER, John: Rank: Private. Regiment or Service: Leinster Regiment. Unit: D Coy, 7th Bn. Date of death: 28 March 1916. Service No. 1962. Born in Clonmel. Enlisted in Cahir while living in Clonmel. Killed in action. Age at death: 26.

Supplementary information: Son of Thomas F. and Ellen Maher, of 48, Rickham St, Clonmel. Grave or Memorial Reference: Sp Mem. 7. Cemetery: St Patricks Cemetery, Loos in France.

MAHER, James: Rank: Gunner. Regiment or Service: Royal Field Artillery. Unit: 'V' Trench Mortar Bty. (Lahore Div) Age at death: 32. Date of death: 11 August 1917. Service No.100515.

Supplementary information: Son of William and Johanna Maher,Victualler, of The Square,Thurles, Co. Tipperary. Grave or Memorial Reference: II. H. 9. Cemetery: Noeux-Les-Mines Communal Cemetery in France.

MAHER, James: Rank: Private. Regiment or Service: Irish Guards. Unit: 1st Bn. Age at death: 22. Date of death: 2 November 1914. Service No.4475. Born in Thurles and enlisted in Clonmel. Died of wounds.

Supplementary information: Son of Thomas and Ellen Maher, of 3 Mountain Rd, Cahir, Co. Tipperary. Grave or Memorial Reference: Has no known grave but is commemorated on Panel 11. Memorial:Ypres (Menin Gate) Memorial in Belgium. He is also commemorated on the Cahir War Memorial.

MAHER, James Berhard: Rank: Lance Corporal. Regiment or Service: Royal Fusiliers (City of London Regiment). Unit: 9th Bn. Date of death: 9 August 1917. Service No.62429. Formerly he was with the 3rd County of London Yeomanry where his number was 3690. Born in Thurles. Enlisted in Finsbury Square while living in Dalston. Killed in action.

Supplementary information: Son of Mr Pat Maher, Stradavoher, Thurles. He has no known grave but is listed in bay 3 on the Arras Memorial in France.

MAHER, Joseph: Rank: Sergeant. Regiment or Service: Connaught Rangers. Unit: 1st Bn. Date of death: 13 July 1918. Service No.9242. Born in Borrisoleigh,Templemore. Enlisted in Templemore while living in Templemore. Died in Mesopotamia (Iraq). Grave or Memorial Reference: He has no known grave but is listed on the Tehran Memorial in Iraq on Panel 5, central Column.

MAHER, Martin: Rank: Private. Regiment or Service: Royal Irish Regiment. Unit: 'C' Coy, 2nd Bn. Date of death: 19 October 1914. Service No.7643. Born in Two Mile Borris, Co. Tipperary. Enlisted in Glasgow while living in Two Mile Borris. Killed in action. Age at death: 34.

Supplementary information: Son of John and Sarah Maher. He has no known grave but is listed on Panels 11 and 12 on the Le Touret Memorial in France.

MAHER, Matthew: Rank: Private. Regiment or Service: Leinster Regiment. Unit: 2nd Bn. Age at death: 27. Date of death: 13 March 1916. Service No.8037. Born in Templemore and enlisted there also. Died of wounds.

Supplementary information: Brother of Sarah Maher, of New Row, Templemore, Co. Tipperary. Grave or Memorial Reference: V. C. 6A. Cemetery: Lijssenthoek Military Cemetary in Belgium.

MAHER, Michael: Rank: Private. Regiment or Service: Connaught Rangers. Unit: 1st Bn. Date of death: 11 July 1917. Service No.7759 and

Grave of Patrick Mahoney.

7799. Born in Portroe Co. Tipperary. Enlisted in Killaloe while living in Killaloe Co. Clare. Died of wounds in Mesopotamia. He has no known grave but is listed on Panel 40 and 64 on the Basra Memorial in Iraq.

MAHER, Patrick: Rank: Gunner. Regiment or Service: Royal Garrison Artillery. Unit: 24th Mountain Bty. Age at death: 35. Date of death: 9 June 1920 Service No. 27089.

Supplementary information: Son of Matthew and Mary Maher, of New Row, Templemore, Co. Tipperary, Republic of Ireland. Grave or Memorial Reference: Face 2. Memorial: Kirkee 1914-1918 Memorial in India.

MAHER, Patrick: Rank: Private. Regiment or Service: Royal Munster Fusiliers. Unit: 2nd Bn. Date of death: 16 November 1914. Service No. 10019. Born in Shinrone, Co. Tipperary. Enlisted in Limerick while living in Roscrea. Killed in action. He has no known grave but is listed on Panel 44 on the Ypres (Menin Gate) Memorial in Belgium.

MAHER, Thomas: Rank: Private. Regiment or Service: Royal Irish Regiment. Unit: 7th Bn. Date of death: 21 September 1918. Service No. 10565. Born in Ballymore Co. Tipperary. Enlisted in Tipperary while living in Cahervillahow, Co. Tipperary. Killed in action. Grave or Memorial Reference: II. F. 10. Cemetery: Wulverghem-Lindenhoek Road Military Cemetery in Belgium.

MAHONEY, Patrick: Rank: Private. Regiment or Service: Royal Irish Regiment. Unit: 3rd Bn. Born in Fethrad. Enlisted in Tipperary while living in Fethard. Died at home. Date of death: 20 August 1914. Service No. 2397. Cemetery, Redcity Cemetery, Tipperary. Grave location: In the north-east part.

Richard Mahood.

MAHONEY, Patrick:. Rank: Private. Regiment or Service: Royal Irish Regiment. Unit: 3rd Bn. Date of death: 20 August 1914. Service No.2397. Born in Fethard. Enlisted in Tipperary while living in Fethard. Died at home. Age at death: 41.

Supplementary information: In the North East Part. Cemetery: Red City Graveyard in Tipperary.

MAHONEY, Thomas: Rank: Driver. Regiment or Service: Royal Field Artillery. Unit: 'C' Bty. 2nd Bty. Age at death: 27. Date of death: 10 October 1918. Service No.W-99. Enlisted in Merthyr while living in Merthyr, Tydvil in Glamorganshire. Killed in action.

Supplementary information: Son of Mr and Mrs Thomas Mahoney, of Fennor, Udingford, Co. Tipperary. Grave or Memorial Reference: VI. D. 5. Cemetery: Highland Cemetery, Le Cateau in France.

MAHONEY/MAHONY, John: Rank: Corporal. Regiment or Service: East Lancashire Regiment. Unit: 2nd Bn. Date of death: 23 March 1916. Service No.9793. Born in Nehagh Co. Tipperary. Enlisted in Blackburn in Lancashire while living in Oswaldtwistle in Lancashire. Died. Grave or Memorial Reference: I. F. 11. Cemetery: Lapugnoy Military Cemetery in France.

MAHONY, Patrick: Rank: Private. Regiment or Service: Leinster Regiment. Unit: 2nd Bn. Age at death: 25. Date of death: 12 April 1917. Service No.5325.

Supplementary information: Son of Thomas and Honora Mahony, of Glenegad Rd, Clonmel, Co. Tipperary. Grave or Memorial Reference: Bay 9. Memorial: Arras Memorial in France.

MAHONY, Thomas: Rank: Captain (Quatermaster). Regiment or Service:

Royal Irish Regiment. Unit: 2nd Bn. Age at death: 43. Date of death: 10 January 1918. Awarded the Military Cross and listed in the *London Gazette*, also mentioned in Despatches.

Supplementary information: Husband of Mary Mahony, of Moor House, Colville Rd, Clonmel, Co. Tipperary. Grave or Memorial Reference: Officers, B. 1. 18. Cemetery: St Sever Cemetery, Rouen in France.

MAHOOD, Richard: Rank: Private. Regiment or Service: Royal Irish Regiment. Unit: South Irish Horse (7th Bn RIR). Age at death: 26. Date of death: 10 November 1917. Service No.1237. Entitled to the 1915 Star, the War Medal and the Vicotry Medal. He was discharged (due to sickness) on 29 June 1916.

Supplementary information: Eldest son of Robert and L. Mahood of 93 Sandymount Avenue Dublin. Cemetery, Saturday Marys Churchyard, Tipperary. Grave location: The old military plot to the west of the church.

MALCOLMSON, Hubert: Rank: Lt. Regiment or Service: Royal Irish Regiment. Unit: 6th Bn. Date of death: 16 September 1916. Clonmel Friends Burial Ground. Grave location: In south-west corner.

MALONE, John: Rank: Gunner. No 37047, Royal Garrison Artillery. Date of death: 4 November 1915. Born in Boherlahan, enlisted in Looe in Cornwall, UK while living in Tipperary. Died of Wounds in Gallipoli. Grave reference I. G. 16.

Buried in Green Hill Cemetery in Turkey.

MALONE, John: Rank: Private. Regiment or Service: East Lancashire Regiment. Unit: 2nd Bn. Date of death: 13 March 1915. Service No.9158. Born in Birdhill, Co. Tipperary. Enlisted in Nenagh. Killed in action. He has no known grave but is listed on Panel 18 on the Le Touret Memorial in France.

MALONEY, E.: Rank: Sub-Lieutenant (A). Regiment or Service: Royal Naval Volunteer Reserve. Unit: Hawke Bn. R. N. Div. Age at death: 20. Date of death: 8 March 1918.

Supplementary information: Son of William Joseph and Mary Frances Maloney (*née* Ryan), of Old Shanbally, Clogheen, Co. Tipperary. Grave or Memorial Reference: I. F. 8. Cemetery: Ribecourt British Cemetery in France. He is also commemorated on the Cahir War Memorial.

MALONEY, Michael: Rank: Private. Regiment or Service: East Lancashire Regiment. Unit: 2nd Bn. Date of death: 5 May 1915. Service No.11274. Born in Tipperary. Enlisted in Blackburn, Lancs while living in Church, Lancs. Killed in action. He has no known grave but is listed on Panel 5 and 6 on the Ploegsteert Memorial in Belgium.

MALONEY, Thomas: Rank: Private. Regiment or Service: Connaught Rangers. Unit: 2nd Bn. Date of death: 4 September 1914. Service No.7476. Born in Nenagh. Enlisted in Nenagh while living in Nenagh. Killed in action. He has no known grave but is listed on the Special Memorial 4 in Vailly British Cemetery in France

MANNING, Patrick: Rank: Private. Regiment or Service: Welsh Regiment. Unit: 1st-5th Bn. Date of death: 3 November 1917. Service No.240646. Born in Waterford. Enlisted in Pontypridd while living in Carrick-on-Suir, Co. Tipperary. Killed in action in Egypt. Age at death: 24.

Supplementary information: Son of Ellen Manning, of Rathgormack, Carrick-on-Suir, Co. Waterford. Grave or Memorial Reference: F. 17. Cemetery: Beersheba War Cemetery in Israel.

MANNING, Thomas: Rank: Private. Regiment or Service: Leinster Regiment. Unit: 6th Bn. Date of death: 12 June 1916. Service No.4488. Formerly he was with the Royal Field Artillery where his number was 100252. Born in Gamonsfield, Co. Tipperary. Enlisted in Clonmel while living in Kilsaheelan. Died at sea. He has no known grave but is listed on the Doiran Memorial in Greece.

MANSFIELD, John: Rank: Private. Regiment or Service: Royal Irish Regiment. Unit: 7th (South Irish Horse) Bn. Age at death: 25. Date of death: 21 March 1918. Service No.5271. Born in Newcastle and enlisted in Cahir while living in New Inn. Killed in action.

Supplementary information: Son of Patrick and Mary Mansfield, of Gargewood, Newcastle, Clonmel, Co. Tipperary. Grave or Memorial

Reference: Has no known grave but is commemorated on Panel 30 and 31. Memorial: Pozieres Memorial in France.

MANSFIELD, Martin: Rank: Corporal. Regiment or Service: Leinster Regiment. Unit: 7th Bn. Date of death: 2 September 1916. Service No.3607. Formerly he was with the Royal Irish Fusiliers where his number was 16031. Born in Clonmel. Enlisted in Cahir. Killed in action. He has no known grave but is listed on Pier and Face 16C on the Thiepval Memorial in France.

MANSFIELD, Maurice: Rank: Rifleman. Regiment or Service: Royal Irish Rifles. Unit: 1st Bn. Date of death: 9 May 1915. Service No.6911. Born in Carrick-on-Suir, Co. Tipperary. Enlisted in Templemore. Killed in action. Age at death: 32.

Supplementary information: Son of the late Maurice and Mary Mansfield. He has no known grave but is listed on Panel 9 on the Ploegsteert Memorial in Belgium.

MARA, Daniel: Rank: Private. Regiment or Service: Irish Guards. Unit: 2nd Bn. Date of death: 23 March 1918. Service No.4638. Born in Cahir. Enlisted in Clonmel. Killed in action. He has no known grave but is listed in Bay 1 of the Arras Memorial in France. He is also commemorated on the Cahir War Memorial.

MARKES, John Carlon: Rank: Major. Regiment or Service: Leinster

Thomas Patrick Marshall.

Regiment, Secondary Regiment: Lancashire Fusiliers Secondary. Age at death: 36. Date of death: 19 July 1916. Awards: Twice Mentioned in Despatches.

Supplementary information: Son of Mr and Mrs Alfred Markes: husband of Philomena Markes, of Glenlara, Tipperary, Ireland. Served in the South African Campaign (Mentioned in Despatches). Grave or Memorial Reference: L. 27. Cemetery: Carnoy Military Cemetery in France. He is also memorialised on a window in St Michael's Catholic church in Tipperary Town.

MARNANE, Patrick: Rank: Private. Regiment or Service: Connaught Rangers. Unit: 6th Bn. Age at death: 20. Date of death: 21 March 1918. Service No.5763. Born in Tipperary and enlisted in Tipperary while living in Tipperary.

Supplementary information: Son of Jeremiah and Kate Marnane, of 31 O'Connell Rd, Tipperary. Grave or Memorial Reference: Has no known grave but is commemorated on Panel 77. Memorial: Pozieres Memorial in France.

MARSHALL, Denis: Rank: Private. Regiment or Service: Connaught Rangers. Unit: 6th Bn. Date of death: 16 August 1917. Service No.4197. Born in Carrick-on-Suir. Enlisted in Clonmel while living in Carrick-on-Suir. Killed in action. Age at death: 44.

Supplementary information: Son of Denis and Elizabeth Marshall, of Long St, Carrick-on-Suir. He has no known grave but is listed on Panel 141 on the Tyne Cot Memorial in Belgium.

MARSHALL, Thomas Patrick: Also listed as **Patrick Thomas**. Rank: Sergt. Regiment or Service: Australian Field Artillery. Unit: 2nd Brigade. Date of death: 11 March 1918. Service No.3842. Born in Cloughjordan, Tipperary. Enlisted in Brisbane, Queensland on 22 December 1914. Age at death: 32. Occupation on enlistment: plumber. Height: 5'5¾". Weight: 130lbs. Complexion: ruddy. Eyes:

Grave of T. Mason.

blue. Religious denomination: R.C. Wounded in action (gunshot wound to the right leg) on 17 August 1917 in Belgium. Served in Southampton, France, Belgium, Lemnos, Alexandria, Gallipoli Peninsula, Roulles, Tel-El-Kebir and Marseilles.

Supplementary information: Mother Annie Marshall, Norman Street, East Brisbane. (Father dead). Eldest Brother: W Marshall, (Principal Lighthouse Keeper) Manham South Head, Swithin, Auckland, NZ. Killed in action. Buried by Revd M. O. O'Brien, attached 1st Aust, Divl Trps at Kemmel on 14 March 1918. Grave or Memorial Reference: O. 21. Cemetery: Kemmal Chateau Military Cemetery. Belgium.

MARSLAND, James Francis: Rank: Lieutenant. Regiment or Service: Leinster Regiment. Unit: 2nd Bn. Age at death: 39. Date of death: 15 August 1915. Awards: M C.

Supplementary information: Son of James Marsland, of Marine View, Helensburgh, Dumbartonshire: husband of Mary Marsland, of 25, Main St, Tipperary. Son-in-law of Mr William Casey, merchant, Main Street Tipperary. He was on a bombing party attacking German trenches with three men when a bomb he was holding was hit by a bomb thrown from the mens trenches causing it to explode. It shattered his head and body. He died the next day without regaining consciousness. Grave or Memorial Reference: I. A. 14. Cemetery: Lijssenthoek Military Cemetary in Belgium.

MARTIN, John: Rank: Lance Corporal. Regiment or Service: Royal Irish Fusiliers. Unit: 2nd Bn. Age at death: 35. Date of death: 17 May 1915. Service No. 5754. Born in Clonmel and enlisted in Newry while living in Oldbridge Co. Waterford. Died of wounds.

Supplementary information: Husband of Annie Martin, of 13, Quin's Lane, Clonmel, Co. Tipperary. Grave or Memorial Reference: I. H. 5A. Cemetery: Wimereux Communal Cemetery, Pas de Calais, France.

MARTIN, Joseph: Rank: Private. Regiment or Service: Irish Guards. Unit: 2nd Bn. Date of death: 2 July 1916. 0
On the second day of the battle of the Somme. Service No.8886. Born in Nenagh and enlisted there also. Killed in action.

Supplementary information: Son of John Martin, of Birr Rd, Nenagh, Co. Tipperary. Grave or Memorial Reference: II. K. 19. Cemetery: Essex Farm Cemetery in Belgium.

MARTIN, Maurice: Rank: Company Sergeant (C.Q.M.S). Regiment or Service: Royal Irish Regiment. Unit: 6th Bn. Date of death: 9 September 1916. Service No.9391. Born in Tipperary. Enlisted in Cahir while living in Tipperary. Killed in action. He has no known grave but is listed on Pier and Face 3A on the Thiepval Memorial in France.

MASON, James: Rank: Private. Regiment or Service: Irish Guards. Unit: 1st Bn. Age at death: 21. Date of death: 6 November 1914. Service No.4489. Born in Cahir and enlisted in Clonmel. Killed in action.

Supplementary information: Son of John and Elizabeth Mason, of Church Street, Cahir, Co. Tipperary. Grave or Memorial Reference: Has no known grave but is commemorated on Panel 11. Memorial: Ypres (Menin Gate) Memorial in Belgium. He is also commemorated on the Cahir War Memorial.

MASON, Patrick: Rank: Private. Regiment or Service: Royal Irish Regiment. Unit: 2nd Bn. Age at death: 25. Date of death: 14 July 1916. Service No.5926. Born in Clogheen and enlisted in Clonmel while living in Clogheen. Killed in action.

Supplementary information: Son of Mrs Ellen Mason, of Convent Rd, Clogheen, Co. Tipperary. Grave or Memorial Reference: Pier and Face 3 A. Memorial: Thiepval Memorial in

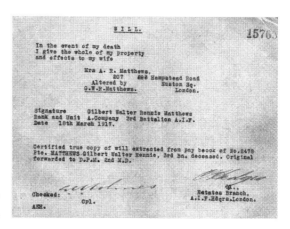

Gilbert Walter Rennis Matthews.

France. He is also commemorated on the Cahir War Memorial.

MASON, T.: Rank: Private. Regiment or Service: Royal Irish Regiment. Unit: A4 Bn. Age at death: 54. Date of death: 24 March 1918. Service No. 4/5042. Cemetery: Nenagh (Barrack Street) Old Graveyard. Grave location: In the north-east part near the North wall.

MASON, Thomas: Rank: Private. Regiment or Service: Royal Irish Regiment. Unit: 'B' Coy. 1st Bn. Age at death: 23. Date of death: 12 March 1915. Service No. 10199. Born in Nenagh and enlisted in Clonmel while living in Nenagh. Killed in action at St Eloi. Thomas had two brothers also serving, one of whom was wounded but both survived.

Supplementary information: Son of Thomas and Mary Mason, of Nenagh, Co. Tipperary. Grave or Memorial Reference: II. B. 17. Cemetery: Voormezeele Enclosures No. 1 and No. 2 in Belgium.

MATTHEWS, Gilbert Walter Rennie: Rank: Private. Regiment or Service: Australian Infantry, A.I.F. Unit: 3rd Bn. Age at death: 27. Date of death: 10 February 1919. Service No. 2478. Age on enlistment 23. Height: 5'8 ¼". Weight: 146lbs. Occupation on enlistment: Labourer. Complexion: fair. Hair: fair. Eyes: blue. Religious denomination: R.C. Passed medical 26 May 1915 in Liverpool, NSW. Born in Tipperary. Wounded in Shrapnel Gulley, Anzac Cove Gallipoli. Served in Tigne, Anzac, Malta, Bermingham, Epsom, Gallipoli, Epsom, Perham Downs, Calais Etaples, Rouen, Buchy, Havre, and Boulogne France. Next of Kin: Mrs E Keany, Church Hill Cottage, Fermoy, Co. Cork. Died of Broncho Pneumonia.

Supplementary information: Son of Joseph and Annie Matthews husband of Alice R Matthews, of 'Lilybrae' Cammeray Rd, Folly Point, North Sydney. Born at Tipperary, Republic of Ireland. His brother is listed as No. 479 Private J. B. Matthews, 3rd Bn, A

Grave of Henry Matthews.

216

I. F. 12 Camp, Longbridge, Deverill, Warminster. Grave or Memorial Reference: A. 76. Cemetery: Tidworth Military Cemetery, UK.

MATTHEWS, Henry: Rank: Sergeant. Regiment or Service: Royal Irish Fusiliers. Unit: 8th Bn. Born in Lurgan, Co. Armagh. Enlisted in Cork while living in Queenstown, Co. Cork. Died at home. Date of death: 9 January 1915. Service No. 15138. Cemetery: St Michael's New Cemetery, Tipperary Town. Grave location: E. H. 99.

MATTHEWS, Michael: Rank: Private. Regiment or Service: Leinster Regiment. Unit: 1st Bn. Age at death: 25. Date of death: 12 May 1915. Service No. 8421. Born in Roscrea and enlisted in Birr. Killed in action.

Supplementary information: Son of Timothy and Eliza Matthews, of 5 Cottage, Bunkershill, Roscrea, Co. Tipperary. Grave or Memorial Reference: Has no known grave but is commemorated on Panel 44. Memorial: Ypres (Menin Gate) Memorial in Belgium.

MAUNSELL, Michael: Rank: Private. Regiment or Service: Royal Irish Regiment. Unit: 2nd Bn. Age at death: 18. Date of death: 3 September 1916. Service No. 11349. Born Ss Peter and Paul in Clonmel and enlisted in Clonmel. Killed in action at Ginchy.

Supplementary information: Son of Michael and Ellen Fraher Maunsell, of 6 Storey's Place, Old Bridge, Clonmel, Co. Tipperary. Grave or Memorial Reference: Pier and Face

3A. Memorial: Thiepval Memorial in France.

McAFEE, Johnston:. Rank: Company Quartermaster Sergeant. Regiment or Service: Royal Irish Fusiliers. Unit: 2nd Bn. Age at death: 36. Date of death: 3 January 1917. Service No. 6717. Born in Portadown Co. Armagh and enlisted in Portadown also. Died in Salonika.

Supplementary information: Son of Mrs McClatchey, of 111 Donegall Rd, Belfast. Husband of Elizabeth Jane McAfee, of Portland School House, Birr, Co. Tipperary. Served in the South African Campaign. Grave or Memorial Reference: 760. Cemetery: Salonika (Lembet Road) Military Cemetery in Greece.

McBRIDE, John Albert: Rank: Sapper. Regiment or Service: Royal Engineers. Unit: 513th Field Coy. Age at death: 24. Date of death: 25 April 1918. Service No. 19807. Born in Borrisokane and enlisted in Birr while living in Borrisokane. Died of wounds.

Supplementary information: Son of D. and Mary Anne McBride, of Ballyhedon House, Borrisokane, Co. Tipperary. Educated at Cork College. Had passed final examination for Commission. Grave or Memorial Reference: III. A. 7. Cemetery: Aubigny Communal Cemetery Extension in France.

McCARTHY, Charles: Rank: Private. Regiment or Service: Irish Guards. Unit: No 4 Coy, 1st Bn. Date of death: 18 May 1915. Service No.3775. Born in Clonmel. Enlisted in Cork. Killed in action. Age at death: 23.

Supplementary information: Son of Michael Charles and Nannie McCarthy, of 2 Little William Street, Cork. A member of the Liverpool City Police. mobilized August, 1914. He has no known grave but is listed on Panel 4 on the Le Touret Memorial in France.

McCARTHY, Daniel: Rank: Driver. Regiment or Service: Royal Field Artillery and Royal Horse Artillery. Unit: 121st Battery. Date of death: 4 March 1915. Service No.14550. Born in Ardfinnan, Co. Tipperary. Enlisted in Clonmel. Died. Age at death: 18.

Supplementary information: Only son of Florence and Bridget McCarthy, of Kerry Street, Fethard, Co. Tipperary. Grave or Memorial Reference: I. A. 48. Cemetery: Longuenesse (St Omer) Souvenir Cemetery in France.

McCARTHY, Daniel: Rank: Corporal. Regiment or Service: Royal Garrison Artillery Secondary. Unit: attd. 'Y' 21st Trench Mortar Bty. Age at death: 45. Date of death: 26 June 1916. Service No.6341 He was awarded the Miltary Medal and mentioned in the *London Gazette*. Born in Carrick-on-Suir and enlisted in Bury. Killed in action.

Supplementary information: Son of Thomas and Kate McCarthy, of Ballyrichard Rd, Carrick-on-Suir, Co. Tipperary. Grave or Memorial Reference: I.C. 68. Cemetery: Norfolk Cemetery, Becordel-Becourt in France.

McCARTHY, Edward: Rank: Private. Regiment or Service: Royal Irish Regiment. Unit: Depot. Age at death: 48. Born St Mary's, Dungarvan, Co. Waterford. Enlisted in Dungarvan. Died at home. Date of death: 20 January 1915. Service No.7096. Data from the letter of final verification.

Supplementary information: Husband of Mary McCarthy of 4 Davis Street, Dungarvan. Cemetery, Clonmel, St Patrick's. Grave location: EA. 115.

McCARTHY, James (Cyprian): Rank: Private. Regiment or Service: Irish Guards. Unit: 2nd Bn. Age at death: 39. Date of death: 15 September 1916. Service No.9288. Born in Drumcondra in Dublin and enlisted in Dublin while living in Emly. Killed in action.

Supplementary information: Son of James McCarthy (S. M. 97th Foot): husband of Mary McCarthy (*née* O'Brien), of Emly, Co. Tipperary. M. A. Classical Teacher. Grave or Memorial Reference: Pier and Face 7 D. Memorial: Thiepval Memorial in France.

McCARTHY, James Francis: Rank: Corporal. Regiment or Service: Royal Irish Regiment. Unit: 1st Bn. Age at death: 33. Date of death: 24 January 1918. Service No.8674. Awarded the Albert Medal. Born in Clonmel and enlisted there also. Died of wounds in Palestine.

Supplementary information: Son of James and Johanna McCarthy, of 24, College St, Clonmel, Co. Tipperary. Grave or Memorial Reference: F. 37.

Cemetery: Jerusalem War Cemetery, Israel. Citation: An extract from *The London Gazette* dated 14 May, 1918, records the following : Albert Medal in Gold.

On the 24th January, 1918, in Palestine, Corporal McCarthy was cleaning grenades in his quarters, when the fuse of one became ignited. He carried it out to throw it into a safe place, but, finding a number of men standing around, he realised that he could not throw it anywhere without injuring his comrades. He clasped the grenade in both hands and held it close to his side. The grenade exploded, killing Corporal McCarthy, who by his devoted courage saved his comrades from serious injury.

McCARTHY, James Ransberry: Rank: Telegraphist. Regiment or Service: Royal Naval Volunteer Reserve. Unit: H.M. Yacht *Goissa*. Age at death: 24. Date of death: 15 November 1918. Service No.London-Z-5486.
Supplementary information: Son of James and Annie Jane McCarthy, of Jossestown, Lisronagh, Clonmel, Co. Tipperary. Grave or Memorial Reference: 31. Memorial: Chatham Naval Memorial, UK. H. M. Yacht *Goissa* was an armed patrol yacht and sank after hitting a mine in the Dardinelles on the 15 November 1918.
McCARTHY, Joseph: Rank: Private. Regiment or Service: Leinster Regiment. Unit: 1st Bn. Date of death: 21 April 1915. Service No.4195.

Born in Clare, Co. Clare. Enlisted in Menagh Co.Tipperary while living in Nenagh. Killed in action. He has no known grave but is listed on Panel 44 on the Ypres (Menin Gate) Memorial in Belgium.

McCARTHY, Michael: Rank: Private. Regiment or Service: Leinster Regiment. Unit: 2nd Bn. Age at death: 19. Date of death: 25 June 1916. Service No.2266. Born in Tiperary and enlisted in Tipperary while living in Tipperary. Died of wounds.
Supplementary information: Son of Daniel and Catherine (McCarthy), of Bansha Rd, Tipperary. Grave or Memorial Reference: II.E.154. Cemetery: Bailleul Communal Cemetery Extension (Nord) in France.

McCARTHY, Patrick: Rank: Private. Regiment or Service: Royal Irish Regiment. Unit: 2nd Bn. Date of death: 14 July 1916. Service No.7485. Born in Fethard. Enlisted in Clonmel while living in Fethard. Killed in action. He has no known grave but is listed on Pier and Face 3A on the Thiepval Memorial in France.

McCARTHY, Thomas Joseph: Rank: A February Cpl. Regiment or Service: Corps of Royal Engineers. Unit: 2nd Field Squadron. Date of death: 25 September 1916. Service No.25280. He won the Military Medal while he was with the 2nd Field Squadron of the Royal Engineers and is listed in the *London Gazette*. Born in Clonmel. Enlisted in Dublin. Killed in action. He won the Military Medal and is listed in the *London Gazette*. Grave or Memorial Reference: IV. G. 10. Cemetery: Guards Cemetery, LesBoeufs in France.

McCONNELL, James: Rank: Private. Regiment or Service: Leinster Regiment. Unit: 2nd Bn. Date of death: 20 October 1914. Service No.6856. Born in Tipperary. Enlisted in Tipperary. Killed in action. He has no known grave but is listed on Panel 10 on the Ploegsteert Memorial in Belgium.

McCORMACK, Daniel: Rank: Private. Regiment or Service: Canadian Infantry (Quebec Regiment) Unit: 14th Bn. Age at death: 32. Date of death: 26 September 1916. Service No.448557

Supplementary information: Son of Daniel and Johanna McCormack, of Kerry St, Fethard, Co. Tipperary, Ireland. Memorial: Vimy Memorial, France. Data from the reverse of the enlistment document: Age on Enlistment: 34 Years. 6 Months. Height: 5' 7". Eye colour: brown. Complexion: black. Hair colour: dark. Religion: R.C. Chest expansion: 3 ½". Girth: 37". He had a tattoo of a Roman's face on his right arm, a scar on his left thigh and a scar on his chin. Date of Enlistment: 12 April 1915. Place of Enlistment: Montreal.

McCORMACK, John Joseph: Rank: Captain. Regiment or Service: Northumberland Fusiliers. Unit: 27th (Tyneside Irish) Bn. Age at death: 27. Date of death: 28 April 1917. Resided at Castle Street, Nenagh.

Supplementary information: Son of John and Sarah McCormack, of Cudville, Nenagh, Co. Tipperary. John had been at the front for about twelve

Grave of Michael McCormack.

Grave of Thomas McDonald.

months. Grave or Memorial Reference: III. E. 22. Cemetery: Brown's Copse Cemetery, Roeux in France.

McCORMACK, Michael: Rank: Private. Number 9902, 3rd Battalion, Royal Irish Regiment. Born in Holycross. Enlisted in Clonmel while living in Holycross (Other records say Waterford). Date of death: 20 January 1916. Age at death: 19. Son of William and Brigid McCormack of Holycross. Buried in Holycross Abbey and moved during renovations to the left of the path in the graveyard. Official records say he died at home but oral tradition indicate his remains were brought home for burial.

McCORMACK, Thomas: Rank: Private. Regiment or Service: Machine Gun Corps (Infantry). Unit: 74th Bn. Formerly 32637 of the Cheshire Regiment. Born in Thurles and enlisted in Thurles. Age at death: 20. Died of wounds on Thursday 14 September 1916. Service No.14574.

Supplementary information: Son of William and Bridget McCormack, of Holy Cross, Thurles, Co. Tipperary. Grave or Memorial Reference: Soldiers' Plot. 178 (Screen Wall). Cemetery: Moston (St Joseph's) Roman Catholic Cemetery, UK.

McCORMACK, William:. Rank: Private. Number 14573. 6th Battalion Machine Gun Corps (Infantry) formerly 32726 Cheshire Regiment. Killed in action on Friday 22 March 1918. Born in Holycross. Enlisted in Thurles while living in Holycross. Son of William and Brigid McCormack of Holycross. Has no known grave but is commemorated on the Arras Memorial, Pas de Calais, France, on Bay 10.

McDERMOTT, Michael Edward: Rank: Sergeant. Regiment or Service: Royal Irish Regiment. Unit: 1st Bn.

Age at death: 29. Date of death: 10 February 1915. Service No.9436.

Supplementary information: Husband of Elizabeth Florence McDermott, of 9 Cross Street, Clonmel, Co. Tipperary. Grave or Memorial Reference: Has no known grave but is commemorated on Panel 33. Memorial: Ypres (Menin Gate) Memorial in Belgium.

McDONALD, Ronald Francis Keith: Rank: Private. Regiment or Service: London Regiment. Unit: 28th (County of London) Battalion (Artists Rifles). Date of death: 25 December 1917. Service No.767182. Born in Newport Co. Tipperary. Enlisted in Gower Street, W. C. while living in London. Age at death 25.

Supplementary information: Son of A. Le Clare Macdonald and Kathleen Macdonald: husband of Mary Ravenscroft (formerly Macdonald), of 86 Burford Lane, Lymm, Warrington. Grave or Memorial Reference: C of E. 2070. Cemetery: Knutsford Cemetery, Cheshire.

McDONALD, Thomas: Rank: Honorary Lieutennant (Quartermaster) Regiment or Service: Royal Irish Regiment. Unit: 5th Bn. Date of death: 23 November 1914. Age at death 42.

Supplementary information: Husband of Mary McDonald of 31 Woodville Terrace, Clonmel. Grave or Memorial Reference: 4 IC. 108. Cemetery: St Patricks Cemetery, Clonmel, Co. Tipperary.

McDONOUGH, Richard: Rank:

Sergeant. Regiment or Service: Irish Guards. Unit: 1st Bn. Age at death: 28. Date of death: 13 May 1918. Service No.3432. Born in Aherlow Co. Tipperary and enlisted in Dublin while living in Lisvernance Co. Tipperary.

Supplementary information: Son of Stephen and Bridget McDonough, of Lisvemane, Aherlow, Co. Tipperary. Grave or Memorial Reference: I. B. 31. Cemetery: Bagneux British Cemetery, Gezauncourt in France.

McDONOUGH, Stephen: Rank: Lance Corporal. Regiment or Service: Irish Guards. Unit: 1st Bn. Age at death: 28. Date of death: 11 September 1916. Service No.7343. Born in Aherlow Co. Tipperary and enlisted in Dublin while living in Castleconnell in Limerick. Killed in action.

Supplementary information: Son of Stephen and Bridget McDonough, of Liswarrinane, Aherlow, Co. Tipperary: husband of Katie Hayes McDonough, of 29 Main Street, Tipperary. A draper's assistant. Grave or Memorial Reference: Pier and Face 7 D. Memorial: Thiepval Memorial in France.

McELLIGOTT, John: Rank: Private. No 9598, Royal Irish Regiment, 1st Bn, Died 14 February 1915, Born: Cashel, Co. Tipperary enlisted in Templemore while living in Kildion Co. Limeick. Killed in action. Enlisted in Templemore while living in Kildimo, Co. Limerick. Has no known grave but is listed on Panel 33 on the Ypres (Menin Gate) Memorial in Belgium. Killed in action during the lull of the

McFALL D.
McFALL J.
McFALL R.
McFARLAND G.
McGEOWN R.
McGIMPSEY R.
McGUGAN J. SERVED AS
        McFADDEN J.
McGUIGGAN J.
McILROY W.
McINTOSH J.
McINTYRE R.
MACKEN F.

THOMA
THOMP
THOMP
THOMS
TORRA
TRIBBI
TURLE
TURNI
UPRICI
VICKE
VINT
VINT

Photograph courtesy of Tommy McClimmonds of Banbridge.

first and second battle of Ypres.

McELLIGOTT, Patrick: Rank: Private. Regiment or Service: Royal Irish Regiment. Unit: 2nd Bn. Date of death: 2 July 1916. Service No. 7525. Born in Tipperary. Enlisted in Cashel. Died of wounds. Grave or Memorial Reference: I. G. 8. Cemetery: Heilly Station Cemetery, Mericourt-l'Abbe in France.

McENIRY, David Bishop Mary: Rank: Gunner. Regiment or Service: Royal Garrison Artillery. Unit: 61st Trench Mortar Battery. Service No. 7637. Born in Clonmel. Enlisted in St Pauls Churchyard in Middlesex while living in Clonmel. Killed in action. Age at death 33.

Supplementary information: Son of Dr David McEniry and Mrs Mary McEniry, of Ballymacarbry, Co. Waterford. Grave or Memorial Reference: I. M. 15. Cemetery: Spoilbank Cemetery in Belgium.

McENIRY, Patrick B.: Rank: Private First Class. Regiment or Service:.

Unit: 6th Bn. Born in Enily, Tipperary. Service Number: not given. Died of wounds. Date of death: 24 August 1918. Grave or Memorial Reference: Plot A, Row 34, Grave 11. Cemetery: Somme Amercian Cemetery, Bony, France.

McFADDEN, James: Alias, correct name is **McGUGAN** P.

McGANN, F. V.: Rank: Lance Corporal. Regiment or Service: 21st (Empress of India's) Lancers Age at death: 48. Date of death: 29 October 1917. Service No. 11587.

Supplementary information: Long Service and Good Conduct Medal. Husband of Bridget McGann, of 30 Fauconberg Rd, Grove Park, Chiswick. Served in the Soudan Campaign (1898). Born at Clonmel, Co. Tipperary. Grave or Memorial Reference: Screen Wall. N. 372. Cemetery: Chiswick Old Cemetery, UK.

McGOWAN, Harry: Rank: Rifleman. Regiment or Service: Royal Irish Rifles. Unit: 18th Bn and 23rd Entrenching Battalion late 14th

The burnt remains of Private McGowran's Victory medal purchased on the internet from a dealer in the UK.

Bn. Date of death: 24 March 1918. Service No.5720. Born in Holyfort, Co. Tipperary. Enlisted in Wicklow while living in Arklow, Co. Wicklow. Killed in action. Grave or Memorial Reference: He has no known grave but is listed in Panels 74 to 76 on the Pozieres Memorial in France.

McGOWRAN, Thomas: Rank: Private. Regiment or Service: Royal Irish Regiment. Unit: 6th Bn. Age at death: 40. Born in St Marys in Dublin and enlisted in Carrick-on-Suir. Died of wounds. Date of death: 3 August 1917. Service No.10065.

Supplementary information: Son of Thomas and Mary McGowran: husband of Bridget McGowran, of Chapel Street, Carrick-on-Suir, Co. Tipperary. Grave or Memorial Reference: III. E. 51. Cemetery: Mendingham Military Cemetery in Belgium.

McGRATH, Chrostopher: Rank: Carpenter's Crew. Regiment or Service: Royal Navy. Unit: HMS *Vanguard* Age at death: 24. Date of death: 9 July 1917. Service No.M-13113.

Supplementary information: Son of John and Anastatia McGrath, of Lattin, Co. Tipperary. Grave or Memorial Reference: 22. Memorial: Plymouth Naval Memorial, UK. An explosion in her magazine brought HMS *Vanguard* to the bottom of the sea taking all 800 of her crew with her.

McGRATH, Denis: Rank: Private. Regiment or Service: Royal Munster Fusiliers. Unit: 2nd Bn. Date of death: 3 September 1916. Service No.6587. Born in Nenagh. Enlisted in Nenagh while living in Nenagh. Died of wounds. Grave or Memorial Reference: II. B. 2. Cemetery: Flatiron Copse, Mametz in France.

McGRATH, D.: Rank: Gunner. Regiment or Service: Royal Garrison Artillery. Age at death: 48. Date of death: 28 January 1919. Service No.275895. Cemetery: Carrick-on-Suir New Cemetery. Grave location: C.T. 37.

McGRATH, Edward: Rank: Private. Regiment or Service: Leinster Regiment. Unit: 2nd Bn. Age at death: 37. Date of death: 20 October 1914. Service No.5910. Born in Nenagh and enlisted in Birr. Killed in action.

Supplementary information: Husband of Mary Flynn Hickman (formerly McGrath), of Silver St, Nenagh, Co. Tipperary. Grave or Memorial Reference: Has no known grave

HMS *Vanguard.*

but is commemorated on Panel 10. Memorial: Ploegsteert Memorial in Belgium.

McGRATH, James: Rank: Private. Regiment or Service: 4th (Queen's Own) Hussars Age at death: 33. Date of death: 23 March 1918. Service No.826. Born in Spittal Co. Tipperary and enlisted in Tipperary. Killed in action.

Supplementary information: Son of Michael and Johanna McGrath, of 35 O'Connell's Road, Tipperary. Grave or Memorial Reference: Has no known grave but is commemorated on Panel 3. Memorial: Pozieres Memorial in France.

McGRATH, James John: Rank: Lt. Regiment or Service: Australian Imperial Force. Unit: 36th Bn. Date of death: 21 January 1917. Age at death: 38. Educated in Trinity College, Dublin. Born 15 February 1879 in Rossmore, Cashel, Co. Tipperary. Enlisted in Lidcombe, NSW 13 March 1916. Aged: 37. Heigth: 5' 11". Wife: Madge McGrath, 'Killarney', Egerton, Lidcombe, NSW. Previous Service, RAF Arty, 2 Years, RAG, 6 Years. Instructional Staff 6 years. Embarked in Sydney on the *Beltana* 13 March 16. Disembarked Plymouth 9 July 1916. Promoted to Lt in Larkhill 1 August 1916. Proceeded overseas from Southampton to France 22 November 1916. Killed in action Wounded in the head and in the body by a shell, death was instantaneous. He was killed on the front line in the Houplines sector at approx. C. 17. c. 80. 20. Ref. Map. Houplines 36. N. W. 1–21000. B. 29. d. 95. 45.

Supplementary information: Son of James John and Sarah McGrath. Born in Ireland. Grave or Memorial Reference: III. D. 12. Cemetery: Buried by Revd J Halpin (36th Bn) in Cite Bonjean Military Cemetery Armentieres, France.

McGRATH, John: Rank: Private. Regiment or Service: Royal Welsh Fusiliers. Unit: 1st Bn. Date of death: 20 October 1914. Service No.10660. Born in Clonmel. Enlisted in Cardiff. Killed in action. He has no known grave but is listed on Panel 22 the Ypres (Menin Gate) Memorial In France.

McGRATH, Martin: Rank: Lance Sergeant. Regiment or Service: Leinster Regiment. Unit: 2nd Bn. Date of death: 13 April 1917. Service No.7603. Born in Silvermines Co. Tipperary. Enlisted in Nenagh. Died of wounds. Grave or Memorial

D. McGrath.

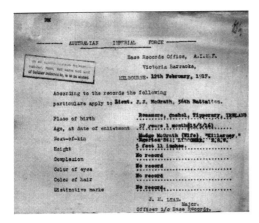

James John McGrath.

Daniel McGuinness.

Reference: I. E. 15 Cemetery: Aire Communal Cemetery in France.

McGRATH, Michael: Rank: Rifleman. Regiment or Service: Royal Irish Rifles. Unit: 2nd Bn. Age at death: 18. Date of death: 17 November 1916. Service No. 8012. Born in Roscrea and enlisted in Waterford. Killed in action.

Supplementary information: Son of Mrs Elizabeth McGrath, of 4 Pound Street, Nenagh, Co. Tipperary. Grave or Memorial Reference: I. J. 5. Cemetery: Berks Cemetery Extension in Belgium.

McGRATH, Michael: Rank: W.O. CL, 11. (CSM). Regiment or Service: Royal Irish Regiment. Unit: 5th Bn. Date of death: 3 September 1915. Service No. 223. Born in St Marys Clonmel, Co. Tipperary. Enlisted in Clonmel. Died of wounds at sea. He has no known grave but is listed on Panel 55 on the Helles Memorial in Turkey.

McGRATH, Roger Adolphud: Rank: Captain. Regiment or Service: Royal Army Medical Corps. Date of death: 5 May 1918. Age at death: 27.

Supplementary information: Son of Dennis and Hannah McGrath, Abbey Farm Clonmel. His nickname was 'Dolphie'. He won the Military Cross and is listed in the *London Gazette*. Grave or Memorial Reference: VII. A. 43. Cemetery: Boulogne Eastern Cemetery in France.

McGRATH, Thomas: Rank: Private. Regiment or Service: Royal

Army Service Corps and Army Service Corps. Unit: Mechanical Transport attached 287th Aux Transport Company. Date of death: 14 February 1918. Service No. M2-132767. Born in Roscrea. Enlisted in Dublin while living in Dublin. Died in the Balkans. Grave or Memorial Reference: IX. D. 8. Cemetery: Struma Military Cemetery in Greece.

McGUGAN, P.: Served under the name **McFADDEN James** Rank: Rifleman. Regiment or Service: Royal Irish Rifles. Unit: B Company, 1st Bn. Date of death: 31 July 1917. Service No. 9272. Born in Clonmel. Enlisted in Clonmel while living in Banbridge, Co. Down. Killed in action. Age at death: 20.

Supplementary information: Son of Mrs Mary McEvoy (formerly McGugan, *née* Small), of Ballyran, Silent Valley, Co. Down, and James McGugan. He has no known grave but is listed on Panel 40 on the Ypres (Menin Gate) Memorial in Belgium and the Banbridge Town War Memorial in Co. Down.

McGUINNESS, Daniel: Rank: Private. Regiment or Service: Royal Irish Fusiliers. Unit: 7th Bn. Born in Portadown, Co. Armagh. Enlisted in Belfast while living in Whitehouse in Co. Antrim. Died at home. Date of death: 12 November 1914. Service No. 16352. Additional information: Husband of Mrs McGuinness of 7 Shamrock Terrace Belfast. Cemetery: St Michael's New Cemetery, Tipperary Town. Grave location: E. H. 96

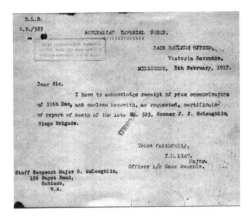

John Joseph McLoughlin.

McKEOWN, Bernard: Rank: Private. Regiment or Service: Loyal North Lancashire Regiment. Unit: 9th Bn. Date of death: 22 March 1918. Service No.3052. Born in Clonmel and enlisted in Manchester. Killed in action. He has no known grave but is listed in Bay 7 on the Arras Memorial in France.

McKEOWN, William: Rank: Rifleman. Regiment or Service: Royal Irish Rifles. Unit: 2nd Bn. Age at death: 20. Date of death: 27 January 1916. Service No.16691. Born in Clonmel and enlisted in Cahir. Killed in action.

Supplementary information: Son of Thomas and Charlotte McKeown, of 15, Kickham St, Clonmel, Co. Tipperary. Grave or Memorial Reference: I. E. 10. Cemetery: Tancrez Farm Cemetery in Belgium.

McKINLEY, Robinson/ Robbinson: Rank: Bombardier. Regiment or Service: Royal Garrison Artillery. Unit: 116th Heavy Battery. Date of death: 29 April 1917. Service No.31612. Born in Templemore. Enlisted in Londonderry. Died

of wounds. Grave or Memorial Reference: B. 1. Cemetery: Bapaume Australian Cemetery in France.

McLAUGHLIN, James Joseph: Rank: Private. Regiment or Service: Kings Liverpool Regiment. Unit: 4th Bn. Date of death: 5 February 1917. Service No.49288. Enlisted in Blackpool while living in Thurles. Killed in action. Grave or Memorial Reference:V. N. 13. Cemetery: Peronne Communal Cemetery Extension in France.

McLEAN, Denis: Rank: Private. Regiment or Service: Royal Munster Fusiliers. Unit: 'C' Coy, 6th Bn. Date of death: 5 August 1915. Service No.1030. Born in Clonmel. Enlisted in Swansea while living in Swansea. Killed in action in Gallipoli. Age at death: 34.

Supplementary information: Son of the late Mrs Mary McLean. Previously served eight years with the Royal Garrison Artillery, and in the South African War. He has no known grave but is listed on Panel 185 to 190 on the Helles Memorial in Turkey.

McLOUGHLIN, John Joseph:

Rank: Gunner. Regiment or Service: Australian Heavy Artillery. Unit: 54th Battery, 36th Group. Date of death: 16 November 1916. Age at death: 19. Service No.323. Born 20 June 1896 in Thurles. Enlisted in Subiaco, Western Australia on 1 June 1915. Passed mediacal examination in Freemantle, WA. Occupation on enlistment: Telegraphist. Height 5' 9½". Weight: 137lbs. Complexion: ruddy. Eyes: brown. Hair: dark brown. Religious Denomination: R.C. Killed in action by a German Shell while laying communications lines for HQ.

Supplementary information: Only son of Gerge Patrick (Staff Sergeant Major) and Mary Elizabeth McLoughlin, of 371, Rokeby Rd, Subiaco, Western Australia. Native of Ireland. Sister, Miss M McLoughlin, C-o Post Office, Subiaco. Grave or Memorial Reference: L. 34. Cemetery: Aveluy Communal Cemetery Extension, France.

McLOUGHLIN, Patrick: Rank: Private. Regiment or Service: Irish Guards. Unit: 1st Bn. Previously he was with the Leicester regiment where his number was 5795. Age at death: 19. Date of death: 27 September 1918. Service No.12951. Born in Roscrea and enlisted in Birr while living in Ballybrack Co. Tipperary.

Supplementary information: Son of Patrick and Mary McLoughlin, of Ballybrack, Roscrea, Co. Tipperary. Grave or Memorial Reference: III. A. 5. Cemetery: Sanders Keep Military Cemetery, Graincourt-Les-Havrincourt in France.

McLOUGHLIN, Patrick: Rank: Private. Regiment or Service: Royal Irish Regiment.
Unit: 2nd Bn. Date of death: 24 November 1914. Age at death 36. Service No.6247. Born in Nenagh. Enlisted in Nenagh. Died of wounds at home.

Grave of F. McMenamin.

Supplementary information: Son of Daniel and Johanna McLoughlin. Grave or Memorial Reference: A. 28. Cemetery: Tidworth Military Cemetery, UK.

McMAHON, James: Rank: Private. Regiment or Service: Royal Irish Regiment. Unit: 1st Bn. Date of death: 29 April 1915. Service No.10356. Born in Clonmel. Enlisted in Clonmel. Died. Grave or Memorial Reference: 24. RC. 99. Cemetery: Newport (St Woolos) Cemetery, UK.

McMAHON, Patrick: Rank: Private. Regiment or Service: Royal Munster Fusiliers. Unit: 1st Bn. Date of death: 1 May 1915. Service No.8674. Born in Cloughjordan, Co. Tipperary. Enlisted in Limerick while living at O'Brien Bridge, Co. Limerick. Killed in action in Gallipoli. Age at death: 27.

Supplementary information: Son of Stephen and Ellen McMahon, of O'Brien's Bridge, Limerick. He has no known grave but is listed on Panel 185 to 190 on the Helles Memorial in Turkey.

McMENAMIN, F.: Rank: Private. Regiment or Service: Royal Irish Regiment transferred to the Labour Corps. where his number was 585518. Unit: 2nd Bn. Age at death: 26. Date of death: 5 March 1919. Service No.1535. Additional information: Husband of Bridget Russell (formerly McMenamin). Cemetery, St John's Famine Cemetery, Tipperary. Grave location: Adjoining the road boundary.

McMULLAN, SAMUEL: Rank: Gunner. Regiment or Service: Royal Garrison Artillery. Unit: 'K' Anti Aircraft Battery. Date of death: 11 April 1918. Service No.34652. Born in Belfast. Enlisted in London while living in Clonmel. Killed in action. Age at death: 26.

Supplementary information: Husband of Mabel Miriam Cole (formerly McMullan), of 72, Rendlesham Rd, Ipswich. Grave or Memorial Reference: II. E. 1. Cemetery: St Nicholas British Cemetery in France.

McNAMARA, John: Rank: Private. Regiment or Service: Royal Irish Regiment. Unit: 2nd Bn. Date of death: 7 June 1917. Service No.4855. Born in Tipperary. Enlisted in Cashel while living in Tipperary. Killed in action. Grave or Memorial Reference: I. B. 4. Cemetery: Wytschaete Military Cemetery in Belgium.

McNAMARA, Michael: Rank: Lance Corporal. Regiment or Service: Connaught Rangers. Unit: 5th Bn. Date of death: 24 January 1916. Service No.4349. Born in Cahir. Enlisted in Pendleton while living in Pendleton in Lancashire. Died in Salonika. Grave or Memorial Reference: I. B. 5. Cemetery: Sofia War Cematery in Bulgaria.

McNAMARA, Thomas: Rank: Private. Regiment or Service: Royal Munster Fusiliers. Unit: 2nd Bn. Date of death: 9 May 1915. Service No.7176. Born in Newport Co. Tipperary. Enlisted in Limerick while living in

Grave of John O'Meara.

Newport. Killed in action. He has no known grave but is listed on Panels 43 and 44 on the Le Touret Memorial in France.

McNEILL, William Edward: Rank: Private. Regiment or Service: Connaught Rangers. Unit: 1st Bn. Date of death: 17 April 1916. Service No. 5672. Born in Clonmel. Enlisted in Fulham. Killed in action in Mesopotamia. He has no known grave but is listed on Panels 40 and 64 on the Basra Memorial in Iraq.

McPHERSON, Charles: Rank: Sergeant. Regiment or Service: Leinster Regiment. Unit: 2nd Bn. Date of death: 20 October 1914. Service No. 7630. Born in Cahir. Enlisted in Drogheda in Co. Louth. Killed in action. Grave or Memorial Reference: I. B. 15. Cemetery: Houplines Communal Cemetery Extension in France.

MEANEY, James: Rank: Private.

Regiment or Service: Royal Munster Fusiliers. Unit: 1st Bn. Date of death: 2 April 1918. Service No. 6759. Born in Thurles. Enlisted in Limerick while living in Kilkee Co. Clare. Killed in action. Age at death: 18.

Supplementary information: Son of Martin and Ellen Meaney, of Ballaney Lane, Kilkee, Co. Clare. Grave or Memorial Reference: VI. E. 2. Cemetery: Villers-Bretonneux Military Cemetery in France.

MEARA/O'MEARA, John: Rank: Private. Regiment or Service: Royal Irish Regiment. Unit: 4th Bn. Date of death: 28 July 1917. Service No. 5399. Nenagh while living in Borrisokane. Died at home. Age at death: 20.

Supplementary information: Also known as **MEARA**. Son of Mrs Kate O'Meara, of Main Street, Borrisokane. Grave or Memorial Reference: In the north-west part. Cemetery: Aglishclohane (Aglish) Church of Ireland Churchyard, Tipperary.

Grave of P. Meara.

MEARA, Martin: Rank: Sapper. Regiment or Service: Corps of Royal Engineers. Unit: 432nd Field Company, Royal Engineers. Date of death: 22 March 1918. Service No.204181. Formerly he was with the Royal Irish Rifles where his number was 7/3719. Born in Tipperary. Enlisted in the Curragh while living in Birr, Co. Offaly. Killed in action. Age at death: 30.

Supplementary information: Son of Martin and Mary Meara, of Townsend Street, Birr, Offaly. He has no known grave but is listed on Panel 10 and 13 on the Pozieres Memorial in France.

MEARA, Michael: Rank: Private. Regiment or Service: Connaught Rangers. Unit: 5th Bn. Previously he was with the Leinster Regiment where his number was 5320. Age at death: 22. Date of death: 10 October 1918. Service No.15148. Born in Lorrha and enlisted in Birr while living in Lorrha. Killed in action.

Supplementary information: Son of Patrick and Kate Meara, of Curragha, Lorrha, Co. Tipperary. Grave or Memorial Reference: Has no known grave but is commemorated on Panel 10. Memorial:Vis-En-Artois Memorial in France.

MEARA P.: Rank: Lance Corporal. Regiment or Service: Irish Guards Age at death: 24. Date of death: 25 September 1918. Service No.4211. Borrisokane New Cemetery. Grave location: In the north-west part.

MEARA, Patrick: Rank: Corporal. Regiment or Service: Royal Irish Regiment. Unit: 1st Bn. Age at death: 39. Date of death: 14 February 1915. Service No.6057. Born in Ardcroney Co. Tipperary and enlisted in Nenagh. Killed in action.

Supplementary information: Son of Patrick Meara: husband of Bridget Meara, of Dublin Rd, Nenagh, Co. Tipperary. Grave or Memorial

Grave of G. Merritt.

Reference: Has no known grave but is commemorated on Panel 33. Memorial: Ypres (Menin Gate) Memorial in Belgium.

MEEHAN, William: Rank: Lance Corporal. Regiment or Service: Royal Irish Regiment. Unit: 6th Bn. Age at death: 32. Date of death: 16 December 1916. Service No. 1739. Born in Moyglass Co. Tipperary and enlisted in Clonmel while living in Killenaule. Killed in action.

Supplementary information: Son of William and Bridget Meehan, of St Johnstown, Killenaule: husband of Kate Fitzgerald Meehan, of Mortlestown, Killenaule, Co. Tipperary. Grave or Memorial Reference: G. 10. Cemetery: Pond Farm Cemetery in Belgium.

MERCER, Robert: Rank: First Engineer. Regiment or Service: Mercantile Marine. Age at death: 67. Date of death: 13 April 1917. Born in Clonmel. Ship: S.S. *Bandon* (Cork.).

Supplementary information: Husband of Ellen Mercer of 9 Pleasant Road, College Road, Cork. The Ship was bound for Liverpool from Cork carrying a cargo of 1,050 tons of coal when she was torpedoed by Submarine UC-33. Only 4 of the crew of 32 survived. The German Submarine, Captained by Obly Alfred Arnold was later rammed in St Georges Channel by Escort Craft HMS PC-61 under the command of Lt Commander F Worsley and sunk. The Submarine Commanding Officer was rescued.

Extracts from Part 1. Vol XXV. No. 121 [January − June, 1919] Journal of the Cork Historical and Archaeological Society:

She sailed from Liverpool for Cork on the 12th April 1917, under the command of Captain P. F. Kelly. The ship was struck by a torpedo on the port side, abreast of the engine room, and immediately began to sink. After a short time, while swimming about amidst the wreckage, he saw the third engineer, Mr Mercer, clinging to one of the life-saving collapsible deck-seats, which floated off the "Bandon's" deck, and grasped it, when it capsized. He then swam round to its end and opening it out it became more buoyant. In addition to Captain Kelly and Mr Mercer the following members of the ill-fated ship were holding on the seat viz., J. OKeeffe, fireman, and the carpenter, also J. McCarthy, A. B. (who afterwards became exhausted, lost his hold of the raft, and was drowned), and a fireman named Walsh.

Robert Mercer has no known grave but is listed on the Tower Hill Memorial, UK.

MERRITT/MERRIT Charles: Rank: Private. Regiment or Service: Royal Irish Regiment. Unit: Depot. Date of death: 9 May 1915. Service No.7993. Born in Cloughjordan. Enlisted in Nenagh while living in Cloughjordan. Died at home. Grave or Memorial Reference: South of the church. Cemetery: Modreeny Church of Ireland Churchyard, Tipperary.

MERRITT, John William: Rank: Private. Regiment or Service: Royal Irish Regiment. Unit: 2nd Bn. Age at death: 26. Date of death: 8 October 1918. Service No.7982 Awarded the Military Medal and listed in The *London Gazette*. Born in Cloughjordan and enlisted in Cloughjordan.

Supplementary information: Son of James and Mary Ann Merritt, of Stoneyacre, Clough Jordan, Co. Tipperary. Grave or Memorial

Reference: Has no known grave but is commemorated on Panel 5. Memorial: Vis-En-Artois Memorial in France.

MESKILL, Thomas: Rank: Private. Regiment or Service: Royal Irish Regiment. Unit: 2nd Bn. Date of death: 14 July 1918. Service No.10795. Born in St Marys, Clonmel Co. Tipperary. Enlisted in Clonmel. Died of wounds. Killed in action. He has no known grave but is listed on Panel 30 and 31 on the Pozieres Memorial in France.

MINIHAN, Patrick: Rank: Private. Regiment or Service: Royal Irish Regiment. Unit: 2nd Bn. Age at death: 38. Date of death: 19 October 1914. Service No.4174. Born in Carrick-on-Suir and enlisted in Tipperary while living in Carrick-on-Suir. Killed in action.

Supplementary information: Husband of Alice Minihan, of Hurley's Lane, Carrick-on-Suir, Co. Tipperary. Grave or Memorial Reference: Has no known grave but is commemorated on Panel 11 and 12. Memorial: Le Touret Memorial in France.

MINOGUE, Joseph: Rank: Private. Regiment or Service: Dorsetshire Regiment. Unit: 5th Bn. Previous to this he was in the Hussars of the line where his number was 1627. Age at death: 27. Date of death: 26 September 1916. Service No.13494. Born in Cloughjordan Co. Tipperary and enlisted in nenagh. Killed in action.

Supplementary information: Son of Jeremiah and Nora Minogue, of Ballinweir, Nenagh, Co. Tipperary.

Grave or Memorial Reference: Pier and Face 7 B. Memorial: Thiepval Memorial in France.

MOCKLAIR/MOCLAIR, John Edward: Rank: Lance Sergeant. Regiment or Service: Royal Irish Regiment. Unit: 8th Bn. Age at death: 26. Date of death: 5 September 1918. Service No.3582 He was formerly with the Leinster Regiment where his number was 3555. Awards: D C M. Born in Cashel, enlisted in Castlebar, Co. Mayo while living in Cashel. Killed in action but originally reported as wounded and missing.

Supplementary information: Son of Patrick and Margaret Mary Moclair (*née* Carew), of Ballinsee House, Cashel, Co. Tipperary. Grave or Memorial Reference: III. H. 10. Cemetery: Le Grand Beaumart British Cemetery, Steenwerck, Nord in France.

MOLLISON/MOLLINSON Charles: Rank: Private. Regiment or Service: Royal Irish Regiment. Unit: 7th Bn. Date of death: 13 December 1917. Service No.25613. Formerly he was with the South Irish Horse where his number was 1533. Born in Cootehill, Co. Cavan. Enlisted in Dublin while living in Nenagh. Died of wounds. Grave or Memorial Reference: I. C. 22. Cemetery: Villiers-Faucon Communal Cemetery Extension in France.

MOLONEY, Martin: Rank: Private. Regiment or Service: Royal Munster Fusiliers. Unit: 2nd Bn. Date of death: 13 October 1915. Service No.6182. Born in Portroe Co. Tipperary. Enlisted in Limerick while living in Portroe. Killed in action. Age at death: 27.

Supplementary information: Son of the late Dan Moloney and Mary Moloney. He has no known grave but is listed on Panel 127 on the Loos Memorial in France.

MOLONEY, Patrick: Rank: Private. Regiment or Service: Royal Irish Regiment. Unit: 2nd Bn. Date of death: 26 October 1915. Service No.4856. Born in Cappawhite Co. Tipperary. Enlisted in Tipperary while living in Cappawhite. Killed in action. Age at death: 23.

Supplementary information: Son of John and Bridget Shannon, of Kildysart, Co. Clare. Grave or Memorial Reference: I.A.7. Cemetery: Auchonvillers Military Cemetery in France.

MONTAGUE, William: Rank: Gunner. Regiment or Service: Royal Horse Artillery and Royal Field Artillery. Unit: 82nd Battery. Date of death: 3 October 1916. Service No.54924. Born in Templemore. Enlisted in Glasgow. Died in Turkey. Age at death: 27.

Supplementary information: Son of John and Matilda Montague. Born in Londonderry. Grave or Memorial Reference: XXI. X. 10. Cemetery: Baghdad (North Gate) War Cemetery in Iraq.

MONTGOMERY, Arthur Samuel: Rank: Lieutenant. Regiment or Service: Royal Inniskilling Fusiliers.

Unit: 5th Bn. Age at death: 39. Date of death: 21 June 1916.

Supplementary information: Son of Thomas B. and Dorothea Maria Montgomery, of Annerville, Clonmel, Co. Tipperary. Grave or Memorial Reference: o. 8. Cemetery: Salonika (Lembet Road) Military Cemetery in Greece.

MOONEY, Edward: Rank: Private. Regiment or Service: Royal Irish Regiment. Unit: 1st Bn. Date of death: 22 February 1915. Service No.9890. Born in Kildare and enlisted in Kilkenny while living in Clonmel. Died of wounds.

Supplementary information: Son of Daniel and Bridget Mooney, of 3 Albert Street, Clonmel, Co. Tipperary. Native of Athy, Co. Kildare. Grave or Memorial Reference: I. B. 9. Cemetery: Etretat Churchyard, France.

MOONEY, Robert James: Rank: Pioneer. Regiment or Service: Corps of Royal Engineers. Unit: 7th Labour Bn. Date of death: 26 April 1917. Service No.118899. Born in Tipperary. Enlisted in Westminster, Middlesex while living in Salford Lancs. Killed in action. Age at death: 43.

Supplementary information: Son of Mrs Anne Mooney. Grave or Memorial Reference: I. A. 7. Cemetery: Strand Military Cemetery in Belgium.

MOORE, Charles: Rank: Private. Regiment or Service: Royal Dublin Fusiliers. Unit: 1st Bn. Age at death: 21. Date of death: 7 September 1918. Service No.43035. Born in Cashel,

enlisted in Fethard while living in Cashel, Killed in action, France. He was formerly with the Royal Irish Regiment where his number was 5214. He was buried in a temporary grave and finally buried in this cemetery after the end of the war.

Supplementary information: Youngest son of William and Margaret Moore, of Friar Street, and Agars Lane, Cashel, Co. Tipperary. His Father William Moore was also serving at the front when he heard the news. Grave or Memorial Reference: II. D. 24. Cemetery: Outtersteene Communal Cemetery Extension, Bailleul in France.

MOORE, Edward: Rank: Private. Regiment or Service: Royal Irish Regiment. Unit: 2nd Bn. Date of death: 1 April 1915. Service No.10785. Born in St Nicholas, Carrick-on-Suir, Co. Tipperary. Enlisted in Clonmel while living in Carrick-on-Suir, Co. Tipperary. Killed in action. He has no known grave but is listed on Panel 4 on the Ploegsteert Memorial in Belgium.

MOORE, Gerald: Rank: Private. Regiment or Service: Royal Irish Regiment Unit: 2nd Bn. Age at death: 24. Date of death: 7 June 1917. Service No.10325. Born in St Michaels in Tipperary and enlisted in Tipperary. Killed in action.

Supplementary information: Son of William Patrick Moore: husband of Mary Moore, of 2 St Nicholas' Lane, Old Bridge, Clonmel, Co. Tipperary. Grave or Memorial Reference: Has no known grave but is commemorated

Thomas Moriarty.
Photograph courtesy of
Thomas Moriarty, Moyne.

on Panel 33. Memorial: Ypres (Menin Gate) Memorial in Belgium.

MOORE, John: Rank: Private. Regiment or Service: Connaught Rangers. Unit: 5th Bn. Date of death: 19 August 1915. Service No.4458. Formerly he was with the Royal Irish Regiment where his number was 321. Born in Carrick-on-Suir, Co. Waterford. Enlisted in Clonmel while living in Clonmel. Killed in action in Gallipoli. He has no known grave but is listed on Panel 181 to 183 on the Helles Memorial in Turkey.

MOORE, Michael: Rank: Private. Regiment or Service: Connaught Rangers. Unit: D Coy, 1st Bn. Date of death: 23 November 1914. Service No.8752. Born in Tipperary. Enlisted in Listowel, Co. Kerry while living in Tralee. Killed in action. Age at death: 33.

Supplementary information: Son of the late John and Anne Moore. He has no known grave but is listed on Panels 43 on the Le Touret Memorial in France.

MORIARTY, Thomas: Rank: Private. Regiment or Service: Royal Irish Regiment. Unit: 6th Bn. Age at death: 37. Date of death: 3 May 1916. Service No.7092. Born in Ballingarry and enlisted in Thurles while living in Ballingarry. Died of wounds.

Supplementary information: Son of Thomas and Margaret Moriarty, of Kylemakill, Moyne, Templemore, Co. Tipperary. Grave or Memorial Reference: V. C. 2. Cemetery: Bethune Town Cemetery in France.

MORONEY, Martin: Rank: Private. Regiment or Service: Irish Guards. Unit: 1st Bn. Date of death: 10 October 1917. Service No.11600. Born in Nenagh. Enlisted in Elswick Northumberland while living in Accrington in Lancashire. Killed in action. He has no known grave but is listed on Panels 10 and 11 on the Tyne Cot Memorial in Belgium.

MORONEY, Thomas: Rank: Private. Regiment or Service: Royal Irish Regiment. Unit: 2nd Bn. Date of death: 21 March 1918. Service No.9691. Born in Carrick-on-Suir,

Co. Tipperary. Enlisted in Clonmel while living in Carrick-on-Suir, Co. Tipperary. Killed in action. He has no known grave but is listed on Panel 30 and 31 on the Pozieres Memorial in France.

MORRIS/MORRISS, Edward: Rank: Sergeant. Regiment or Service: Tank Corps. Date of death: 9 August 1918. Service No. 307231. Formerly he was with the Royal Engineers where his number was 120832. Born in Clonmel. Enlisted in Cork. Killed in action.

Supplementary information: Son of the late John Morris. He has no known grave but is listed on Panel 11 on the Vis-En-Artois Memorial in France.

MORRIS, Kenneth D.: Rank: Private. Regiment or Service: Highland Light Infantry. Unit: 53rd Bn. Date of death: 26 October 1918. Service No. TR February 48570 and TR2-48570. Born in Roscrea. Enlisted in Edinburgh while living in Kelso in Berwickshire. Died at home. Grave or Memorial Reference: North West Div. 25 (3). Cemetery: Froickheim Cemetery, UK.

MORRIS, Michael F.S.: Rank: Private. Regiment or Service: Leinster Regiment. Unit: 7th Bn. Date of death: 11 May 1916. Service No. 5356. Formerly he was with the Connaught Rangers where his number was 3819. Born in Kilkenny. Enlisted in Clonmel while living in Clonmel. Killed in action. Age at death: 36.

Supplementary information: Son of Mr and Mrs Samuel Morris, of Newrath House, Waterford. Grave or Memorial Reference: I.B.4. Cemetery: Philosophe British Cemetery, Mazingarbe in France.

MORRIS, Thomas: Rank: Private. Regiment or Service: Royal Irish Regiment. Unit: 1st Bn. Age at death: 19. Date of death: 26 February 1915. Service No. 4410. Born in Ballingarry and enlisted in Kilkenny while living in Ballingarry. Killed in action.

Supplementary information: Son of Mr P. and Annie Morris, of 38, Clashawaun, Clara, King's Co. Native of Tipperary. Grave or Memorial Reference: I. C. 3. Cemetery: Elzenwalle Brasserie Cemetery in Belgium.

MORRISSEY, Daniel: Rank: Sergeant. Regiment or Service: Royal Irish Regiment. Unit: 6th Bn. Date of death: 19 February 1917. Service No. 5773. Born in Templemore. Enlisted in Templemore. Grave or Memorial Reference: I. C. 25. Cemetery: Loker Churchyard in Belgium.

MORRISSEY, David: Rank: Private. Regiment or Service: Royal Irish Regiment. Unit: 2nd Bn. Age at death: 35. Date of death: 5 September 1915. Service No. 7471. Born in Mullinahone Co. Tipperary and enlisted in Manchester.

Supplementary information: Son of David and Johanna Morrissey, of Tipperary, Grave or Memorial Reference: Plot 1. Row B. Grave 14. Cemetery: Forceville Communal

Cemetery and Extension in France.

MORRISSEY, Edward: Rank: Sergeant. Regiment or Service: Royal Dublin Fusiliers. Unit: 6th Bn. Age at death: 20. Date of death: 10 August 1915. Service No.12163. Born in Templemore and enlisted in Dublin while living in Templemore. Killed in action in Gallipoli.

Supplementary information: Son of Matthew and Kate Morrissey, of Mary St, Templemore, Co. Tipperary. Grave or Memorial Reference: Has no known grave but is commemorated on Panel 190 to 196. Memorial: Helles Memorial in Turkey.

MORRISSEY, Michael: Rank: Private. Regiment or Service: Royal Irish Regiment. Unit: 'C' Coy. 2nd Bn. Age at death: 21. Date of death: 24 August 1914. Service No.10319. Born in Templemore and enlisted in Templemore. Killed in action.

Supplementary information: Son of Stephen and Kate Morrissey, of Barrack St, Templemore, Co. Tipperary. Grave or Memorial Reference: I. A. 2. Cemetery: Cement House Cemetery in Belgium.

MORRISSEY, Patrick: Rank: Private. Regiment or Service: Royal Irish Regiment. Unit: 6th Bn. Date of death: 5 April 1917. Service No.5297. Born in Lisnaguar Co. Tipperary. Enlisted in Tipperary while living in Ballyglass, Co. Tipperary. Killed in action duning a trench raid. Age at death: 30. The Regimental history records states that on 5 April 1917 'a most successful raid was carried out on the enemy's trenches. Twenty-one of the 4th Grenadier Regiment were taken as prisoners, from whom very much valuable information was obtained. Our casualties were: Captain J. E. Day and six men killed, seven men missing, Lieutenant E. Williams, 2nd Lieutenant R. E. W. Burke and 66 men wounded. Congratulations on their achievement were received from the G. O. C. 2nd Army and the divisional and brigade commanders personally visited the battalion and congratulated them.'

Supplementary information: Son of William and Nora Morrissey: husband of Catherine Dalton (formerly Morrissey), of Kilchane, Tipperary. He has no known grave but is listed on Panel 33 on the Ypres (Menin Gate) Memorial in Belgium.

MORRISSEY, Timothy Edward: Rank: Sailor. Regiment or Service: Mercantile Marine. Unit: S. S. *Saint Ninian* (Glasgow) Age at death: 21. Date of death: 7 February 1917.

Supplementary information: Son of Anastasia Morrissey, of the Strand, Carrick-on-Suir, Co. Tipperary, and the late Thomas Morrissey. Born at Carrick-on-Suir. Memorial: Has no known grave but is commemorated on the Tower Hill Memorial, London. When the Steamer Corsican Prince was torpedoed by a German Sub off Whitby in 1917. the S.S. *Saint Ninian* went to their aid and pick up survivors. The Submarine surfaced and attacked the SS *Saint Ninian* with a torpedo which hit the ship between the engine room and No.3 hold. She sank almost immediately only half of her crew survived.

MORRISSEY, William: Rank: Private. Regiment or Service: Royal Irish Regiment. Unit: 'B' Coy. 2nd Bn. Age at death: 28. Date of death: 8 May 1915. Service No. 5919. Born in Carrick-on-Suir and enlisted in Clonmel while living in Carrick-in-Suir. Killed in action.

Supplementary information: Son of William O'Brien Morrissey and Margret Morrissey: husband of Bridget O'Brien (formerly Morrisey), of Long Lane, Carrick-on-Suir, Co. Tipperary. Grave or Memorial Reference: Has no known grave but is commemorated on Panel 33. Memorial: Ypres (Menin Gate) Memorial in Belgium.

MORRISSEY, William: Rank: Private. Regiment or Service: Royal Irish Regiment. Unit: 2nd Bn. Date of death: 9 October 1914. Service No. 4706. Born in St Nicholas Carrick-on-Suir, Co. Tipperary. Enlisted in Waterford while living in Carrick-on-Suir. Killed in action. Age at death: 20.

Supplementary information: Son of Patrick and Margaret Morrissey, of Greystone St, Carrick-on-Suir, Co. Tipperary. He has no known grave but is listed on Panels 11 and 12 on the Le Touret Memorial in France.

MOULSON/MOULSTON, Charles Edmond: Rank: Sergeant. Regiment or Service: Regiment or Service: Household Cavalry and Cavalry of the line including the Yeomanry and Imperial Camel Corps. Unit: 11th (Prince Alberts Own) Hussars. Date of death: 19 November 1914. Service No. 13128. Born in Wolverhampton. Enlisted in Cahir while living in Cloghan Barracks, Co. Tipperary. Won the DCM when he was a Corporal of Horse and listed in the *London Gazette* on 7 December 1914. The citation reads: Led his troop on 6 November, after his Officer was shot, with great resolution and gallantry under heavy fire, and assisted materially to restore confidence amongst the troops'. Killed in action. Age at death: 38.

Supplementary information: Husband of Mrs B. Moulson, of 216, Convamore

Death of Corporal James Moylan.

The news reached Nenagh this week of the death in Salonica from enteric fever of Corporal James Moylan, of the Connaught Rangers, son of the late Mr Jas Moylan, Queen street, Nenagh. The deceased who belonged to a well-known Nenagh family, saw service in the Boer War, and when the present war broke out was on pension but he again offered his services which were accepted and re-joined his old regiment. He was one of the drill instructors of the Nenagh Volunteers, and acted as their first secretary. Most popular with all classes he was a prominent member of the Nenagh Ivy Dance Class. His demise is deeply regretted. He leaves a wife and family to mourn his loss.

James Moylan.

Rd, Grimsby. He has no known grave but is listed on Panel 5 on the Ypres (Menin Gate) Memorial in Belgium.

MOYLAN, James: Rank: Lance Sergeant. Regiment or Service: Royal Irish Fusiliers. Unit: 2nd (Garrison) Bn. Previously he was with the Connaught Rangers where his number was 4276. Date of death: 28 December 1916. Service No.G-1625. Born in Nenagh and enlisted there also.

Supplementary information: Husband of Bridget Moylan, of Grace's Street, Nenagh, Co. Tipperary. Grave or Memorial Reference: 571. Cemetery: Salonika (Lembet Road) Military Cemetery in Greece.

MOYLER, George: Rank: Private. Regiment or Service: Royal Dublin Fusiliers. Unit: 2nd Bn. Previously he was with the Royal Irish Regiment where his number was 5322. Age at death: 23. Date of death: 21 March 1918. Service No.43034. Born in Thurles and enlisted there also.

Supplementary information: Son of George and Margaret Moyler, of Quarry St, Thurles, Co. Tipperary. Grave or Memorial Reference: II. D. 6. Cemetery: Templeux-Le-Guerard British Cemetery in France.

MOYNIHAN, Cornelius: Rank: Private. Regiment or Service: Royal Irish Regiment. Unit: 2nd Bn. Age at death: 24. Date of death: 19 October 1914. Service No.5089. Born in St Marys in Clonmel and enlisted in Tipperary while living in Clonmel. Killed in action.

Supplementary information: Son of Cornelius and Bridget Moynihan, of 12 George's Court, Clonmel, Co. Tipperary. Grave or Memorial Reference: Has no known grave but is commemorated on Panel 11 and 12. Memorial: Le Touret Memorial in France.

MULCAHY, John: Rank: Private. Regiment or Service: Royal Irish Regiment. Unit: 1st Bn. Date of death: 31 May 1915. Service No.10147. Born in Fethard. Enlisted in Clonmel while living in Fethard. Died of wounds. Grave or Memorial Reference: IX. C.

P. Mulqueen.

14. Cemetery: Cite Bonjean Military Cemetery, Armentaires in France.

MULCAHY, John: Rank: Lance Corporal. Regiment or Service: Machine Gun Corps (Infantry). Unit: 5th Coy. Previously he was with the Royal Irish regiment where his number was 5074. Age at death: 18. Date of death: 1 May 1917. Service No.60827. Born in Ardfinnan Co. Tipperary and enlisted in Clonmel while livening in Ardfinnan. Killed in action.

Supplementary information: Son of Mrs Mary Murray, of Chapel Street, Clogheen, Co. Tipperary. Grave or Memorial Reference: Bay 10. Memorial: Arras Memorial in France. He is also commemorated on the Cahir War Memorial.

MULLANY, Thomas: Rank: Private. Regiment or Service: Royal Munster Fusiliers. Unit: 1st Bn. Date of death: 11 August 1917. Service No.15056. Formerly he was with the Manchester Regiment where his number was 33266. Born in Tipperary. Enlisted in Manchester while living in Manchester. Died of wounds. Age at death: 28.

Supplementary information: Son of John Mullany and Maria Concannon, his wife, of Shamrock House, Ballinrobe, Co. Mayo. He has no known grave but is listed on Panel 44 on the Ypres (Menin Gate) Memorial in Belgium.

MULLINS, John: Rank: Driver. Regiment or Service: Canadian Field Artillery. Unit: 1st Div Ammunition Col. Age at death: 45. Date of death: 25 January 1919.

Supplementary information: Son of John and Bridget Mullins of Clonmel, Ireland and husband of Mary Mullins, 65 Dresden Row, Halifax, Nova Scotia. Grave or Memorial Reference: I. A. 9. Cemetery: Huy (La Sarte) Communal Cemetery in Belgium.

MULQUEEN, P: Rank: Air Mechanic, 3rd class. Regiment or Service: Royal Air Force. Unit: 45th Training Depot Squadron. Date of death: 28 January 1919. Service No.106614. Age at death: 55.

Supplementary information: Husband of Bridget Mulqueen of 3 College Street Clonmel. Tipperary. Grave or Memorial Reference: 5.1.132. Cemetery: St Patricks Cemetery, Clonmel. Co. Tipperary.

MURPHY, Alfred Durham: Rank: Lieutenant Colonel. Regiment or Service: Leinster Regiment. Unit: 2nd Bn. Age at death: 27. Date of death: 6 November 1917. Died, Home. His rank is also down as Bt-Major (A-Lt Col). As well as his WWI medals he won the Distinguished Service Order and the Military Cross. All Military Cross winners are listed in the *London Gazette*.

Supplementary information: Son of Lt. Col. E. W. Murphy and Mary Ellen Murphy, of Ballinamona, Cashel, Co. Tipperary. Educated at Downside College. In 1911 he entered the Army through the special reserve. At the very outbreak of hostilities in 1914, as a sub-altern he went with his Regiment to France and had been continuously in the fighting since September, 1914. Sir John French mentioned Lt Murphy's courageous actions in dispatches, and after some short time he was made a member of the Distinguished Service Order. Grave or Memorial Reference: III. B. 5. Cemetery: Roisel Communal Cemetery Extension in France.

MURPHY, Charles: Rank: Private. Regiment or Service: Royal Welsh Fusiliers. Unit: 9th Bn. Date of death: 17 August 1918. Service No.12528. Born in Tipperary. Enlisted in Machynlleth while living in Tipperary. Died of wounds. Grave or Memorial Reference: IV.C.9. Cemetery: Sandpits British Cemetery, Fouquereuil in France.

MURPHY, Cornelius: Rank: Private. Regiment or Service: Royal West Surrey Regiment. Unit: 2nd Bn. Date of death: 21 May1915. Service No.3719 and G-3719. Formerly he was with the Royal West Kent Regiment where his number was 4444. Born in Clonmel. Enlisted in Tonbridge in Kentwhile living in Fulham in

Middlesex. Died of wounds.

Supplementary information: Brother of Mr D.W. Murphy of 65 Mirabel Road, Fulham, London. Grave or Memorial Reference: I. A. 128. Cemetery: Longuenesse (St Omer) Souvenir Cemetery in France.

MURPHY, Daniel: Rank: Gunner. Regiment or Service: Royal Garrison Artillery. Date of death: 9 May 1916. Service No.26129. Born in Templetouhy, Co. Tipperary. Enlisted in Templemore while living in Templetouhy. Died in Mesopotamia. Age at death: 27.

Supplementary information: Son of Thomas and Ellen Fogarty, of Shamrock Street, Urlingford, Co. Kilkenny. Grave or Memorial Reference: VII. F. 3. Cemetery: Amara War Cemetery in Iraq.

MURPHY, David: Rank: Private. Regiment or Service: Manchester Regiment. Unit: 2nd Bn. Age at death: 36. Date of death: 28 October 1914. Service No.8093. Born in Tipperary

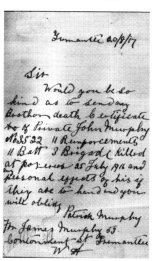

John Murphy.

and enlisted in Manchester while living in Tipperary. Killed in action.

Supplementary information: Son of Michael and Margaret Murphy, of Old Rd, Tipperary. Grave or Memorial Reference: Panels 34 and 35. Memorial: Le Touret Memorial in France.

MURPHY, James: Rank: Lance Corporal. Regiment or Service: Leinster Regiment. Unit: 2nd Bn. Previously he was with the Royal Irish regiment where his number was 9919. Age at death: 25. Date of death: 31 July 1917. Service No. 10733. Born in Templemore and enlisted in Nenagh. Killed in action.

Supplementary information: Son of James and Mary Murphy, of County Home, Thurles, Co. Tipperary. Grave or Memorial Reference: IX. L. 19. Cemetery: Hooge Crater Cemetery Zillebeke, Belgium.

MURPHY, John: Rank: Sergeant. Regiment or Service: Army Service Corps. Unit: 16th Lines of Communication Supply Coy. Age

at death: 42. Date of death: 18 May 1918. Service No. S2-015597. Born in Carrick-on-Suir and enlisted in Clonmel while living in Carrick-on-Suir. Killed in action.

Supplementary information: Son of Pat Murphy, of Ash Park, Carrick-on-Suir, Co. Tipperary: husband of the late Bridget Cash (formerly Murphy). Grave or Memorial Reference: V.B. 17. Cemetery: Longuenesse (St Omer) Souvenir Cemetery in France.

MURPHY, John: Rank: Private. Regiment or Service: Australian Infantry. Unit: 11th Bn. Date of death: 25 July 1916. Service No. 3522. Born in Tipperary. Enlisted in Freemantle, Western Australia while living at 53 Contanment Street. Occupation on enlistent: Barman. Age on enlistment: 30. Height: 5'7". Complexion: fair. Eyes: blue. Hair: light brown. Religious Denomination: R.C. Attested in Perth on 16 August 1915. Served in Habiatia, Alexandria, Marsellies, Sailly, Strazelle, Hazebruick, France and trained in the Bull Ring in Etaples where he

Michael Murphy.

sprained his ankle. Personal effects were sent to his brother Mr J. Murphy, Hopkins Street, Boulder City, Western Austraila. Killed in action. He has no known grave but is listed on the Villers Bretonneux Memorial in France.

MURPHY, George Charles: Rank: Sapper. Regiment or Service: Corps of Royal Engineers. Unit: 105th Field Coy. Date of death: 27 May 1918. Service No.24467. Formerly he was with the 10[sth] Field Company Royal Engineers. Born in Clonmel. Enlisted in Chatham Kent while living in Gillingham in Kent. Killed in action. Age at death: 19.

Supplementary information: Son of Ellen Murphy, of 8 Park Rd, Gillingham, Kent, and the late Cpl. (26496, Royal Engineers) G. Murphy. Grave or Memorial Reference: II. G. 15. Cemetery: La Ville-Aux-Bois Military Cemetery in France.

MURPHY, Martin: Rank: Sergeant. Regiment or Service: Royal Irish Regiment. Unit: 2nd Bn. Date of death: 22 July 1916. Service No.6101. Born in St Johns, Tipperray. Enlisted in Clonmel while living in Tipperary. Died of wounds. Grave or Memorial Reference: II. C. 21. Cemetery: Heilly Station Cemetery, Mericourt-l'Abbe in France.

MURPHY, Michael: Rank: Corporal. Regiment or Service: Leinster Regiment. Unit: 2nd Bn. Age at death: 32. Date of death: 27 April 1915. Service No.6179. Born in Tipperary on 12 February 1883 to Michael and Mary Murphy (*née* O'Kieffe) and enlisted there also. Killed in action. Shot by a sniper during the 2nd Battle of Ypres. His brother Bill was a member of the 4th Bn, 3rd Tipperary Brigade IRA and his other brother Jim served in the Royal Irish Constabulary in Co. Clare.

Supplementary information: Son

Grave of Walter Murphy.

of Michael and Mary Murphy, of 5 Bansha Rd, Tipperary Town, County Tipperary. Served in the South African Campaign. Prior to outbreak of the war he was training to be a teacher in the Army. Grave or Memorial Reference: B. 31. Cemetery: Ferme Buterne Military Cemetery, Houplines in France.

MURPHY, Patrick: Rank: Private. Regiment or Service: South Irish Horse. Date of death: 22 June 1917. Service No. 1825. Entitled to the War Medal and the Vicotry Medal. Born in Moycarke and enlisted in Limerick while he was living in Dublin. Killed in action.

Supplementary information: Son of Daniel and Johanna Murphy, of Ballymore, Goold's Cross, Co. Tipperary. Grave or Memorial Reference: XIX. A. 9. Cemetery: Loos British Cemetery in France.

MURPHY, Thomas: Rank: Private. Regiment or Service: Royal Irish Regiment. Unit: 2nd Bn. Date of death: 22 November 1917. Service No. 11436. Born in Drom. Enlisted in Fethard while living in Drom. Killed in action. He has no known grave but is listed on Bay 5 on the Arras Memorial in France.

MURPHY, Thomas: Rank: Private. Regiment or Service: Royal Irish Fusiliers. Unit: 7th Bn. Age at death: 32. Date of death: 1 May 1916. Service No. 19905. Born in Tipperary and enlisted there also. Died of wounds.

Supplementary information: Son of Michael and Ellen Murphy, of Spittal Street, Tipperary. Grave or Memorial Reference: III. H. 89. Cemetery: Bethune Town Cemetery in France.

MURPHY, Walter: Rank: Private. Regiment or Service: Royal Irish Fusiliers. Unit: 8th Bn. Born in Cork. Enlisted in Cork. Died at home. Date of death: 9 March 1915. Service No. 16025. Cemetery: St Michael's New Cemetery, Tipperary Town. Grave location: E. H. 102.

MURPHY, William: Rank: Private. Regiment or Service: Leinster Regiment. Unit: 1st Bn. Age at death: 25. Date of death: 28 April 1915. Service No. 9640. Born in Tipperary and enlisted in Limerick. Killed in action.

Supplementary information: Son of John and Ellen Murphy, of 4 Upper New Rd, Tipperary. Grave or Memorial Reference: Has no known grave but is commemorated on Panel 44. Memorial: Ypres (Menin Gate) Memorial in Belgium.

MURPHY, William: Rank: Private. Regiment or Service: Irish Guards. Unit: 1st Bn. Date of death: 9 September 1917. Service No. 10337. Born in Moycarkey, Co. Tipperary. Enlisted in Thurles. Killed in action. Grave or Memorial Reference: V. D. 2. Cemetery: Artillery Wood Cemetery in Belgium.

MURPHY, William: Rank: Private. Regiment or Service: Royal Irish Regiment. Unit: 2nd Bn. Date of death: 21 July 1916. Service No. 9690. Born in

Ballinaclough, Co. Tipperary. Enlisted in Cashel while living in Ballinaclough. Killed in action. He has no known grave but is listed on Pier and Face 3A on the Thiepval Memorial in France.

MURPHY, William Patrick: Rank: Sapper. Regiment or Service: Corps of royal Engineers. Unit: 172nd Tunnelling Company. Royal Engineers. Date of death: 10 March 1916. Service No. 86885. Born in Tipperary. Enlisted in London while living in Hammersmith, Middlesex. Killed in action. He has no known grave but is listed on Panel 1 on the Ploegsteert Memorial in Belgium.

MURRAY, Cornelius: Rank: Lance Corporal. Regiment or Service: Royal Irish Regiment. Unit: 2nd Bn. Date of death: 13 June 1917. Service No. 8692. Born in Crimlin Co. Tipperary and enlisted in Roscrea while living in Crimlin. Died of wounds.

Supplementary information: Son of Mary Murray, of Crumlin, Moneygill, Co. Tipperary. Alternative Commemoration – buried in Castletown Old Graveyard, Co. Offaly. Has no known grave but is commemorated on Panel 5 (Screen Wall). Memorial: Grangegorman Memorial in Dublin.

MURRAY, Denis: Rank: Gunner. Regiment or Service: Royal Garrison Artillery. Unit: 86th Heavy Battery. Date of death: 31 December 1916. Service No. 34068.

Supplementary information: Son of Mr Michael Murray, Chapel Street, Nenagh and brother of Thomas Murray listed below. Had six years army service before his death and three of his brothers also served. Born in Templederry. Enlisted in Nenagh. Died in Turkey. He has no known grave but is listed on the Doiran Memorial in Greece.

MURRAY, Patrick: Rank: Private. Regiment or Service: Irish Guards. Unit: 2nd Bn. Date of death: 27 September 1915. Service No. 6497. Born in Nenagh.

Supplementary information: Son of Mr Muchael Murray, Chapel Street, Nenagh. Patrick was a member of the Nenagh Shamrock Club. Shot by a German sniper 'conveying a can of water for his comrades in the trenches'. Enlisted in Nenagh while living in Nenagh. Killed in action. He has no known grave but is listed on Panels 9 and 10 on the Loos Memorial in France.

MURRAY, Thomas: Rank: Private. Regiment or Service: Royal Irish Regiment. Unit: 'E' Coy. 2nd Bn. Age at death: 29. Date of death: 4 August 1917. Service No. 7453. Born in Fethard and enlisted in Clonmel while living in Fethard.

Supplementary information: Son of Patrick and Mary Murray, of Upper Green, Fethard, Co. Tipperary. Three of his brothers also served. (see Denis Murray above). Grave or Memorial Reference: Has no known grave but is commemorated on Panel 33. Memorial: Ypres (Menin Gate) Memorial in Belgium.

MURRAY, William Frederick: Rank: Private. Regiment or Service: Machine Gun Corps (Infantry). Unit: 36th Coy. Age at death: 34. Date of death: 27 November 1916. Service No.46384. Born in Kello Co. Meath and enlisted in Willesden Green while living in Cricklewood.

Supplementary information: Son of William Murray, of Tipperary: husband of Emily Maud Smith (formerly Murray), of 5 Belgrave Terrace, Stanhope Rd, Finchley, London. Grave or Memorial Reference: F. 31. Cemetery: Agny Military Cemetery in France.

MYERS, John: Rank: Sergeant. Regiment or Service: Manchester Regiment. Unit: 11th Bn. Age at death: 26. Date of death: 26 September 1916. Service No.3326. Born in clonmel and enlisted in Oldham in Lancashire.

Supplementary information: Son of Jeremiah and Catherine Myers, of 18 Thomas Street, Clonmel, Co. Tipperary. Grave or Memorial Reference: Pier and Face 13 A and 14 C. Memorial: Thiepval Memorial in France.

N

NAGLE/NEAGLE, John: Rank: Private. Regiment or Service: Leinster Regiment. Unit: 2nd Bn. Age at death: 19. Date of death: 18 October 1914. Service No.9808. Born in Tipperary and enlisted in Birr. Killed in action.

Supplementary information: Son of John and Mary Nagle, of Church Street, Tipperary. Grave or Memorial Reference: Has no known grave but is commemorated on Panel 10. Memorial: Ploegsteert Memorial in Belgium.

NAGLE, William: Rank: Private. Regiment or Service: Royal Irish Regiment. Unit: 5th Bn. Date of death: 16 August 1915. Service No.477. Born in Bansha Co. Tipperary. Enlisted in Limerick. Killed in action in Gallipoli. He has no known grave but is listed on Panel 55 on the Helles Memorial in Turkey.

NAGLE, William: Rank: Corporal. Regiment or Service: Connaught Rangers. Unit: 2nd Bn. Date of death: 6 November 1914. Service No.10183. Born in Tipperary. Enlisted in Tipperary while living in Tipperary. Killed in action. Grave or Memorial Reference: C. 5. Cemetery: Railway Chateau in Belgium.

NANGLE, Michael: Rank: Private. Regiment or Service: West Riding Regiment. Unit: 8th Bn. Date of death: 14 September 1915. Service No.14312. Born in Boyle, Co. Roscommon. Enlisted in Guiseley, Yorks while living in Carrick-on-Suir, Co. Tipperary. Died of wounds. Grave or Memorial

Grave of Martin Nevin.

Reference: E. EA. A. 669. Cemetery: Addolorata Cemetery in Malta.

NEVIN, Martin: Rank: Private. Regiment or Service: Royal Irish Regiment. Unit: 2nd Bn. Age at death: 24. Date of death: 12 November 1916. Service No. 10166.

Supplementary information: Son of Francis and Mary Nevin of Frolic, Carney. Husband of Ellie Nevin of Prospect, Nenagh, Co. Tipperary. Cemetery: Cloughprior Cemetery, Tipperary.

NEVIN, Thomas: Rank: Sergeant. Regiment or Service: East Lancashire Regiment. Unit: 1st Bn. Date of death: 1 September 1914. Service No. 8748. Born in Borrisokane, Co. Tipperary. Enlisted in Birr while living in Woking in Surrey. Died of wounds. Killed in action. He has no known grave but is listed on the La Ferte-Sous-Jouarre-Memorial in France.

NICHOLLS, Wallace Douglas: Rank: Saddler-Corporal. Regiment or Service: Household Cavalry and Cavalry of the line including the Yeomanry and Imperial Camel Corps. Unit: 4th Royal Irish Dragoon Guards. Date of death: 7 March 1917. Service No. 4943. Born in Tipperary. Enlisted in Woolwich, Kent. Died. Age at death: 26.

Supplementary information: Son of Samuel and Annie Nicholls: husband of Fanny Nicholls, of 51 Ordnance Rd, Woolwich Common, London. He has no known grave but is listed on Panel 1 on the Loos Memorial in France.

NICHOLSON, Albery Henry: Rank: Private. Regiment or Service: Royal Inniskilling Fusiliers. Unit: 6th Bn. Date of death: 7 September 1915. Service No. 8438. Born in Caher Lesmore, Co. Tipperary. Enlisted in Canterbury while living in Walmer. Killed in action. Age at death 23.

Supplementary information: Son of Capt. J. S. Nicholson (R. M.), of Stanley Gardens, Hastings. Grave or Memorial Reference: B. 38. Cemetery: Authuile Military Cemetery in France.

Grave of A. Noble.

NIXON, Adam: Rank: Lance Corporal. Regiment or Service: Leinster Regiment. Unit: 6th Bn. Age at death: 19. Date of death: 10 August 1915. Service No.257. Born in Aghancon Co. Tipperary and enlisted in Birr. Killed in action in Gallipoli.

Supplementary information: Son of John and Jane Nixon, of Parkmore, Roscrea, Co. Tipperary. He had five brothers who also served with the British Army in the First World War. Grave or Memorial Reference: Has no known grave but is commemorated on Panel 184 and 185. Memorial: Helles Memorial in Turkey.

NIXON, James: Rank: Lance Corporal. Regiment or Service: Leinster Regiment. Unit: 'D' Company, 1st Bn. Date of death: 19 April 1915. Service No.9146. Age at death: 25. Born in Birr, Kings County. Enlisted in Maryborough, Queens County. Died of wounds.

Supplementary information: Son of Johna and Jane Nixon of Parkmore, Roscrea. He had five brothers who also served with the British Army in WW1. Grave or Memorial Reference: Enclosure No.2. V. A. 9. Cemetery: Bedford House Cemetery in Belgium.

NOBLE, A: Rank: Lance Corporal. Regiment or Service: Yorkshire Regiment. Unit: 2nd Bn. Date of death: 16 June 1920. Service No.62561. Cemetery, Mary's Churchyard, Tipperary. Grave location: The old military plot to the west of the church.

NOLAN, Bevan John: Rank: Second Lieutenant. Regiment or Service: Royal Irish Regiment. Unit: 4th Bn, attd. 'C' Coy. 2nd Bn. Age at death: 21. Date of death: 3 September 1916.

Supplementary information: Son of Walter and Frances Marion Nolan, of Garnavilla, Cahir, Co. Tipperary. Grave or Memorial Reference: XIV. K. 7. Cemetery: Delville Wood Cemetery, Longueval in France. He is also commemorated on the Cahir War Memorial.

NOLAN, James: Rank: Sergeant. Regiment or Service: South Lancashire Regiment. Unit: 2nd Bn. Date of death: 24 October 1914. Service No.7391. Born in Templemore. Enlisted in Nenagh while living in Templemore. Killed in action. He has no known grave but is listed on Panel 23 on the Le Touret Memorial in France.

NOLAN, John: Rank: Private. Regiment or Service: Connaught Rangers. Unit: 1st Bn. Date of death: 7 July 1915. Service No.9691. Born in Templemore. Enlisted in Templemore while living in Templemore. Died of wounds. Grave or Memorial Reference: 11. B. 14. A. Cemetery: Etaples Military Cemetery in France.

NOLAN, John: Rank: Private. Regiment or Service: Royal Irish Regiment. Unit: 2nd Bn. Date of death: 5 July 1916. Service No.6258. Born in Ss Peter and Paul, Clonmel, Co. Tipperary. Enlisted in Clonmel. Killed in action. He has no known grave but is listed on Pier and Face

3 A on the Thiepval memorial in France.

NOLAN, Patrick: Rank: Sergeant. Regiment or Service: Royal Irish Regiment. Unit: 2nd Bn. Age at death: 34. Date of death: 28 October 1917. Service No.182. Born in New-Ross in Wexford and enlisted in Leith while living in Carrick-on-Suir.

Supplementary information: Brother of Margaret Hanlon, of Upper Bally Richard Rd, Carrick-on-Suir, Co. Tipperary. Grave or Memorial Reference: VIII. I. 86. Cemetery: Boulogne Eastern Cemetery in France.

NOONAN/NUNAN, James: Rank: Lance Corporal. Regiment or Service: Irish Guards Age at death: 19. Date of death: 13 May 1916. Service No.9723. Born in Tipperary and enlisted in Holborn in Middlesex while living in Ardvullane Co. Tipperary. Died at home.

Supplementary information: Son of Mr and Mrs John Noonan. Born at Ardavullane, Tipperary. Grave or Memorial Reference: N. 173650. Cemetery: Brompton Cemetery, UK.

NOREMAC, John: Rank: Lance Corporal. Regiment or Service: Cameronians (Scottish Rifles). Unit: 2nd Bn. Date of death: 10 March 1915. Service No.10288. Born in Clonmel. Enlisted in Glasgow. Killed in action during the Bombardment of Neuve Chappele. He has no known grave but is listed on Panels 15 and 16 on the Le Touret Memorial in France.

NORRIS, John: Rank: Lance Corporal. Regiment or Service: South Wales Borderers. Unit: 6th Bn. Date of death: 18 January 1917. Service No.16943. Born in Waterford, Tipperary, Ireland and enlisted in Tredegar while living in Clonmel, Ireland. Died of wounds.

Supplementary information: Son of Thomas Norris, of Sillaheen, Ballymacarheny, Clonmell, Co. Tipperary. Grave or Memorial Reference: III. A. 119. Cemetery: Bailleul Communal Cemetery Extension (Nord) in France.

NORTH, John: Rank: Rifleman. Regiment or Service: London Regiment. Unit: 8th (City of London) Battalion) Battalion (Post Office Rifles). Date of death: 15 September 1916. Service No.4986. Born in Callai. Enlisted in Killenaule while living in Killenaule. Killed in action. Age at death: 25.

Supplementary information: Son of Honorah North, of Causeway View Lane, Portrush, Co. Antrim, and the late William Charles North. He has no known grave but is listed on Pier and Face 9 C and 9 D on the Thiepval Memorial in France.

NUGENT, John: Rank: Private. Regiment or Service: Machine Gun Regiment. Unit: 30th Bn. Date of death: 21 March 1918. Service No.43299. Formerly he was with the Royal Irish Regiment where his number was 11125. Born in Four Mile Water, Co. Tipperary. Enlisted in Clonmel while living in Ballymacarbury. Killed in action. Grave or Memorial Reference: I. H. 23. Cemetery: Savy British Cemetery in France.

NUGENT, Thomas: Rank: Private. Regiment or Service: King's Own Scottish Borderers. Unit: 1st–5th Bn. He was previously with the Royal Irish regiment where his number was 3525. Date of death: 1 August 1918. Service No.31164. Born in Cahir and enlisted in Tipperary while living in Cahir. Killed in action.

Supplementary information: Husband of B. Nugent of Upper Abbey Street, Cahir, Co. Tipperary. Grave or Memorial Reference: X. E. 3. Cemetery: Raperie British Cemetery, Villemontoire in France. He is also commemorated on the Cahir War Memorial.

NUGENT, Maurice: Rank: Private. Regiment or Service: Royal Irish Regiment. Unit: 2nd Bn. Age at death: 19. Date of death: 2 June 1916. Service No.10798. Born in Ballymacarberry in Waterford and enlisted in Clonmel while living in Ballymacarberry. Died of wounds.

Supplementary information: Son of James and Johanna Nugent, of 4 Kickham Row, Clonmel, Co. Tipperary.

Late of Ballymacarbery, Co. Waterford. Grave or Memorial Reference: Plot 1. Row A. Grave 20. Cemetery: Corbie Communal Cemetery Extension in France.

NUNAN/NOONAN, James: Rank: Lance Corporal. Regiment or Service: Irish Guards Age at death: 19. Date of death: 13 May 1916. Service No.9723. Born in Tipperary and enlisted in Holborn in Middlesex while living in Ardvullane Co. Tipperary. Died at home.

Supplementary information: Son of Mr and Mrs John Noonan. Born at Ardavullane, Tipperary. Grave or Memorial Reference: N. 173650. Cemetery: Brompton Cemetery, UK.

NYHAN, Thomas: Rank: Private. Regiment or Service: Irish Guards. Unit: 1st Bn. Date of death: 26 September 1916. Service No.8158. Born in Emly, Co. Tipperary. Enlisted in Tipperary. Died of wounds. Grave or Memorial Reference: I. E. 43. Cemetery: Grove Town Cemetery, Meaulte, France.

O

OAKLEY, James: Rank: Gunner. Regiment or Service: Royal Garrison Artillery. Unit: 20th T. M. Bty. Age at death: 27. Date of death: 14 March 1916. Service No.43097. Born in Cloughjordan and enlisted in Dublin while living in Cloughjordan. Killed in action.

Supplementary information: Son of Hubert and Penelope Oakley, of Deer Park, Cloughjordan, Co. Tipperary. Grave or Memorial Reference: Bay 1. Memorial: Arras Memorial in France.

O'BRIEN, Christopher: Rank: Private. Regiment or Service: Royal Irish Regiment. Unit: 2nd Bn. Date of death: 17 April 1915. Service No.6400. Born in Irishtown, Clonmel, Co. Tipperary. Enlisted in Clonmel. Killed in action. He has no known grave but is listed on Panel 4 on the Ploegsteert Memorial in Belgium.

O'BRIEN, Daniel: Rank: Private (Lance Corporal). Regiment or Service: Royal Irish Regiment. Unit: 2nd Bn. Date of death: 16 January 1918. Service No.11146. Born in Ballyporeen, Co. Tipperary. Enlisted in Cahir while living in Cooladerry, Co. Tipperary. Killed in action. Grave or Memorial Reference: V. C. 3. Cemetery: Epehy Wood Farm Cemetery, Epehy in France. He is also commemorated on the Cahir War Memorial.

O'BRIEN, Edmond: Rank: Private. Regiment or Service: Irish Guards. Unit: 1st Bn. Date of death: 17 September 1916. Service No.8362. Born in Dundrum, Co. Tipperary. Enlisted in Thurles. Killed in action. He was a member of the Local Volunteer Force before enlistment. He has no known grave but is listed on Pier and Face 7D on the Thiepval Memorial in France.

O'BRIEN, Edmond: Rank: Bombardier. Regiment or Service: Royal Garrison Artillery. Unit: 11th Siege Bty. Age at death: 34. Date of death: 23 April 1917. Service No.26101. Born in Ardfinnan and enlisted in Cahir. Died of wounds.

Supplementary information: Son of Bridget O'Brien: husband of

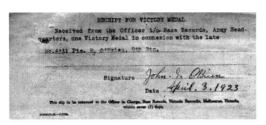

Hugh O'Brien.

Ellen O'Brien, Ardfinnan, Cahir, Co. Tipperary. Grave or Memorial Reference: IV. C. 29. Cemetery: Duisans British Cemetery, Etrun in France. He is also commemorated on the Cahir War Memorial.

O'BRIEN, Henry Edward: Rank: Captain. Regiment or Service: Royal Army Medical Corps. Unit: No. 2 Gen. Hosp. Age at death: 27. Died of wounds. Attached to 99th Field Ambulance. Date of death: 8 September 1916.

Supplementary information: Son of Richard R. and Elizabeth O'Brien, of 3 Jervis Place, Clonmel, Co. Tipperary. Grave or Memorial Reference: Div. 3. F. 3. Cemetery: Ste Marie, Cemetery, Le Havre in France.

O'BRIEN, Hugh: Rank: Private. Regiment or Service: A. I. F. Unit: 9th Bn. Date of death: 23 July 1916. Service No. 4331 Born in Tipperary. Date of enlistment: 7 October 1915. Weight: 100lbs. Height: 5'8". Eyes: grey. Complexion: ruddy. Hair: black. Religious denomination: R.C. Occupation on enlistment: labourer. Next of kin address, Mr H O'Brien, 54 Pratten Street, Petria Terrace, Brisbane, Queensland, and also at Tarron, Queensland. Served in Alexandria, Marseilles, the Bull Ring in Etaples, and France. He was court-martialled earlier in the war for drunkenness while on active service, leaving his piquet without orders from his Superior Officer. He was sentenced with two others to forty-five days' field punishment No 1 which is a very severe sentence. Field punishment No 1 is where a soldier is tied spread-eagled to wagon wheel for long periods of time. He was still serving this sentence when he was killed in action. His sister Marie O'Brien received a pension 10 shillings a week from the government from 12 October 1916. Killed in action. He has no known grave but is listed on the Villers Bretonneux Memorial in France.

O'BRIEN, James: Rank: Private. Regiment or Service: Irish Guards. Unit: 1st Bn. Age at death: 24. Date of death: 8 January 1915. Service No. 4699. Born in Dunhall Co. Tipperary and

Grave of J. O'Brien.

James O'Brien.

enlisted in Clonmel. Killed in action.

Supplementary information: Son of Mr and Mrs O'Brien, of Mountain Rd, Cahir, Co. Tipperary. Grave or Memorial Reference: Has no known grave but is commemorated on Panel 4. Memorial: Le Touret Memorial in France. He is also commemorated on the Cahir War Memorial.

O'BRIEN, James: Rank: Private. Regiment or Service: Royal Irish Regiment. Unit: 2nd Bn. Date of death: 21 March 1918. Service No. 5962. Born in St Michaels in Tipperary. Enlisted in Tipperary. He won the Military Medal and is listed in the *London Gazette*. Killed in action. Age at death: 26.

Supplementary information: Son of Mrs Johanna Hanley, of Doon, Co. Limerick. He has no known grave but is listed on Panel 30 and 31 on the Pozieres Memorial in France.

O'BRIEN, J: Rank: Sapper. Regiment or Service: Royal Engineers. Date of death: 27 December 1919. Service No. 365924. Age at death: 50.

Supplementary information: Husband of Elizabeth O'Brien, of Saint Vincent's Avenue, Wood Quay, Galway. Grave or Memorial Reference: E. H. 109. Cemetery: St Michaels New Cemetery, Tipperary.

O'BRIEN, James: Rank: Private. Regiment or Service: Royal Warwickshire Regiment. Unit: 2nd– 5th Bn. Age at death: 28. Date of death: 3 December 1917. Service No. 235066.

Supplementary information: Son of Michael O'Brien, of Tipperary: husband of Bridget Merrick, (formerly O'Brien), of Long St, Cappamore, Limerick. Grave or Memorial Reference: Has no known grave but is commemorated on Panel 3. Memorial: Cambrai Memorial in Louveral in France:

Driver James F O'Brien RFA upon whom has been conferred the Medal Militaire of the French Legion of Honour is among the hundred wounded British soldiers who have just arrived at the Huddersfield Royal Infirmary. In an interview he describes the circumstances in which he gained the distinction, "this little affair" he said, "occurred on August 26th at Ligny, between Mons and Le Chateau. We were retiring, and the whole of my battery, with the exception of one gun, had reached safety. The remaining gun was the one to which I was attached. Shells were dropping around me wholesale, and several trees about ten yards away were lopped off. The gun was in danger of being smashed by the Germans. I went to the wagon lines, secured a couple of horses, and went back to my gun. Corporal Rimmer, a burly Yorkshireman, came up and helped me limber up. One who had previously tried to help me had been shot clean through the head. We ran to the gun up a steep narrow road. I subsequently found that during the short run the mare I was riding had been hit nine times, and one of the bullets had passed through the riding pads of my saddle. We galloped along and brought the gun safely into the position taken up by the remainder of the battery. I did not know what happened to Corporal Rimmer, but I have seen him since. We waited in the new position until the Prussian Guard advanced, and then we smashed them". Driver O'Brien also mentioned that helped another gunner, who had been shot through the head, out of the firing line, and then found out that the gunner had had both legs shot off. That affair occurred near Soissons. At Ballieul, Driver O'Brien saw a remark-able incident. Two women were taking shelter at a shrine. A shell dropped four yards in front and killed both. When Driver O: Brien sings "It's a long long way to Tipperary" he means it seriously, for he was born at Cashel, Tipperary. He enlisted in 1909 when he was 19, being attached to the 35th Battery, Royal Field Artillery (Howitzer Section).

In a late 1914 letter to his Mother, Mrs Mary Anne O'Brien, Cashel, he says:

We arrived in France on the 23 August, and came straight up the country. On Wednesday 26 August, we got into action at a place called Ligny: we didn't fire but the enemy shelled us. Oh! It was dreadful to hear their shells come screaming over our heads. We remained in the same position for about an hour when we got the order to retire. Our Battery was the first to make a move: all went well for about 400 Yards until we came into a road covered with trees. And then it seemed as if hell itself was let loose. My God I will never forget it: bursting shells, horses falling, men shouting. I cannot explain it: it is impossible. Our centre horse was shot and before he fell, the driver just jumped clear from what I should say was certain death. In the confusion everyone was saying and doing things at random. I remember looking around at the officer and he was laughing. We unlimbered our big gun and as I was trying to get clear, another

team and wagon came crashing into my limber: it seemed as if I was going to be killed, everything I was doing for the good appeared to be upset at the last moment. We remained on the road for what I thought to be an hour, but I suppose it only lasted about five minutes. But still no one came my way to get our gun out of danger. Of course all the remainder of our team had gone, leaving me with five horses to try and save the gun which was 3 ½ ton in weight. One young Officer, Lieutenant Browning from Fermoy, was with me on the road. I asked him what was to become of us and he said "We must get that gun out" I replied "Yes, Sir, or we both down," He laughed and we both got on our horses: He shouted "Ireland forever". Away we went into the thick of it. Oh God it was a glorious ride: a sharp gallop, halt, right about, and then a Sergeant and a Farrier helped to limber up the gun. As I was just starting to get away again my horse was shot about eight or nine times: my own cap was blown off my head, and one gunner was killed. It is awful to see a chum get killed. I saw him fall: it makes you long for a chance to avenge their deaths. At last I got the horses to start (my own was limping badly but she kept on) and in about ten minutes we were safe for a time at least, but my dear old pal- my horse-died at Ligny after taking part in the now famous Battle of Mons. My Major sent in my name, and I have been awarded a great French honour called the Medaille Militaire of the legion of Honour. It is like the Victoria Cross, but of course not quite so great. I am asking my major to get it sent home to you so that you may be able to see that I have done my duty. It is a splendid decoration: I have some of the ribbon on my breast; I do feel so proud of it too. I need not say that I was delighted to receive high distinction for doing what was my simple duty. As I write this letter on the same gun limber, the shells keep on coming over but I don't think they will find us. Mum, you should see the Germans: they look a nice lot of fellows, but by gum they ain't. I am longing for one good sleep, and I mean to have it if I can possibly get home alive. It is a big chance, but if dangerous, well Irishmen are never afraid to die. I would gladly give my life if I know I have been the cause of killing a few of my 'Chums'---the Germans. Now how are all the old friends in Cashel? I trust you will not worry, because we must all be reconciled to whatever happens. God's will be done. You may never know I may, with God's help walk up from the old station with my chest adorned with my French Medaille Militaire. Give my love to my sisters and brothers. Tell them that they should not fret, I shall be O. K. I was never born to die with my boots on. I hear Ireland has got Home Rule, I am proud of it. Well good luck to our beloved country, may all her sons join in the happy times to come.
I am your loving Son
Jim.

Grave of James Francis O'Brien.

O'BRIEN, James Francis: Rank: Driver, 58270, Royal Field Artillery, 5th Reserve Bde, 16 December 1915. Born in Cashel and enlisted in Templemore. Died at home. Buried in Cashel (Rock of Cashel) Graveyard, north of the North tower. Son of J. O'Brien, of William Street, Cashel. Born in Cashel and enlisted in Templemore. See his photograph and other information above. Grave location: North of the North tower.

O'BRIEN, James Francis: Rank: Lieutenant. Regiment or Service: Royal Munster Fusiliers. Unit: 2nd Bn. Age at death: 24. Date of death: 21 December 1914. Killed in action.

Supplementary information: Son of Clarissa Clare O'Brien, (*née* Webster) of Ardport House Thurles and the late Denis Bray O'Brien. Cemetery: He has no known grave but is listed on Panels 43 and 44 the Le Touret Memorial in France.

O'BRIEN, Jeremiah: Rank: Gunner. Regiment or Service: Royal Garrison Artillery. Unit: 14th Siege Bty. Age at death: 42. Date of death: 19 June 1918. Service No. 41941. Born in Tipperary and enlisted in Clonmel. Died of wounds.

Supplementary information: Son of Jeremiah and Mrs E. O'Brien, of Tipperary. Served in the South African War. Grave or Memorial Reference: I. A. 39. Cemetery: Terlincthun British Cemetery, Wimille in France.

O'BRIEN, John: Served as **GORMAN**. Rank: Private. Regiment or Service: Royal Irish Regiment. Unit: 2nd Bn. Age at death: 30. Date of death: 19 October 1914. Service No. 4438.

Supplementary information: Husband of Bridget O'Brien of 33 River Street,

Clonmel, Co. Tipperary. Grave or Memorial Reference: Has no known grave but is commemorated on Panel 11 and 12. Memorial: Le Touret Memorial in France.

O'BRIEN, John: Rank: Sergeant. Regiment or Service: Irish Regiment. Unit: 3rd Bn. Age at death: 42. Born in Wexford. Enlisted in Clonmel. Date of death: 22 March 1915. Service No.5739.

Supplementary information: Husband of M. O'Brien of 5 Davis Rd. Clonmel. Cemetery, Clonmel, St Patrick's Cemetery. Grave location: 4. D. 128.

O'BRIEN, Laurence: Rank: Private. Regiment or Service: Royal Munster Fusiliers. Unit: 8th Bn. Age at death: 18. Date of death: 7 June 1916. Service No.4880. Born in Thurles and enlisted in Templemore while living in Thurles.

Supplementary information: Son of Bridget O'Brien, of Upper Pike Street, Thurles, Co. Tipperary, and James O'Brien. Grave or Memorial Reference:V.D.94. Cemetery: Bethune Town Cemetery in France.

O'BRIEN, Michael: Rank: Private (Lance Corporal). Regiment or Service: Royal Irish Regiment. Unit: 6th Bn. Date of death: 3 September 1916. Service No.6279. Born in St Michael's in Tipperary. Enlisted in Scartnaglorane, Co. Tipperary. Killed in action. He has no known grave but is listed on Pier and Face 3A on the Thiepval Memorial in France.

O'BRIEN, Patrick: Rank: Lance Corporal. Regiment or Service: Royal Irish Fusiliers. Unit: 1st Bn. Date of death: 24 August 1918. Service No.16221. Born in Clonmel. Enlisted in Clonmel. Killed in action. Grave or Memorial Reference: II. G. 26. Cemetery: Bailleul Communal Cemetery Extension (Nord) in France.

O'BRIEN, Timothy: Rank: Private. No 1247, Royal Irish Regiment, 5th Bn. Date of death: 12 September 1915 in, Cashel, Co. Tipperary. Enlisted in Cashel. Killed in action. Gallipoli. He has no known grave but is listed on Panel 55 of the Helles Memorial in Turkey.

O'BRIEN, Thomas: Rank: Private. Regiment or Service: Royal Irish Regiment. Unit: 5th Bn. Age at death: 19. Date of death: 27 October 1915. Service No.4967.

Supplementary information: Son of Mrs Mary O'Brien, of St Joseph's Hospital, Clogheen, Co. Tipperary. Grave or Memorial Reference: 1593. Cemetery: Salonika (Lembet Road) Military Cemetery in Greece.

O'BRIEN, Thomas: Rank: Private. Regiment or Service: Royal Irish Regiment. Unit: 1st Bn. Age at death: 25. Date of death: 10 March 1918. Service No.2623. Born in Killenaule and enlisted in Clonmel while living in Killenaule. Killed in action in Palestine.

Supplementary information: Son of Thomas and Kate O'Brien, of

Cattaganstown, Killenaule, Co. Tipperary. Grave or Memorial Reference: A. 69. Cemetery: Jerusalem War Cemetery, Israel.

O'BRIEN, Thomas Dominick: Rank: Boy 1st Class. Regiment or Service: Royal Navy. Unit: HMS. *Viknor* Age at death: 16. Date of death: 13 January 1915. Service No.J-28235.

Supplementary information: Son of Thomas O'Brien, of Clonmel, Co. Tipperary. Grave or Memorial Reference: 8. Memorial: Portsmouth Naval Memorial. HMS *Viknor* was an armed Merchant Cruiser. She struck a sea mine off Tory Island and went down with all 295 crew. There were no survivors.

O'BRIEN, William: Rank: Private. Regiment or Service: Royal Irish Fusiliers. Unit: 7th Bn. Date of death: 21 April 1916. Service No.20583. Born in Nenagh. Enlisted in Tipperary while living in Doon Co. Limerick. Killed in action. Age at death: 25.

Supplementary information: Son of John and Margaret O'Brien, of Doon, Limerick. Grave or Memorial Reference: II.J.37. Cemetery:Vermelles British Cemetery in France.

O'CALLAGHAN, John Joseph: Rank: Acting Corporal. Regiment or Service: Royal Dublin Fusiliers. Unit: 1st Bn. Date of death: 1 July 16, the first day of the Battle of the Somme. Service No.19942. Born in Clonmel. Enlisted in Cork while living in Clonmel. Killed in action. Age at death: 22.

Supplementary information: Son of Patrick O'Callaghan, of Knocklofty, Clonmel. Grave or Memorial Reference: B. 78. Cemetery: Hawthorn Ridge Cemetery No 2, Auchonvilliers in France.

O'CALLAGHAN, M: Rank: Lance Bombardier. Regiment or Service: Royal Garrison Artillery. Date of death: 1 April 1919. Service No.128160. Born in Clonmel, Co. Tipperary. Grave or Memorial Reference: R405. Cemetery: Liverpool (Ford) Roman Catholic Cemetery in Liverpool.

O'CALLAGHAN, P: Rank: Private. Regiment or Service: Munster Fusiliers. Unit: 1st Garrison Bn. Date of death: 15 March 1920. Service No.G/1397. Cemetery, Clonmel, St Patricks Cemetery. Grave location: 6. L. 117.

O'CONNELL, Daniel: Rank: Private. Regiment or Service: Royal Munster Fusiliers. Unit: 2nd Bn. Age at death: 29. Date of death: 4 October 1918. Service No.8259. Born in Rathkeale in Limerick and enlisted in Tralee Co. Kerry while living in Dysart Co. Limerick.

Supplementary information: Son of James O'Connell, of Kyle, Tipperary: husband of Norah O'Connell. Grave or Memorial Reference: V. M. 15. Cemetery: Niederzwehren Cemetery in Germany.

O'CONNELL, F: Rank: Private. Regiment or Service: Royal Dublin Fusiliers. Unit: 3rd Bn. Age at death: 21.

A postcard of the SS *Lapland* from 1910.

Date of death: 10 May 1917. Service No.25188. Additional information: Son of Mrs Johanna O'Connell of 5 Raheen Terrace Clonmel. Grave location: 3. EA. 103. Cemetery, Clonmel, St Patricks Cemetery.

O'CONNELL, Francis: Rank: Private. Regiment or Service: Household Cavalry and Cavalry of the line including the Yeomanry and Imperial Camel Corps. Unit: South Irish Horse, B. Squadron. Date of death: 19 March 1917. Service No.2061. Entitled to the War Medal and the Vicotry Medal. Born in Tipperary. Enlisted in Dublin in May 1916 while living in Tipperary. Killed in action. Grave or Memorial Reference: III. D. 11. Cemetery: Douchy-Les-Ayette British Cemetery in France.

O'CONNELL, John: Rank: Private. Regiment or Service: Royal Inniskilling Fusiliers. Unit: 1st Bn. Date of death: 2 May 1915. Service No.8963. Born in Cashel, Co. Tipperary. Enlisted in Coleraine. Killed in action in Gallipoli. He has no known grave but is listed on Panel 97 to 101 on the Helles Memorial in Turkey.

O'CONNOR, James: Rank: Trimmer. Regiment or Service: Mercantile Marine. Unit: SS *Lapland* (Liverpool) Age at death: 25. Date of death: 7 April 1917.

Supplementary information: Born at Tipperary. Has no known grave but is commemorated on the Tower Hill Memorial, London.

O'CONNOR, John: Rank: Private. Regiment or Service: East Lancashire Regiment. Unit: 11th Bn. Date of death: 1 July 1916, the first day of the Battle of the Somme. Service No.18035. Born in Nenagh. Enlisted in Accrington in Lancashire while living in Church in Lancashire. Killed in action. He has no known grave but is listed on Pier and Face 6 C. on the Thiepval Memorial in France.

O'CONNOR, Martin: Rank: Private. Regiment or Service: Cheshire Regiment. Unit: 13th Bn. Date of death: 10 August 1917. Service No.49201. Formerly he was with the Manchester Regiment where his number was 22716. Born in Clonmel. Enlisted in Manchester. Killed in action. He has no known grave but is listed on Panels 9-22 on the Ypres (Menin Gate) Memorial in Belgium

O'CONNOR, Michael Joseph: Rank: Private. Regiment or

Service: Royal Irish Regiment. Unit: 3rd Bn. Age at death: 30. Born in Kilmackthomas Co. Waterford. Enlisted in Waterford while living in Kilmackthomas. Died at home. Date of death: 27 September 1916. Service No.8504. Additional information: Son of William O'Connor. Husband of Margaret O'Connor of 135 East Main Street Annadale, West Lothian. Cemetery: Templemore Catholic Cemetery. Grave location: plot 2.

O'CONNOR, Patrick: Alias, correct name is **HOWLEY, Roger Francis**. Rank: Private. Regiment or Service: 5th Reinforcements, 15th Bn, 4th Australian Infantry Brigade. Date of death: 13 August 1915. Service No.1986. Born in Tipperary. Enlisted on 15 May 1915 at Toowoomba. Age on enlistment: 26 years 3 months. Height: 5' 9". Complexion: fresh. Hair: dark brown. Weight: 11st 6lbs, Eyes: blue. Before the outbreak of war he left home due to parental cruelty and went to sea. He deserted his ship in Sydney having arrived there from Chile and worked his way up to the Warling Downs where he worked in Bowenville. Enlisted in Toowoomba and trained in Enoggera Camp. Shot in the bladder in the Gallipoli Peninsula on 8 August 1915 and transferred from 29th Field Ambulance to a hospital ship. He died of wounds on the hospital ship H. S. Dongola and was buried at sea. H is effects were sent to Elizabeth T Howley, 7 Grosvenor Rd, Leyton, E. 10. His sister is listed as Mrs F Mann, 64 Valentine Road, Woods Street, Walthamstone, Essex.

Supplementary information: Age 26. Son of Thomas and Elizabeth Ann Howley, of 14, King Edward Rd, Leyton, London, England. He has no known grave but is listed on the Lone Pine Memorial, Memorial in Gallipoli.

O'CONNOR, Thomas: Rank: Private. Regiment or Service: Irish

Grave of Michael Joseph O'Connor.

Guards. Unit: 1st Bn. Age at death: 34. Date of death: 9 October 1915. Service No. 5593. Born in Clonmel and enlisted there also. Killed in action.

Supplementary information: Son of James and Mary O'Connor, of Heywood Rd, Clonmel: husband of Margaret O'Connor, of 23 Heywood Rd, Clonmel, Co. Tipperary. Grave or Memorial Reference: VII. A. 2. Cemetery: St Mary's A. D. S. Cemetery, Haisnes in France.

O'DONNELL, Denis: Rank: Private. Regiment or Service: Irish Guards. Unit: 2nd Bn. Date of death: 15 September 1916. Service No. 5846. Born in Tipperary. Enlisted in Liverpool. Killed in action. He has no known grave but is listed on Pier and Face 7D on the Thiepval Memorial in France.

O'DONNELL, James: Rank: Private. Regiment or Service: Royal Irish Regiment. Unit: 5th Bn. Date of death: 4 November 1918. Service No. 2786. Born in Templemore. Enlisted in Londonderry. Killed in action. Grave or Memorial Reference:

I. B. 31. Cemetery: Cross Roads Cemetery, Fontaine-Au-Bois in France.

O'DONNELL, JOHN: Rank: Private. Regiment or Service: Royal Irish Regiment. Unit: 2nd Bn. Age at death: 31. Date of death: 24 May 1915. Service No. 3938. Born in Tipperary and enlisted there also. Died of wounds.

Supplementary information: Husband of Nellie O'Donnell, of Monastery Rd, Tipperary. Grave or Memorial Reference: I. F. 51. Cemetery: Bailleul Communal Cemetery Extension (Nord) in France.

O'DONNELL, Percy: Rank: Second Lieutenant. Regiment or Service: Royal Field Artillery. Unit: 81st Bty. 5th Bde. Age at death: 31. Date of death: 6 May 1916.

Supplementary information: Son of Michael and Maria O'Donnell, of Bannixtown House, Clonmel, Co. Tipperary. Grave or Memorial Reference: V. A. 35. Cemetery: Lijssenthoek Military Cemetary in Belgium.

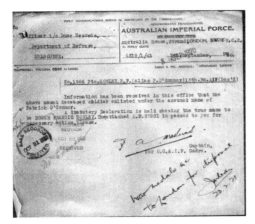

Patrick O'Connor.

O'DONNELL, Richard: Rank: Private. Regiment or Service: Australian Infantry. Unit: 43rd Bn. Date of death: 4 July 1918. Service No.2429. Born in Clonmel, Co. Tipperary. Enlisted 4 June 1916 in Perth, NSW while living at Brittania Coffee Palace, Perth. Occupation on enlistment: labourer. Age: 33 years 10 months. Height: 5'5". Weight: 14st 1lbs, Hair: auburn. Eyes: blue. Complexion: fresh. Religious denomination: R.C. Served in Freemantle, Devonport, England, Folkstone, Armentiereas, and the famous Bull Ring in Etaples. Gassed in the trenches on 27 May 1918, hospitalised and returned to duty 12 June 1918. Four weeks later he died of wounds received in action (gunshot wound to the head). His effects were to be sent to: Mrs Mary Ryan, Peninsula Road, Meylands, Perth. Western Australia. Brother is named as James O'Donnell, Fethard, Co. Tipperary. His parents were dead when he enlisted. Grave or Memorial Reference: III. D. 41. Cemetery: Daours Communal Cemetery Extension, France.

O'DONNELL, Richard: Rank: Private. Regiment or Service: Royal Irish Regiment. Unit: 6th Bn. Age at death: 27. Date of death: 9 September 1916. Service No.5039. Born in Ballylooby in Tipperary and enlisted in Ballylomasna Co. Tipperary while living in New Graigue Co. Tipperary. Killed in action.

Supplementary information: Son of Thomas and Bridget O'Donnell, of New Graigue, Clogheen, Co.Tipperary. Grave or Memorial Reference: I. D.

20. Cemetery: Combles Communal Cemetery Extension in France. He is also commemorated on the Cahir War Memorial.

O'DONOGHUE, David Hugh: Rank: Private. Regiment or Service: Australian Infantry, A. I. F. Unit: 9th Bn. Age at death: 25. Date of death: 20 June 1918. Service No.6076

Supplementary information: Son of Edward and Mary O'Donoghue, of Lakeview, Marlfield, Clonmel, Tipperary, Ireland. Grave or Memorial Reference: II. A. 20. Cemetery: Borre British Cemetery in France.

O'DONOHUE, John: Rank: Private. No 15012, Leinster Regiment, 2nd Bn, Previously he was with the Royal Irish regiment where his number was 5590. Date of death: 11 January 1917. Age at death: 52. Born in Cashel. Enlisted in Cashel while living in Cashel.

Supplementary information: Buried Cahel (Rock of Cashel) Graveyard. In north-west angle of Cathedral. (Also known as **DONOHUE**). Son of John and Catherine O'Donohue of Camas Rd., Cashel, Co. Tipperary. Served in the South African Campaign, and on the north- west Frontier of India. He was born in Cashel and enlisted in Cashel. Died in France and Flanders. This man died in foreign parts during the First World War and is buried at home.

O'DONOGHUE, Michael: Rank: Private. Regiment or Service: Royal Dublin Fusiliers. Unit: 2nd Bn. Previously he was with the Royal

Grave of J. O'Donoghue.

Irish Regiment where his number was 5427. Age at death: 20. Date of death: 23 October 1916. Service No.43041. Born in Cahir and enlisted in Cashel while living in Cahir. Killed in action.

Supplementary information: Son of John O'Donoghue, of Market St, Cahir, Co. Tipperary. Grave or Memorial Reference: Has no known grave but is commemorated on Panel 44 and 46. Memorial: Ypres (Menin Gate) Memorial in Belgium. He is also commemorated on the Cahir War Memorial.

O'DONOGHUE, Timothy: Rank: Driver. Regiment or Service: Royal Horse Artillery and Royal Field Artillery. Date of death: 11 April 1917. Service No.74997. Born in Clonmel. Enlisted in Cardiff, Glam. Grave or Memorial Reference: B. 12. Cemetery: Bapaume, Australian Cemetery in France

O'DWYER, John: Rank: 2nd Lt (TP).

Regiment or Service: General List, New Armies and Royal Irish Fusiliers. Unit: 7th Bn. Secondary Unit: Trench Mortar Battery. Date of death: 10 September 1916. Residence: Barrack Street, Thurles. Enlisted in London. Died of wounds. Grave or Memorial Reference: II. C. 61. Cemetery: La-Neuville British Cemetery, Corbie in France.

O'DWYER, Patrick: Rank: Private. Regiment or Service: Royal Irish Regiment. Unit: 6th Bn. Date of death: 16 June 1917. Service No.3674. Born in Tipperary and enlisted in Mallow Co. Cork while living in Tipperary. Died of wounds at home.

Supplementary information: Son of Mrs H. O'Dwyer, of Upper New Rd, Tipperary.

O'DWYER, Patrick Michael: Rank: Private. Regiment or Service: Canadian Infantry (Alberta Regiment)

Unit: 50th Bn. Age at death: 45. Date of death: 10 April 1917. Service No.812192

Supplementary information: Son of Mr and Mrs James M. O'Dwyer, of Cappagh White, Tipperary, Ireland: husband of Nancy O'Dwyer, of Vibank, Saskatchewan, Canada. Data from the reverse of the enlistment document: Age on Enlistment: 39 Years. 7 Months. Height: 5'5 ½". Eye colour: brown. Hair colour: dark. Religious denomination: R.C. Chest expansion: 3 ½". Girth: 37 ½". Date of enlistment: 25 May 1916. Place of enlistment: Edmonton. Grave or Memorial Reference: 2. C. 20. Cemetery: Canadian Cemetery No. 2, Neuville-St Vaast in France.

O'DWYER, Thomas: Rank: Private. Regiment or Service: Royal Army Medical Corps. Unit: 1st Malta Coy. Is also listed under the name DWYER. Age at death: 29. Date of death: 14 July 1916. Service No.30436. Born in Bansha and enlisted in Clonmel. Died in Malta.

Supplementary information: Son of Thomas and Mary O'Dwyer, of Upper Abbey St, Cahir, Co. Tipperary. Grave or Memorial Reference: E. EA. A. 688. Cemetery: Addolorata Cemetery in Malta. He is also commemorated on the Cahir War Memorial.

O'FARRELL, John: Rank: Private. Regiment or Service: Royal Irish Regiment. Unit: 2nd Bn. Date of death: 9 July 1916. Service No.4862. Born in Templekenny, Co. Tipperary. Enlisted in Clonmel while living in Ballyporeen. Died of wounds. Grave or Memorial Reference: VIII. C. 118. Cemetery: Boulogne Eastern Cemetery in France. He is also commemorated on the Cahir War Memorial.

O'FLAHERTY, John: Rank: Private. Regiment or Service: Royal Munster Fusiliers. Unit: 1st Bn. Age at death: 22. Date of death: 7 November 1917. Service No.6748. Born in Rossmore and enlisted in Limerick while living in Goolds Cross Co. Tipperary. Killed in action.

Supplementary information: Son of Thomas and Catherine O'Flaherty, of Doorish, Goold's Cross, Co. Tipperary. Grave or Memorial Reference: I. C. 32. Cemetery: Croisilles Railway Cemetery in France.

O'GRADY, John: Rank: Private. Regiment or Service: Unit: Army Service Corps. Born in Cork. Enlisted in London while living in Cork. Died of wounds at home. Date of death: 19 May 1918. Service No.M/372831.

Supplementary information: Son of John and Margaret O'Grady of Chapel Street, Cloyne Co. Cork: husband of Margaret Sweeney (formerly O'Grady) of 74 Gairymore Clonmel. Buried in Inishlounaght Cemetery, Co. Tipperary. Grave location: Near the East boundary.

O'GRADY, Timothy: Rank: Private. Regiment or Service: Irish Guards. Unit: 1st Bn. Age at death: 20. Date of death: 9 October 1917. Service No.10864. Born in Moycarkey and

Grave of John O'Grady.

enlisted in Clonmel. Killed in action.

Supplementary information: Son of the late Mr and Mrs James O'Grady, of Cloughmartin, Holycross, Thurles, Co. Tipperary. Grave or Memorial Reference: Has no known grave but is commemorated on Panel 10 to 11. Memorial: Tyne Cot Memorial in Belgium.

O'GRADY, Patrick: Rank: Sergeant. Regiment or Service: South Wales Borderers. Unit: 4th Bn. Date of death: 9 April 1916. Service No. 125665. Born in Thurles. Enlisted in Newport, Mon. Killed in action in Mesopotamia. Grave or Memorial Reference: He has no known grave but is listed on Panel 16 and 62 on the Basra Memorial in Iraq.

O'HOULIHAN, Patrick: Rank: Private. Regiment or Service: Australian Army Medical Corps. Unit: 1st Field Ambulance. Date of death: 18 September 1917. Service

No. 1256. From Abbeyville, Lorrha. Co. Tipperary.

Supplementary information: Brother of Thomas Houlihan who died with the Newzealenders. Grave or Memorial Reference: XIX. D. 15A. Cemetery: Lijssenthoek Military Cemetery in Belgium. According to his records he enlisted in Perth on the 10 October 1914. His place of birth was put down as Lorrha in or near the town of Birr in the county of Tipperary. Age at death: 22½. Height: 5' 8'. He worked as a farmhand. His wife's name was Ruby and she was born in Australia but lived in London. Eyes: blue. Hair: brown. Complexion: ruddy. Weight: 12st. During his training and service he was in Tidworth, Folkstone and London. He was also in Boulogne, Alexandria, Egypt, Tel-El-Kabir, Abbassia, Rouen, Belgium and also trained in the famous Bull Ring in Etaples. He had some illnesses during his service including Mumps and Myalgia which was common in those days in the trenches. On

Patrick O'Houlihan.

the 18 of September he received two bullet wounds. The first fractured his left thigh and the second hit him in the head. He was brought by a field ambulance to a Candadian Casualty Clearing Station where he died later. Two months later his widow received a pension of 40 shillings which she got every two weeks for the rest of her life.

O'KEEFE, Denis: Rank: Driver. Regiment or Service: Royal Horse Artillery and Royal Field Artillery. Date of death: 24 March 1916. Service No.90999. Born in Lisgool, Co. Tipperary. Enlisted in Cork. Died in Mesopotamia. Age at death: 22.

Supplementary information: Son of Denis O'Keeffe, of Corbally, Ballincurrig, Midleton, Co. Cork. He has no known grave but is listed on Panels 3 and 60 on the Basra Memorial in Iraq.

O'KEEFE, John: Rank: Private. Regiment or Service: Royal Irish Regiment. Unit: 5th Bn. Date of death:

22 October 1918. Service No.179. Born in Fethard. Enlisted in Clonmel while living in Fethard. Killed in action. Age at death: 20.

Supplementary information: Son of William and Hannah O'Keefe, of Dournane, Mooncoin, Co. Kilkenny. Grave or Memorial Reference: II. E. 6. Cemetery: Zantvoorde British Cemetery in Belgium.

O'KELLY, Michael: Rank: Private. Regiment or Service: Royal Army Medical Corps. Unit: 17th Field Ambulance. Date of death: 23 April 1917. Service No.843. Born in Tipperary and enlisted in Wakefield. Killed in action.

Supplementary information: Son of Mrs M. O'Kelly, of Old Church Street, Cahir, Tipperary. Grave or Memorial Reference: I. O. 49. Cemetery: Philosophe British Cemetery, Mazingarbe in France. He is also commemorated on the Cahir War Memorial.

O'LOUCHLIN/O'LOUGHLIN, James: Rank: Sergeant. Regiment or Service: Irish Guards. Unit: 1st Bn. Age at death: 25. Date of death: 6 September 1914. Service No.3123. Born in Newross in Co. Wexford and enlisted in Tipperary. Died of wounds.

Supplementary information: Son of James O'Louchlin, of Cordangan, Tipperary. Grave or Memorial Reference: Sp. Mem. Cemetery: Vaudoy Communal Cemetery in France.

O'LOUGHLIN, Patrick: Rank: Private. Regiment or Service: Irish Guards. Unit: 1st Bn. Age at death: 20. Date of death: 29 December 1914. Service No.4762. Born in Tipperary and enlisted in Cork while living in Tipperary. Killed in action.

Supplementary information: Son of James and Margaret M. O'Loughlin, of Cordangan, Tipperary. Grave or Memorial Reference: I. D. 16. Cemetery: Le Touret Military Cemetery, Richebourg-L'Avoue in France.

O'MAHONY, James: Rank: Private. Regiment or Service: Royal Irish Regiment. Unit: 7th Bn. Age at death: 43. Date of death: 12 December 1918. Service No.10048.

Supplementary information: Son of James and Mary O'Mahony, of Elm Cottage, Kilcommon, Cahir: husband of Catherine O'Mahony, of Garryroan, Cahir, Co. Tipperary. Grave or Memorial Reference: XII. B. 2. Cemetery: Brookwood Military Cemetery, UK. He is also commemorated on the Cahir War Memorial.

O'MARA, John Francis: Rank: Gunner. Regiment or Service: Royal Field Artillery. Unit: 'A' Bty. 11th Bde. Age at death: 35. Date of death: 12 July 1916. Service No. W-1374. Born in Cashel and enlisted in Darwen in Lancashire. Killed in action.

Supplementary information: Son of John and Johanna O'Mara, of Cashel, Co. Tipperary: husband of Jane O'Mara, of 13 Ellen Street, Darwen. Grave or Memorial Reference: V. F. 9. Cemetery: Gordon Dump Cemetery, Ovilliers-La-Boiselle in France.

O'MARA, Michael: Rank: Private. No 8198, Manchester regiment, 2nd Bn. Died 29 October 14, Aged 36. Born in Cashel, enlisted in Ashton-Under-Lyne in Lancashire while living in Manchester. Husband of Caroline Lomas (*née* O'Mara), of 101, Jersey Street. Dwellings, Ancoats, Manchester. These two O'Mara lads may be brothers. He has no known grave but is listed on the Le Touret Memorial in France on Panels 34 and 35. Killed in action, France.

O'MARA/O'MEARA, Patrick: Rank: Private. Regiment or Service: Leinster Regiment. Unit: 7th Bn. Age at death: 23. Date of death: 15 April 1916. Service No.2776. Born in Clonmel and enlisted in Waterford. Killed in action.

Supplementary information: Son of Michael and Margaret O'Mara, of Merlin Lodge, Clonmel, Co. Tipperary. Grave or Memorial Reference: II. K. 26. Vermelles British Cemetery in France

O'MEARA/MEARA John: Rank: Private. Regiment or Service: Royal Irish Regiment. Unit: 4th Bn. Date of death: 28 July 1917. Service No.5399. Nenagh while living in Borrisokane. Died at home. Age at death: 20.

Supplementary information: Also known as MEARA. Son of Mrs Kate O'Meara, of Main Street, Borrisokane. Grave or Memorial Reference: In the North West Part. Cemetery: Aglishclohane (Aglish) Church of Ireland Churchyard, Tipperary

O'MEARA, Thomas: Rank: Private. Regiment or Service: Leinster Regiment. Unit: 6th Bn. Age at death: 38. Date of death: 23 October 1915. Service No.421. Born in Roscrea and enlisted in Birr. Killed in action in Gallipoli.

Supplementary information: Husband of Ellen O'Meara, of Abbey Street, Roscrea, Co. Tipperary. Grave or Memorial Reference: III. B. 63. Cemetery: East Mudros Military Cemetery in Greece.

O'NEILL, Annesley/Abraham: Rank: Private. Regiment or Service: Canadian Infantry Unit: 101st Bn. Age at death: 32. Date of death: 10 February 1916. Service No.700394

Supplementary information: Son of the late George and Sarah O'Neill, of Glantane, Templederry, Thurles, Co. Tipperary, Ireland. Grave or Memorial Reference: L. 400. S. 13. G. 10. Cemetery: Winnipeg (Elmwood) Cemetery in Canada. Note the different name on page 1 above of his enlistment document. Data from

the reverse of the enlistment document: Age on Enlistment: 32 Years 9 Months. Height: 5' 9 ½". Eye colour: blue. Complexion: dark. Hair: dlack. Religious denomination: C. of E. Chest expansion: 2 ½". Girth: 39 ½". Date of enlistment: 21 December 1915. Place of enlistment: Winnipeg.

O'REILLY, Christopher Joseph: Rank: Lance Corporal. Regiment or Service: Irish Guards. Unit: 1st Bn. Age at death: 21. Date of death: 28 March 1918. Service No.6366. Born in Clonmel and enlisted there also. Died of wounds.

Supplementary information: Son of William and Mary O'Reilly, of 9, Cross Street, Clonmel, Co. Tipperary. Grave or Memorial Reference: IV. A. 14. Cemetery: St Hilaire Cemetery, Frevent in France.

O'RIORDAN, William: Rank: Private. Regiment or Service: Royal Dublin Fusiliers. Unit: 10th Bn. Date of death: 3 November 1916. Service No.26072. Born in Ballyporeen, Co. Tipperary. Enlisted in Cork while living in Kilcolman, Co. Cork. Killed in action. Age at death: 17.

Supplementary information: Son of Helena O'Riordan, of 16, Leinster Street, North Strand Rd, Dublin, and the late Michael O'Riordan, of Kilcolman, Enniskean, Co. Cork. He has no known grave but is listed on Pier and Face 16 C on the Thiepval Memorial in France.

O'ROURKE, Henry: Rank: Gunner. Regiment or Service: Royal Horse

Grave of John O'Meara.

Artillery and Royal Field Artillery. Date of death: 3 September 1917. Service No.5793. Born in Clonmel. Enlisted in Cork. Died of wounds. Grave or Memorial Reference: I. H. 49. Cemetery:Voormezeele Enclosures No1 and No2 in Belgium.

O'ROURKE, John: Rank: Lance Corporal. Regiment or Service: Durham Light Infantry. Unit: 10th Bn. Date of death: 12 August 1916. Service No.12043. Born in Tipperary and enlisted in Bishop, Auckland while living in Tipperary. Killed in action.

Supplementary information: Son of Daniel O'Rourke: husband of Johanna O'Rourke, of Lower Ballingarry, Thurles, Co. Tipperary. Grave or Memorial Reference: Pier and Face 14 A and 15 C. Memorial: Thiepval Memorial in France.

O'SHAUGHNESSY, Patrick: Rank: Gunner. Regiment or Service: Australian Field ArtilleryUnit: 5th Division Trench Mortar Battery. Date of death: 26 October 1916. Service No.3301. Previous

Supplementary information: Service, Royal Field Artillery in Dublin for 12 ½ years. Next of kin, Brother, James O'Shaughnessy, Cappawhite, Co. Tipperary. Served in Gallipoli (received bullet wound to the ankle), Alexandria, Moascar, Marseilles, Helouan, Egypt, Suez, Tel-El-Kebir and France. Born in Cappawhite, Tipperary. Date of enlistment: 8 September 1914 in Perth, Western Australia. Occupation on enlistment: labourer, Age on enlistment: 34years 4 mths, Height: 5'5". Eyes: green. Hair: black. Complexion: dark. Religious denomination: R,C. His brother: James O'Shaughnessy, Ayle Oola, Tipperary received his effects on 8 March 1917. Killed at 2nd Army

Trench Mortar School on 24 October 16 as a result of premature explosion in trench mortar practice. Buried in Mont Des Cats outside the Monastery, 1 mile south-east of Godewaerswelde 4½ miles north-west of Bailleul. Cemetery: Meteren Military Cemetery, France. Ref IV. F. 723.

O'SHEA, James: Rank: Private. Regiment or Service: Leinster Regiment. Unit: 1st Bn. Age at death: 24. Date of death: 16 March 1915. Service No.9097. Born in Clonmel and enlisted there also. Died of wounds.

Supplementary information: Brother of Thomas O'shea, of 30, River Street, Clonmel, Co. Tipperary. Grave or Memorial Reference: B. 30. Cemetery: Dickiebusch New Military Cemetery in Belgium.

O'SHEA, James: Rank: Private. Regiment or Service: Royal Irish Regiment. Unit: 2nd Bn. Date of death: 29 October 1916. Service No.8026. Born in Roscrea. Enlisted in Dungarvan Co. Waterford while living in Modeligo Co. Waterford. Killed in action. Age at death: 25.

Supplementary information: Husband of Mary Frances O'Shea of Modeligo, County Waterford. Grave or Memorial Reference: X. 36. Cemetery: Kemmel Chateau Military Cametery.

O'SHEA/SHEA John: Rank: Private. Regiment or Service: Leinster Regiment. Unit: "C" Coy. 2nd Bn. Previously he was with the Royal Irish Regiment where his number was

10224. Born in Clonmel and enlisted in Clonmel while living there also. Died of wounds. Age at death: 29. Date of death: 19 October 1918. Service No.10727.

Supplementary information: Son of Thomas and Catherine O'Shea, of Clonmel, Co. Tipperary. Grave or Memorial Reference: VI. A. 54. Cemetery: Terlincthun British Cemetery, Wimille in France.

O'SHEA, Thomas: Rank: Private. Regiment or Service: Royal Irish Regiment. Unit: 2nd Bn. Age at death: 23. Date of death: 25 May 1915. Service No.6410. Born in St Mary's in Clonmel and enlisted in Clonmel also. Died of wounds.

Supplementary information: Son of Thomas and Cathleen O'Shea, of Clonmel, Co. Tipperary. Grave or Memorial Reference: Poelcapelle Com. Cem. Mem. 1. Cemetery: Poelcapelle British Cemetery in Belgium.

O'SHEA, Timothy: Rank: Private. Regiment or Service: Royal Irish Fusiliers. Unit: 8th Bn. Date of death: 27 April 1916. Service No.185525 and 18525. Born in Hollyfort, Co. Tipperary. Enlisted in Belfast. Killed in action. He has no known grave but is listed on Panel 124 on the Loos Memorial in France.

O'SHEA, John: Rank: Lance Corporal. Regiment or Service: Royal Irish Regiment. Unit: 6th Bn. Age at death: 32. Date of death: 7 June 1917. Service No.4899. Born in Carrick-

Patrick O'Shaughnessy.

on-Suir and enlisted in Wigan.

Supplementary information: Son of James and Margaret O'Shea, of Clasnasmuth, Ahenna, Carrick-on-Suir, Co. Tipperary. Grave or Memorial Reference: Has no known grave but is commemorated on Panel 33. Memorial: Ypres (Menin Gate) Memorial in Belgium.

O'SHEA/SHEA, John: Rank: Private. Regiment or Service: Irish Guards. Unit: 1st Bn. Age at death: 22. Date of death: 15 May 1915. Service No.4309. Born in Carrick-on-Suir and enlisted in Clonmel. Died of wounds.

Supplementary information: Son of Walter and Mary O'Shea, of Bally-lynch, Carrick-on-Suir, Co. Tipperary. Grave or Memorial Reference: III. D. 1. Cemetery: Bethune Town Cemetery in France.

O'SHEA, John: Rank: Private. Regiment or Service: Royal Irish Regiment. Unit: 2nd Bn. Age at death: 36. Date of death: 5 July 1916. Service

No.4775. Born in Callan Co. Kilkenny and enlisted in Cashel while living in Thurles. Died of wounds.

Supplementary information: Son of John and Bridget Osborne O' Shea, of Friar Street, Thurles, Co. Tipperary. Native of Callan, Co. Kilkenny. Grave or Memorial Reference: Plot 1. Row B. Grave 43. Cemetery: Corbie Communal Cemetery Extension in France.

O'SULLIVAN, Michael: Rank: Private. Regiment or Service: Royal Dublin Fusiliers. Unit: 10th Bn. Date of death: 4 April 1918. Service No.26648. Born in Killendale Co. Tipperary. Enlisted in Manchester. Killed in action. He has no known grave but is listed on Panel 79 and 80 on the Pozieres Memorial in France.

O'SYRETT, Rory: Rank: Acting Lance Corporal. Regiment or Service: Corps of Military Police. Unit: Mounted Branch. Date of death: 3 December 1914. Service No.P-120. Born in Templemore. Enlisted

274

in Shepherd's Bush while living in Ealing Common. Grave or Memorial Reference: I.K.18. Cemetery: Merville Communal Cemetery in France.

OWENS, J. J: Rank: Battery Sergeant Major. Regiment or Service: Royal Garrison Artillery. Unit: 1st Bty. 1st Reserve Bde. Age at death: 38. Date of death: 5 January 1920 Service No.6383.

Supplementary information: Long Service and Good Conduct Medal. Son of Joseph Owens: husband of E. E. Owens, of 'Ferndale' South East Rd, Sholing, Southampton. Born at Clonmel, Tipperary. Grave or Memorial Reference: In South part. Cemetery: Totland (St Saviour) Roman Catholic Churchyard, UK.

P

PARSONS, Andrew: Rank: Sergeant, No 9956, Leinster Regiment, 2nd Bn. Died 28 June 1916, Born, St Mary's, Cashel, and enlisted in Clonmel. Died of wounds. Age at death: 20.

Supplementary information: Brother of William Parsons, below is the letter from his Chaplain to his brother Michael states: 'He was good fellow and died as every Catholic soldier should. He was at the altar two days previously and received the last Sacraments after being wounded. He was quite conscious then and I was hoping he would pull through, but he had lost a lot of blood and was not over strong'. Buried in Bailleul Communal Cemetery Extension (Nord) in France. Grave reference II. E. 141. Died of Wounds, France.

PARSONS, Mervyn Merefield: Rank: Rifleman. Regiment or Service: Rifle Brigade. Unit: A Coy, 7th Bn. Date of death: 8 September 1915. Service No.S-7709. Born in Tippeary. Enlisted in London while living in Willesden, Middlesex. Killed in action. Age at death: 26.

Supplementary information: Son of Herbert and Mary Sortain Parsons, of Merefield House, 17, Heathfield Park, Willesden Green, London. Gave up his position as 1st Assistant on a Rubber Estate at Sungei Siput, Malay States, to come to England to enlist. Grave or Memorial Reference: X. 28. Cemetery: Potijze Burial Ground Cemetery in Belgium.

PARSONS, William: Rank: Lance Sergeant, No 8997, Royal Munster Fusiliers, 2nd Bn, Date of death: 27

Grave of John Perry.

August 1914, Born: Cashel, enlisted in Dublin while living in Cashel. Killed in action at the battle of Mons. Brother of Andrew Parsons above. Buried in St Souplet British Cemetery in France. Grave reference I. F. 11. Killed in action, France.

PARSONS, W: Rank: Private. Regiment or Service: Devonshire Regiment. Unit: Age at death: 28 Date of death: 1 December 1920. Service No. 5609973.

Supplementary information: Son of Mrs Henrietta Parsons of Kingsbridge Devon. Cemetery, Clonmel, St Patrick's Cemetery. Grave location: 8. N. 12.

PARTON, Albert: Rank: Private. Regiment or Service: King's Shropshire Light Infantry. Unit: 1st Bn. Age at death: 23. Date of death: 4 December 1917. Service No. 9784. Born in St Mary's in Brignorth and enlisted in Brignorth. Killed in action.

Supplementary information: Son of Mrs S. Parton, of II, St John Street, Low Town, Bridgnorth, Salop: husband of Mary Parton, of 4 Brewery Place, Clonmel, Co. Tipperary. Grave or Memorial Reference: Has no known grave but is commemorated on Panel 8 and 9. Memorial: Cambrai Memorial in Louveral in France.

PATTERSON, Ernest: Rank: Private. Regiment or Service: Royal Irish Regiment Age at death: 17. Date of death: 8 April 1917. Service No. 9545.

Supplementary information: Son of

Robert John and Matilda Patterson, of Ballyphilips, Roscrea, Co. Tipperary. Grave or Memorial Reference: C. C. 59. Cemetery: Bath (Locksbrook) Cemetery, UK.

PAUL, Cedric Franklyn/Franklin: Rank: Acting Lance Corporal. Regiment or Service: Royal Sussex Regiment. Unit: 11th Bn. Date of death: 29 July 1917. Service No. G-20442. British Expeditionary Force. Born in Killenaule. Enlisted in Eastbourne. Killed in action. Age at death: 27.

Supplementary information: Son of Maud Paul, of 23 Morehampton Rd, Dublin, and the late Revd. Henry Paul, M A. He has no known grave but is listed on Panel 20 on the Ypres (Menin Gate) Memorial in Belgium.

PEARSE/PEARCE, William John Hore: Rank: Sergeant. Regiment or Service: Royal Warwickshire Regiment. Unit: 1st Bn. Date of death: 15 April 1918. Service No. 16-1703. Born in Tipperary. Enlisted in Birmingham while living in Egbaston, Birmingham. Killed in action. He has no known grave but is listed on Panel 2 and 3 on the Ploegsteert Memorial in Belgium.

PEILOW, Benjamin John: Rank: Private. Regiment or Service: Australian Infantry, A. I. F. Unit: 20th Bn. Age at death: 29. Date of death: 11 August 1918. Service No. 5629

Supplementary information: Son of Benjamin Francis and Anna Peilow. Born at Castle Lough, Portroe, Nenagh, Co. Tipperary, Ireland. Memorial:

Villers-Bretonneux Memorial. Villers-Bretonneux Military Cemetery in France.

PERCY, Samuel: Rank: Private. Regiment or Service: Royal Irish Regiment. Unit: 5th Bn. Age at death: 33. Date of death: 15 April 1917. Service No. 3-7960 and 7960. Born in Cloughjordan and enlisted there also. Died in a torpedoe attack on a Hospital ship in Salonika.
Supplementary information: Eldest son of Fanny Percy, of Main Street, Cloughjordan, Co. Tipperary, and the late Benjamin Percy. Grave or Memorial Reference: IX. C. 5. Cemetery: Struma Military Cemetery in Greece.

PERRY, John: Rank: Private. Regiment or Service: Royal Irish Fusiliers. Unit: 7th Bn. Date of death: 4 April 1918. Service No. 19874. Cemetery, St John's Famine Cemetery, Tipperary. Grave location: Around the centre of the south part.

PHELAN, Edward: Rank: Private. Regiment or Service: Irish Guards. Unit: 2nd Bn. Age at death: 22. Date of death: 31 July 1917. Service No. 7765. Born in Gortnahoe and enlisted in Cork while living in Gortnahoe. Killed in action.
Supplementary information: Son of William and Anne Phelan, of Gortnahoe, Thurles, Co. Tipperary. Grave or Memorial Reference: II. D. 17. Cemetery: Artillery Wood Cemetery in Belgium.

PHELAN, James: Rank: Private. Regiment or Service: Royal Dunlin Fusiliers. Unit: 1st Bn. Date of death: 30 April 1915. Service No. 11209. Born in Tipperary. Enlisted in Carlow. Died of wounds. Killed in action in Gallipoli. Age at death: 21.
Supplementary information: Son of Elizabeth Phelan, of Charlotte Street, Carlow, and the late James Phelan. He has no known grave but is listed on the Special Memorial, B, 80. V Beach Cemetery in Turkey.

PHELAN, Kieran: Rank: Private. Regiment or Service: Leinster Regiment. Unit: 2nd Bn. Date of death: 15 April 1917. Service No. 9246. Born in Dunkerrins, Co. Tipperary. Enlisted in Birr. Died of wounds. Grave or Memorial Reference: I. A. 19. Cemetery: Barlin Communal Cemetery Extension in France.

PHELAN, Patrick: Rank: Private. Regiment or Service: South Lancashire Regiment. Unit: 1st – 5th Bn. Date of death: 23 December 1917. Service No. 241999. Enlisted in Earlestown, Lancs while living in Clonmel, Co. Tipperary. Killed in action.
Supplementary information: Nephew of Mary Cooney, of 109 Irishtown, Clonmel, Co. Tipperary. He has no known grave but is listed on Panel 7 on the Cambrai Memorial in Louveral in France.

PHILLIPS, Edward George Dunscombe: Rank: Captain. Regiment or Service: Royal Irish Regiment. Unit: 2nd Bn. att. 6th Bn.

Age at death: 22. Date of death: 14 November 1916.

Supplementary information: Son of Major John Hopkinson Phillips and Georgina Violet Mary Masters Phillips, of Parkville, Clonmel, Co. Tipperary. Grave or Memorial Reference: X. 39. Cemetery: Kemmel Chateau Military Cemetery in Belgium.

POULTEN/POULTON, Ernest Edward: Rank: Private. Regiment or Service: Royal Warwickshire Regiment. Unit: 16th Bn. He was previously with the Hussars where his number was 5817. Age at death: 30. Date of death: 9 October 1917. Service No.32913. Born in St Mary's, Southampton and enlisted in Southampton. Killed in action.

Supplementary information: Son of Harry and Alice Poulten, of Southampton: husband of Mary Annie Poulten, of New Rd, Tipperary. Grave or Memorial Reference: Has no known grave but is commemorated on Panel 23 to 28 and 163A. Memorial: Tyne Cot Memorial in Belgium.

POWELL, George Henry: Rank: Second Lieutenant. Regiment or Service: Machine Gun Corps (Infantry). Unit: 5th Coy. Age at death: 27. Date of death: 29 April 1917.

Supplementary information: Son of the late G. H. Powell, M. D, of Nenagh Co. Tipperary, and of Mrs Powell, of Cookstown, Co. Tyrone. Grave or Memorial Reference: Bay 10. Memorial: Arras Memorial in France.

POWELL, Thomas: Rank: Private.

Regiment or Service: Manchester Regiment. Unit: 2nd Bn. Date of death: 23 October 1914. Service No.249. Born in Tipperary. Enlisted in Aldershot while living in Reading, Berks. Died of wounds.

Supplementary information: Husband of M. A. Phillips (formerly Powell), of 84, Albany Rd, Reading. Grave or Memorial Reference: I. D. 4. Cemetery: Gorre British and Indian Cemetery in France

POWER, Edmond: Rank: Company Sergeant Major. Regiment or Service: Royal Irish Regiment. Unit: 2nd Bn. Age at death: 38. Date of death: 8 August 1917. Service No.6037 Awarded the Military Cross and listed in the *London Gazette*. Born in Ballybacon and enlisted in Clonmel while living in Clogheen. Died of wounds.

Supplementary information: Son of Edmond and Johanna Power, of Ballyvera, Ardfinane, Cahir, Co. Tipperary. Grave or Memorial Reference: III. E. 5. Cemetery: Brandhoek New Military Cemetery in Belgium. He is also commemorated on the Cahir War Memorial.

POWER, Henry Richard: Rank: 2 Lt. Regiment or Service: 3rd Bn, Royal Irish Rifles attached to Royal Flying Corps. Unit: 48th Squadron. Date of death: 22 August 1917. Age at death: 27.

Supplementary information: Son of the late Mr Jas H Power and Mrs Power, Ballydavid House Thurles. Grave or Memorial Reference: I. A.

7. Cemetery: Zuydcoote Military Cemetery in France.

POWER, James: Rank: Private. Regiment or Service: Manchester Regiment. Unit: 1st Bn. Date of death: 21 December 1914. Service No.1021. Born in Fethard. Enlisted in Clonmel while living in Fethard. Killed in action. He has no known grave but is listed on Panels 34 and 35 of the Le Touret Memorial In France.

POWER, Jeremiah: Rank: Sergeant. Regiment or Service: Cameronians (Scottish Rifles). Unit: 9th Bn. Date of death: 22 July 1918. Service No.9207. Born in Bansha. Enlisted in Dublin while living in Bansha. Killed in action.

Supplementary information: Brother of Mrs B. Quirke, of The Grapes, 13 Limekiln Lane, Liverpool. He has no known grave but is listed on Panel 5 on the Ploegsteert Memorial in Belgium.

POWER, Maurice: Rank: Private. Regiment or Service: Royal Irish Regiment. Unit: 2nd Bn. Date of death: 19 October 1914. Service No.6573. Born in St Mary's, Clonmel Co. Tipperary. Enlisted in Waterford. Killed in action. He has no known grave but is listed on Panels 11 and 12 on the Le Touret Memorial in France.

POWER, Michael: Rank: Private. Regiment or Service: Irish Guards. Unit: 1st Bn. Date of death: 17 February 1915. Service No.2260. Born in Stradbally Co. Waterford and enlisted in Waterford while living in Thurles.

Supplementary information: Husband of K. Power, of Quarry Street, Thurles, Co. Tipperary. Grave or Memorial Reference: II. D. 5. Cemetery: Cuinchy Communal Cemetery in France.

POWER, Michael: Rank: Private. Regiment or Service: Royal Irish Regiment. Unit: 5th Bn. Date of death: 16 November 1915. Service No.4935 and 4-4935. Born in St Mary's, Clonmel. Enlisted in Clonmel. Died in Egypt. Grave or Memorial Reference: A. 24. Cemetery: Alexandria (Chatby) Military and War memorial Cemetery in Egypt.

POWER, Michael: Rank: Private. Regiment or Service: Irish Guards. Unit: 1st Bn. Date of death: 7 May 1918. Age at death: 25. Service No.10188. Enlisted in Dublin while living in Killenaule. Died of wounds at home. Grave or Memorial Reference: RC. 557. Cemetery: Grangegorman Military Cemetery in Dublin.

POWER, Michael: Rank: Private. Regiment or Service: Royal Irish Regiment. Unit: 1st Bn. Age at death: 19. Date of death: 16 March 1915. Service No.6392. Born in Ballyneale Co. Tipperary and enlisted in Carrick-on-Suir while living in Ballinacluna Co. Tipperary.

Supplementary information: Son of Mrs Margaret Power, of Ballinacluna, Carrick-on-Suir, Co. Tipperary. Grave or Memorial Reference: Has no known grave but is commemorated on Panel 33. Memorial: Ypres (Menin

Gate) Memorial in Belgium.

POWER, William: Rank: Private. Regiment or Service: Royal Irish Regiment. Unit: 2nd Bn. Date of death: 19 October 1914. Service No.6463. Born in Ballyneil, Co. Tipperary. Enlisted in Clonmel while living in Carrick-on-Suir. Killed in action. He has no known grave but is listed on Panels 11 and 12 on the Le Touret Memorial in France.

PRENDERGAST, James: Rank: Private. Regiment or Service: Leinster Regiment. Unit: 2nd Bn. Date of death: 8 May 1918. Service No.4492. Formerly he was with the Royal Field Artillery where his number was 100205. Born in Waterford. Enlisted in Clonmel while living in Clonmel. Died of wounds. Grave or Memorial Reference: I. E. 35. Cemetery: Ebblinghem Military Cemetery in France.

PRENDERGAST, Maurice Philip: Rank: Lance Corporal. Regiment or Service: Royal Irish Regiment. Unit: 2nd Bn. Age at death: 18. Date of death: 7 June 1917. Service No.3-9742 Awards: Mentioned in Despatches. Born in Clogheen and enlisted in Clonmel while living in Clogheen. Killed in action.

Supplementary information: Son of Geoffrey and Margaret Matilda Prendergast (*née* Carson), of The Hermitage, Clogheen, Co. Tipperary. Grave or Memorial Reference: Has no known grave but is commemorated on Panel 33. Memorial: Ypres (Menin

Gate) Memorial in Belgium. He is also commemorated on the Cahir War Memorial.

PRENDERGAST, Walter: Rank: Sergeant. Regiment or Service: Royal Irish Regiment. Unit: Depot. Date of death: 21 February 1918. Service No.7278. Born in St Mary's, Clonmel, Co. Tipperary. Enlisted in Clonmel. Died at home.

Supplementary information: Husband of M. Prendergast, of 8 Mitchell Rd, Clonmel. Grave or Memorial Reference: 4. HA. 138. Cemetery: Clonmel (St Patrick's) Cemetery

PRICE, Robert: Rank: Private. Regiment or Service: Royal Irish Regiment. Unit: 2nd Bn. Age at death: 27. Date of death: 14 May 1915. Service No.5632. Born in St Nicholas, Carrick-on-Suir and enlisted in Carrick-on-Suir. Killed in action.

Supplementary information: Son of Robert and Bridget Price, of Hurleys Lane, Carrick-on-Suir, Co. Tipperary. Grave or Memorial Reference: Has no known grave but is commemorated on Panel 33. Memorial: Ypres (Menin Gate) Memorial in Belgium.

PRICE, Thomas: Rank: Private. Regiment or Service: Royal Irish Regiment. Unit: 2nd Bn. Age at death: 24. Date of death: 7 June 1917. Service No.4692. Born in Carrick-on-Suir and enlisted in Waterford while living in Carrick-on-Suir. Died of wounds.

Supplementary information: Son of Robert and Bridget Price, of Hurley's Lane, Carrick-on-Suir, Co. Tipperary.

Grave or Memorial Reference: I. A. 6. Cemetery: Locre Hospice Cemetery in Belgium.

PRICE, William: Rank: Private. Regiment or Service: Leinster Regiment. Unit: 1st Bn. Date of death: 12 May 1915. Service No.3464. Born in Cahir. Enlisted in Cork. Killed in action. Age at death: 19.

Supplementary information: Son of the Late Patrick and Mary Price. He has no known grave but is listed on Panel 44 of the Ypres (Menin Gate) Memorial in Belgium.

PRITTIE, The Hon. Francis Reginald D: Rank: Captain. Regiment or Service: Rifle Brigade. Unit: 1st Bn. Age at death: 34. Date of death: 19 December 1914. Awards: Twice Mentioned in Despatches.

Supplementary information: Legion of Honour. Son of 4th Baron Dunalley and Baroness Dunalley, of Kilboy, Nenagh, Co. Tipperary. Assistant Commissioner, Uganda Boundary Commission, 1910-1914. Grave or Memorial Reference: IV. F. 5. Cemetery: Rifle House Cemetery in Belgium.

PURCELL, Edward: Rank: Private. Regiment or Service: Royal Irish Regiment. Unit: 1st Bn. Date of death: 27 March 1915. Service No.8939. Born in Moyne Co. Tipperary. Enlisted in Kilkenny while living in Templemore. Died of wounds. Age at death: 29.

Supplementary information: Son of Robert and Ellen Purcell, of Monamondra, Errill, Ballybrophy, Offaly. Ten years' service. Grave or Memorial Reference: J. 49. Cemetery: Bailleu Communal Cemetery (Nord) in France

PURCELL, Philip/Phillip: Rank: Private. Regiment or Service: Royal Irish Regiment. Unit: 2nd Bn. Date of death: 14 July 1916. Service No.7615. Born in Ballingarry. Enlisted in Ballingarry while living in Thurles. Killed in action. Age at death: 30.

Supplementary information: Brother of Edmond Purcell, of 6 Grange Urlingford, Co. Kilkenny. He has no known grave but is listed on Pier and Face 3 A on the Thiepval Memorial in France.

Q

QUANNE/QUANN/QUANE, James: Rank: Sergeant/Sergeant Major. Regiment or Service: Royal Irish Regiment Unit: 3rd Bn. Age at death: 43. Date of death: 17 August 1916. Service No.8012. Born in Tipperary and enlisted there also. Died at home. Extract from the *Tipperary Star* 1916:

Late Sergeant-Major Quann, Tipperary. The death has occurred in Tipperary of Sergeant major James Quann, 3rd Bn. Royal Irish Regiment, who before he re-joined the army, over a year ago, had been a drill instructor of the National Volunteers in Tipperary District. The deceased, who was aged about 46 years, was a native of Tipperary. At an early age he joined the army, in which he had 21 years service. He served in India, and went through the Samaria (1897) and Punjab frontier engagements (1897-8). He passed unscathed through the South African War, in which he had some interesting and excit-ing experiences. About three years ago he retired on pension and when the Volunteer movement started he was appointed Drill Instructor for Tipperary Town and the surrounding districts. He had a magnificent voice for drill-ing, and through the excellence of his methods those under his tui-tion made exceptionally rapid and satisfactory progress. At the great review of the Volunteers in Dublin on Easter Sunday, 1915, the fine military bearing of the Volunteers from Tipperary District, under the command of the deceased, was very favourably commented on all sides. Some months after the Dublin review he re-joined the Army. Less than a fortnight ago he came home to Tipperary from Dublin on sick leave, having been ailing for some weeks. His leave was to have expired on Wednesday last, but feeling very unwell he went to the Military Hospital at Tipperary, where he was detained, and where he passed away on Tuesday evening, the cause of

1914-15 Star. British War Medal.

John Quinane.

death being heart failure. His demise was totally unexpected, and was received with sincere regret by everybody in the town and district, where he was universally and exceptionally popular. Deep sympathy is felt with his bereaved wife and five children. The funeral took place at 10:30 on Saturday morning from the Military Barracks to the new Cemetery, with full military honours. The remains were carried on a gun carriage drawn by four horses. In front of the bier marched a firing party of 25 men of the Royal Irish Regiment with arms reversed, under the command of Sergeant O'Brien, Dublin Fusiliers. Following them, came the band of the Irish Command Depot, Tipperary, under the direction of Captain Patterson. Behind the bier marched a party of 200 men at the Depot. The band played the Dead March in 'Saul', and Chopin's Funeral March, and as the procession slowly passed up Bridget Street, and through the main Street to the New Cemetery, a very large and representative number of the Townspeople joined in. The burial service was read by Right Revd. Monsignor Ryan P.P., V. G, assisted by Revd M. S. Ryan, Chaplain. Three volleys were fired over the grave by the firing party after they presented arms, and the Last Post was sounded by eight buglers with thrilling effect. The chief mourners at the graveside were: Mrs Quann (wife of the deceased), Christopher and Cornelius Quann (sons).

Supplementary information: Husband of Annie Quanne, of 5, Davitt St, Tipperary. Grave or Memorial Reference: E. H. 1. Cemetery: St Michaels New Cemetery, Tipperary Town.

QUIGLEY, Daniel: Rank: Private. Regiment or Service: Royal Irish Regiment. Unit: 3rd Bn. Age at death: 28. Date of death: 2 February 1915. Service No. 7051. Born in Nenagh and enlisted there also. Died at home.

Supplementary information: Husband of Johsons Kennedy, of 4 Cottage, Portland Row, Nensgh, Co. Tipperary. Grave or Memorial Reference: RC. 439. Cemetery: Grangegorman Military Cemetery in Dublin.

Grave of John Quinane.

QUIGLEY, Denis: Rank: Private. Regiment or Service: Royal Munster Fusiliers. Unit: 1ˢᵗ Bn. Age at death: 24. Date of death: 9 September 1916. Service No.4479. Born in Clogheen and enlisted in Bruree Co. Limerick while living in Clogheen. Killed in action.

Supplementary information: Son of Martin and Johanna Quigley, of Chapel St, Clogheen, Co. Tipperary. Grave or Memorial Reference: Pier and Face 16 C. Memorial: Thiepval Memorial in France. He is also commemorated on the Cahir War Memorial.

QUIGLEY, Patrick: Rank: Private. Regiment or Service: Royal Dublin Fusiliers. Unit: 9ᵗʰ Bn. Age at death: 30. Date of death: 9 September 1916. Service No.21286. Born in Cahir and enlisted there also. Killed in action.

Supplementary information: Son of Patrick and Catherine Quigley, of Suttonrath Cahir, Co. Tipperary. Grave or Memorial Reference: Pier and Face 16 C. Memorial: Thiepval Memorial in France.

QUIGLEY, William: Rank: Private. Regiment or Service: Irish Guards. Unit: 2ⁿᵈ Bn. Date of death: 9 October 1917. Service No.11620. Born in Killenaule. Enlisted in Wexford while living in Killenaule. Killed in action. He has no known grave but is listed on Panels 10 and 11 on the Tyne Cot Memorial in Belgium.

QUINANE, John: Rank: Private. Regiment or Service: Australian Infantry A. I. F. Unit: 45ᵗʰ Bn. Age at death: 29. Date of death: 19 June 1918. Service No.2225.

Supplementary information: Son of Elizabeth Quinane of Warrini Victoria and the late Michael Quinaue. Grave location: South-West of the ruins on West boundary. His grandfather, John Quinane left Gortahalla in 1852 and emigrated to Australia. John Height: 5'8" Age on enlistment: 27 ½. Occupation: labourer when he enlisted in Victoria Barracks in New South Wales on 18 February 1916. His postal address at that time was

Coffee Palace, Georges Street, Sydney. John received a gunshot wound on the 6 April 1918 when he was with A Coy 45th Battalion in France and was transferred from the trenches by the 12th Field Ambulance. He is listed in the 395th and 396th Casualty lists. John was admitted to the 18th General Hospital. On the 13 April he sailed on the Hospital Ship *Queen Elizabeth* to England, was admitted to Reading War Hospital and then transferred to King George V Hospital in Dublin on 15 June 1918. Previously his only illness with the AIF was trench feet in March 1917. He died from Pneumonia and was buried by his cousin John Cahill, Holycross, Co. Tipperary. The funeral took place at noon on Saturday 22 June 1918 and £5 was allocated by the Army to John Cahill for his burial. His coffin of polished elm was supplied by Michael Hickey, Undertaker in Thurles. The officiating Clergyman was Dr Michael Dwyer, Thurles. Thomas M Hayes (British Army) No. 41758. Died in Mesopotamia, John Quinane (Australian Army) No 2225 Died of disease and Patrick Cahill (Canadian Army) were all related. Buried in Glenkeen Cemetry outside Borrisoleigh, Co. Tipperary.

QUINLAN, John: Rank: Private. Regiment or Service: Royal Irish Regiment. Unit: 5th Bn. Age at death: 27. Date of death: 21 October 1918. Service No. 8045. Born in Roscrea and enlisted there also.

Supplementary information: Son of Patrick and Margaret Quinlan, of Cloonan Cottage, Roscrea, Co. Tipperary.

Grave or Memorial Reference: III. E. 18. Cemetery: Highland Cemetery, Le Cateau in France.

QUINLAN, Joseph: Rank: Private. Regiment or Service: Irish Guards. Unit: 2nd Bn. Date of death: 27 September 1916. Service No. 10215. Born in Thurles. Enlisted in Clonmel. Killed in action. He has no known grave but is listed on Pier and Face 7D on the Thiepval Memorial in France.

QUINLAN, Patrick: Rank: Private. Regiment or Service: Royal Inniskilling Fusiliers. Unit: 6th Bn. Date of death: 27 December 1917. Service No. 27722 and 7-27722. Formerly he was with the Royal Irish Regiment where his number was 9016. Born in Tipperary. Enlisted in Tipperary. Killed in action in Egypt. Grave or Memorial Reference: F 40. Cemetery: Jerusalem War Cemetery in Israel.

QUINN, Henry: Rank: Private. Regiment or Service: Royal Irish Regiement. Unit: 2nd Bn. Date of death: 2 September 1918. Service No. 6879. Born in Cahir. Enlisted in Cahir. Killed in action. Grave or Memorial Reference: V. C. 12. Cemetery: Wulverghem-Lindenhoek Road Military Cemetery in Belgium. He is also commemorated on the Cahir War Memorial.

QUINN, James: Rank: 2 Lt. Regiment or Service: Royal Garrison Artillery. Date of death: 29 July 1916. Residence, Fethard, Tipperary Died of wounds.

Grave of G.P. Raynham.

Supplementary information: Residence, Fethard, Tipperary He had three brothers who also served, Thomas John and Edmond, Sergeant Edmond Quinn, RGA who was elected to the English Poor Law Boards and Rural District Councils. Grave or Memorial Reference: I. L. 49. Cemetery: Albert Communal Cemetery Extension in France.

QUINN, John: Rank: Private. Regiment or Service: South African Infantry. Unit: 3rd Regt. Age at death: 37. Date of death: 16 April 1917. Service No. 8244.

Supplementary information: Son of Margaret Corcoran and Patrick Quinn, of Roscrea, Co. Tipperary, Ireland. Grave or Memorial Reference: XXII. J. 2. Etaples, Military Cemetery in France.

QUINN, John: Rank: Private. Regiment or Service: South African Infantry. Unit: 3rd Regt. Age at death: 37. Date of death: 16 April 1917. Service No: 8244.

Supplementary information: Son of Margaret Corcoran and the late Patrick Quinn, of Roscrea, Co. Tipperary, Ireland. Grave or Memorial Reference: XXII. J. 2. Cemetery: Etaples Military Cemetery in France.

QUINN, John: Rank: Private. Regiment or Service: Connaught Rangers. Unit: 5th Bn. Age at death: 44. Date of death: 22 August 1915. Service No. 4212. Born in Templemore and enlisted in Dublin while living in Templemore. Killed in action in Gallipoli.

Supplementary information: Son of the late John Quinn, of Bank Street, Templemore, Co. Tipperary. Served in the South African War. Grave or Memorial Reference: Has no known grave but is commemorated on Panel 181 to 183. Memorial: Helles Memorial in Turkey.

QUINN, Philip: Rank: Private. Regiment or Service: Royal Irish Regiment. Unit: 1st Bn. Age at death: 42. Date of death: 23 March 1915.

Service No. 6605. Born in Templemore and enlisted there also. Killed in action.

Supplementary information: Brother of Michael Quinn, of Bank Street, Templemore, Co. Tipperary. Grave or Memorial Reference: Has no known grave but is commemorated on Panel 33. Memorial: Ypres (Menin Gate) Memorial in Belgium.

QUINN, Thomas: Rank: Private. Regiment or Service: Connaught Rangers. Unit: 1st Bn. Age at death: 23. Date of death: 19 March 1915. Service No. 10310. Born in Nenagh and enlisted in Limerick while living in Nenagh. Killed in action.

Supplementary information: Son of the late Denis Quinn, of Silver Street, Nenagh, Co. Tipperary. Grave or Memorial Reference: Has no known grave but is commemorated on Panel 43. Memorial: Le Touret Memorial in France.

QUINN, Walter William: Rank: Private. Regiment or Service: Connaught Rangers. Unit: 1st Bn. Date of death: 26 April 1915. Service No. 6834. Born in Tipperary. Enlisted in Dublin while living in Ballinrobe. Killed in action. Grave or Memorial Reference: I. U. 24. Cemetery: La Brique Military Cemetery, No. 2 in Belgium.

QUINN, William: Rank: Private. Regiment or Service: Royal Munster Fusiliers. Unit: 2nd Bn. Date of death: 10 November 1917. Service No. 9074. Born in St Mary's, Co. Tipperary,

Clogheen. Enlisted in Limerick while living in Clogheen. Killed in action. Age at death: 27.

Supplementary information: Husband of Catherine Quinn, of 7 Mill View Terrace, Tralee, Co. Kerry. Grave or Memorial Reference: VIII. C. 20. Cemetery: Passchendaele New British Cemetery in Belgium.

QUIRKE, James: Rank: Lance Corporal. Regiment or Service: Irish Guards. Unit: 2nd Bn. Age at death: 20. Date of death: 31 March 1918. Service No. 11727. Born in Cappauniack and enlisted in Liverpool while living in Cappauniack Co. Tipperary. Killed in action.

Supplementary information: Son of Thomas and Kate Quirke, of Cappauniac, Bansha, Co. Tipperary. Grave or Memorial Reference: IV. F. 2. Cemetery: Douchy-Les-Ayette British Cemetery in France. He is also commemorated on the Cahir War Memorial.

QUIRKE, John: Rank: Private. Regiment or Service: Irish Guards. Unit: 1st Bn. Age at death: 22. Date of death: 15 March 1917. Service No. 10464. Born in Fethard and enlisted in Fethard also. Killed in action.

Supplementary information: Son of Robert and Johanna Quirke, of Lower Green, Fethard, Co. Tipperary. Grave or Memorial Reference: III. F. 3. Cemetery: Sailly-Saillisel British Cemetery in France.

QUIRKE, David: Rank: Private. Regiment or Service: Royal

Irish Regiment. Date of death: 15 January 1918. Service No.9884. Born in Cahir. Enlisted in Clonmel while living in Clonmel. Killed in action. Grave or Memorial Reference: II. D. 4. Cemetery: Jeancourt Communal Cemetery Extension in Jeancourt Communal Cemetery Extension in France.

QUIRKE, David Leo: Rank: Driver. Regiment or Service: Royal Field Artillery. Unit: 'B' By. 180th Bde. Age at death: 21. Date of death: 4 April 1918. Service No.100982. Born in Tipperary and enlisted in Athlone. Killed in action.

Supplementary information: Son of Thomas and Mary Quirke (*née* O'Leary), of Clonmel, Co. Tipperary. Grave or Memorial Reference: II. K. 21. Cemetery: Adelaide Cemetery, Villers-Bretonneux in France.

QUIRKE, James: Rank: Gunner. Regiment or Service: Royal Field Artillery. Unit: 112th Bty. 24th Bde. Date of death: 21 March 1918. Service No.101000. Born in Bansha and enlisted in Tipperary. Killed in action.

Supplementary information: Son of Mrs Edmond Quirke, of Rossadrehid, Bansha, Co. Tipperary. Grave or Memorial Reference: Bay 1. Memorial: Arras Memorial in France.

QUIRKE, Michael Francis: Rank: Private. Regiment or Service: Royal Irish Regiment. Unit: 7th Bn. Date of death: 18 December 1917. Age at death: 30. Service No.25719. Formerly he was with the South Irish Horse where his number was 1440. Born in Tipperary. Enlisted in Dublin while living in Pallas Co. Tipperary. Died of wounds.

Supplementary information: Son of Edmond and Maria Quirke of Tipperary. Grave or Memorial Reference: P. V. F. 5A. Cemetery: St Sever Cemetery Extension, Rouen in France.

QUIRKE, Michael Francis: Rank: Private. Regiment or Service: London Regiment (Post Office Rifles). Unit: 1st–8th Bn. Age at death: 32. Date of death: 17 September 1916. Service No.3056. Born in Tipperary and enlisted in London while living in Tipperary. Killed in action during the fierce battle of High Wood.

Supplementary information: Son of the late Denis and Mary Rahilly, of Murgasty Cottages, Tipperary. Patricks brother was with the Munster Fusiliers and although he was wounded he survided the war. Grave or Memorial Reference: Pier and Face 9 C and 9 D. Memorial: Thiepval Memorial in France.

R

RAHILLY, Patrick: Rank: Rifleman. Regiment or Service: London Regiment. Unit: 1st-8th Bn, (Post Office Rifles). Date of death: 15 September 1916. Service No. 3056. Age at death: 32. Born in Tipperary. Enlisted in London while living in Tipperary. Killed in action.

Supplementary information: Son of Denis and Mary Rahilly, of Murgasty Cottages, Tipperary. He has no known grave but is listed on Pier and Face 9 C and 9 D the Thiepval Memorial in France. He is also commemorated on the Cahir War Memorial.

RAYNHAM, G.P: Rank: Private. Regiment or Service: Northamptonshire Regiment Service No. 10987.

Supplementary information: Son of Mr and Mrs H. Raynham of Mildenhall Suffolk. Cemetery, St Mary's COI Churchyard, Templemore. Grave location: In the south-west part.

READ, George Averil: Rank: Captain. Regiment or Service: Leinster Regiment. Unit: 3rd Bn. att. 11th Bn. Age at death: 30. Date of death: 8 March 1917.

Supplementary information: Son of Turner and Emily M. Read, of Dungar, Roscrea, Co. Tipperary. Grave or Memorial Reference: K. 14. Cemetery: Pond Farm Cemetery in Belgium.

REANEY, Michael: Rank: Guardsman. Regiment or Service: Grenadier Guards. Unit: 1st Bn. Date of death: 17 October 1915. Service No. 17119. Born in Mullinahone. Enlisted in Tipperary. Killed in action. He has no known grave but is listed on Panels 5 to 7 on the Loos Memorial in France.

Warington War Memorial. Photo courtesy of Tommy McClimonds, Co. Down.

Grave of John Riordan.

REGAN, Martin: Rank: Private. Regiment or Service: Royal Irish Regiment. Unit: 6th Bn. Age at death: 20. Date of death: 6 April 1917. Service No.2005. Born in Cahir and enlisted in Clonmel while living in Cahir. Died of wounds.

Supplementary information: Son of Mrs Mary O'Regan, of Old Church Street, Cahir, Co. Tipperary. Grave or Memorial Reference: III. B. 51. Cemetery: Bailleul Communal Cemetery Extension (Nord) in France. He is also commemorated on the Cahir War Memorial.

REGAN, Michael: Rank: Private. Regiment or Service: Royal Irish Regiment. Unit: 7th (South Irish Horse) Bn. Age at death: 28. Date of death: 21 March 1918. Service No.10501. Joined the 7th Bn in February 1918. Born in Boston USA and enlisted in Swansea while living in Pontardawe in Glam. Killed in action.

Supplementary information: Son of Timothy and Margaret Regan (*née* Power), of Ahenny, Carrick-on-Suir, Co. Tipperary. Grave or Memorial Reference: Has no known grave but is commemorated on Panel 30 and 31. Memorial: Pozieres Memorial in France.

REID, Lestock Henry: Rank: Second Lieutenant. Regiment or Service: New Zealand Pioneer Battalion. Serial Number: 4/52A. Killed by Machine Gun Fire in Armentieres in France. Date of death: 20 December 1916

Supplementary information: Husband of Muriel G. Reid, of Kilkefernan, Clonmel, Irish Free State, and eldest son of Arthur Ironside Reid and Mary Sidney Reid, of 122 Richardson Street, Opawa, Christchurch, New Zealand. In first landing on Anzac Cove, 25 April. Served in Egypt: gazetted in France March 7, 1916. Grave or Memorial Reference: I. B. 38. Cemetery: Cite Bonjean Military Cemetery, Armentieres, France. He is also recorded on the Family Headstone

291

in St Patrick's Cemetery, Waterford Road Clonmel.

REILLY, James: Rank: Private. Regiment or Service: Connaught Rangers. Unit: 2nd Bn. Date of death: 1 November 1914. Service No.7728. Born in Nenagh. Enlisted in Birr while living in Nenagh. Died of wounds. Killed in action. Age at death: 28.

Supplementary information: Son of Joseph Reilly and Mary Delaney, his wife: husband of Mary Ray Reilly, of William Street, Nenagh, Co. Tipperary. He has no known grave but is listed on Panel 42 on the Ypres (Menin Gate) Memorial in Belgium.

REILLY, Michael: Rank: Lance Corporal. Regiment or Service: Royal Irish Regiment. Unit: 6th Bn. Age at death: 24. Date of death: 27 January 1916. Service No.2087. Born in Grangemockler and enlisted in Clonmel while living in Redmondstown Co. Tipperary. Killed in action.

Supplementary information: Son of Michael Reilly, of Grangemockles, Co. Tipperary. Grave or Memorial Reference: Has no known grave but is commemorated on Panel 44. Memorial: Loos Memorial in France.

RENTOUL, James Lawrence: Rank: Private. Regiment or Service: Royal Army Medical Corps Unit: 91st Field Ambulance. Age at death: 33. Date of death: 30 September 1918. Service No.129116. Born in Darlington and enlisted in Newry. Killed in action.

Supplementary information: Son of the Revd R. W. R. and Mrs Rentoul (*née* Wylie) of Clonmel, Co. Tipperary: husband of B. Eileen Rentoul (née Moore), of Fircroft, Hawthornden Rd, Knock, Co. Down. Grave or Memorial Reference: A. 28. Cemetery: La Baraque British Cemetery in France.

REYNER/REYNOR Joseph: Rank: Private. Regiment or Service: Royal Dublin Fusiliers. Unit: 8th Bn. Date of death: 3 February 1917. Service No.24802. Born in Nenagh. Enlisted in Dublin. Died of wounds. Age at death 38.

Supplementary information: Husband of Caroline Hannan (formerly Reynor), of 5 McNamara Terrace, Limerick. Native of Dublin. Grave or Memorial Reference: III. A. 74. Cemetery: Bailleul Communal Cemetery Extension (Nord) in France.

REYNOLDS, James: Rank: Lance Corporal. Regiment or Service: Leinster Regiment. Unit: 2nd Bn. Date of death: 23 June 1917. Service No.5316. Born in Nenagh. Enlisted in Nenagh while living in Nenagh. Killed in action. He has no known grave but is listed on Panel 44 on the Ypres (Menin Gate) Memorial in Belgium.

RICHARDSON, Thomas Robert: Rank: Sergeant and Acting Sergeant. Regiment or Service: Corps of Royal Engineers. Unit: 4th Signal Company, Royal Engineers. Date of death: 10 July 1916. Service No.23166. Formerly he was with the Royal Irish Rifles where his number was 9015. Born in Norgraffin Co. Tipperary. Enlisted in Belfast while living in Warringstown in Co. Down. Died of wounds. Age at death: 25.

Supplementary information: Son of Robert and Sarah Jane Robertson. Grave or Memorial Reference: II. D. 14. Cemetery: Etretat Churchyard, France. He is also commemorated on the Waringstown War Memorial in Banbridge Co. Down.

RICHINGS, David George: Rank: Driver. Regiment or Service: Royal Horse Artillery and Royal Field Artillery. Unit: 63rd Battery. Date of death: 1 May 1916. Service No. 35417. Born in Clonmel. Enlisted in Potchefstroom in South Africa. Died in Turkey.

Supplementary Information: Son of Major Joseph Richings, of Church View, Windlesham, Surrey, and the late Jane Elizabeth Richings. He has no known grave but is listed on Panel 3 and 60 the Basra Memorial in Iraq. He is also commemorated on the Cahir War Memorial.

RILEY, Patrick: Rank: Private. Regiment or Service: Kings Liverpool Regiment. Unit: 11th Bn. Date of death: 29 March 1916. Service No. 13297. Born in Tipperary. Enlisted in Liverpool while living in Liverpool. Grave or Memorial Reference: Plot 2, Row K, Grave 4. Cemetery: Le Treport Military Cemetery in France.

RIORDAN, John: Rank: Private. Regiment or Service: Royal Irish

Fusiliers. Unit: 7th Bn. Born in Clerihan, Co. Tipperary. Enlisted in Clonmel while living in Clerihan. Died at home. Date of death: 19 May 1915. Service No. 16551. Cemetery: St Michael's New Cemetery, Tipperary Town. Grave location: E. H. 97

RIORDAN, Michael: Rank: Private. Regiment or Service: Royal Irish Regiment. Unit: 2nd Bn. Age at death: 38. Date of death: 14 May 1915. Service No. 5987. Born in Ardfinnan and enlisted in Clonmel while living in Clogheen. Killed in action.

Supplementary information: Son of Martin and Mary Riordan, of Convent Rd, Clogheen: husband of Bridget Riordan, of Cockpit Street, Clogheen, Co. Tipperary. Grave or Memorial Reference: Has no known grave but is commemorated on Panel 33. Memorial: Ypres (Menin Gate) Memorial in Belgium. He is also commemorated on the Cahir War Memorial.

RIORDAN, Thomas: Rank: Private. Regiment or Service: Royal Irish Regiment. Unit: 2nd Bn. Age at death: 20. Date of death: 14 July 1916. Service No. 6368. Born in St Nicholas's in Carrick-on-Suir and enlisted in Clonmel while living in Carrick-on-Suir. Killed in action.

Supplementary information: Son of William and Elizabeth Riordan, of Upper Bally Richard Rd, Carrick-on-Suir, Co. Tipperary. Grave or Memorial Reference: Pier and Face 3 A. Memorial: Thiepval Memorial in France.

RIORDAN, William: Rank: Corporal. Regiment or Service: Royal Irish Regiment. Unit: 7th (South Irish Horse where his number was 449) Bn. Age at death: 26. Date of death: 21 March 1918. Service No.25753. Entitled to the 1915 Star, the War Medal and the Vicotry Medal. Born in Templemore and enlisted there also in April 1910. Killed in action.

Supplementary information: Son of Thomas and Annie Riordan, of Bank Street, Templemore, Co. Tipperary. Grave or Memorial Reference: Has no known grave but is commemorated on Panel 30 and 31. Memorial: Pozieres Memorial in France.

ROBERTS, Sir Frederick Sleigh: Rank: Field Marshal. Regiment or Service: Commands and Staff, General Staff and Colonel Commandant, Royal Artillery and Colonel in the Irish Guards: From the CWGC: Awards: V C, K G, K P, G C B, O M, G C S I, G C I E. Age at death: 82. Date of death: 14 November 1914. 1st Earl of Kandahar, Pretoria and Waterford. Born at Cawnpore, India. Privy Counsellor. Son of the late Gen. Sir Abraham Roberts, G.C.B., and the late Lady Roberts: husband of the late Countess Roberts, C.I., R.R.C., of Englemere, Ascot, Berks. Educated at Eton, Sandhurst and Addiscombe. Commissioned to the Bengal Artillery (December, 1851): served throughout the Indian Mutiny 1857 (V.C.): and the Abyssinian (1867-68) and Lushai (1871-72) Expeditions. Also served in the Afghanistan Campaign (1878-80) and Commanded the Kabul-Kandahar Field Force August-September, 1880. Commanded the Forces in Ireland (1895-99): Commander-in-Chief in the South African War (1899-1900). Commander-in-Chief in India (1885-93) and at Home (1901-04). Master Gunner of St James' Park and Colonel-in-Chief of Overseas and Indian Forces in the United Kingdom during the Great War. An extract from the *London Gazette* dated 24 December 1858, records the following:

On the 2nd January 1858 at Khodagunge, India, on following up the retreating enemy, Lieutenant Roberts saw in the distance two sepoys going away with a standard. He immediately gave chase, overtaking them just as they were about to enter a village. Although one of them fired at him the lieutenant was not hit and he took possession of the standard, cutting down the man who was carrying it. He had also on the same day saved the life of a sowar who was being attacked by a sepoy. His Mother was from Kilfeacle in Tipperary and he died of Pneumonia in St Omer in France on 14 November 1914 while visiting Indian Troops. Buried in St Paul's Cathedral in London. He is also commemorated on the Cahir War Memorial.

ROBERTS, Hedley Vicars: Rank: Lance Corporal. Regiment or Service: Norfolk Regiment. Unit: 7th Bn. Age at death: 45. Date of death: 24 January 1918. Service No.12234. Born in

William John
Rudd.

Co. Carlow and enlisted in St Paul's Churchyard in Middlesex.

Supplementary information: Son of David and Ellie Roberts (*née* Magill) of Roscrea, Co. Tipperary: husband of Ethel A. Roberts, of 2 Damer Terrace, West Chelsea, London. Grave or Memorial Reference: II. C. 12A. Cemetery: Les Baraques Military Cemetery, Sangatte in France.

ROBERTS, William: Rank: Private. Regiment or Service: Royal Irish Regiment. Unit: 2nd Bn. Date of death: 19 October 1914. Service No.10941. Born in Ss Peter and Paul, Clonmel, Co. Tipperary. Enlisted in Clonmel. Killed in action. Grave or Memorial Reference: VII. L. 8. Cemetery: Cabaret Rouge British Cemetery, Souchez, France.

ROBERTSON, Alexander: Rank: Gunner. Regiment or Service: Royal Field Artillery. Unit: 'B' Bty. 312th Bde. Age at death: 24. Date of death: 31 October 1917. Service No.68456. Born in South Shields and enlisted in Durham. Killed in action.

Supplementary information: Son of Mrs A. Robertson, of 6, Montgomery Street, Montreal, Canada: husband of Mrs M. K. Maws (*née* Robertson), of II, Georges Court, Clonmel, Co.

Tipperary, Ireland. Grave or Memorial Reference: I. D. 3. Cemetery: St Martin Calvaire British Cemetery, St Martin-Sur-Cojeul in France.

ROBINSON, William: Rank: Lance Corporal. Regiment or Service: Manchester Regiment. Unit: 11th Bn. Date of death: 7 August 1916. Service No.9412. Born in Clonmel. Enlisted in Manchester. Died of wounds. Grave or Memorial Reference: III. C. 13. Cemetery: Heilly Station Cemetery, Mericourt-L'Abbe in France.

ROBINSON, William Charles: Rank: Second Lieutenant. Regiment or Service: 30th Punjabis. Date of death: 7 January 1917.

Supplementary information: Son of Thomas and Isabella Caroline Robinson of Kilcommon, Cahir. Grave or Memorial Reference: IV.B.6. Cemetery: Morogoro Cemetery in Tanzania. He is also commemorated on the Cahir War Memorial.

ROCHE, James: Rank: Private. Regiment or Service: Royal Irish Fusiliers. Unit: 8th Bn. Date of death: 6 September 1916. Service No.43008. Formerly he was with the Royal Irish Regiment where his number was 2125. Born in Carrick-on-Suir,

Co. Tipperary. Enlisted in Clonmel while living in Carrick-on-Suir, Co. Tipperary. Killed in action. He has no known grave but is listed on Pier and Face 15 A on the Thiepval Memorial in France.

ROCHE, John: Rank: Lance Corporal. Regiment or Service: Irish Guards. Unit: 2nd Bn. Age at death: 20. Date of death: 7 December 1915. Service No.6334. Born in Templemore and enlisted in Clonmel. Died of wounds.

Supplementary information: Son of Martin and Kate Roche, of Lower Pike Street, Thurles, Co. Tipperary. Letter from his Commanding Officer to his Mother:

Madam I very much regret that your son 6334 Lance Corporal Roche J. of No 15 Platoon, No 4 Company, 2nd Bn, Irish Guards was shot on December 3 by a German sniper. I regret to say that the wound was a serious one being in the head but he showed great pluck about it and there seems to be every chance of his recovery. Your son was operated on the evening of the 3rd inst. at Merville Hospital and Father Knapp of this Regiment visited him and reported to me that the operation had been entirely successful, his pulse, heart and temperature all being good. I ask you to please accept my sincere sympathy for you in your trouble, and I can also assure you I feel his loss very much in my Company, as apart

from his congenial disposition, and his very plucky character, he was a most promising non-commissioned officer, and would have undoubtedly have done very well. I only hope he may have a speedy recovery. I am yours very truly, D. Hudson-Kinahan, O. C. No 4 Coy, 2nd Bn, Irish Guards B. E. F. France.

To Mrs Roche, Thurles. December 10 1915.

Dear Madam, I deeply regret to have to report to you that your son, 6334 Lance Corporal J. Roche, died from his wounds on December 7th, not having recovered consciousness after his operation. He was buried on the following day and a cross was erected over his grave by his comrades. Allow me to offer you my most sincere sympathy in the loss of one so brave and true, and I can assure you he will be greatly missed by many friends out here, and I personally much deplore his loss. -Yours Truly, D Hudson-Kinahan. O. C.

Letter from Sergeant P Nolan, 4 Coy, 2nd Bn, Irish Guards, B. E. F. France, 10 December 1915.

Dear Mrs Roche.

Please excuse me as a stranger, in addressing you in above manner, but I wish to sympathise with you on the death of your son. As

Grave of D. Ryan.

E. Ryan.

Heny Joseph Ryan.

his platoon Sergeant I was very well acquainted with him since we came out together last August and a better nor a kinder hearted lad ever donned the khaki. I was beside him when he was wounded and I had hopes that he would have been all right but such was not to be God's will. Our Good Priest Father Knapp saw him several times after being wounded and administered the last Sacraments to him before he died. He is in Heaven praying for you and for us all. In concluding I would state all the men in No 4 Company sincerely sympathise with you in the loss you have sustained. I enclose your lads cap star which you might like to keep in his memory. -Yours Sincerely. P Nolan.

Note: Sgt Peter Nolan won the Distinguished Conduct Medal as well as the Military medal and Bar. He was killed in action on 27 November 1917. Grave or Memorial Reference: IV. O. 4. Cemetery: Merville Communal Cemetery in France.

ROCHE, John: Rank: Private. Regiment or Service: Royal Irish Regiment. Unit: 5th Bn. Date of death: 12 May 1918. Service No.6231 and 116231. Born in St Mary's, Clonmel, Co. Tipperary. Enlisted in Clonmel. Killed in action. Grave or Memorial Reference: I. K. 17. Cemetery: La Targette British Cemetery, Neuville-St Vaast in France.

ROCHE, Michael: Rank: Private. Regiment or Service: Royal Irish Regiment. Unit: 6th Bn. Date of death: 3 September 1916. Service No.5373. Born in Powerstown, Co. Tipperary. Enlisted in Clonmel while living in Redmondstown Co. Tipperary. Killed in action. He has no known grave but is listed on Pier and Face 3 A on the Thiepval Memorial in France.

RONAN, Edward: Rank: Private. Regiment or Service: Royal Dublin Fusiliers. Unit: 2nd Bn. Date of death: 1 July 16, first day of the Battle of the Somme. Service No.22723. Born in Tipperary. Enlisted in Kildare while living in Tipperary. Killed in action. He has no known grave but is listed on Pier and Face 16 C on the Thiepval Memorial in France.

ROSE, James: Rank: Lance Sergeant. Regiment or Service: Irish Guards. Unit: 1st Bn. Date of death: 27 July 1916. Service No.2880. Born in Clonmel. Enlisted in Mullingar. Killed in action. Age at death: 31.

Supplementary information: Son of the late Joshua Rose, of Kilduff House, Philipstown, King's County: husband of Sarah Rose, of Bandon, Co. Cork. Grave or Memorial Reference: I. X. 2. Cemetery: La Brique Military Cemetery, No 2 in Belgium.

ROWLAND, Robert David: Rank: Driver. Regiment or Service: Corps of Royal Engineers. 1st Signal Coy. Date of death: 15 September 1914. Service No.16172. Formerly he was with the 1st Division Signal Company Royal

Engineers. Born in Roscrea. Enlisted in Dublin while living in Roscrea. Killed in action. Grave or Memorial Reference: II. B. 16. Cemetery: Vendresse British Cemetery in France.

RUDD, William John: Rank: Private. Regiment or Service: Royal Dublin Fusiliers. Unit: 10th Bn. Age at death: 20. Date of death: 13 November 1916. Service No. 26683. Born in Roscrea and enlisted in Dublin while living in Roscrea. Killed in action.

Supplementary information: Son of William John and Ellen Sophia Rudd, of Abbey Mills, Roscrea. Co. Tipperary. Grave or Memorial Reference: Pier and Face 16 C. Memorial: Thiepval Memorial in France.

RUSSELL/RUSSEL, Edmond: Rank: Private. Regiment or Service: Royal Inniskilling Fusiliers. Unit: 7th–8th Bn. He was previously with the Royal Irish Regiment where his number was 4829. Age at death: 22. Date of death: 19 August 1918. Service No. 48319. Born in Greenside Carrick-on-Suir and enlisted in Carrick-on-Suir. Died of wounds. *Supplementary information*: Son of Patrick and Norah Russell, of Green Side, Carrick-on-Suir, Co. Tipperary. Grave or Memorial Reference: III. E. 5. Cemetery: Arneke British Cemetery in France.

RUSSELL, John: Rank: Private. Regiment or Service: Royal Irish Regiment. Unit: 7th Bn. Date of death: 21 March 1918. Service No. 8936. Born in Killenaule and enlisted in Cashel while living in Killenaule. Killed in action.

Supplementary information: Son of William and Katherine Russell, of Spring Hill, Killenaule, Thurles, Co. Tipperary. Grave or Memorial Reference: Has no known grave but is commemorated on Panel 30 and 31. Memorial: Pozieres Memorial in France.

RYALL, Charles: Rank: Private. Regiment or Service: Irish Guards. Unit: 1st Bn. Age at death: 39. Date of death: 13 September 1917. Service No. 2105. Born in Fethard and enlisted in Chester. Killed in action.

Supplementary information: Son of Richard and Annie Ryall, of Buffanagh, Fethard, Co. Tipperary. Grave or Memorial Reference: III. B. 36. Cemetery: Canada Farm Cemetery in Belgium.

RYAN, Andrew: Rank: Corporal. Regiment or Service: Royal Irish Regiment. Unit: 5th Bn. Age at death: 45. Date of death: 4 September 1915. Service No. 328. Born in Thurles and enlisted there also. Killed in action in Gallipoli.

Supplementary information: Son of Thomas Ryan, of Thurles: husband of Mrs B. Ryan, of Limekiln Lane, Thurles, Co. Tipperary. Volunteered in August 1914 at the beginning of the war. Brother in law of Private James Sheehan who died at sea on 24 August 1915. Grave or Memorial. Reference: II. A. 4. Cemetery: Lala Baba Cemetery in Turkey.

RYAN, Connie: Rank: Corporal. Regiment or Service: Royal Irish Regiment. Unit: 1st Bn. Age at death: 32. Date of death: 4 January 1918. Service No. 8872. Awarded the Military Medal and listed in the *London Gazette*. Born in Cappawhite and enlisted in Tipperary. Died in Palestine.

Supplementary information: Son of Mrs Julia Crowe, of 20 New Cottages, Cashel Rd, Tipperary. Grave or Memorial Reference: J. 43. Cemetery: Ramleh War Cemetery in Israel.

RYAN, David: Rank: Private. No 1209, Royal Munster Fusiliers, 2nd Bn. Date of death: 7 March 1917. Born in Borelaghuan(Boherlahan), enlisted in Limerick while living in Bruff, Co. Limerick. Died of wounds. Buried in Bray Military Cemetery in the village of Bray-sur-Somme in France. Grave reference II. B. 14. Died of Wounds.

RYAN, Denis: Rank: Private. Regiment or Service: Irish Guards. Unit: 2nd Bn. Age at death: 20. Date of death: given as both 13 September 1916 and 15 September 1916. Service No. 4817 Awarded the Military Medal and listed in the *London Gazette*. Born in Drombane and enlisted in Glasgow while living in Dromane. Killed in action.

Supplementary information: Son of Daniel and Johanna Ryan, of Glebe Cross, Drombane, Thurles, Co. Tipperary. Grave or Memorial Reference: Pier and Face 7 D. Memorial: Thiepval Memorial in France.

RYAN, D: Rank: Lance Corporal. Regiment or Service: Queen's Own Royal West Kent Regiment. Unit: Age at death: 23. Date of death: 25 March 1920. Service No. G/6484.

Supplementary information: Husband of Mary Ryan of 28 Dungarvan Rd. Clonmel. Cemetery, Clonmel, St Patrick's Cemetery. Grave location: 2. F. 66.

RYAN, E: Rank: Private. Regiment or Service: Royal Irish Regiment. Unit: Depot. Date of death: 7 November 1918. Service No. 257.

Supplementary information: Husband of M. Ryan, of Knockenrawley, Tipperary. Grave or Memorial Reference: E. H. 105. Cemetery: Tipperary (St Michael's) New Cemetery, Tipperary Town.

RYAN, E: Rank: Private. Regiment or Service: Leinster Regiment. Unit: 2nd Bn. Age at death: 29. Date of death: 2 April 1916. Service No. 7377.

Supplementary information: Son of Mrs Nora Ryan: of "Ballaby" Silver Street, Nenagh, Co. Tipperary. Grave or Memorial Reference: II. D. 236. Cemetery: Bailleul Communal Cemetery Extension (Nord) in France.

RYAN, G: Rank: Shoeing Smith. Regiment or Service: Royal Field Artillery. Unit: 66th Div. Ammunition Col. Age at death: 26. Date of death: 9 March 1919. Service No. 119621.

Supplementary information: Son of Michael and Annie Ryan, of Ballyscanlon, Coolbawn, Borrisokane,

Grave of John Ryan.

Co. Tipperary: husband of A. J. Kisby (formerly Ryan), of 29 Holmrook Rd, Preston. Grave or Memorial Reference: B. 6. Cemetery: Houyet Churchyard in France.

RYAN, Henry Joseph: Rank: Lt. Regiment or Service: Australian Infantry. Unit: 25th Bn. Date of death: 17 July 1918.

Supplementary information: Educated in De La Salle's College, Castletown, Ireland. Commissioned Officer of the Armed Constabulary. Served in Plymouth, Folkstone, Havre, Cobham, Tidowrth, Wisques, Brisbane, England, France. Wounded (gunshot to left arm) 18 April 1917 in France. Date of birth: 31 January 1878. Age at enlistment: 37. Enlisted in Port Moresby, New Guinea. Height: 5' 11", Weight: 175 lbs. Complexion: fresh. Eyes: brown. Hair: black. Religious denomination: R.C. Killed in action. Age at death: 40. Sister listed as Mrs J. Kennedy, Upper Fox Street, Poultry Farm, Gisborne. Embarked overseas on the 7 September 1916.

Lt Ryan was killed in action on 17 July 1918, by a burst of Machine Gun bullets. At the time he was commanding 'C' Company, 25th Bn. and leading them in attack against enemy trenches at about 6.40pm. He died almost instantly. His body was brought in the following morning by a party of Battalion Headquarter Lewis gunners acting as stretcher bearers under the command of Lt W Harrison (MC) (MM) (Since returned to Australia). His body was buried in the presence of his brother Officers and his men in the cemetery beside the Amiens Villers Brettoneux Road about 200 or 300 yards west of Villers Brettoneux. A cross was erected by the Battalion on his grave.

Supplementary information: Son of Henry Joseph and Margaret Mary Ryan. Native of Tipperary, Ireland. Grave or Memorial Reference: I. C. 10. Cemetery: Adelaide Cemetery Villers-Bretonneux. France.

Grave of Martin Ryan.

RYAN, J: Rank: Private. Regiment or Service: Royal Irish Regiment. Unit: 2nd Bn. Age at death: 52. Date of death: 3 December 1914. Service No.6591. Born in Clogheen and enlisted in Nenagh while living in Clogheen. Died.

Supplementary information: Husband of Johanna Quigley (*née* Ryan), of Cloyheen, Co. Tipperary. Grave or Memorial Reference: A. 19. Cemetery: Sainghin-En-Weppes Communal Cemetery in France.

RYAN, James: Rank: Gunner. Regiment or Service: Royal Garrison Artillery. Unit: 155th Heavy Bty. Date of death: 2 May 1917. Service No.97573. Born in Clonsingle Co. Tipperary and enlisted in Manchester while living in Newport Co. Tipperary.

Supplementary information: Son of Mary Ryan of Clonsingle, Newport, Co. Tipperary. Grave or Memorial Reference: P. I. E. 4A. Cemetery: St Sever Cemetery Extension, Rouen in France.

RYAN, James: Rank: Private. Regiment or Service: Royal Irish Regiment. Unit: 2nd Bn. Date of death: 23 August 1914. Service No.8613. Born in New Birmingham, Co. Tipperary. Enlisted in Thurles. Killed in action. Age at death: 28.

Supplementary information: Son of Michael and Bridget Ryan, of New Birmingham, Thurles, Co. Tipperary. He has no known grave but is listed on the La Ferte-Sous-Jouarre-Memorial in France.

RYAN, James: Rank: Sergeant. Regiment or Service: Manchester Regiment. Unit: 21st Bn. Date of death: 14 July 1917. Service No.21951. Born in Clonmel. Enlisted in Manchester.

Supplementary information: Son of John and Margaret Ryan: husband of Annie Ryan, of 195 Hamilton Street, Rochdale Rd, Manchester. Native of Manchester. Grave or Memorial Reference: XXV K. 12A. Cemetery: Etaples Military Cemetery in France.

RYAN, James: Rank: Private.

Regiment or Service: Royal Irish Regiment. Unit: 2nd Bn. Date of death: 5 July 1916. Service No.8117. Born in Ballina Co. Tipperary. Enlisted in Nenagh while living in Killaloe Co. Clare. Killed in action. Grave or Memorial Reference: VII. C. 6. Cemetery: Flatiron Cemetery: Flatiron Copse Cemetery. Mametz in France.

RYAN, James: Rank: Private. Regiment or Service: Lincolnshire Regiment. Unit: 1st Bn. Date of death: 1 November 1914. Service No.6518. Born in Thurles. Enlisted in Dublin while living in Thurles. Killed in action. He has no known grave but is listed on Panel 21 on the Ypres (Menin Gate) Memorial in Belgium.

RYAN, James: Rank: Private. Regiment or Service: Machine Gun Corps (Infantry). He was previously with the Royal Army Service Corps where his number was 8952. Date of death: 28 October 1918. Service No.37786. and 37780. Born in Cloneganna Co. Tipperary and enlisted in Dublin while living in Roscrea.

Supplementary information: Alternative Commemoration, buried in Killea Graveyard, Co. Tipperary. Grave or Memorial Reference: Has no known grave but is commemorated on Panel 8 (Screen Wall). Memorial: Grangegorman Memorial in Dublin.

RYAN, James: Rank: Private. Regiment or Service: Royal Irish Regiment. Unit: 'A' Coy. 2nd Bn. Age at death: 27. Date of death: 13 September 1917. Service No.2278. Born in Cashel and enlisted in Clonmel while living in Cashel. Died of wounds.

Supplementary information: Son of James Ryan, of Golden. Husband of Ann Ryan, of William Street, Cashel, Co. Tipperary. Grave or Memorial Reference: XII. D. 12. Cemetery: Harlebeke New British Cemetery in Belgium.

RYAN, James: Rank: Private. Regiment or Service: Royal Irish Regiment. Unit: 2nd Bn. Age at death: 28. Date of death: 23 August 1914. Service No.8613. Born in New Birmingham and enlisted in Thurles. Killed in action.

Supplementary information: Son of Michael and Bridget Ryan, of New Birmingham, Thurles, Co. Tipperary. Memorial: La Ferte-Sous-Jouarre-Memorial in France.

RYAN, James: Rank: Sergeant. Regiment or Service: (Duke of Wellingtons) West Riding Regiment. Unit: 2nd Bn. Date of death: 6 May 1915. Service No.6944. Born in Tipperary. Enlisted in Bradford, Yorks while living in Walworth. Died of wounds. Grave or Memorial Reference: I. E. 184. Cemetery: Bailleul Communal Cemetery Extension (Nord) in France.

RYAN, John: Rank: Private. Regiment or Service: Manchester Regiment. Unit: 19th Bn. Date of death: 31 May 1915. Service No.12818. Born in Clonmel. Enlisted in Manchester while living in Rotherham. Died at home. Grave or Memorial Reference: M CE 1017. Cemetery: Manchester Southern Cemetery, UK.

RYAN, John: Rank: Private. Regiment or Service: Royal Irish Regiment. Unit: 8th Bn. Date of death: 3 November 1918. Service No.9948. Born in Carrick-on-Suir, Co. Tipperary. Enlisted in Carrick-on-Suir, Co. Tipperary. Killed in action. Grave or Memorial Reference: C. R. 45. Cemetery: Carrick-on-Suir New Cemetery, Co. Tipperary.

RYAN, John: Rank: Private. Regiment or Service: Royal Irish Regiment. Unit: 2nd Bn. Age at death: 30. Killed in action, Monday 19 October 1914. Service No.5972. He was one of the 'old Contemptables'. Born in Ballycahill. Enlisted in Templemore while living in Thurles. Killed in action.

Supplementary information: Son of Bill and Ellie Ryan, of Quarry Street, Thurles, Co. Tipperary: husband of Bridget Higgiston (*née* Ryan), of Birr Rd, Nenagh, Co. Tipperary. Grave or Memorial Reference: Has no known grave but is commemorated on Panel 11 and 12. Memorial: Le Touret Memorial in France. Pas de Calais, France. There are over 13, 000 names on this memorial to men that died in this area during WW1 that have no known grave.

RYAN, John: Rank: Private. Regiment or Service: Royal Munster Fusiliers. Unit: 8th Bn. Date of death: 8 January 1915. Service No.3282. Born in Nenagh. Enlisted in Limerick while living in Nenagh. Died at home. Grave or Memorial Reference: Screen Wall. Cemetery: Fermoy Military Cemetery, Co. Cork.

RYAN, John: Rank: Gunner. Regiment or Service: Royal Garrison Artillery. Unit: B Siege Battery. Date of death: 19 June 1916. Service No.48063. Born in Cappawhite Co. Tipperary. Enlisted in Tipperary while living in Cunahun Hollyfort Co. Tipperary. Died at home. Grave or Memorial Reference: CC. K. 9. Cemetery: Bexhill Cemetery, UK.

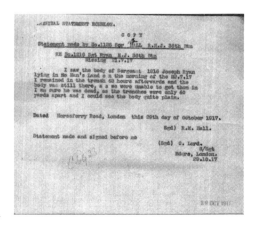

Myles Joseph Ryan.

RYAN, John Joseph: Rank: Private. Regiment or Service: Machine Gun Corps (Infantry). Unit: 106th Coy. He was previously with the Royal Irish regiment where his number was 9804. Age at death: 28. Date of death: 20 October 1917. Service No.26017. and 2607. Born in Tipperary and enlisted there also. Killed in action.

Supplementary information: Son of Jeremiah and Mary Ryan, of 37, O'Connell Row, Tipperary. Grave or Memorial Reference: Has no known grave but is commemorated on Panel 154 to 159 and 163A. Memorial: Tyne Cot Memorial in Belgium.

RYAN, Joseph: Rank: Lance Corporal. Regiment or Service: Royal Dublin Fusiliers. Unit: 1st Bn. Age at death: 21. Date of death: 17 August 1917. Service No.11212. Born in Nenagh and enlisted there also.

Supplementary information: Son of Mrs A. Ryan, of Summer Hill, Nenagh, Co. Tipperary. Grave or Memorial Reference: Has no known grave but is commemorated on Panel 144 to 145. Memorial: Tyne Cot Memorial in Belgium.

RYAN, Martin: Alias, correct name is **TUOHY, Martin**. Rank: Private. Regiment or Service: Royal Irish Rifles. Unit: 2nd Garrison Bn. Enlisted in Ballyvonare Co. Cork. while living in Thurles. Died at home. Previously he was with the Royal Irish Rifles where his number was 7/4494. Extract from the Tipperary Star dated March, 1917: Killed on Duty. While doing sentry duty on the railway bridge, Malahide, Co. Dublin, Lance Corporal M Ryan, Pike Street, Thurles was knocked down by a passing train as a result of which he died almost immediately afterwards. The engine driver at an inquest on the remains yesterday, said he did not see the deceased but the whistle of the engine was blown and the strong wind might have prevented it being heard-a statement which was corroborated by the fireman. The jury exonerated the driver and recommended the widow of the deceased to the consideration of the Railway Company and Military Authorities. Date of death: 20 March 1917. Service No.1718

Supplementary information: Grave location: Between the church and the East boundary.

RYAN, Martin: Rank: Lance Corporal. Regiment or Service: Royal Irish Rifles. Unit: 7th Bn. Date of death: 16 August 1917. Service No.40054. Formerly he was with the West Riding Regiment where his number was 20250. Born in Tipperary. Enlisted in Halifax while living in Cronovone, Co. Tipperary. Killed in action. He has no known grave but is listed on Panels 138 to 140 and 162 to 162A and 163A on the Tyne Cot Memorial in Belgium.

RYAN, Michael: Rank: Private. Regiment or Service: Machine Gun Corps (Infantry) He was previously with the Royal Irish regiment where his number was 1170. Age at death: 22. Date of death: 8 July 1916. Service No.26015. Born in Kellenaule and enlisted there also. Died of wounds.

Supplementary information: Son of Michael Ryan, of Lurgoe: Killenaule, Thurles, Co. Tipperary. Grave or Memorial Reference: C. 429. Cemetery: Ashburton Roman Catholic Cemetery, Gosforth, UK.

RYAN, Michael: Rank: Private. Regiment or Service: Lancashire Fusiliers. Unit: 2nd-5th Bn. Date of death: 20 November 1917. Service No.41642. Born in Thurles. Enlisted in Manchester. Killed in action. Grave or Memorial Reference: XXXI. F. 16-1917. Cemetery: Cabaret-Rouge British Cemetery, Souchez in France.

RYAN, Michael: Rank: Private. Regiment or Service: Royal Irish Regiment. Unit:3rd Bn. Date of death: 25 June 1916. Service No.9912. Born in Nenagh. Enlisted in Limerick while living in Cloughjordan. Died of wounds. Age at death: 21.

Supplementary information: Son of John Ryan, New Street, Lismore, County Waterford. Grave or Memorial Reference: 30693. Cemetery: Limerick (St Lawrence's) Catholic Cemetery, County Limerick.

RYAN, Michael: Rank: Gunner. Regiment or Service: Royal Horse Artillery and Royal Field Artillery. Unit:5th Reserve Brigade. Date of death: 26 July 1916. Service No.76155. Born in Tipperary. Enlisted in Cahir. Died at home. Grave or Memorial Reference: 2. FB. 65. Cemetery: Clonmel (St Patrick's) Cemetery.

RYAN, Michael: Rank: Private. Regiment or Service: South Wales Borderers. Unit:6th Bn. Date of death: 25 March 1918. Service No.17488. Born in Tipperary. Enlisted in Newport, Mon. Killed in action. He has no known grave but is listed in Bay 6 on the Arras Memorial in France.

RYAN, Michael: Rank: Lance Corporal. Regiment or Service: Royal Irish Fusiliers. Unit: 8th Bn. Date of death: 5 May 1916. Service No.20467. Born in Tipperary. Enlisted in Bury, Lancs while living in Heywood, Lancs. Died of wounds. Age at death: 29.

Supplementary information: Son of Michael and Ellen Ryan, of Cappamore, Co. Limerick. Grave or Memorial Reference: A. 20. 27. Cemetery: St Sever Cemetery, Rouen in France.

RYAN, Michael: Rank: Private. Regiment or Service: Royal Irish Regiment. Unit: 3rd Bn. Date of death: 21 April 1916. Service No.9929. Born in Anacarty in County Tipperary, enlisted in Cashel, while living in Golden. Died at home. He is commemorated on the Addenda Panel. (Screen Wall) on the Grangegorman Memorial in Dublin but buried in Kilpatrick Old Graveyard, Co. Tipperary.

RYAN, Myles Joseph: Rank: Sergeant (promoted on 5 November 1916). Regiment or Service: Australian Infantry, A. I. F. Unit: 36th Bn. Age at death: 24. Born: Tipperary. Date of death: 22 July 1917. Service No.1216.

Enlisted on 4 February 1916. Age on enlistment: 23, Occupation: labourer, Weight: 147lbs, Complexion: Fair, Eyes: Grey, Hair: Fair. Religious Denomination: RC. Served in Southampton, England, Belgium, Sydney and Devonport. Attested in Broadmeadows Camp on 21 February 1916 and joined D Coy 36th Bn. Reported as Missing in action on 23 July 1917 and after a Court of Inquiry (15 January 1918) this was changed to Killed in action. Location of death: Armentieres.

Original Statement Echelon, by No 1126 Sapper Hall, R. H. J. 36th Bn.

> I saw the body of Sgt 1216 Joseph Ryan lying in No Mans Land on the morning of 22 July 1917. I remained in the trench 48hrs afterwards and the body was still there, as we were unable to get them in. I am sure he was dead, as the trenches were only 40 yards apart and I could see the body quite plain

Dated 29 October 1917.

Statement by No 1237, Private Seeblink:

> Private M. J. Ryan 36th Bn. was killed in Armentieres Sector by gas. Sgt M Ryan went over with me but was missing later on. I lost sight of him but I can clearly say for certain that he was killed

Dated 11 January 1918.

Statement by 1279 Sgt Webster, 36th Bn.:

This NCO was one of a party detailed for an attack on an enemy strong-post opposite Messines in the morning of 21 July 1917. The objective was not gained and severe casualties were inflicted on our party. I was not one of the party myself but was at the time acting as CQM Sergeant and one of my duties was to report casualties to Battalion Hedaquarters. Previous to the operation Private Ryan handed me his personal effects and asked me to forward these to his Mother in Ireland should anything happen to him.

Several of our party who returned to the trenches stated that Private Ryan was seen to fall wounded and as he lay on the ground continued to fire his rifle at the enemy, but he was subsequently killed by a grenade. Sgt Ryan always maintained that he would never be taken as prisoner and when handing me his personal effects prior to the enterprise made the same statement again...Attempts were made to recover the bodies...but owing to the close proximity of the enemy stronghold to or front line [35 Yards] this was found impossible.

Dated 13 December 1917.

Supplementary information: Son of Daniel Bourke Ryan and Annie Dwyer Ryan, of 13 Emmett Street, New Tipperary, Ireland. Native of Tipperary. Grave or Memorial Reference: II. G. 26. Cemetery: Wulverghem-Lindenhoek Road Military Cemetery in Belgium.

Grave of W. Ryan.

RYAN, Peter: Rank: Sergeant. Regiment or Service: Gloucestershire Regiment. Unit 1ˢᵗ–4ᵗʰ Bn. Age at death: 31. Date of death: 24 September 1917. Service No.200621. Grave or Memorial reference: Screen Wall War Plot. Cemetery: Bristol (Arnos Vale) Catholic Cemetery, UK.

RYAN, Patrick: Rank: Private. Regiment or Service: Royal Irish Regiment. Unit:'D' Coy. 6ᵗʰ Bn.Age at death: 31. Date of death: 9 September 1916. Service No.9872. Born in Thurles and enlisted there also.

Supplementary information: Son of Jack and Kate Ryan, of Stradavoher, Thurles: husband of Mary Ryan, of Quarry Street, Thurles, Co. Tipperary. Grave or Memorial Reference: Pier and Face 3 A. Memorial: Thiepval Memorial in France.

RYAN, Patrick: Rank: Private. Regiment or Service: Irish Guards. Unit: 2ⁿᵈ Bn. Date of death: 28 March 1918. Service No.10318. Born in Borrisokane. Enlisted in Borrisokane. Killed in action. He has no known grave but is listed in Bay 1 on the Arras Memorial in France.

RYAN, Richard: Rank: Private. Regiment or Service: Leinster Regiment. Unit: 1ˢᵗ Bn. Date of death: 28 April 1915. Service No.8456. Born in Drom, Co. Tipperary. Enlisted in Templemore. Killed in action. Age at death: 25.

Supplementary information: Son of the late Richard and Margaret Ryan. He has no known grave but is listed on Panel 44 on the Ypres (Menin Gate) Memorial in Belgium

RYAN, Richard: Rank: Sergeant. Regiment or Service: Royal Irish Regiment. Unit: 2ⁿᵈ Bn. Date of death: 14 May 1915. Service No.6802. Born in Carrick-on-Suir, Co. Tipperary. Enlisted in Kilkenny while living in Ballineen, Co. Cork. Killed in action.

Age at death: 42.

Supplementary information: Son of Michael and Bridget Ryan. He has no known grave but is listed on Panel 33 on the Ypres (Menin Gate) Memorial in Belgium.

RYAN, Stephen: Rank: Private. Regiment or Service: Royal Irish Regiment. Unit: 1st Bn. Date of death: 10 March 1918. Service No.4828 and 4-4828. Born in Carrick-on-Suir, Co. Tipperary. Enlisted in Carrick-on-Suir, Co. Tipperary. Killed in action in Palestine. Grave or Memorial Reference: A. 48. Cemetery: Jerusalem War Cemetery in Israel.

RYAN, Stephen: Rank: Private. Regiment or Service: Royal Irish Regiment. Unit: 2nd Bn. Age at death: 33. Date of death: 23 August 1914. Service No.6726. Born in Cashel, enlisted in Clonmel while living in Cashel. Killed in action. This cemetery was made by the Germans and Stephen was one of the first casualties of the Great War.

Supplementary information: Son of Timothy and Mary Ryan, of Cashel, Co. Tipperary: husband of Mary Ryan, of the Green, Cashel, Co. Tipperary. Grave or Memorial Reference: II. B. 15. Cemetery: St Symphorien Military Cemetery in Belgium.

RYAN, Thomas: Rank: Private. Regiment or Service: Royal Dublin Fusiliers. Unit: 8th Bn. Date of death: 27 April 1916. Service No.16515. Born in Tipperary. Enlisted in Dublin while living in Tipperary. Killed in action.

He has no known grave but is listed on Panels 127 to 129 on the Loos Memorial in France.

RYAN, Thomas: Rank: Driver. No 12116, Royal Horse Artillery and Royal Field Artillery. Date of death: 23 September 1918. Born in Golden, enlisted in Preston in Lancashire while living in Golden. Died in Salonika. Buried in Sarigol Military Cemetery, Kriston in the Town of Sarigol in Turkey. Grave reference D. 674. Died during the attacks on Pip Ridge and the Grand-Couronne north of Thessalonika in Salonika.

RYAN, Thomas: Rank: Private. Regiment or Service: Royal Dublin Fusiliers. Unit: 2nd Bn. Age at death: 42. Date of death: 22 March 1918. Service No.5179.

Supplementary information: Son of Edmund and Anne Ryan, of Pike Street, Thurles, Co. Tipperary: husband of Anne Ryan, of 144 Grenville Street, Edgeley, Stockport. Twenty-two years Service. Grave or Memorial Reference: CA. R. C. 298. Cemetery: Stockport Borough Cemetery, UK.

RYAN, Thomas: Rank: Company Quartermaster Sergeant. Regiment or Service: Royal Fusiliers. Unit: 25th Bn. Date of death: 29 June 1916. Service No.13601. Born in Tipperary and enlisted in Bolton while living in Bolton. Died in East Africa.

Supplementary information: Husband of M. R. Ryan, of Lidwells Lane, Goudhurst, Kent. Born at Tipperary, Ireland. twenty-one years' service in

Royal Irish Regt. Grave or Memorial Reference: III. B. 1. Cemetery: Moshi Cemetery in Tanzania.

RYAN, Thomas: Rank: Private. Regiment or Service: Irish Guards. Unit: 1st Bn. Age at death: 26. Date of death: 4 September 1914. Service No.3441. Born in Gurtnahoe Co. Tipperary and enlisted in Clonmel. Killed in action.

Supplementary information: Brother of Mr J. Ryan, of New Birmingham, Thurles, Co. Tipperary. Grave or Memorial Reference: 26. Cemetery: Guards Grave, Villers Cotterets Forest in France.

RYAN, Thomas: Rank: Private. Regiment or Service: Royal Irish Regiment. Unit: 2nd Bn. Date of death: 4 August 1917. Service No.5613. Born in Ballybacon Co. Tipperary. Enlisted in Clonmel while living in Kilcommon. Died of wounds. Grave or Memorial Reference: II. B. 40. Cemetery: Mendingham Military Cemetery in Belgium. He is also commemorated on the Cahir War Memorial.

RYAN, Thomas: Rank: Private. Regiment or Service: Royal Dublin Fusiliers. Unit: 10th Bn. Date of death: 13 November 1916. Service No.27111. Born in Templemore. Enlisted in Marylebone in Middlesex. Killed in action. He has no known grave but is listed on Pier and Face 16 C on the Thiepval Memorial in France

RYAN, Timothy: Rank: Driver. Regiment or Service: Royal Field Artillery Secondary. Unit: att. 9th Rest Camp. Age at death: 39. Date of death: 11 October 1918. Service No.13355. Born in Tipperary and enlisted there also. Died in Italy.

Supplementary information: Son of Timothy Ryan and his wife Catherine O'Brien, of Tipperary: husband of Mary Ryan, of Bansha Rd, Tipperary. Served in the South African Campaign. Grave or Memorial: Reference: III. K. 7. Cemetery: Taranto Town Cemetery Extension in Italy.

RYAN, Timothy: Rank: Private. Regiment or Service: Leinster Regiment. Unit: 2nd Bn. Age at death: 28. Date of death: 4 May 1915. Service No.3369. Born in Tipperary and enlisted in Birr. Died of wounds.

Supplementary information: Son of John Ryan, of Bansha Rd, Tipperary, and the late Johanna Ryan. Grave or Memorial Reference: C. 113. Cemetery: Shorncliffe Military Cemetary.

RYAN, William: Rank: Private. Regiment or Service: Irish Guards. Unit: 1st Bn. Date of death: 9 October 1917. Service No.10592. Born in Castletown, Co. Tipperary. Enlisted in Nenagh while living in Killaloe, Co. Clare. Killed in action. Age at death: 27.

Supplementary information: Son of Matthew and Mary Ryan, of Cloneybrien, Killaloe, Co. Clare. He has no known grave but is listed on Panels 10 to 11 on the Tyne Cot Memorial in Belgium.

RYAN, William: Rank: Guardsman. Regiment or Service: Scots Guards. Date of death: 16 June 1915. Service No.5175. Born in Tipperary. Enlisted in Falkirk, Stirling. Grave or Memorial Reference: A. 8. 39. Cemetery: St Sever Cemetery, Rouen in France.

RYAN, William: Rank: Private. Regiment or Service: Irish Guards. Unit: 1st Bn. Age at death: 18. Date of death: 18 May 1915. Service No.5807. Born in Annacarty and enlisted in Clonmel. Killed in action.

Supplementary information: Son of William and Mary Ryan, of Greenfields, Tipperary. Grave or Memorial Reference: Has no known grave but is commemorated on Panel 4. Memorial: Le Touret Memorial in France.

RYAN, W. Rank: Driver. Regiment or Service: Royal Field Artillery. Age at death: 47. Date of death: 22nd July 1919. Service No.90812.

Supplementary information: Husband of E. Ryan of Friar Street Cashel. Cemetery: Rock of Cashel Cemetery, north-west angle of the Cathedral, Tipperary.

RYAN, William John: Rank: Gunner. Regiment or Service: Royal Horse Artillery and Royal Field Artillery. Unit, D Battery, 231st Brigade. Date of death: 29 September 1918. Service No.76949. Born in Clonmel. Enlisted in Clonmel. Killed in action. He has no known grave but is listed on Panels 3 and 4 on the Vis-En-Artois Memorial in France.

S

SAMPSON, John: Rank: Private. Regiment or Service: Royal Irish Regiment. Unit: 6th Bn. Age at death: 17. Date of death: 27 October 1917. Service No. 11526. Born in Tipperary and enlisted in Clonmel. Killed in action.

Supplementary information: Son of John and Mary Sampson, of 51 O'Connell's Rd, Tipperary. Grave or Memorial Reference: I. B. 23. Cemetery: Croisilles Railway Cemetery in France.

SARGINT, Edward Eaton: Rank: Captain. Regiment or Service: Royal Irish Fusiliers. Unit: 7th Bn. Age at death: 21. Date of death: 16 August 1917. Awards: M C.

Supplementary information: Son of Edward Richmond Sargint and Amy Maud Sargint, of 61 Fonthill Rd, Hove, Brighton. Born in Tipperary. Grave or Memorial Reference: Has no known grave but is commemorated on Panel 140 to 141. Memorial: Tyne Cot Memorial in Belgium.

SAVAGE, Robert: Rank: Private. Regiment or Service: Royal Dublin Fusiliers. Unit: 1st Bn. Formerly he was with the Royal Irish Rifles where his number was 9022. Age at death: 31. Date of death: 8 August 1918. Service No. 25880. Born in Templemore. Enlisted in Ballinasloe Co. Galway while living in Templemore. Killed in action.

Supplementary information: Son of Robert and Frances Savage, of Co. Meath. Grave or Memorial Reference: II. G. 13. Cemetery: Borre British Cemetery in France.

SAVAGE, William: Rank: Lance Sergeant. Regiment or Service: Irish Guards. Unit: 2nd Bn. Date of death: 9 April 1916. Service No. 7204. Born in Roscrea. Enlisted in Nenagh. Killed in action. Grave or Memorial Reference: I. H. 33. Cemetery: Menin Road South Military Cemetery in Belgium.

SCALLY, Patrick: Rank: Sergeant. Regiment or Service: Middlesex Regiment. Unit: 'C' Coy. 4th Bn. Age at death: 34. Date of death: 15 November 1916. Service No. G-926. and G-958. Born in Thurles and enlisted in Fulham in Middlesex. Killed in action.

Supplementary information: Son of Maurice and Johanna Scally, of Co. Tipperary: husband of Hannah Mary Scally, of big, Aylmer Street, St Catherine Street, Montreal, Canada. Grave or Memorial Reference: Pier and Face 12 D and 13 B. Memorial: Thiepval Memorial in France.

SCOTT, Alexander: Rank: Corporal. Regiment or Service: Royal Munster Fusiliers. Unit: Depot. Serial

Grave of B.C. Shreeve.

Number: 2/6361. Date of death: 9 December 1917.

Supplementary information: Husband of M Scott of 60 Queen Street, Clonmel. Grave or Memorial Reference: In the north part, left of the main path. Cemetery: Currykippane Cemetery, Co. Cork.

SCULLY, J: Rank: Recruit. Regiment or Service: Royal Engineers. Unit: 4th Provisional Company. Date of death: 7 May 1915.

Supplementary information: Husband of Ellen Scully of 87 Irishtown, Clonmel. Grave or Memorial Reference: 1312. Cemetery: Fort Pitt Military Cemetery in Kent, UK.

SEALE, Thomas/Theophilus/ Theobald: (sources vary regarding his first name) Rank: Temp 2nd Lt and 2nd Lt. Regiment or Service: Royal Munster Fusiliers. Unit: 7th Bn attached to the 2nd Bn. Date of death: 22 August 1916. Killed in action.

Supplementary information: Son of Richard Seale, Parnell Street, Clonmel.

He had only been in France one month with the 2nd Bn of the Munster Fusiliers and only entered the 1st line trenches two weeks before he died. Before the war he was a cashier in the Bank of Ireland, Dublin and received his commission with the South Irish Horse. Grave or Memorial Reference: I. D. 47. Cemetery: Flatiron Copse Cemetery. Mametz in France.

SEAVOR, Stephen: Rank: Private. Regiment or Service: Connaught Rangers. Unit: 5th Bn. Date of death: 7 December 1915. Service No.6255. Born in Tipperary. Enlisted in Liverpool while living in New York. Died of wounds. He has no known grave but is listed on the Doiran Memorial in Greece.

SHANAHAN, Patrick: Rank: Private. Regiment or Service: Royal Scots. Unit: 17th Bn. Previously he was with the West Yorkshire regiment where his Number was 34262. Killed in action. Age at death: 30. Date of death: 20 October 1917. Service No.40606.

Born in Clonmel and enlisted in York while living in Clonmel. Killed in action.

Supplementary information: transf. from Scots Greys. Son of Walter and Margaret Shanahan, of 4 Irishtown, Upper Clonmel, Co. Tipperary. Grave or Memorial Reference: Has no known grave but is commemorated on Panel 11 to 14 and 162. Memorial: Tyne Cot Memorial in Belgium.

SHANAHAN, Thomas: Rank: Private. Regiment or Service: Royal Irish Regiment. Unit: 2nd Bn. Date of death: 9 May 1915. Service No.6077. Born in St Nicholas's, Carrick-on-Suir, Co. Tipperary. Enlisted in Carrick-on-Suir, Co. Tipperary. Died of wounds. Killed in action. He has no known grave but is listed on Panel 33 on the Ypres (Menin Gate) Memorial in Belgium.

SHARPE, Thomas Cronan: Rank: Private. Regiment or Service: East Lancashire Regiment. Unit: 8th Bn. Previously he was with the Manchester Regiment where his number was 29595. Age at death: 36. Date of death: 4 October 1917. Service No.29552. Born in Dublin and enlisted in Manchester while living in Dublin. Killed in action.

Supplementary information: Son of Joseph and Mary Ellen Sharpe, of Limerick Street, Roscrea, Co. Tipperary: husband of Eva Fullam (née Sharpe), of 95 Lower Mount Street, Dublin. Grave or Memorial Reference: Has no known grave but is commemorated on Panel 77 to 79 and

163A. Memorial: Tyne Cot Memorial in Belgium.

SHAW, John: Rank: Private. Regiment or Service: Royal Irish Regiment. Unit: 2nd Bn. Date of death: 19 October 1914. Service No.6674. Born in St Mary's, Clonmel, Co. Tipperary. Enlisted in Clonmel. Killed in action. He has no known grave but is listed on Panels 11 and 12 on the Le Touret Memorial in France.

SHAWE, J: Rank: Private. Regiment or Service: Royal Irish Regiment. Unit: 4th Bn. Age at death: 34. Date of death: 12 November 1916. Service No.4804. Cemetery, Clonmel, St Patrick's Cemetery. Grave location: 5. LB. 133.

SHEA/O'SHEA, John: Rank: Private. Regiment or Service: Leinster Regiment. Unit: 'C' Coy. 2nd Bn. Previously he was with the Royal Irish Regiment where his number was 10224. Born in Clonmel and enlisted in Clonmel while living there also. Died of wounds. Age at death: 29. Date of death: 19 October 1918. Service No.10727.

Supplementary information: Son of Thomas and Catherine O'Shea, of Clonmel, Co. Tipperary. Grave or Memorial Reference: VI. A. 54. Cemetery: Terlincthun British Cemetery, Wimille in France.

SHEA/O'SHEA, JOHN: Rank: Private. Regiment or Service: Irish Guards. Unit: 1st Bn. Age at death: 22. Date of death: 15 May 1915. Service

No.4309. Born in Carrick-on-Suir and enlisted in Clonmel. Died of wounds.

Supplementary information: Son of Walter and Mary O'Shea, of Bally-lynch, Carrick-on-Suir, Co. Tipperary. Grave or Memorial Reference: III. D. 1. Cemetery: Bethune Town Cemetery in France.

SHEEDY, James: Rank: Private. Regiment or Service: Royal Irish Regiment. Unit: 6th Bn. Date of death: 2 June 1916. Service No.9418. Born in Clonmel and enlisted in Fethard. Killed in action.

Supplementary information: Son of Margaret Carroll (*née* Sheedy), of Cashel Rd, Fethard, Co. Tipperary. Grave or Memorial Reference: IV. A. 2. Cemetery: Dud Corner Cemetery, Loos in France.

SHEEHAN, James: Rank: Private. Regiment or Service: Royal Irish Regiment. Unit: 5th Bn. Date of death: 24 August 1915. Service No.309. Born in Thurles. Enlisted in Thurles. Died of wounds at sea.

Supplementary information: Son of William and Ellen Sheehan, of 6, Skerrin Rd, Thurles. Brother in Law of Corporal Andrew Ryan Killed on 4 September 1915. He has no known grave but is listed on Panel 55 on the Helles Memorial in Turkey.

SHEPPARD, Robert: Rank: Lance Corporal. Regiment or Service: Irish Guards. Unit: 1st Bn. Age at death: 32. Date of death: 18 May 1915. Service No.1262. Born in Kilcolman in Kings

County and enlisted in Birr while living in Portland Co. Tipperary, Killed in action.

Supplementary information: Son of Benjamin and Hester Sheppard, of Portland, Birr, Co. Tipperary. Grave or Memorial Reference: Has no known grave but is commemorated on Panel 4. Memorial: Le Touret Memorial in France.

SHERIDAN, Thomas: Rank: Private. Regiment or Service: Leinster Regiment. Unit: 7th Bn. Age at death: 21. Date of death: 1 December 1918. Service No.1862. Born in Nenagh and enlisted in Birr while living in Nenagh. Died of wounds.

Supplementary information: Son of Pat and Bridget Sheridan, of White Walls, Nenagh, Co. Tipperary. Grave or Memorial Reference: III. D. 2. Cemetery: Hamburg Cemetery in Germany.

SHIELS, Matthew Joseph: Rank: Sergeant. Regiment or Service: Royal Irish Regiment. Unit: 2nd Bn. Date of death: 15 August 1917. Service No.9268. He won the Military Medal and is listed in the *London Gazette*. Born in Thurles. Enlisted in Dublin. Killed in action. Age at death 28.

Supplementary information: Son of Edward Matthew Shiels: husband of Annie Irene Pattimore (née Shiels), of Marlboro' House, Delaricey, St Sampson's, Guernsey. He has no known grave but is listed on Panel 33 on the Ypres (Menin Gate) Memorial in Belgium.

Grave of Albert Smith.

Grave of James Somers.

Grave of Patrick Stapleton.

SHINE, The Revd James: Rank: Chaplain 4th Class. Regiment or Service: Army Chaplains' Department Secondary Regiment: Middlesex Regiment Secondary. Unit: Att. 21st Bn. Age at death: 37. Date of death: 21 April 1918.

Supplementary information: Son of Thomas and Mary Shine, of Ballylaffin (also recorded as Ballyfinnan), Ardfinnan, Cahir, Co. Tipperary. He was a Priest for the Waterford RC Diocese on loan to Dunkeld RC Diocese Scotland and died of wounds in France. Grave or Memorial Reference: VII. B. 40. Cemetery: Boulogne Eastern Cemetery in France. He is also commemorated on the Cahir War Memorial and the Aldershot Memorial.

SHINE, John Joseph: Rank: Private. Regiment or Service: Royal Irish Regiment. Unit: C Coy, 2nd Bn. Date of death: 14 September 1914. Age at death: 18. Service No.10537. Born in Powerstown Co. Tipperary. Enlisted in Clonmel while living in Powerstown. Killed in action.

Supplementary information: Son of John and Kate Shine, Croanwalsh, Clonmel. Cemetery: La Ferte-Sous-Jouarre-Memorial in France.

SHORTT, Charles H: Rank: Private. Regiment or Service: Shropshire Light Infantry. Unit: 1st Bn. Date of death: 21 July 1916. Service No.19793. Born in Templemore. Enlisted in Camberley. Died of wounds.

Supplementary information: Husband of M. A. Shortt, of 18 Gordon Villas, Park Street, Camberley, Surrey. Grave or Memorial Reference: VIII. C. 40. Cemetery: Lijssenthoek Military Cemetery in Belgium.

SHORTT, Patrick: Alias, correct first name is John. Rank: Lance Corporal. Regiment or Service: Royal Irish Regiment. Unit: 1st Bn. Age at death: 28. Date of death: 10 March 1918. Service No.9508. Born in Drom Co. Tipperary and enlisted in Templemore. Killed in action in Palestine.

Supplementary information: Son of John and Margaret Shortt, of Templemore, Co. Tipperary. Grave or Memorial Reference: J. 88. Cemetery: Jerusalem War Cemetery, Israel.

SHREEVE, B.C.: Rank: Lance Bombardier. Regiment or Service: 129th Bty. 42nd Bde. Royal Field Artillery. Unit: Date of death: 9 February 1920. Service No.147966. Cemetery: Cahir Military Plot. Grave location: Between the main path and the west boundary.

SIMPSON, Alan: Rank: Lance Corporal. Regiment or Service: Royal Irish Regiment. Unit: 7th (South Irish Horse where his number was 1574) Bn. Age at death: 22. Date of death: 15 March 1918. Service No.25782. Entitled to the War Medal and the Vicotry Medal. Born in Clonoulty and enlisted in Thurles In October/November 1915 while living in Clonoulty. Killed in action.

Supplementary information: Son of James and Arabella Simpson, of Clonouity, Gooldscross, Co. Tipperary.

Grave or Memorial Reference: Pier and Face 3 A. Memorial: Thiepval Memorial in France.

SLATEN, Patrick: Rank: Private. Regiment or Service: Leinster Regiment. Unit: 2nd Bn. Age at death: 25. Date of death: 30 April 1916. Service No.2268. Born in Tipperary and enlisted in Tipperary while living there also.

Supplementary information: Son of Patrick and Mary Slaten, of 4 Bansha Rd, Tipperary. Grave or Memorial Reference: II. C. 6. Cemetery: Ration Farm (La Plus Douve) Annexe in Belgium.

SLATER/SLATOR, John: Rank: Sergeant. Regiment or Service: Machine Gun Corps (Infantry). Unit: 6th Coy. Previously he was with the Royal Irish regiment where his number was 9977. Age at death: 25. Date of death: 29 May 1918. Service No.18051. Born in St Mary's in Clonmel and enlisted in Clonmel. Killed in action.

Supplementary information: Son of Mr A. Slater, of 44 Albert Street, Clonmel, Co. Tipperary, and the late Mrs M. Slater. Grave or Memorial Reference: Has no known grave but is commemorated on Panel 154 to 159 and 163A. Memorial: Tyne Cot Memorial in Belgium.

SLATTERY, John: Rank: Rifleman. Regiment or Service: Royal Irish Rifles. Unit: 2nd Bn. Previously he was with the Royal Field Artillery where his number was 100328. Age at death:

25. Date of death: 7 July 1916. Service No.7764. Born in Lisornagh Co. Tipperary and enlisted in Clonmel. Killed in action.

Supplementary information: Son of Thornas and E. Slattery, of Baptistgrange, Lisronagh, Clonmel, Co. Tipperary. Grave or Memorial Reference: Pier and Face 15 A and 15 B. Memorial: Thiepval Memorial in France.

SLOAN/SLOANE, John: Rank: Private. Regiment or Service: Irish Guards. Unit: 1st Bn. Date of death: 4 September 1914. Service No.1176. Born in Clonmel. Enlisted in Clonmel. Killed in action. Grave or Memorial Reference: 27. Cemetery: Guards Grave, Villers Cotterets Forest in France.

SMITH, Albert E: Rank: Gunner. Regiment or Service: Royal Field Artillery. Unit: 232nd Bty. 74th Bde. Born in Cheltenham and enlisted in Newport Monmouthshire. Date of death: 11 January 1915. Service No.19879. Cemetery: Cahir Military Plot. Grave location: Between the main path and the west boundary

SMITH, Frederick: Rank: Private. Regiment or Service: Royal Dublin Fusiliers. Unit: 2nd Bn. Date of death: 21 March 1918. Service No.21257. Born in Cahir. Enlisted in Dublin. Killed in action. He has no known grave but is listed on Panels 79 and 80 on the Pozieres Memorial in France. He is also commemorated on the Cahir War Memorial.

SMITH, John: Rank: Private. Regiment or Service: York and Lancaster Regiment. Unit: 1ˢᵗ Bn. Age at death: 25. Date of death: 23 April 1915. Service No. 33132 and 3-3132. Born in Carrick-on-Suir and enlisted in Sheffield. Killed in action.

Supplementary information: Son of Joseph Smith, of Mill Street, Carrick-on-Suir, Co. Tipperary. Grave or Memorial Reference: Has no known grave but is commemorated on Panel 36 and 55. Memorial: Ypres (Menin Gate) Memorial in Belgium.

SMYTHE, Patrick Dowling: Rank: Private. Regiment or Service: Royal Army Service Corps. Unit: 302ⁿᵈ M. T. Company. Date of death: 9 May 1916. Service No. M2-079471. Born in Clonmel. Enlisted in Dublin while living in Dublin. Died at Home. Age at death: 25.

Supplementary information: Son of Patrick and Mary Smythe, of 3 St Teresa's Rd, Glasnevin, Dublin. One of four brothers who served. Grave or Memorial Reference: 283. Cemetery: Marlborough Old Cemetery, UK.

SOMERS, Albert J: Rank: Sergeant. Regiment or Service: Royal Irish Regiment. Unit: 2ⁿᵈ Bn. Age at death: 20. Date of death: 2 October 1918. Service No. 3-7984 and 7984. Awarded the Military Medal and Bar and listed in the *London Gazette*. Born in Wexford and enlisted in Cloughjordan. Died of wounds.

Supplementary information: Son of Robert Wilson Somers and Charlotte Somers, of Cloughjordan, Co. Tipperary. Grave or Memorial Reference: III. F. 10. Cemetery: Sunken Road Cemetery, Boiusleux-St Marc in France.

SOMERS, James: Victoria Cross Winner. Rank: Sergeant, Regiment or Service: Army Service Corps and Royal Inniskilling Fusiliers. Unit: 1ˢᵗ Bn. Age at death: 24. Date of death: 7 May 1918. Service No. M-39117. Son of W Somers, Cloughjordan.
From the *London Gazette* supplement 31 August 1915:

> For most conspicuous bravery on the night of 1- 2 July 1915. In the Southern Zone of the Gallipoli Peninsula when owing to hostile bombing some of our troops had retired from a sap Sergeant Somers remained alone on the spot until a party brought up bombs. He then climbed over into the Turkish trench and bombed the Turks with great effect. Later on he advanced into the open under very heavy fire and held back the enemy by throwing bombs into their flank until a barricade had been established. During this period he frequently ran to and from our trenches to obtain fresh supplies of bombs. By his great gallantry and coolness Sergeant Somers was largely instrumental in effecting the recapture of a portion of our trench which had been lost.

Died in his home in Cloughjordan from lung trouble brought on by gas poisoning. Buried in Modreeny Church of

Ireland Cemetery, west of the church.

SPARLING, Philip Richard: Rank: Lance Corporal. Regiment or Service: Manchester Regiment. Unit: 1st-7th Bn. Age at death: 20. Date of death: 22 August 1918. Service No.276368. Born in Temple Park in Queens County and enlisted in Manchester. Died of wounds.

Supplementary information: Son of Montgomery and Adeliza E. Sparling, of 1 Caistor Street, Everton Rd, Chorlton-on-Medlock, Manchester. Native of Templepark, Cloughjordan, Co. Tipperary. Grave or Memorial Reference: IV. F. 23. Cemetery: Bagneux British Cemetery, Gezauncourt in France.

SPENCER, Charles Horatio: Rank: Private. Regiment or Service: Duke of Cornwalls Light Infantry. Unit: 6th Bn and A Company 3rd Bn. Date of death: 17 April 1918. Age at death: 40. Service No.28663. Born in Fethard. Enlisted in Devonport in Devon. Died at home.

Supplementary information: Son of Charles Horatio and Sarah Spencer, of Devonport and was previously wounded in France. Grave or Memorial Reference: Church R. 37.16. Cemetery: Ford Park Cemetery in England. He is also commemorated on the Cahir War Memorial.

SPLAIN, Timothy: Rank: Shoeing Smith. Regiment or Service: Royal Field Artillery and Royal Field Artillery. Unit: 31st Div Ammunition Col. Date of death: 29 October 1918. Service No.20413. Born in Templemore. Enlisted in Leeds. Died at Home. Grave or Memorial Reference: Screen Wall, New Part, 12. 43. Cemetery: Bramley (St Peter) Churchyard, UK.

SPRINGFIELD, Humphrey Osborn: Rank: 2ndLt. Regiment or Service: Warwickshire Yeomanry. Date of death: 5 August 1916. Age at death: 29. Killed in action.

Supplementary information: He attended Framlingham College and is listed on the Old Framlinghamians Roll of Honour, All Saints Church, Norfolk. Born in Tipperary. Mentioned in Dispatches. Rode with Viscount Portman's hounds and the Norfolk and Irish packs. Brother of Captain George Patrick Osborn Springfield who was killed in action on 12 September 1914. Son of Thomas Osborn Springfield and Maud Beatrice Springfield. Native of Norfolk. He was previously wounded in Gallipoli. Grave or Memorial Reference: A. 30. Cemetery: Kantara War Memorial Cemetery in Egypt.

STAPLETON, Edward: Rank: Private. Regiment or Service: Royal Irish Regiment. Unit: 7th Bn (South Irish Horse). Date of death: 22 October 1918. Service No.7101. Joined the 7th Bn in February 1918. Born in Carrick-on-Suir, Co. Tipperary. Enlisted in Waterford while living in Kilmacow Co. Cork. Killed in action. Grave or Memorial Reference: V. E. 5. Cemetery: Tournai Communal Cemetery Allied Extension in Belgium.

STAPLETON, John: Rank: Private. Regiment or Service: Royal Irish Fusiliers. Unit: 1st Bn. Date of death: 6 July 1916. Service No. 20486. Born in Thurles. Enlisted in Dundrum while living in Thurles. Killed in action. Grave or Memorial Reference: I. D. 41. Cemetery: Sucrerie Military Cemetery, Colinclamps in France.

STAPLETON, Patrick: Rank: Q. M. S. Regiment or Service: Leinster Regiment. Unit: Depot. Date of death: 10 August 1917. Service No. 3570. Born in Tipperary. Enlisted in Maryborough while living in Tipperary. Died at home. Grave or Memorial Reference: E. H. 101. Cemetery: Tipperary (St Michael's) New Cemetery, Tipperary Town.

STAPLETON, Robert: Rank: Private. Regiment or Service: Royal Dublin Fusiliers. Unit: 2nd Bn. Age at death: 27. Date of death: 16 October 1916. Service No. 25622. Born in Clonmore Co. Tipperary and enlisted in Templemore. Killed in action.

Supplementary information: Son of Robert and Mary Stapleton, of Groffin Street, Clonmore, Templemore, Co. Tipperary. Grave or Memorial Reference: Has no known grave but is commemorated on Panel 44 and 46. Memorial: Ypres (Menin Gate) Memorial in Belgium.

STAPLETON, Thomas J: Rank: Private. Regiment or Service: 5th (Royal Irish) Lancers Age at death: 41. Date of death: 22 June 1917. Service No. GS-4830 and 4830. Born in

Roscrea and enlisted in Birr while living in Roscrea. Killed in action.

Supplementary information: Son of Patrick and Winifred Stapleton, of Millpark, Roscrea: husband of Winifred Stapleton, of Dublin Rd, Roscrea, Co. Tipperary. Grave or Memorial Reference: II. F. 27. Cemetery: Unicorn Cemetery, Vend'huile in France.

STARR, Denis: Rank: Private. Regiment or Service: Irish Guards. Unit: 1st Bn. Age at death: 21. Date of death: 1 November 1914. Service No. 3951. Born in Portroe Co. Tipperary and enlisted in Nenagh. Killed in action.

Supplementary information: Son of Patrick Starr, of Slate Quarries, Nenagh, Co. Tipperary. Grave or Memorial Reference: Has no known grave but is commemorated on Panel 11. Memorial: Ypres (Menin Gate) Memorial in Belgium.

STEELE, John: Rank: Rifleman. Regiment or Service: Royal. Irish Rifles. Unit: 1st Bn. Date of death: 5 May 1915. Age at death: 39. Service No. 3358. Born in Clogheen, Co. Tipperary. Enlisted in Clydebank, Dunbarton while living in Renfrew. Killed in action.

Supplementary information: Son of Thomas and Susan Steele. Husband of Agnes Jane Steele, of 19 Meadowside Street, Renfrew. Grave or Memorial Reference: I. B. 10. Cemetery: Royal Irish Rifles Graveyard, Laventie in France.

STEPHENS, John: Rank: Private. Regiment or Service: Royal Irish Regiment. Unit: 2nd Bn. Date of death: 19 October 1914. Service No.4906. Born in Nenagh. Enlisted in Tipperary. Killed in action. He has no known grave but is listed on Panels 11 and 12 on the Le Touret Memorial in France.

STOKES, Edward: Rank: Lance Corporal. Regiment or Service: East Lancashire Regiment. Unit: 2nd Bn. Date of death: 28 April 1917. Service No.9524. Born in Clonmel. Enlisted in Accrington in Lancashire while living in Nenagh. Killed in action. He has no known grave but is listed on Pier and Face 6C on the Thiepval Memorial in France.

STONEY, George Francis: Rank: Private. Regiment or Service: Canadian Infantry (British Columbia Regiment) Unit: 72nd Bn. Age at death: 46. Date of death: 3 November 1918. Service No.2204595.

Supplementary information: Son of Capt. George Francis and Emilie Stoney, of Kyle Park, Co. Tipperary, Ireland. On the Editorial Staff of *The Oregonian*, Portland, Oregon, U.S.A. Grave or Memorial Reference: B. 2. 18. Cemetery: Aulnoy Communal Cemetery in France. Data from the reverse of the enlistment document: Age on Enlistment: 45 Years 10 Months. Height: 5'7". Eye colour: grey. Complexion: fair. Hair colour: dark brown. Religious denomination: C. of E. Chest expansion: 5". Girth: 35". Vision: R-D 20-30, L-D 20-60. Hearing: normal. Date of Enlistment: 17 January 1918. Place of Enlistment: Vancouver.

STORAN/STARAN Edward: Rank: Private. Regiment or Service: Royal Inniskilling Fusiliers. Unit: 7th Bn. He was previously with the Royal Munster Fusiliers where his number was 5528. Age at death: 30. Date of death: 27 April 1916. Service No.26477. Born in Castleconnell in Limerick and enlisted in Limerick also. Killed in action.

Supplementary information: Son of Edward and Kate Storan, of O'Brien's Bridge, Co. Limerick: husband of Kate Ryan (*née* Storan), of Gortlandroe, Nenagh, Co. Tipperary. Grave or Memorial Reference: I. E. 6. Cemetery: Philosophe British Cemetery, Mazingarbe in France.

SULLIVAN, Frank: Rank: Private. Regiment or Service: 9th (Queen's Royal) Lancers. Unit: 'A' Sqdn. Age at death: 27. Date of death: 9 August 1918. Service No.L-11522 and 11522. Born in Ardfinnan Co. Tipperary and enlisted in Newmarket while living in Cahir. Killed in action.

Supplementary information: Son of Thomas Sullivan, of Rochestown, Ardfinnan, Co. Tipperary. Grave or Memorial Reference: A. 9. Cemetery: Warvillers Churchyard Extension in France. He is also commemorated on the Cahir War Memorial.

SULLIVAN, John William: See **DOHENY, JOHN**. Served as SULLIVAN.

SULLIVAN, John William: Rank: Rifleman (Acting Corporal). Regiment or Service: Kings Royal Rifle Corps. Unit: 9th Bn. Date of death: 24 August 1916. Service No.9911. Born in Tipperary. Enlisted in London while living in Finsbury Park, Middlesex. Killed in action. Age at death: 24.

Supplementary information: Son of the late J. Sullivan. He has no known grave but is listed on Pier and Face 3A on the Thiepval Memorial in France.

SULLIVAN, Patrick: Rank: Private. Regiment or Service: Machine Gun Corps. Unit: Infantry-16th Bn. Date of death: 9 October 1918. Service No.74004. Formerly he was with the Connaught Rangers where his number was 6370. Born in Tipperary. Enlisted in Merthyr. Grave or Memorial Reference: XVIII. B. 8. Cemetery: Berlin South-Western Cemetery in Germany.

SULLIVAN, William: Rank: Private. Regiment or Service: Royal Irish Regiment. Unit: 2nd Bn. Date of death: 4 July 1916. Service No.5158. Born in Tipperary. Enlisted in Tipperary. Killed in action. He has no known grave but is listed on Pier and Face 3 A on the Thiepval Memorial in France.

SULLIVAN, William: Rank: Private. Regiment or Service: Royal Munster Fusiliers. Date of death: 28 June 1916. Service No.4233. Born in Ballingarry. Enlisted in Kilkenny, while living in Ballingarry. Killed in action. He has no known grave but is listed on Panels 127 on the Loos Memorial in France.

SUTTON, John: Rank: Lance Corporal. Regiment or Service: Leinster Regiment. Unit: 7th Bn. Date of death: 10 September 1916. Service No.3153. Born in Tipperary. Enlisted in Maryborough. Died of wounds. Age at death: 23.

Supplementary information: Husband of Nellie Sutton, of 10 Oldway House

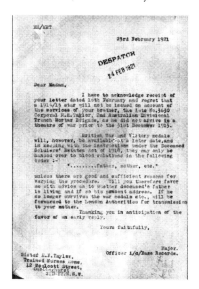

Richard Hamilton Taylor.

Lane, Barrack Street, Cork. Grave or Memorial Reference: Plot 2, Row C, Grave 59. Cemetery: Corbie Communal Cemetery Extension in France.

SWEENEY, William: Rank: Private. Regiment or Service: Royal Irish Regiment. Unit: 6th Bn. Date of death: 27 November 1916. Service No.5602. Born in Ss Peter and Paul, Clonmel, Co. Tipperary. Enlisted in Clonmel. Killed in action. Grave or Memorial Reference: X. 42. Cemetery: Kemmel Chateau Military Cemetery in Belgium.

SWEETMAN, Edward: Rank: Private. Regiment or Service: Royal Irish Regiment. Unit: 2nd Bn. Date of death: 5 July 1916. Service No.10378. Born in St Mary's, Clonmel. Enlisted in Clonmel. Killed in action. He has no known grave but is listed on Pier and Face 3 A on the Thiepval Memorial in France.

T

TALBOT, Ainslie Douglas: Rank: Captain. Regiment or Service: Lancashire Fusiliers. Unit: 1st Bn. Age at death: 28. Date of death: 4 June 1915.

Supplementary information: Son of Col. J. S. Talbot and Eileen, his wife, of Ashgrove, Co. Tipperary. Grave or Memorial Reference: E. 63. Cemetery: Lancashire Landing Cemetery in Turkey.

TALBOT, Joseph: Rank: Private. Regiment or Service: Leinster Regiment. Unit: 2nd Bn. Date of death: 27 April 1916. Service No.4891. Born in Roscrea. Enlisted in Birr while living in Roscrea. Died of wounds. Age at death: 40.

Supplementary information: Son of Laurence and Mary Talbot: husband of Maggie Talbot (now Delahunty), of Dunkerrin, Roscrea, Co. Tipperary. Native of Roscrea. Grave or Memorial Reference: V. B. 15. Cemetery: Etaples Military Cemetery in France.

TAYLOR, John: Rank: Corporal. Regiment or Service: Machine Gun Corps. Unit: 204th Coy, Infantry. Date of death: 29 July 1917. Service No.66615. Formerly he was with the Royal Irish Regiment where his number was 7315. Born in Templemore. Enlisted in Templemore. Killed in action. Grave or Memorial Reference: I. L. 47. Cemetery: Coxyde Military Cemetery in Belgium.

TAYLOR, John Robert: Rank: Leading Telegraphist. Regiment or

Grave of Patrick Tobin.

Service: Royal Navy. Unit: H. M.T.B. 'No. 13.'Age at death: 24. Date of death: 27 January 1916. Service No.239890.

Supplementary information: Son of Philip and Annie Nelson Taylor, of Philipstown House, Cappawhite, Co. Tipperary. Grave or Memorial Reference: 13. Memorial: Plymouth Naval Memorial, UK.

TAYLOR, Richard Hamilton: Rank: Corporal. Regiment or Service: Australian Field Artillery. Unit: 2nd Div Trench Mortar Bty. Date of death: 30 October 1917. Service No.3630. Born in Finnoe, Borrisokane, Co. Tipperary. Enlisted 8 September 1915 in Sydney, NSW. Age on enlistment, 28 Years 2 Months, occupation on enlistment, Conductor on the Sydney trams. Height: 5' 11". Weight: 5st 11lbs. Complexion: fair. Eyes: grey. Hair: brown. Religious Denomination: C. of E.. Served in France, Belgium, Marseilles and Alexandria. Mother, Mrs Ada Taylor, 'Inchmore Cottage' Borrisokane, Co. Tipperary. In a letter, written in 1921, by her daughter to the Australian Records that Mrs Taylor had to leave Tipperary and emigrate to London due to Sin Fein persecution. Killed in action. Sister, E, F, Taylor, Trained Nurses Home, 12 Woolcott Street, Darlinghurst, Sydney, NSW.

Supplementary information: Son of Richard Hamilton Taylor and Ada de Beauchamp Taylor, of 79, Albert Rd, Kingstown, Ireland. Grave or Memorial Reference: I. I. 52. Cemetery: Ypres Reservoir Cemetery. Belgium.

TAYLOR, William Isaac: Rank: Bombardier. Regiment or Service: Royal Field Artillery. Unit: 98th Bty.1st Bde. Age at death: 28. Date of death: 16 November 1918. Service No.55953. Born in Tipperary and enlisted Manchester. Died in Salonika. Nicknamed 'Dick'.

Supplementary information: Son of Isaac and Elizabeth Taylor, of Dovea, Thurles, Co. Tipperary. Grave or Memorial Reference: 834. Cemetery: Mikra British Cemetery, Kalamaria in Greece.

TEEHAN, Matthew: Rank: Private. Regiment or Service: Connaught Rangers. Unit: 6th Bn. Date of death: 21 March 1918. Service No.8325. Formerly he was with the Royal Irish Regiment where his number was 3938. Born in Ballingarry. Enlisted in Kilkenny while living in Ballingarry. Killed in action. He has no known grave but is listed on Panel 77 on the Pozieres Memorial in France.

TERRY, Timothy: Rank: Lance Corporal. Regiment or Service: Royal Irish Regiment. Unit: 1st Bn. Age at death: 28. Date of death: 15 March 1915. Service No.9176. Born in St Mary's in Clonmel and enlisted in Clonmel while living in Thurles. Killed in action.

Supplementary information: Husband of Martha Terry, of Upper Pike Street, Thurles, Co. Tipperary. Grave or Memorial Reference: Has no known grave but is commemorated on Panel 33. Memorial: Ypres (Menin Gate) Memorial in Belgium.

THOMAS, Charles W: Rank: Private. Regiment or Service: Argyll and Southerland Highlanders. Unit: 10th Bn. Date of death: 14 July 1916. Service No.10199 and 10159. Born in Tipperary. Enlisted in London, while living in Southampton. Killed in action. Age at death: 24.

Supplementary information: Husband of Elizabeth Mary Thomas, of II Lower Banister Street, Bedford Place, Southampton. He has no known grave but is listed on Pier and Face 15 A and 16 C on the Thiepval Memorial in France.

THOMPSON, Albert: Rank: Private. Regiment or Service: Royal Irish Regiment. Unit: 1st Bn. Date of death: 30 December 1917. Service No.9868. Born in Paddington, Middlesex. Enlisted in London, while living in Clonmel. Died at sea. He has no known grave but is listed on the Chatby Memorial in Egypt.

THOMPSON, Cuthbert Henry: Rank: Private. Regiment or Service: Royal Irish Regiment. Unit: 2nd Bn. Age at death: 28. Date of death: 12 June 1916. Age at death: 28. Service No.5123. Born in Cullen in Co. Tipperary and enlisted in Clonmel while living in Monard. Died of wounds received on 8 May 1916.

Supplementary information: Known as 'Bertie' to all who knew him. Son of Herbert B.H. Thompson, of Acraboy House, Tipperary and grandson of the late Mr Cuthbert Clayton, Golden Hills, Golden, Tipperary. He joined the Cadet Corps of the Royal Irish Regiment in Fermoy on September 1915 and volunteered for active service after three months training. He was being considered for a commission when he was wounded but died before it could happen. Grave or Memorial Reference: Plot 2. Row K. Grave 7B. Cemetery: Le Treport Military Cemetery in France.

THWAITES, Alexander: Rank: Staff Sergeant. Regiment or Service: Royal Army Pay Corps. Date of death: 23 December 1916. Service No.1167. Born in Tipperary. Enlisted in Chatham. Died at home. Age at death: 35.

Supplementary information: Son of Alexander Thwaites: husband of Caroline Thwaites, of 7 Livingstone Place, Edinburgh. Enlisted in Royal Scots. Twenty-one years service. Grave or Memorial Reference: Near the West End. Cemetery: Brentwood Roman Catholic Cemetery, UK.

TIERNEY, Denis: Rank: Private. Regiment or Service: Cameronians (Scottish Rifles). Unit: 9th Bn. Date of death: 25 September 1915. Service No.17715. Born in Venagh Co. Tipperary. Enlisted in Accrington while living in Oswaldtwistle. Killed in action. Age at death: 19.

Supplementary information: Son of Mr and Mrs Michael Tierney, of 16 Higher Heys, Oswaldtwistle, Lancs. He has no known grave but is listed on Panels 57 to 59 on the Loos Memorial in France.

TIERNEY, John: Rank: Private. Regiment or Service: South Wales Borderers. Unit: 11th Bn. Date of death: 7 July 1916. Service No.21632. Born in Tipperary. Enlisted in Newport, Mon, while living in Basslaeg, Mon. Killed in action. He has no known grave but is listed on Face 4 Aon the Thiepval Memorial in France.

TIERNEY, Michael: Rank: Lance Corporal. Regiment or Service: Royal Irish Regiment. Unit: 1st Bn. Age at death: 27. Date of death: 24 March 1915. Service No.10985. Born in Nenagh and enlisted there also. Killed in action.

Supplementary information: Son of John and Bridget Tierney, of White Walls, Nenagh, Co. Tipperary. Grave or Memorial Reference: Has no known grave but is commemorated on Panel 4. Memorial: Ploegsteert Memorial in Belgium.

TIERNEY, Patrick: Rank: Private. Regiment or Service: Royal Irish Regiment. Unit: 1st Bn. Date of death: 24 April 1915. Service No.10027. Born in Roscrea. Enlisted in Clonmel, while living in Roscrea. Killed in action. He has no known grave but is listed on Panel 33 on the Ypres (Menin Gate) Memorial in Belgium.

TIERNEY, Patrick: Rank: Private. Regiment or Service: London Regiment. Unit: 15th (County of London) Bn. P. W. O Civil Service Rifles. Date of death: 22 March 1918. Service No.533124. Born in Tipperary. Enlisted in Marlebone while living in

Paddington. Killed in action. He has no known grave but is listed in Bay 10 on the Arras Memorial in France.

TIERNEY, Peter: Rank: Private. Regiment or Service: Royal Dublin Fusiliers. Unit: 8th-9th Bn. Date of death: 29 November 1917. Service No.26119. Born in Bansha. Enlisted in Dublin while living in Bansha. Killed in action. Grave or Memorial Reference: II. F. 9. Cemetery: Croisilles British Cemetery in France.

TOBIN, Edward: Rank: Lance Corporal. Regiment or Service: Royal Irish Regiment. Unit: 2nd Bn. Date of death: 3 May 1915. Service No.9462. Born in Ss. Peter & Paul, Clonmel. Enlisted in Clonmel. Killed in action. Age at death: 26.

Supplementary information: Son of Edward and Margaret Usher Tobin. He has no known grave but is listed on Panel 33 on the Ypres (Menin Gate) Memorial in Belgium.

TOBIN, Francis: Rank: Private. Regiment or Service: Irish Guards. Unit: 1st Bn. Date of death: 1 December 1917. Service No.12003. Born in Clonmel. Enlisted in Clonmel. Killed in action. Grave or Memorial Reference: VII. H. 11. Cemetery: Gouzeaucourt New British Cemetery in France.

TOBIN, Michael: Rank: Stoker 1st Class. Regiment or Service: Royal Navy. Unit: HMS *Marmion*. Age at death: 26. Date of death: 21 October 1917. Service No.SS-115153. Date of

Birth: 12 April 1892.

Supplementary information: Son of Michael and Nora Tobin, of 6 Catherine Street, Clonmel, Co. Tipperary. Grave or Memorial Reference: 22. Memorial: Plymouth Naval Memorial, UK. HMS *Marmion* sank after she collided with HMS *Tirade* in the North Sea. The ship was only in service for two years.

TOBIN, Patrick: Rank: Private. Regiment or Service: Leinster Regiment. Unit: 7th Bn. Age at death: 22. Date of death: 21 March 1918. Service No.2088. Awarded the Military Medal and listed in the *London Gazette*. Born in Templetouny Co. Tipperary and enlisted in Thurles while living in Templetouny. Killed in action.

Supplementary information: Son of Bridget Tobin, of Brownstown, Loughmore, Thurles, Co. Tipperary. Grave or Memorial Reference: Has no known grave but is commemorated on Panel 78. Memorial: Pozieres Memorial in France.

TOBIN, Patrick: Rank: Private. Regiment or Service: Royal Irish Regiment. Unit:4th Bn. Age at death: 18. Date of death: 7 September 1918. Service No.8083. Born in Bansha and enlisted in Tipperary. Died at home.

Supplementary information: Son of Mrs Mary Tobin, of New Rd, Tipperary. Grave or Memorial Reference: In south-east part. Cemetery: St Mary's Churchyard in Tipperary.

TOHER, William: Rank: Gunner. Regiment or Service: Royal Garrison Artillery Unit: 212th Siege Btn. Age at death: 30. Date of death: 1 December 1917. Service No.172559. Born in Grange Co. Limerick and enlisted in Camberwell in Surrey while living in Peckham, S. E. Surrey. Killed in action.

Supplementary information: Son of Patrick and Frances M. Toher, of Ballinure, Thurles, Co. Tipperary. Born Grange, Co. Limerick. Grave or Memorial Reference: II. D. 5. Cemetery: Duhallow A. D. S. Cemetery in Belgium.

TRACEY, William: Rank: Private. Regiment or Service: Leinster Regiment. Unit: 2nd Bn. Age at death: 42. Date of death: 20 October 1914. Service No.6919. Killed in action. Born in Templemore and enlisted there also.

Supplementary information: Brother of Andrew Tracey, of Church Street, Templemore, Co. Tipperary. Grave or Memorial Reference: Has no known grave but is commemorated on Panel 10. Memorial: Ploegsteert Memorial in Belgium.

TRAINER, Robert James: Rank: Sergeant. Regiment or Service: East Yorkshire Regiment. Unit: 7th Bn. Formerly he was with the Yorkshire Regiment where his number was 6679. Date of death: 31 March 1918. Service No.8956. Born in Tipperary, Ireland. Enlisted in Richmond, Yorks while living in Headingley, Leeds. Killed in action. He has no known grave but is listed on Bay 4 and 5 of the Arras Memorial in France.

TRAVERS, Patrick: Rank: Private. Regiment or Service: Royal Irish Regiment. Unit: Depot. Born in Tralee. Enlisted in Limerick, while living in Tralee. Died at home. Date of death: 23 December 1916. Service No. 11370. Cemetery, Clonmel, St Patrick's Cemetery. Grave location: 4. DA. 117

TREACY, Thomas: Rank: Private. Regiment or Service: Royal Irish Regiment. Unit: 3rd Bn. Date of death: 24 April 1916. Service No. 11162. Born in Mordyke Co. Tipperary. Enlisted in Clonmel while living in Mordyke Co. Tipperary. Died of wounds at home. Grave or Memorial Reference: Collective Grave. Cemetery: Eastern Health Board Offices Grounds of Kilmainham in Dublin.

TREACY, William: Rank: Private. Regiment or Service: Royal Irish Regiment. Unit: 6th Bn. Date of death: 3 September 1917. Service No. 9113. Formerly he was with the Royal Field Artillery where his number was 134399. Born in Moneygall, Kings Co. Enlisted in Roscrea while living in Moneygall. Died of wounds. Age at death: 42.

Supplementary information: Son of Michael Treacy, of Moneygall: husband of Norah Treacy, of Moneygall, King's Co. Grave or Memorial Reference: I. L. 3. Cemetery: Bucquoy Road Cemetery, Ficheux in France

TRIPHOOK, Owen Leech: Rank: Major. Regiment or Service: Royal Field Artillery Secondary Regiment: Military Accounts Department, India Secondary. Unit: attd. Age at death: 36. Date of death: 6 April 1919. Born at Cashel, Co. Tipperary. His rank is also down as LT A-CPT and he is also listed on the Colchester War memorial. Awards: Twice Mentioned in Despatches.

Supplementary information: Son of the Revd. John Crampton Triphook and Emma Saunders Triphook: husband of Margaret Triphook, of 44 St John's Park Mansions, Pemberton Gardens, London. Born at Cashel, Co. Tipperary. Grave or Memorial Reference: VII. E. 5. Cemetery: Baghdad (North Gate) War Cemetery in Iraq.

TROY, Edward: Rank: Corporal. Regiment or Service: Leinster Regiment. Unit: 2nd Bn. Date of death: 24 August 1916. Service No. 8891 and 8801. Born in Moneygall, Co. Tipperary. Enlisted in Nenagh. Killed in action. Grave or Memorial Reference: III. A. 25. Cemetery: Peronne Road Cemetery, Maricourt in France.

TULLY, Martin: Rank: Private. Regiment or Service: Leinster Regiment. Unit: 2nd Bn. Date of death: 20 October 1914. Age at death: 34. Service No. 7246. Born in Tipperary. Enlisted in Birr, Kings County. Killed in action.

Supplementary information: Son of Patrick and Mary Tully. He has no known grave but is listed on Panel 10 of the Ploegsteert Memorial in Belgium.

TUOHY, Martin: This man served under the name MARTIN RYAN. Rank: Private. Regiment or Service: Royal Irish Rifles. Unit: 2ⁿᵈ Garrison Bn. Enlisted in Ballyvonare Co. Cork. While living in Thurles. Died at home. Previously he was with the Royal Irish Rifles where his number was 7/4494. Extract from the *Tipperary Star* dated March, 1917: Killed on duty. While doing sentry duty on the railway bridge, Malahide, Co. Dublin, Lance Corporal M Ryan, Pike Street Thurles was knocked down by a passing train as a result of which he died almost immediately afterwards. The engine driver at an inquest on the remains yesterday, said he did not see the deceased but the whistle of the engine was blown and the strong wind might have prevented it being heard–a statement which was corroborated by the fireman. The jury exonerated the driver and recommended the widow of the deceased to the consideration of the Railway Company and Military Authorities. Date of death: 20 March 1917. Service No.1718. Additional information: Grave location: Between the church and the East boundary.

TURNER, Alan Norman: Rank: Private. (Lance Corporal). Regiment or Service: Royal Irish Regiment. Unit:1ˢᵗ. Date of death: 30 December 1917. Service No.5604. Born in St Thomas', Dublin. Enlisted in Clonmel while living in Carrick-on-Suir, Co. Tipperary. Died at sea. Age at death: 19.

Supplementary information: Son of Mr and Mrs John Tyrie Turner, of 17 Main Street, Carrick-on-Suir. He has no known grave but is listed on the Chatby Memorial, UK

TURNER, Walter: Rank: Lance Corporal. Regiment or Service: Royal West Kent Regiment. Unit:1ˢᵗ Bn. Date of death: 1 August 1916. Service No.L-7484. Born in Clonmell Co. Tipperary. Enlisted in Woolwich in Kent. Died of wounds. Grave or Memorial Reference: II. E. 55. Cemetery: Heilly Station Cemetery, Mericourt-L'Abbe in France.

TUTTLE, Henry: Rank: C-S (A-S. M.). Regiment or Service: Royal Irish Regiment. Unit: 1ˢᵗ Bn. Date of death: 21 July 1915. Service No.5877. Born in Nenagh. Enlisted in Clonmel while living in Nenagh. Died in India. He has no known grave but is listed on Face 12 on the Madras 1914-18 War Memorial, Chikmagalur Cemetery, Chennai, India.

TYDD, William John Stern: Rank: Second Lieutenant. Regiment or Service: Connaught Rangers. Unit:4ᵗʰ Bn. Age at death: 20. Date of death: 22 January 1917.

Supplementary information: Son of Francis Edward Tydd, LL. B, and Isobel Tydd, of Richmond House, Clonmel, Co. Tipperary. Grave or Memorial Reference: III. A. 193. Cemetery: Bailleul Communal Cemetery Extension (Nord) in France.

TYLER, George: Rank: Private. Regiment or Service: East Surrey Regiment. Unit: 13ᵗʰ Bn. Date of death:

26 November 1917. Service No.30597. Formerly he was with the Middlesex Regiment where his number was 24178. Born in Clonmel, Waterford, Ireland. Enlisted in Shoreditch, Middlesex. He has no known grave but is listed on Panel 6 on the Cambrai Memorial in Louveral in France.

TYNAN, Matthew: Rank: Gunner. Regiment or Service: Royal Garrison Artillery.4th Mountain I Battery. Date of death: 9 September 1916. Service No.25382. Born in Killenaule. Enlisted in Clonmel while living in Kilsheelan Co. Tipperary. Died in India. Grave or Memorial Reference: 2221. Cemetery: Quetta Government Cemetery. Although he has a known grave he is also listed on face 1 on the Delhi (India Gate) Memorial in India.

V

VEALE, John: Rank: Private. Regiment or Service: Royal Dublin Fusiliers. Unit: 8th Bn. Date of death: 1 April 1916. Service No.18253 and 5-18253. Born in Carrick-on-Suir, Co. Tipperary. Enlisted in Bury while living in Heywood. Killed in action. He has no known grave but is listed on the Special Memorial 9 in Bois-Carre Military Cemetery in France

VERRENT, Alfred Donald: Rank: Private. Regiment or Service: Royal Dublin Fusiliers. Unit: 1st Bn. Age at death: 17. Date of death: 25 April 1915. Service No.11660. Born in Nenagh and enlisted in Dublin while living in Newport Co. Tipperary. Killed in action in Gallipoli.

Supplementary information: Son of Charles J. and Margaret Verrent, of Glenstal, Murroe, Newport, Co. Limerick. Native of Kilboy, Nenagh, Co. Tipperary. Grave or Memorial Reference: Special Memorial B. 113. Cemetery: V Beach Cemetery in Turkey.

VERRENT, David Charles: Rank: Private. Regiment or Service: Gloucestershire Regiment. Unit: 10th (Service) Bn. Date of death: 1 May 1917. Age at death: 22. Service No.13191. Born in Silvermine Co. Tipperary. Enlisted in Birmingham, while living in Silvermine. Killed in action.

Supplementary information: Son of Charles J. and Margaret Verrent, of Glenstal, Murroc, Co. Limerick. Grave or Memorial Reference: VI. A. 7. Cemetery: Heath Cemetery, Harbonnieres in France.

W

WADE, Timothy: Rank: Private. Regiment or Service: Royal Irish Regiment. Unit: 2nd Bn. Date of death: 24 January 1917. Service No. 7682. Born in Clonoulty. Enlisted in Cashel while living in Goolds Cross. Died at home. Grave or Memorial Reference: Screen Wall, War Plot C. Cemetery: Bristol (Arnos Vale) Roman Catholic Cemetery

WALL, John: Rank: Bombardier. Regiment or Service: Royal Field Artillery. Unit: 120th Btn. Age at death: 25. Date of death: 20 October 1918. Service No. 12047 Awards: Distinguished Service Medal. Born in Cahir and enlisted in Clonmel. Died of wounds.

Supplementary information: Son of Edmond Wall and Ellen O'Higgins (wife), of Derrygrath, Co. Tipperary. Grave or Memorial Reference: D. 8. Cemetery: Bethercourt Communal Cemetery in France. He is also commemorated on the Cahir War Memorial.

WALL, Frank Tobin: Rank: Assistant Paymaster. Regiment or Service: Royal Naval Reserve. Unit: HMS *Triumph* Age at death: 25. Date of death: 25 May 1915.

Supplementary information: Son of William and Ellen Wall, of Mainstown, Carrick-on-Suir, Co. Tipperary. Grave or Memorial Reference: 8. Memorial: Plymouth Naval Memorial, UK. HMS *Triumph* was a pre-dreadnaught battleship and was sunk by the German Submarine U21 in 1915. Seventy-three members of her crew died.

WALLACE, George: Rank: Sergeant. No 7675, Leinster Regiment, 2nd Bn. Date of death: 31 July 1916. Born in Golden, enlisted in Birr while living in Golden. Has no known grave but

Maurice Walsh.
Photography courtesy of Maurice Walsh, Clogheen.

Grave of Daniel Joseph Whelan.

is listed on the Thiepval Memorial in France on Pier and Face 16 C. Killed in action during the battle of Gommecourt where losses were catastrophic. This battle lasted from the 1 July until the end of September.

WALSH, Edward: Rank: Private. Regiment or Service: Royal Irish Regiment. Unit: 7th Bn. Age at death: 20. Date of death: 24 August 1918. Service No. 5194. Born in Nicholas's in Carrick-on-Suir and enlisted in Carrick-on-Suir. Killed in action.

Supplementary information: Son of James Walsh: husband of Mary Walsh, of Walls Lane, Graystone Street, Carrick-on-Suir, Co. Tipperary. Grave or Memorial Reference: II. C. 10. Cemetery: Godewaersvelde British Cemetery in France.

WALSH, James: Rank: Private. Regiment or Service: Royal Irish Regiment. Unit: 2nd Bn. Date of death: 3 September 1916. Service No. 11057. Born in Carrick-on-Suir, Co. Tipperary. Enlisted in Carrick-on-Suir, Co. Tipperary. Killed in action. He has no known grave but is listed on Pier and Face 3 A on the Thiepval Memorial in France.

WALSH, James: Rank: Private. Regiment or Service: Royal Irish Regiment. Unit: 2nd Bn. Date of death: 30 June 1915. Service No. 5833. Born in Thurles. Enlisted in Nenagh while living in Gort Co. Galway. Died of wounds. He has no known grave but is listed on Panel 33 on the Ypres (Menin Gate) Memorial in Belgium.

WALSH, James: Rank: Private. Regiment or Service: Royal Irish Fusiliers. Unit: 7th Bn. Age at death: 37. Date of death: 21 May 1916. Service No. 18501. Born in Tipperary and enlisted there also. Killed in action.

Supplementary information: Husband of Bridget Walsh, of Carronready, Tipperary. Grave or Memorial

Grave of John Whelan.

Reference: Has no known grave but is commemorated on Panel 124. Memorial: Loos Memorial in France.

WALSH, Joseph: Rank: Private. No 42159, East Yorkshire Regiment, 1ˢᵗ-4ᵗʰ Bn, Died 27 May 18, Born: Cashel, Co. Tipperary. Enlisted in Manchester. Has no known grave but is listed on the Soissons memorial in France. Killed in action in France when the British Army found themselves facing an overwhelming German attack. Despite fierce opposition, the Germans pushed the Allies back across the Aisne to the Marne, the allies lost 15,000 men including Joseph Walsh.

WALSH, Joseph: Rank: Private. Regiment or Service: Royal Irish Regiment. Unit: 2ⁿᵈ Bn. Date of death: 19 October 1914. Service No.4693. Born in Carrick-on-Suir, Co. Waterford. Enlisted in Waterford. Died. He has no known grave but is listed on Panels 11 and 12 on the Le Touret Memorial in France.

WALSH, Maurice: Rank: Private. Regiment or Service: Duke of Wellington's (West Riding Regiment). Unit: 2ⁿᵈ-7ᵗʰ Bn. Age at death: 23. Date of death: 9 December 1917. Service No.26357. Born in Ballyporeen and enlisted in Clonmel while living in Ballyporeen. Died of wounds.

Supplementary information: Son of Maurice and Mary O'Brien Walsh, of Carrigavistale, Ballyporeen, Co. Tipperary. Grave or Memorial Reference: P.V.M. 6A. Cemetery: St Sever Cemetery Extension, Rouen in France

WALSH, Michael: Rank: Driver. Regiment or Service: Royal Field Artillery. Unit: 'B' Bty. 148ᵗʰ Bde. Age at death: 27. Date of death: 9 July 1916. Service No.L-10681. Born in Tipperary and enlisted in Liverpool.

Grave of Lawrence Joseph Whelan.

Killed in action.

Supplementary information: Son of Thomas and Ellen Walsh, of Mooncrea, Ardfinnan, Co. Tipperary. Grave or Memorial Reference: Pier and Face 1 A and 8 A. Memorial: Thiepval Memorial in France. He is also commemorated on the Cahir War Memorial.

WALSH, Stephen: Rank: Private. No 9524, Royal Irish Regiment, 2nd Bn. Date of death: 23 March 1918, Born: Cashel, Co. Tipperary. Enlisted in Cashel. Died of wounds. Grave reference I.A. 10. D Buried in Honnechy British Cemetery in the little village of Honnechy, eight kilometres south-west of Le Cateau, in France.

WALSH, Thomas: Rank: Private. Regiment or Service: Royal Irish Regiment. Unit: 2nd Bn. Date of death: 18 November 1918. Service No.5059. Born in Kilrane Co. Tipperary and enlisted in Nenagh while living in Kilrane.

Supplementary information: Cousin of John Spain, of Rapla, Nenagh, Co. Tipperary. Grave or Memorial Reference: VI. D. 4. Cemetery: Berlin south-western cemetery in Germany.

WALSH, Thomas: Rank: Private. Regiment or Service: Royal Irish Regiment. Unit: 2nd Bn. Date of death: 14 July 1916. Service No.8023. Born in Roscrea. Enlisted in Roscrea. Killed in action. He has no known grave but is listed on Pier and Face 3A on the Thiepval Memorial in France.

WALSH, William: Rank: Private. Regiment or Service: Royal Irish Regiment. Unit:6th Bn. Date of death: 2 August 1917. Service No.5193. Born in St Nicholas's, Carrick-on-Suir, Co. Tipperary. Enlisted in Clonmel while living in Carrick-on-Suir, Co. Tipperary. Killed in action. He has no known grave but is listed on Panel 33 on the Ypres (Menin Gate) Memorial in Belgium.

WALSH, William: Rank: Private. Regiment or Service: Connaught

Robert Henry White.

Rangers. Unit: 6th Bn. Age at death: 30. Date of death: 16 August 1917. Service No.8475. Born in Clonmel and enlisted in Clonmel while living there also. Killed in action.

Supplementary information: Son of Thomas and Statia Walsh, of Clonmel, Co. Tipperary. Grave or Memorial Reference: E. 23. Cemetery: Potijze Chateau Lawn Cemetery in Belgium.

WALSHE, John: Rank: Private. Regiment or Service: Royal Marine Labour Corps Age at death: 49. Date of death: 24 November 1918. Service No.Deal-13001(S).

Supplementary information: Son of Patrick and Ellen Walshe, of Cashel, Co. Tipperary. Served at the Battle of Mons (1914). Grave or Memorial Reference: Div. 62. IV. D. 7. Cemetery: Ste Marie, Cemetery, Le Havre in France.

WARD, Henry Michael: Rank: Private. Regiment or Service: Duke of Wellingtons (West Riding Regiment). Unit: 3rd Bn. Date of death: 13 January

1916. Service No.12891. Born in Templemore. Enlisted in Huddersfield while living in Huddersfield. Died at Home. Age at death: 39.

Supplementary information: Son of George and Sarah Ward: husband of Ellen Ward, of 17 Back Silver Street, Moldgreen, Huddersfield. Born at Templemore, Co. Tipperary. Grave or Memorial Reference: 63. 135. Cemetery: Huddersfeild (Edgerton) Cemetery, UK.

WARD, John Christopher: Rank: C. S. M. Regiment or Service: Kings Liverpool Regiment. Unit: 9th Bn. Date of death: 12 August 1916. Service No.2212. Born in Tipperary. Enlisted in Liverpool while living in Liverpool. Killed in action. Age at death: 39.

Supplementary information: Son of Frances Ward, of 115, Carisbrooke Rd, Walton, Liverpool, and the late Francis Ward. He has no known grave but is listed on Pier and Face 1 D and 8 B and 8 C on the Thiepval Memorial in France.

A Christmas present from Princess Mary to the soldiers at the front in 1914. It contained a .303 bullet pencil, a Christmas card with a photo of the King, Queen and Princess and cigarettes or chocolate.

WARMINGTON/WORMINGTON, Arthur: Rank: Acting Lance Corporal. Regiment or Service: Royal Army Service Corps. Attached to the 17th Divisional Headquarters. Date of death: 24 April 1918. Service No.M2-018649. Born in Fethered, Co. Tipperary. Enlisted in London while living in Willesbourne, Warwick. Died of wounds. Age at death: 23.

Supplementary information: Son of Joseph and Alma Maude Wormington, of Friz Hill, Wellesbourne, Warwick. Grave or Memorial Reference: VI. B. 57. Cemetery: Doullens Communal Cemetery Extension, No 1 in France.

WARNOCK, John: Rank: Private. Regiment or Service: Household Cavalry and Cavalry of the line including the Yeomanry and Imperial Camel Corps. Unit: 4th (Queens Own) Hussars. Date of death: 31 October 1914. Service No.2268. Born in Dublin. Enlisted in Surgan while living in Clonmel. Died of wounds. He has no known grave but is listed on Panel five on the Ypres (Menin Gate) Memorial in Belgium

WATERS, James: Rank: Private. Regiment or Service: Royal Irish Regiment. Unit: 1st Bn. Age at death: 41. Date of death: 11 June 1917. Service No.6152. Born in St Nicholas's in Carrick-on-Suir and enlisted in Carrick-on-Suir also. Died in Solonika.

Supplementary information: Son of Thomas and Bridget Waters, of Cross Lane, Carrick-on-Suir, Co. Tipperary. Grave or Memorial Reference: 27. Cemetery: Mikra British Cemetery, Kalamaria in Greece.

WATERS, Martin: Rank: Private. Regiment or Service: Royal Munster Fusiliers. Unit: 2nd Bn. Age at death: 20. Date of death: 9 May 1915. Service No.5724. Born in Nenagh and enlisted in Nenagh while living there also. Killed in action.

Supplementary information: Son of Thomas and Mary Waters, of Birr Rd, Nenagh: husband of Margaret Waters (*née* Hayden), of Ormond Street, Nenagh, Co. Tipperary. Grave or Memorial Reference: Has no known grave but is commemorated on Panel 43 and 44. Memorial: Le Touret Memorial in France.

WATERS, William: Rank: Sergeant. Regiment or Service: Royal Irish

Grave of Eastwood Wilson.

Regiment. Unit: 6th Bn. Date of death: 7 June 1917. Service No.6084. Born in St Nicholas's, Carrick-on-Suir, Co. Tipperary. Enlisted in Carrick-on-Suir. Died of wounds. Grave or Memorial Reference: A. 5. Cemetery: Irish House Cemetery in Belgium.

WATKINS, George: Rank: Corporal. Regiment or Service: Leinster Regiment. Unit: 1st Bn. Date of death: 15 March 1915. Service No.8975. Born in Roscrea. Enlisted in Birr. Killed in action. Age at death: 23.

Supplementary information: Son of John S. and Margaret Watkins, of Ettagh Brosna, Roscrea, King's Co. He has no known grave but is listed on Panel 44 on the Ypres (Menin Gate) Memorial in Belgium

WEBSTER, George: Rank: Private. Regiment or Service: Royal Irish Regiment. Unit: 6th Bn. Date of death: 2 August 1917. Service No.11007. Born in Ballingarry. Enlisted in Clonmel, while living in Ballingarry. Killed in action. He has no known grave but is listed on Panel 33 on the Ypres (Menin Gate) Memorial in Belgium.

WEBSTER, Richard: Brother of Robert Webster Rank: Private. Regiment or Service: Royal Irish Regiment. Unit: 1st Bn. Date of death: 26 June 1915. Service No.10561. Born in Gurtnahoe Co. Tipperary. Enlisted in Clonmel while living in Gurtnahoe. Killed in action. Age at death: 25.

Supplementary information: Son of John and Ellen Webster, of Sallypark, Gurtnahoe, Thurles, Co. Tipperary. Grave or Memorial Reference: III. A. 29. Cemetery: Houplines Communal Cemetery Extension in France.

WEBSTER, Robert: Rank: Private. Regiment or Service: Royal Irish Regiment. Unit: 'C' Coy, 1st Bn. Date of death: 2 May 1915. Service No.10544. Born in Gurtnahoe Co. Tipperary. Enlisted in Clonmel while living in Gurtnahoe. Killed in action. Age at death: 26. Killed in action.

Supplementary information: Son of John and Ellen Webster, of Sallypark,

Urlingford, Co. Kilkenny. He has no known grave but is listed on Panel 11 on the Ypres (Menin Gate) Memorial in Belgium.

WESTMAN, Michael: Rank: Private. Regiment or Service: Royal Munster Fusiliers. Unit: 4th Bn. Secondary Regiment: Labour Corps Secondary. Unit: transf. to (42828) Agriculture Coy. Age at death: 26. Date of death: 15 October 1918. Service No. 7305. Born in Dublin and enlisted in Cork while living in Kilsham Co. Tipperary. Died.

Supplementary information: Son of Mrs M. Westman: husband of Mary Westman, of Knockfoble, Kilshane, Tipperary. Born at Dublin. Grave or Memorial Reference: C. 380. Cemetery: Ashburton Roman Catholic Cemetery, Gosforth, UK.

WESTON, Thomas: Rank: Private. Regiment or Service: Royal Irish Regiment. Unit: 2nd Bn. Age at death: 34. Date of death: 21 March 1918. Service No. 8033. Born in Rathgormac Co. Tipperary and enlisted in Carrick-on-Suir. Killed in action.

Supplementary information: Son of Mrs Catherine Weston, of Greystone Street, Carrick-on-Suir, Co. Tipperary. Grave or Memorial Reference: Has no known grave but is commemorated on Panel 30 and 31. Memorial: Pozieres Memorial in France.

WHATLING, Fred: Rank: Lance Corporal. Regiment or Service: Coldstream Guards. Unit: 3rd Bn. Age at death: 30. Date of death: 14 September 1914. Service No. 6225. Born in Halsham in Yorkshire and enlisted in hull while living in Preston near Hull. Died of wounds at Soupir.

Supplementary information: Son of Theophilus Willfreda Whatling: husband of Sarah Ann Whatling, of Cloncourse, Balloughmore, Roscrear, Co. Tipperary. Memorial: La Ferte-Sous-Jouarre-Memorial in France.

WHELAN, Daniel Joseph: Rank: Private. Army Service Corps transferred to 662nd H. S. Army Employment Coy, Labour Corps. Age at death: 41. Date of death: 12 October 1918. Service No. 17816.

Supplementary information: None. Buried in Ardcroney Old Graveyard. Grave location: Near the cemetery wall south-east of the ruins.

WHELAN, James: Rank: Private. Regiment or Service: Royal Irish Regiment transferred to the Labour Corps where his number was 390529. Unit: 3rd Bn. Age at death: 27. Date of death: 6 November 1918. Service No. 8970.

Supplementary information: Son of Mrs Whelan of Abbey Lane Nenagh Co. Tipperary. Cemetery: Nenagh (Barrack Street) Old Graveyard. Grave location: In the north-west part near the North wall.

WHELAN, John: Rank: Private. Regiment or Service: Royal Army Medical Corps. Age at death: Unknown. Date of death: 23 April 1919. Service No. 69405. Cemetery: Nenagh (Barrack Street) Old Graveyard. Grave location: In the north-west part near the north wall.

WHELAN, John: Rank: Private. Regiment or Service: Royal Irish Regiment. Unit: 'H' Coy. 2nd Bn. Age at death: 19. Date of death: 24 May 1915. Service No. 4568. Born in Carrick-on-Suir and enlisted in Waterford while living in Carrick-on-Suir. Died of wounds.

Supplementary information: Son of William and Bridget Whelan, of Strand, Carrick-on-Suir, Co. Tipperary. Grave or Memorial Reference: Has no known grave but is commemorated on Panel 33. Memorial: Ypres (Menin Gate) Memorial in Belgium.

WHELAN, John: Rank: Private. Regiment or Service: Royal Irish Regiment. Unit: 6th Bn. Age at death: 20. Date of death: 14 June 1915. Service No. 1655. Born in Grange Co. Tipperary and enlisted in Clonmel while living in Cahir. Died at home.

Supplementary information: Son of Mrs Mary Whelan, of Derrygrath, Cahir, Co. Tipperary. Grave or Memorial Reference: Near North boundary. Cemetery: Buttevant (St Mary's) Catholic Cemetery, Cork.

WHELAN Lawrence Joseph: Rank: Fusilier. Regiment or service: Royal Irish Fusiliers. Unit: 2nd Bn. Service No. 6978850. Date of death: 2 January 1946. Age at death: 42.

Supplementary information: Son of Patrick and Elizabeth Whelan of Nenagh, Co. Tipperary. Cemetery: Nenagh (Barrack Street) Old Graveyard.

WHELAN, Michael: Rank: Private. Regiment or Service: Leinster Regiment. Unit: 1st Bn. Age at death: 30. Date of death: 15 March 1915. Service No. 3282. Born in Nenagh and enlisted in Birr. Died of wounds.

Supplementary information: Son of William and Margaret Whelan, of Monanore, Toomevara, Nenagh, Co. Tipperary. Grave or Memorial Reference: Has no known grave but is commemorated on Panel 44. Memorial: Ypres (Menin Gate) Memorial in Belgium.

WHELAN, Michael: Rank: Private. Regiment or Service: Royal Irish Regiment. Unit: 1st Bn. Age at death: 25. Date of death: 27 March 1915. Service No. 4157. Born in Ballingarry and enlisted in Kilkenny while living in Ballingarry. Died of wounds.

Supplementary information: Son of Edmond Whelan, of Ballingarry: husband of Mary Condon (formerly Whelan), of Ballingarry, Thurles, Co. Tipperary. Grave or Memorial Reference: J.30. Bailleul Communal Cemetery Extension (Nord) in France.

WHITAKER, Louis: Rank: Third Engineer. Regiment or Service: Mercantile Marine. Unit: SS *Gravina* (Liverpool) Age at death: 45. Date of death: 7 February 1917.

Supplementary information: Son of Cecilia Whitaker, of 72 St Alphonsus Rd, Drumcondra, Dublin, and the late James Whitaker. Born at Mooresfoot, Tipperary. Memorial: Has no known grave but is commemorated on the Tower Hill Memorial, London.

WHITE, David Joseph: Rank: Private. Regiment or Service: Royal Irish Fusiliers. Unit: 1st Bn. Age at death: 41. Date of death: 26 May 1915. Service No. 12700. Born in Templemore and enlisted in Liverpool while living in Garston in Lancashire. Died of wounds.

Supplementary information: Son of the late Colour Serjt. Michael J. White. Born at Templemore, Co. Tipperary. Served Mashonaland, 1897: and in the South African Campaign. Grave or Memorial Reference: II. B. 18. Cemetery: Hazebrouck Communal Cemetery, Nord, in France.

WHITE, E: Rank: Private. Regiment or Service: Connaught Rangers Age at death: 31. Date of death: 11 March 1919. Service No. 10909.

Supplementary information: Son of Mrs J. White, of 9 Bansha Rd, Tipperary. Grave or Memorial Reference: E. H. 106. Cemetery: Tipperary (St Michael's) New Cemetery, Tipperary Town.

WHITE, John Lawrence William: Rank: Sergeant. Regiment or Service: Army Service Corps. Unit: 56th Siege Bty. AmmUnit: Ion Col. Age at death: 44. Date of death: 15 August 1916. Service No. M1-05612 and M1-5612. Enlisted in London while living in Hove.

Supplementary information: Son of William and Emily White, of Tipperary. Served in the South African Campaign. Grave or Memorial Reference: II. D. 56. Cemetery: Puchevillers British Cemetery in France.

WHITE, Michael: Rank: Private. Regiment or Service: Royal Inniskilling Fusiliers. Unit: 7th-8th Bn. Age at death: 29. Date of death: 21 March 1918. Service No. 23056. Born in Cappawhite and enlisted in Tipperary. Killed in action.

Supplementary information: Son of the late Michael and Mary White, of Newtown, Cappawhite, Tipperary. Grave or Memorial Reference: Has no known grave but is commemorated on Panel 38 to 40. Memorial: Pozieres Memorial in France.

WHITE, Patrick Foley: Rank: Sergeant. Regiment or Service: Royal Horse Artillery. Unit: "D" Bty. 14th Bde. Age at death: 26. Date of death: 5 September 1916. Service No. 35685. Born in Clonmel and enlisted there also. Killed in action.

Supplementary information: Son of Alexander White (R. Q. M. S, Royal Artillery), and Margaret White, of 18, Dillon Street, Clonmel, Co. Tipperary. Grave or Memorial Reference: VI. A. 6. Cemetery: Quarry Cemetery, Montauban in France.

WHITE, Robert Henry: Rank: Private. Regiment or Service: Canadian Infantry (Central Ontario Regiment) Unit: 'C' Coy. 3rd Bn. Age at death: 19. Date of death: 23 April 1915. Service No. 9733.

Supplementary information: Son of the late Robert and Elizabeth White, of Roscrea, Co. Tipperary, Ireland. Grave or Memorial Reference: Panel 18 - 24 - 26 - 30. Memorial: Ypres (Menin Gate) Memorial in Belgium

WHITE, William: Rank: Sergeant. Regiment or Service: Royal Irish Fusiliers. Unit: 2nd Bn. Date of death: 14 May 1915. Service No. 2287. Born in Tipperary. Enlisted in Dublin while living in Cappawhite Co. Tipperary. Killed in action. He has no known grave but is listed on Panel 42 on the Ypres (Menin Gate) Memorial in Belgium.

WHITEHEAD, Walter: Rank: 2Lt. Regiment or Service: Royal Dublin Fusiliers. Unit: 3rd Bn attached to the 8th Bn.

Supplementary information: Lived in Roscrea, Son of George and Harriet Whitehead of 86 Drumcondra Road, Dublin. Age at death: 25. Date of death: 6 September 1916. Killed in action. He has no known grave but is listed in Pier and Face C on the Thiepval Memorial in France.

WIGZELL, Reginald: Rank: Corporal (Lance Sergeant). Regiment or Service: Royal Irish Regiment. Unit: 6th Bn. Date of death: 15 June 1917. Service No. 6987. Born in Clonmel. Enlisted in Dublin while living in Clonmel. Died of wounds at home. Age at death: 30.

Supplementary information: Son of John and Johanna Wigzell, Dublin. Grave or Memorial Reference: 16 (Screen Wall). Cemetery: Kensal Green (St Mary's) Roman Catholic Cemetery, UK.

WILKINS, Charles Frederick: Rank: Rifleman. Regiment or Service: Rifle Brigade. Unit: 3rd Bn.

Age at death: 28. Date of death: 21 October 1914. Service No. 2699. Born in Reading and enlisted in Reading while living in Berkhamstead, Herts. Killed in action.

Supplementary information: Son of Charles Wilkins, of 77 Ellesmere Rd, Berkhamsted, Herts: husband of Mrs Bridget Byrne, (formerly Wilkins), of 8 Ex-Servicemen's Cottages, Brookville, Tipperary. Grave or Memorial Reference: Has no known grave but is commemorated on Panel 10. Memorial: Ploegsteert Memorial in Belgium.

WILLIAMS, George: Rank: Lance Corporal. Regiment or Service: East Lancashire Regiment. Unit: 6th Bn. Date of death: 19 August 1916. Service No. 10526. Born in Tipperary. Enlisted in Blackburn, Lancs while living in Wombwell, Lancs. Died in Mesopotamia. He has no known grave but is listed on the Shaikh Old Cemetery Memorial in Amara War Cemetery in Iraq.

WILLIAMS, John: Rank: Acting Bombardier. No 15939, and L-15939. Royal Field Artillery, 'A' Bty. 23rd Bde. Aged 33. Died 8 November 1917. Died of Wounds. Born: Cashel, Co. Tipperary. Enlisted in Manchester. Son of John and Mary Williams, of 4 Junction Street, Ancoats, Manchester. Grave reference II. D. 2. Buried in Minty Farm Cemetery in Belgium.

WILLIAMS, Walter George: Rank: Gunner. Regiment or Service: Royal Field Artillery. Unit: 3rd Bty. 45th Bde.

Age at death: 32. Date of death: 23 June 1917. Service No.12275. Born in Tipperary and enlisted Chatham in Kent. Killed in action.

Supplementary information: Son of George and Mary Ann Williams, of 37 Balmoral Rd, Gillingham, Kent. Born in the 2nd Bn. Royal Welch Fusiliers, at Templemore Barracks, Co. Tipperary. Grave or Memorial Reference: I. D. 16. Cemetery: Ypres Town Cemetery Extension in Belgium.

WILLINGTON, James Vernon Yates: Rank: 2Lt.(TP). Regiment or Service: Prince of Wales Leinster Regiment (Royal Canadians). Killed in action in Gallipoli aged 20.

Supplementary information: Son of James T. C. and Alice Willington of St Kieran's (Lorrha) Birr King's County. He has no known grave but is listed on the Helles Memorial on Panel 184 and 185.

WILSON, Eastwood: Rank: Driver. Regiment or Service: Royal Field Artillery. Unit: C Bty. 74th Bde. Born in Dewsbury and enlisted in Dewsbury. Date of death: 20 June 1915. Service No.13621. Cahir Military Plot. Grave location: Between the main path and the west boundary.

WYNDHAM, Clifford: Rank: Lance Corporal. Regiment or Service: East Surrey Regiment. Unit: 8th Bn. Age at death: 23. Date of death: 9 August 1917. Service No.10435. Born in Wimbledon Surrey and enlisted in Kingston in Surrey. Killed in action.

Supplementary information: Husband of Anastatia Dooley (formerly Wyndham), of St Mary's Avenue, Thurles, Co. Tipperary. Grave or Memorial Reference: Has no known grave but is commemorated on Panel 34. Memorial: Ypres (Menin Gate) Memorial in Belgium.

Y

YARROW, R.R.: Rank: Private. Regiment or Service: Northumberland Fusiliers. Unit: 8th Bn. Secondary Regiment: Labour Corps Secondary. Unit: transf. to (710143) Age at death: 45. Date of death: 4 July 1920 Service No. 4854.

Supplementary information: Son of Robert Yarrow, of Newcastle-on-Tyne: husband of Bridget Yarrow, of Church Street, Tipperary. Grave or Memorial Reference: M. C. 486. Cemetery: Newcastle-Upon-Tyne (St John's Westgate and Elswick) Cemetery, UK.

YEABSLEY, Desmond: Rank: Drummer. Regiment or Service: Suffolk Regiment. Unit: 2nd Bn. Date of death: Two are given, 9 April 1915 and 26 August 1914. Service No. 8696. Born in Tipperary. Enlisted in Aldershot. Killed in action. Age at death: 17.

Supplementary information: Son of Laura Sarah Yeabsley, of 213 Hole Lane, Northfield, Birmingham, and the late George N. Yeabsley. He has no known grave but is listed on the La Ferte-Sous-Jouarre-Memorial in France.

YEAMAN, William: Rank: Gunner. Regiment or Service: Royal Garrison Artillery. Date of death: 8 June 1916. Service No. 86. Formerly he was with the Royal Garrison Artillery Hull Heavy Battery where his number was

Another Nenagh Man Killed in Action.

Since the outbreak of hostilies there can be no doubt about the fact that Nenagh has magnificently responded to the call of King and Country, and this has been unmistakably shown by the reference to the large number of men who joined the colours from the Nenagh Shamrock Club and the town and district generally, and to which special mention has been recently made in the English Press. No doubt that Club will never again record the names of many of its former valued members. The latest who has nobly fallen on the battle field, and an esteemed member of the Club named, is Sergeant Con Young, of the 1st Battalion Connaught Rangers, son of Mr Bryan Young of Silver View, Nenagh, an old and much respected employee for a long number of years of the G.S. & W. Railway The deceased was well known and highly esteemed in his native town, and the greatest sympathy is felt for his bereaved parents in the loss they have sustained on the death of their gallant son.

Cornelius Young.

86 also. Born in Cahir. Enlisted in Hull. Died in East Africa.

Supplementary information: Husband of Mary Ann Yeaman, of 15 Boxwood Avenue, Lee Smith Street, Hull, England. Grave or Memorial Reference: 7. F. 17. Cemetery: Dar Es Salaam War Cemetery in Tanzania.

YOUNG, Cornelius: Rank: Lance Corporal. Regiment or Service: Connaught Rangers. Unit: 1st Bn. Date of death: 21 January 1916. Service No.9779. Born in Nenagh. Enlisted in Tipperary while living in Nenagh. Died of wounds. Killed in action in Mesopotamia. Age at death: 28.

Supplementary information: Son of Brian and Mary Young, of Silver View, Nenagh, Co. Tipperary. He has no known grave but is listed on Panel 40 and 64 on the Basra Memorial in Iraq.

Epilogue

The final word we will leave to Poet Laurence Bunyan:

For The Fallen

With proud thanksgiving, a mother for her children,
England mourns for her dead across the sea.
Flesh of her flesh they were, spirit of her spirit,
Fallen in the cause of the free.
Solemn the drums thrill: death august and royal
Sings sorrow up into immortal spheres,
There is music in the midst of desolation
And a glory that shines upon our tears.
They went with songs to the battle, they were young,
Straight of limb, true of eye, steady and aglow.
They were staunch to the end against odds uncounted:
They fell with their faces to the foe.
They shall grow not old, as we that are left grow old:
Age shall not weary them, nor the years contemn.
At the going down of the sun and in the morning
We will remember them.
They mingle not with their laughing comrades again:
They sit no more at familiar tables of home:
They have no lot in our labour of the day-time:
They sleep beyond England's foam.
But where our desires are and our hopes profound,
Felt as a well-spring that is hidden from sight,
To the innermost heart of their own land they are known
As the stars are known to the Night:
As the stars that shall be bright when we are dust,
Moving in marches upon the heavenly plain:
As the stars that are starry in the time of our darkness,
To the end, to the end, they remain.

Bibliography

The Commonwealth War Graves Commission.
Soldiers Died in the Great War. Soldiers of the Great War.
The New Library and Archives Canada.
The National Archives of Australia.
Nominal Rolls of the New Zealand Expeditionary Force.
De Ruvigny's Roll of Honour.
The 1901 and 1911 Census for Tipperary.
The Public Records Office in Kew, UK.
The National Roll of the Great War, London.
Tipperary Star archives.
The Freemans Journal and *National Press.*
The Nationalist Archives.
Nenagh Guardian Archives.
The War Graves of the British Empire.
Commonwealth War Graves Commission registers for the Irish Free State and Ireland's Memorial Records.